TRANSATLANTIC SENSATIONS

Bringing together sensation writing and transatlantic studies, this collection makes a convincing case for the symbiotic relationship between literary works on both sides of the Atlantic. *Transatlantic Sensations* begins with the 'prehistories' of the genre, looking at the dialogue and debate generated by the publication of sentimental and gothic fiction by William Godwin, Susanna Rowson, and Charles Brockden Brown. Thus establishing a context for the treatment of works by Louisa May Alcott, Mary Elizabeth Braddon, Dion Boucicault, Wilkie Collins, Charles Dickens, George Lippard, Charles Reade, Harriet Beecher Stowe, and George Thompson, the volume takes up a wide range of sensational topics including sexuality, slavery, criminal punishment, literary piracy, mesmerism, and the metaphors of foreign literary invasion and diseased reading. Concluding essays offer a reassessment of the realist and domestic fiction of George Eliot, Charlotte Yonge, and Thomas Hardy in the context of transatlantic sensationalism, emphasizing the evolution of the genre throughout the century and mapping a new transatlantic lineage for this immensely popular literary form. The book's final essay examines an international kidnapping case that was a journalistic sensation at the turn of the twentieth century.

Ashgate Series in Nineteenth-Century Transatlantic Studies

Series Editors: Kevin Hutchings and Julia M. Wright

Focusing on the long nineteenth century (ca. 1750–1900), this series offers a forum for the publication of scholarly work investigating the literary, historical, artistic, and philosophical foundations of transatlantic culture. A new and burgeoning field of interdisciplinary investigation, transatlantic scholarship contextualizes its objects of study in relation to exchanges, interactions, and negotiations that occurred between and among authors and other artists hailing from both sides of the Atlantic. As a result, transatlantic research calls into question established disciplinary boundaries that have long functioned to segregate various national or cultural literatures and art forms, challenging as well the traditional academic emphasis upon periodization and canonization. By examining representations dealing with such topics as travel and exploration, migration and diaspora, slavery, aboriginal culture, revolution, colonialism and anti-colonial resistance, the series will offer new insights into the hybrid or intercultural basis of transatlantic identity, politics, and aesthetics.

The editors invite English language studies focusing on any area of the long nineteenth century, including (but not limited to) innovative works spanning transatlantic Romantic and Victorian contexts. Manuscripts focusing on European, African, US American, Canadian, Caribbean, Central and South American, and Indigenous literature, art, and culture are welcome. We will consider proposals for monographs, collaborative books, and edited collections.

Transatlantic Sensations

Edited by

JENNIFER PHEGLEY
University of Missouri-Kansas City, USA

JOHN CYRIL BARTON
University of Missouri-Kansas City, USA

and

KRISTIN N. HUSTON
University of Missouri-Kansas City, USA

with a Preface by

DAVID S. REYNOLDS

ASHGATE

Published by
Ashgate Publishing Limited
Wey Court East
Union Road
Farnham
Surrey, GU9 7PT
England

Ashgate Publishing Company
Suite 420
101 Cherry Street
Burlington
VT 05401-4405
USA

www.ashgate.com

British Library Cataloguing in Publication Data
Transatlantic sensations. – (Ashgate series in nineteenth-century transatlantic studies)
   1. Sensationalism in literature. 2. English literature – 19th century – History and criticism.
   3. American literature – 19th century – History and criticism. 4. English literature – 18th century – History and criticism. 5. American literature – 18th century – History and criticism.
   I. Series II. Phegley, Jennifer. III. Barton, John Cyril. IV. Huston, Kristin N.
   820.9'008-dc23

Library of Congress Cataloging-in-Publication Data
Transatlantic sensations: edited by Jennifer Phegley, John Cyril Barton, and Kristin N. Huston, with a preface by David S. Reynolds.
      p. cm.—(Ashgate series in nineteenth-century transatlantic studies)
   Includes bibliographical references and index.
   ISBN 978-1-4094-2715-5 (hardcover: alk. paper) — ISBN 978-1-4094-2716-2 (ebook)
   1. English fiction—19th century—History and criticism. 2. American fiction—19th century—History and criticism. 3. Sensationalism in literature. 4. Literature and society—Great Britain—History—19th century. 5. Literature and society—United States—History—19th century. 6. Comparative literature—English and American. 7. Comparative literature—American and English. I. Phegley, Jennifer. II. Barton, John Cyril. III. Huston, Kristin N.
   PR878.S44.T73 2012
   823'.0870908—dc23
                                                                                    2011044076
ISBN: 9781409427155 (hbk)
ISBN: 9781409427162 (ebk)

Printed and bound in Great Britain by the
MPG Books Group, UK

Contents

List of Figures

Notes on Contributors

Christopher Apap teaches American literature at Oakland University. He is currently working on a monograph studying the literary representation of local and national identities in the early republic. His research has appeared in *Comparative American Studies*, *The Journal of the Early Republic*, and *Early American Literature*.

John Cyril Barton is Assistant Professor of English at the University of Missouri–Kansas City. His essays have appeared in journals such as *Arizona Quarterly*, *Law-and-Literature*, *REAL: Research in English and American Literature*, *Studies in American Fiction*, *Critical Horizons*, as well as the book *Integrating Literature* (MLA 2008). He recently finished a monograph titled *Literary Executions: Capital Punishment and American Culture, 1820–1920*.

Susan David Bernstein, Professor of English, and Gender and Women's Studies, the University of Wisconsin–Madison, is the author of *Confessional Subjects: Revelations of Gender and Power in Victorian Literature and Culture* (North Carolina, 1997) and the editor of two novels by Amy Levy, *The Romance of a Shop* and *Reuben Sachs* (Broadview, 2006), as well as the co-editor of *Victorian Vulgarity: Taste in Verbal and Visual Culture* (Ashgate, 2009). She is completing her next book, *Roomscape: Women Readers in the British Museum from George Eliot to Virginia Woolf*.

Holly Blackford is an Associate Professor of English at Rutgers University–Camden. She teaches and publishes literary criticism on American, children's, and adolescent literature. Her books include *Out of this World: Why Literature Matters to Girls* (2004), *Mockingbird Passing: Closeted Traditions and Sexual Curiosities in Harper Lee's Novel* (2011), *The Myth of Persephone in Girls' Fantasy Literature* (forthcoming), and an edited volume *100 Years of Anne with an 'e': The Centennial Study of* Anne of Green Gables (2009). She chairs the article award committee of the International Children's Literature Association and serves as professor of Rutgers's Ph.D. program in Children and Childhood Studies.

David Bordelon is an Associate Professor of English at Ocean County College in Toms River, New Jersey. His publications include essays and chapters on nineteenth-century popular fiction, American book history, and graphic narratives.

Julia McCord Chavez is an Assistant Professor of English at Saint Martin's University in Lacey, Washington. She has published articles on the Gothic qualities of Victorian serial fiction and the serialization of Mary Elizabeth Braddon's sensation fiction within *Temple Bar Magazine*. Currently, she is working on a book titled *Victorian Wanderers and the Serial Form*.

Dorice Williams Elliott is Associate Professor in the English Department at the University of Kansas. Her book, *The Angel out of the House: Philanthropy and Gender in Nineteenth-Century England,* was published in 2002 by the University Press of Virginia. She has published articles on Elizabeth Gaskell, Hannah More, Sarah Scott, and Jane Austen, and on servants, class, and Australian convicts. She is currently working on a book manuscript about class and colonialism in Australian convict literature.

Narin Hassan is an Associate Professor in the School of Literature, Communication, and Culture at the Georgia Institute of Technology where she teaches courses in Victorian literature and culture, gender studies, and postcolonial studies. Her book, *Diagnosing Empire: Women, Medical Knowledge, and Colonial Mobility* (Ashgate, 2011), traces the relationship of female doctoring to travel and colonial progress. She is currently researching a new project on representations of gender and botany in the nineteenth century which examines sensation fiction along with other texts such as gardening guides, travel memoirs, and scientific accounts.

Kristin Huston is a doctoral candidate at the University of Missouri–Kansas City, where she also teaches composition and literature classes. Her research interests include gender and sexuality studies, the history of the body, nineteenth-century transatlantic literature and art, and periodical studies. Her dissertation involves the study of representations of Creole women in four nineteenth-century periodicals published in Jamaica and Louisiana.

Kimberly Snyder Manganelli is Assistant Professor of English at Clemson University, where she teaches nineteenth-century British and American literature. She is the author of *Transatlantic Spectacles of Race: The Tragic Mulatta and the Tragic Muse* (forthcoming from Rutgers University Press).

Kate Mattacks is a Senior Lecturer in Drama at the University of West England, Bristol. After completing a Ph.D. on M.E. Braddon at Keele, she worked on two AHR-funded projects within the field of Victorian drama: The Victorian Plays Project, a web-based resource of more than 350 Victorian plays; and the 'Buried Treasures' Project based at Royal Holloway and the British Library, extending the catalogue for the Lord Chamberlain's Collection of licensing manuscripts. She has written articles on a variety of subjects, including Braddon, the theatrical publisher T.H. Lacy, Victorian anti-feminism, spiritualism, dramatic piracy, and speech disability on stage. She is currently working on a monograph entitled *After Lady Audley: M.E. Braddon and Staging Sensationalism*.

Ana Savic Moturu is a senior lecturer at the University of Texas at Arlington. Her dissertation, entitled *Intimate Antagonists: British Images of the Balkans, 1853–1914*, theorizes the conflictual relationship between the Balkans and the West, examining political, cultural, and historical factors that led to Western constructions of the Balkans as an internal other.

Alexander Moudrov received his Ph.D. in Comparative Literature from The City University of New York's Graduate Center. His dissertation, *The Rise of the American Culture of Sensationalism: 1620–1860*, traces the formation of the American literary tradition while emphasizing the importance of various forms of sensationalism in its history. His recent publications include "Early American Crime Literature" and "Nabokov's Invitation to Plato's Beheading." Currently an instructor in the Department of Comparative Literature at Queens College, he teaches courses in global literatures and intercultural relations, as well as interdisciplinary courses that bridge literary studies with other disciplines, particularly philosophy, religion, and history.

Jennifer Phegley, Professor of English at the University of Missouri–Kansas City, is the author of *Educating the Proper Woman Reader: Victorian Family Literary Magazines and the Cultural Health of the Nation* (2004) and *Courtship and Marriage in Victorian England* (2011). She has also co-edited *Reading Women: Literary Figures and Cultural Icons From the Victorian Age to the Present* (2005) and *Teaching Nineteenth-Century Fiction* (2010).

David S. Reynolds is Distinguished Professor of English and American Studies at the Graduate Center of the City University of New York. His books include *Beneath the American Renaissance: The Subversive Imagination in the Age of Emerson and Melville* (1988), *George Lippard* (1982), *Faith in Fiction: The Emergence of Religious Literature in America* (1981), *Walt Whitman's America: A Cultural Biography* (1995), *John Brown, Abolitionist: The Man Who Killed Slavery, Sparked the Civil War, and Seeded* Civil *Rights* (2005), *Waking Giant: America in the Age of Jackson* (2008), and *Mightier than the Sword: "Uncle Tom's Cabin" and the Battle for America* (2011). He is also the editor of George Lippard's *The Quaker City; or, The Monks of Monk Hall* (1995), the anthology *George Lippard, Prophet of Protest: Writings of an American Radical* (1986), Walt Whitman's *Leaves of Grass: The 150th Anniversary Edition* (2005)**,** Harriet Beecher Stowe's *Uncle Tom's Cabin: The Splendid Edition* (2011), *A Historical Guide to Walt Whitman* (1999), and coeditor, with Kimberly Gladman, of George Thompson's *Venus in Boston and Other Tales of Nineteenth-century City Life* (2001) and, with Debra Rosenthal, *The Serpent in the Cup: Temperance and American Literature* (1997). He is the winner of the Christian Gauss Award, the Bancroft Prize, the Ambassador Book Award, and finalist for the National Book Critics Circle Award. He is listed in *Who's Who in America* and *Who's Who in the World* (2000 edition to the present).

Tamara S. Wagner obtained her Ph.D. from Cambridge University in 2002 and is currently Associate Professor at Nanyang Technological University in Singapore. Her books include *Financial Speculation in Victorian Fiction: Plotting Money and the Novel Genre, 1815–1901* (2010), *Longing: Narratives of Nostalgia in the British Novel, 1740–1890* (2004), and *Occidentalism in Novels of Malaysia and Singapore, 1819–2004* (2005), as well as edited collections on *Consuming Culture* *in the Long Nineteenth-Century* (2007; paperback edition 2010), *Antifeminism and the Victorian Novel: Rereading Nineteenth-Century Women Writers* (2009), and *Victorian Settler Narratives: Emigrants, Cosmopolitans and Returnees in Nineteenth-Century Literature* (2011). Wagner has also guest edited special issues on silver-fork fiction (2009) and on the religious writer Charlotte Yonge (2010) for the journal *Women's Writing* and co-edited a guest issue on the Victorian Orient for *Critical Survey* (2009). Her current projects include a special issue on Frances Trollope and a study of Victorian narratives of failed emigration.

Preface

David S. Reynolds

This book traces the rise of sensational fiction between 1790 and 1890, revealing analogies and interchange among American, British, and Continental writers of novels and stories that featured crime, mystery, illicit sex, or other transgressive, startling, or racy themes. Such literature, immensely popular in its time but long minimized by literary scholars, puts the lie to the standard image of Victorian culture as a tame, prim environment against which certain forward-thinking writers—e.g., Lord George Gordon Byron, Charles Dickens, Charlotte, Emily, and Anne Brontë, and Thomas Hardy in England; Victor Hugo, Charles Baudelaire, and Emile Zola in France; Edgar Allan Poe, Nathaniel Hawthorne, and Herman Melville in America—rebelled in their dark, often subversive writings. Actually, the popular culture surrounding these authors swirled with currents of criminality, perversity, and eroticism that surged in best-selling sensational fiction and in turn were absorbed and transmuted by the major authors. While revealing fresh dimensions of the sensation genre, the current book taps into a prominent trend in recent literary studies: transnational criticism, which challenges standard conceptions of national literatures by revealing a ceaseless flow of transatlantic and hemispheric cultural exchange. Although there have appeared studies of the sensational literature of individual nations, to date there is no full-length exploration of the complex and ongoing cross-fertilization between the sensational writings of various cultures.

Sensationalism is as old as literature itself. Most literary genres from the ancient Greek epics and tragedies onward have elements of what later would be called sensationalism. An Irish journalist noted in the 1860s, "Without the sensational nothing in art or literature would be worth a straw. All genius is more or less sensational" (*Freeman's* 7 February 1868). True enough, but the period between 1790 and 1890 saw a number of new cultural and social phenomena that exponentially increased the popularity and variety of sensational literature. Urbanization and improved travel created a mobile reading public that feasted on cheap sensational novels, many of them gaudily colored pamphlets that were sold in sidewalk bookstalls, in train stations, or on wharves. Advances in printing technology facilitated the inexpensive production of this literature, whose distribution was sped by the advent of steam-powered ships and the railroad. The market revolution, which saw a shift from the bygone subsistence economy toward capitalism, fostered a "go-ahead" mentality that thrived on constant diversion and stimulation.

Sensational literature appeared in overlapping phases during this period. Early on came the Gothic novel, which began in earnest with Horace Walpole's *The*

Castle of Otranto (1764), followed over the next four decades by Clara Reeve's *The Old English Baron*, William Beckford's *Vathek*, Anne Radcliffe's *The Mysteries of Udolpho*, and hundreds of lesser known Gothic novels, many of them published by William Lane's Minerva Press. The typical Gothic novel featured a persecuted heroine, a villainous monk or baron, and apparently supernatural occurrences that took place in a mysterious setting, usually a medieval castle in Germany or one of the Latin countries. Variations on the Gothic rapidly appeared. One, *Schauerromantik* (horror-Romantic), was produced by German authors such as E.T.A. Hoffmann, Ludwig Tieck, and Friedrich Schiller, who dwelt on horrific scenes of rape, torture, murder, ghosts, and devils. This gruesome mode caused a shift from Radcliffe's "gentle" Gothic (emphasizing the heroine's virtue, the villain's punishment, and the explained supernatural) toward a more sensational brand of fiction represented by Matthew Gregory Lewis's *The Monk* and Charles Robert Maturin's *Melmoth, the Wanderer*, in which devil worship, witchcraft, magic, and spectacular villainy were prominent. Another offshoot of the Gothic was William Godwin's *Things As They Are; or, The Adventures of Caleb Williams*, an early detective novel, whose protagonist, falsely accused of murder, cleverly exposes the actual villain. Godwin's interest in experimenting with the sensational was shared by one of his greatest admirers, the Philadelphia novelist Charles Brockden Brown, who found fresh American settings for the Gothic, which Brown directed toward inward, psychological themes in a way that anticipated Poe's notion that "terror is not of Germany, but of the soul" (Poe 129).

While Gothic fiction continued to be a strong cultural presence through the first half of the nineteenth century, more contemporary brands of sensationalism arose in the 1830s, which witnessed increasingly popular crime literature in several countries. British readers had long enjoyed the Newgate Calendar, a series of nonfictional pamphlets, periodically collected in anthologies, that recounted the lives of notable inmates of London's Newgate Prison. The Newgate Calendar enjoyed a lively sale from the early eighteenth century onward mainly because of its appeal to the public's thirst for the details of crime. This popularization of criminal escapades was enhanced by the Newgate novel, represented by Edward Bulwer-Lytton's *Pelham* and *Eugene Aram*, William Harrison Ainsworth's *Rookwood* and *Jack Sheppard*, Charles Dickens's *Oliver Twist*, and about a dozen other British novels that appeared between 1830 and 1850. During the same period, France produced a steady stream of crime novels, many of which appeared serially in feuilletons and then came out in book form; the most prolific feuilletonist was Frédérick Soulié, who wrote scores of novels about unusual crimes, with an emphasis, as one commentator noted, on "blood, corpses, ghastly murders, ghoulishness, revolting details of disease, or torture, or decomposition" (Mary Elizabeth Braddon qtd. in Wolff 128). America witnessed a succession of popular crime pamphlets and collections such as *Record of Crimes in the United States* (1833), *The Pirates Own Book* (1837), and *The Lives of the Felons, or American Criminal Calendar* (1847) that fed into popular sensational fiction by Joseph Holt Ingraham, Ned Buntline, Sylvanus Cobb, and others, much of it published in so-called mammoth story weeklies.

This literature, under a thin veil of didacticism, often presented criminals as dashing, clever, cool, or no more corrupt than outwardly respectable types. The engaging villain came in various guises, including the likable criminal who won the reader's sympathy, the justified outlaw whose crimes were said to be motivated by a corrupt social system, and the reverend rake who used religion as a vehicle for seduction. In the eyes of conservative critics, the engaging villain was a real threat to society. The Brooklyn preacher Henry Ward Beecher blasted "French and English novels of the infernal school," with their "humane murderers, lascivious saints, holy infidels, honest robbers." Beecher used apocalyptic metaphors to describe what he regarded as the pernicious influence of such novels. "The Ten Plagues have visited our literature," he declared. "Water is turned to blood; frogs and lice creep and hop over our most familiar things,—the couch, the cradle, and the bread-trough; locusts, murrain, and fire, are smiting every green thing" (Beecher 210–11). His sister, Harriet Beecher Stowe, likewise complained of the "great rage for pickpockets, highwaymen, murderers" in imported European fiction and insisted that American imitations were even worse; she wrote that "the *trash* literature of the day"—particularly fiction that "figured largely in our mammoth sheets"—ran "very much in a foul and muddy current, full of the slang and filth of low and degraded society" (Stowe, "Literary Epidemics—1" and "Literary Epidemics—2").

Stowe was hardly alone in highlighting the sensationalism of the American popular press. Penny newspapers, aimed at the wallets and tastes of America's increasingly rowdy working class, supplanted the stodgy sixpennies of the past with a new brand of journalism that was brash, zestful, and above all sensational. Anything lively—a "Secret Tryst, a "Double Suicide," an "Awful Accident"— was fit news to print in the penny papers. By the 1840s, every major American city had one or more penny papers. Emerson noted in his journal that most of his countrymen spent their time "reading all day murders & railroad accidents" in newspapers (Porte 433). Thoreau similarly spoke of the "startling and monstrous events as fill the daily papers" (Gilman 267). A number of foreign visitors were appalled by the American penny newspapers. Dickens, despite his own interest in criminality, charged them with "pimping and pandering for all degrees of vicious taste" (*American Notes* 114); in *Martin Chuzzlewit* he portrayed American newsboys peddling papers with scabrous titles like the *New York Sewer* and the *New York Stabber* Three decades later, the visiting British woman Emily Faithfull declared that "the American newspaper very often startles its more cultured reader with extraordinary sensational headings and the prominence it gives to horrors of all kinds" (Faithfull 336).

American sensationalism reflected a boisterous, frequently violent culture whose turbulent energies were unleashed by freedom of the press, ever-expanding suffrage, and competing factions. American mobs who targeted different groups— abolitionists, blacks, and immigrants in particular—became so common that Abraham Lincoln warned that an "absolutely unrestrained ... mobocratic spirit" was overtaking the nation (Lincoln 31). In the South, bowie knives, guns, or hempen rope were frequently used to enforce vigilante justice, and duels and deadly family feuds were part of the accepted code of honor. In Northern cities, what the historian Sean Wilentz has described as the "republicanism of the streets" erupted in gang warfare and in the daily activities of a working-class urban type known as the b'hoy, or Bowery Boy, who was always itching for a "muss" and loved running aside fire engines in noisy competition with rival fire companies (Wilentz 263). In 1842, Phineas T. Barnum, the quintessential American entrepreneur of sensationalism, opened his famous New York museum of freaks and oddities, fueling the "—est" factor, or Americans' curiosity in the larg*est*, small*est*, the thinn*est*, the fatt*est*, the most outrageous, and so forth (Reynolds, *Waking Giant* 276–277).

Such national idiosyncrasies gave a special American flavor to the most popular sensational genre of the 1840s and 1850s, the city-mysteries novel. This genre transferred Gothic darkness to the complex urban environment. The city was suddenly perceived as a strange and overwhelming place, full of secret recesses, hidden crime, and working-class wretchedness. This urban genre arose with the publication of *The Mysteries of Paris* (1842) by the French author Eugene Sue, who turned his well-honed talents as a sensational novelist to depicting the city's underworld of prostitutes, pimps, thieves, and murderers while exposing upper-class hypocrisy and venality. Sue's novel was quickly followed by G.W.M. Reynolds's novel *The Mysteries of London* (1844) and similar fiction by other authors about numerous European cities (including Berlin, Hamburg, Brussels, and Vienna). In America, there appeared "mysteries and miseries" of numerous locales, such as New York, Philadelphia, Boston, New Orleans, San Francisco, and even Lowell and Nashua. American authors tried to outdo each other in the vividness with which they described urban sensations. The winners in this grisly competition were George Lippard and George Thompson. Lippard's *The Quaker City* (1845), America's best-selling novel before the appearance of Stowe's *Uncle Tom's Cabin* (1852), made the labyrinthine Monk Hall, a fictional gentlemen's club, the nineteenth-century equivalent of the Gothic castle, whose "monks" were secretly depraved Philadelphians and whose keeper was the lowly, monstrous Devil-Bug, perhaps the most sadistic character in American literature. George Thompson wrote scores of urban novels, typified by *City Crimes*, whose freakishly disfigured protagonist, the Dead Man, and his ghoulish son, known as The Image, live among criminals in the excrement-filled Dead Vaults, a subterranean sewer system below New York where "the crime of incest is as common among them as dirt! I have known a mother and her son—a father and his daughter—a brother and sister—to be guilty of criminal intimacy" (131). Like their European counterparts, American city-mysteries novels were enlivened by street slang and the "flash" lingo of criminals, though an American novel like *The Quaker City* was far richer in its linguistic variations than any European novel due to America's uniquely polyglot urban environment. American city-mysteries novels also tended to be more gory than the European fiction—a reflection of the turbulence of Jacksonian society itself—although vestigial Puritanism limited the eroticism of the American works to the titillating and suggestive.

Two leading American writers, Hawthorne and Poe, represented other aspects of the transformed American sensationalism that contributed to transatlantic fiction. Hawthorne, a Democrat devoted to Andrew Jackson, absorbed the wildest and most subversive themes and characters of his contemporary culture—hidden sin, the engaging villain, the reverend rake, the fallen woman, and so on—and crafted them in symbolic, richly psychological fiction by coupling them with Puritanism, a defining feature of his own and his nation's past. In his era, Hawthorne could be viewed as a fountainhead of transatlantic sensationalism. For instance, the Scottish author Margaret Oliphant, seeking to identify influential sensational writers, pointed to Hawthorne, whose fiction, Oliphant wrote, represented a "class of books abounding in sensation," with "here a Scarlet Letter and impish child of shame, there a snake-girl, horrible junction of reptile and woman," and many other instances of "horror and mystery" reflective of an American culture that offered "little else" than sensations (Oliphant 564). Poe, a Southern Whig who absorbed his party's devotion to inventiveness, brought both artistry and intensity to the horrific or sensational through his careful regulation of prosody, plot, and the first-person narrator. Poe had a strong effect in Europe. His influence on such craftsmen of evil as Baudelaire, Mallarmé, and Lautréamont has often been described, but actually he was first known in Europe as a popular writer of what one reviewer called "tales of horror which make the flesh creep and the hair stand on end" with their "strange, ghastly mixture of the fantastic and the horrible" (*New-York Evangelist* 1).

But it took more than Poe and Hawthorne to direct sensationalism toward what was officially called "the sensation novel," a name assigned to a hybrid genre of the 1860s that combined the transgressiveness of sensationalism with the realistically described, contemporary settings and characters of an altogether different kind of fiction: the sentimental-domestic novel. From the start, sensational fiction was engaged in a dialectical relationship with the sentimental novel. The rise of the novel in the eighteenth century was defined by this dialectic, as evidenced by the contrast between Daniel Defoe's Newgate-inspired crime novels *Jack Shepard*, *Jonathan Wild*, and *Moll Flanders*, on one side, and Samuel Richardson's depictions of female virtue in his sentimental novels *Pamela* and *Clarissa*, on the other. The battle between the two modes continued when lurid Gothic fiction was answered by Maria Edgeworth, Hannah More, Jane West, Jane Austen, and others who parodied the Gothic and drew textured portraits of middle-class life. America, even with its surging sensational culture, witnessed the popularity of domestic fiction and nonfiction, evidenced by novels, domestic manuals, and religious tracts by a range of authors who reinforced the cult of domesticity, based on the values of piety, purity, and the sanctity of woman's sphere.

It is understandable that, in the interest of revising the literary canon and doing justice to overlooked writers, many recent critics have chosen to focus on domesticity and sentimentality. But it is important to recognize that the majority of novels and stories written by American authors during this period were *not* of the sentimental-domestic variety.[1] Also, the readership of the different types of novels was not defined by sex: women were just as likely as men to read sensational fiction and in fact were often described as its main audience.[2] Since there was no international copyright, foreign sensational fiction was inexpensively printed and sold in America, leading a Chicago physician in 1855 to devote an entire book decrying popular "Yellow-Jacket Literature" featuring "the murderer, robber, pirate, swindler," and so on which, he estimated, had "an enormous circulation of 2.5 million volumes" and formed an "ocean of immorality" threatening to engulf America's twenty-four million citizens in "public poison" (*Confessions* 11).

In this perfervid atmosphere, domestic novels could be viewed as anomalies. Susan Warner's *The Wide, Wide World* (1851) struck a reviewer as a surprise best-seller because it had "no stirring adventure, no romantic incidents, not a word of love, and not a tittle of war" but was rather "a quiet, peaceable, moral, religious, domestic story." The reviewer hoped that Warner's novel would help "check that flood of vicious fiction which, issuing from the press under every guise, fosters folly,…and never benefits the mind or guides the wanderer on his way" (*London Observer*). Similarly, another commentator saw no "condescension to popular taste," in "pure, modest, refined" novels like *The Wide, Wide World*, which had "no mystery of concealment that keeps the reader in breathless suspense—…no intensity of passion—no exciting disclosures" (*New-York Tribune*).

The distance between the sensational and sentimental-domestic modes began to be bridged in the 1850s, thanks in part to the worldwide popularity of Harriet Beecher Stowe's *Uncle Tom's Cabin* (1852). Stowe took the innovative step of fusing the two modes. On the one hand, *Uncle Tom's Cabin* was full of sensational adventures: the daring race to freedom across ice floes by the fugitive slave Eliza Harris, the shoot-out in the rocky pass between Eliza's husband George and his pursuers, the bloody lashing of Uncle Tom, and so forth. At the same time, the novel emphasized piety, purity, and domesticity like a typical domestic novel. Soon thereafter, American women writers like Fanny Fern, E.D.E.N. Southworth, Alice Carey, and Harriet Prescott Spofford discovered other ways of melding the sensational or trangressive with the conventional and domestic—a strategy that fed into the multilayered poetic guises of Emily Dickinson.

The stage was set for what was officially called "the sensation novel," produced by the likes of Wilkie Collins, Mary Elizabeth Braddon, Charles Reade, and Ellen Wood in England and by Louisa May Alcott and others in America. Although

---

[1]   See my statistical analysis in *Beneath the American Renaissance: the Subversive Imagination in the Age of Emerson and Melville* (New York: Alfred A. Knopf, 1988), 338.

[2]   See, for instance, the discussions of women's taste for sensation fiction in "Your Reading," *Christian Secretary* 24 (6 February 1846): 4; "Yellow-Colored Literature," *The Literary Union* 1 (14 April 1849): 24, "Cheap Fiction," *American Publishers' Circular and Literary Gazette* 2 (15 March 1856): 158; "Pen-Poison," *Hours at Home: A Popular Monthly* 6 (February 1868): 289; "Mr. Hardhack on the Sensational in Literature and Life," *The Atlantic Monthly* 26 (August 1870): 195–200; "Working Girls and Their Literature," *The Golden Age* 29 July 1871; and "The New Dangers of Sensational Fiction," *The Critic*, 258 (Dec. 8 1888): 281.

some of these authors were capable of gory sensationalism of the Newgate variety—Braddon, for instance, churned out grisly magazine tales filled with what she called "crime, treachery, murder, slow poisoning, and general infamy"—their most innovative fiction was that in which they mixed the sensational with the everyday (Wolff 126). Henry James credited sensation fiction of the 1860s with revealing "those most mysterious of mysteries, the mysteries which are at our own doors" and tying terror "at a hundred points with the common objects of life" (742). Collins in *The Woman in White* (1860) converted the stock character of the engaging villain into the *average* villain through his portrait of Count Fosco, a fat, genial man with a taste for pastry, cigars, pet mice, and canaries (Collins explained that he wanted to make his villain "common-place,…in opposition to the recognised type of villain" ("History"). Even more representative of the sensation novel were its ambiguous heroines, who cunningly aped the sweetness and virtue of the domestic moral exemplar to achieve often amoral goals. Lydia Gwilt of Collins's *Armadale* is a former governess and an ex-convict who successfully passes herself off as a Victorian lady. The low-born Lucy Wallace of Braddon's *Lady Audley's Secret* uses charm and apparent innocence to win the hand of the wealthy Sir Michael Audley, even though she turns out to be a bigamist who has abandoned her child and attempted to commit murder. Jean Muir, the heroine of Alcott's *Behind a Mask*, disguises herself with false teeth, make-up, and outward virtue so convincingly that she seems "meek, modest, faithful, and invariably sweet-tempered," a charade that enables her to marry a rich man and become Lady Coventry, even though she actually has a murky past as a kept woman and an abandoned wife (Stern 25).

The prominence of sensation fiction in the 1860s has led some to associate the genre with that decade alone. One scholar typically speaks of "the virtual restriction of the sensation novel to the one decade of the 1860s" (Rance 129). But, as we have seen, and as this volume demonstrates, sensationalism had a long history. It rose to unprecedented visibility in the late eighteenth century and then became increasingly popular in the nineteenth century. It took different shapes in various countries, but national distinctions were in fact moot, since advances in printing and distribution made each nation's sensational literature readily available elsewhere.

Nor did sensationalism die out after 1870, as some have claimed. To the contrary, it intensified, as did its dialectical relationship with sentimental-domestic modes. Just as authors like Braddon, Southworth, and Alcott switched between writing sensational fiction and so-called "moral pap" (Alcott's phrase for *Little Women* (Cheney 296)), and as nineteenth-century story papers and book publishers regularly issued contrasting kinds of fiction, so both the sensational and the sentimental—and piquant mixtures of the two—have continued to pervade society right up to today, in fiction, sermons, political campaigns, advertising, TV shows, pop music, celebrity culture, and tabloids. Instead of speaking of sensationalism's demise, scholars would be well advised to consider its ever-expanding reach. *Transatlantic Sensations* helps lay the historical groundwork for further explorations of this global phenomenon.

Works Cited

Beecher, H.W. *Lectures to Young Men, on Various Important Subjects*. New York: M.H. Newman and Co., 1849.

"Cheap Fiction." *American Publishers' Circular and Literary Gazette* 2 (15 March 1856): 158.

Cheney, Ednah D. Ed. *Louisa May Alcott: Her Life, Journals, and Letters*. Boston: Roberts Brothers, 1890.

Collins, Wilkie. "History of *The Woman in White*." *North Wales Chronicle* (December 29, 1877).

Confessions and Experiences of a Novel Reader. Chicago: William Stacey, 1855.

Dickens, Charles. *American Notes and Pictures from Italy*. London: Macdonald and Sons, n.d.

Faithfull, Emily. *Three Visits to America*. Edinburgh: David Douglas, 1884.

Freeman's Journal and Daily Commercial Advertiser. February 7, 1868.

Gilman, William H. et al. eds. *The Journal of Henry David Thoreau*. New York: Dover, 1962.

James, Henry. "Mary Elizabeth Braddon." *Literary Criticism*. New York: Library of America, 1984.

Lincoln, Abraham. *Speeches and Writings, 1832–1858*. New York: Library of America, 1980.

London Observer. January 25, 1852.

"Mr. Hardhack on the Sensational in Literature and Life." *The Atlantic Monthly* 26 (August 1870): 195–200.

"The New Dangers of Sensational Fiction." *The Critic* 258 (December 8, 1858): 281.

New-York Evangelist 30. January 20, 1859.

New-York Tribune. May 1, 1852.

Oliphant, Margaret. "Sensation Novels." *Blackwood's Edinburgh Magazine* 91 (1862).

"Pen-Poison." *Hours at Home: A Popular Monthly* 6 (February 1868): 289.

Poe, Edgar Allan. "Preface." *Tales of the Grotesque and Arabesque*. New York: Library of America, 1980.

Porte, Joel. Ed. *Emerson in His Journals*. Cambridge, Mass.: Harvard University Press, 1982.

Rance, Nicholas. *Wilkie Collins and Other Sensation Novelists: Walking the Moral Hospital*. Rutherford: Farleigh Dickinson University Press, 1991.

Reynolds, David S. *Beneath the American Renaissance: The Subversive Imagination in the Age of Emerson and Melville*. New York: Alfred A. Knopf, 1988.

———. *Waking Giant: America in the Age of Jackson*. New York: Harper Collins, 2008.

Stern, Madeline. Ed. *Behind a Mask: The Unknown Thrillers of Louisa May Alcott*. New York: William Morrow and Co., 1975.

Stowe, Harriet Beecher. "Literary Epidemics—No.1." *New-York Evangelist* 13 (28 July1842).

———. "Literary Epidemics—No. 2." *New-York Evangelist* 14 (13 July1843).

Thompson, George. *City Crimes; or, Life in New York and Boston.* New York: William Berry and Co., 1849.

Wilentz, Sean. *Chants Democratic: New York City and the Rise of the American Working Class, 1788–1850.* New York: Oxford University Press, 1984.

Wolff, Robert Lee. *Sensational Victorian: The Life and Fiction of Mary Elizabeth Braddon.* New York: Garland, 1979.

"Working Girls and Their Literature." *The Golden Age* (29 July 1871).

"Yellow-Colored Literature." *The Literary Union* 1 (14 April 1849): 24.

"Your Reading." *Christian Secretary* 24 (6 February 1846): 4.

Acknowledgments

We are indebted to many people for their support of *Transatlantic Sensations*. First and foremost, we would like to thank our editor Ann Donahue for her enthusiasm, good humor, and expert advice throughout the publication process. We also thank Kevin Hutchings and Julia M. Wright, the series editors for Ashgate's "Nineteenth-Century Transatlantic Studies," as well as the press's external reader, for valuable comments that sharpened the project as a whole and helped shape particular contributions to it. We likewise appreciate the generous financial assistance provided by the co-chairs of the English Department at the University of Missouri–Kansas City, Virginia Blanton and Jeffrey Rydberg-Cox.

Our contributors were a pleasure to work with, and we would like to extend our appreciation to them for their genuine engagement with the project. In particular, we would like to thank David S. Reynolds for offering encouragement and writing the preface. Finally, we are grateful to the students in John Barton and Jennifer Phegley's 2008 "Transatlantic Sensations" course for helping us develop our ideas about the transatlantic exchange of nineteenth-century sensationalism. This class provided a crucial foundation for the book and brought Kristin Huston to the project.

Introduction
"An Age of Sensation ... Across the Atlantic"

John Cyril Barton and Jennifer Phegley

> Some would have it an age of Sensation,
> If the age one of Sense may not be—
> The Word's not *Old* England's creation,
> But New England's over the sea,—
> Where all's in the high-pressure way,
> In life just as in locomotion,
> And where, though you're here for today,
> Where to-morrow you'll be, you've no notion ...
> And now that across the Atlantic
> Worn threadbare "Sensation" we've seen,
> And the people that lately were frantic,
> Blush to think such madmen they've been;
> *Mr. Punch* sees with pain and surprise,
> On the part of this common sense nation,
> Every here and there, on the rise,
> This pois'nous exotic "Sensation." (31)
>
> "Sense v. Sensation" *Punch* (July 1861)

From the late eighteenth century to the late nineteenth century, "sensation" was understood to be a transatlantic phenomenon. Nineteenth-century critics often traced the origins of sensationalism as far back as classical Greek drama, but its association with contemporary seduction tales, Gothic fiction, Newgate novels, city-mysteries romances, middle-class sensation fiction, melodramatic stage productions, dime novels, imperial and frontier adventures, and detective stories made it symptomatic of the modern world on both sides of the Atlantic.[1] While scholars today usually consider these forms as discrete literary phenomena from distinct national contexts, these genres were often interrelated by nineteenth-

---

[1] Amanda Claybaugh argues that nineteenth-century readers and critics often saw literature in English as one common tradition and discussed English and American writers "alongside one another without alluding to national difference" (13). While this trend may well be true in regard to the high-culture writers she mentions—Henry James, George Eliot, Walt Whitman, and Alfred, Lord Tennyson—we focus here on English and American writers who sought to draw distinctions by blaming each other for the popular phenomenon of sensationalism. Despite this significant difference, we agree with Claybaugh's contention that the Anglo-American literary world was indeed a single, if diverse, tradition in English throughout most of the century.

century critics in terms of an emerging notion of "sensationalism" that gained currency in the popular press of the era. In its various manifestations, sensation was thus intimately linked to an era of mass production, mass readership, and mass culture. Sensationalism was judged in vastly conflicting ways as either the sign of cultural decline or the harbinger of a new and more energetic age. Either way, it was certainly something to debate—sometimes seemingly endlessly—and to condemn or celebrate, depending on one's perspective (and often on whether one happened to be an elite critic, a middle-class writer, or a common reader).

As Karen Halttunen has pointed out, the first use of the term "sensation" recorded by the *Oxford English Dictionary* was in 1779 in relation to the production of "excited or violent feeling" (67). The tales of crime, violence, and punishment compiled in the five-volume *Newgate Calendar,* which first appeared in 1773, were an early source of such sensationalism. Widely read in both England and the United States, the *Newgate Calendar*, named for the London prison that housed notorious criminals, contained accounts originally featured in newspapers, ballads, and broadsides. Sensation, then, was often a press-driven phenomenon, which expanded as printing was modernized and cheap newspapers became more affordable and widely accessible. Sensational news, in turn, spawned sensational fiction, as was the case with the Newgate novel. Novels ripped from the criminal chronicles in the news such as Edward Bulwer-Lytton's *Eugene Aram* (1832), Charles Dickens's *Oliver Twist* (1839), and William Harrison Ainsworth's *Jack Sheppard* (1840) were condemned by critics who feared they would inspire the growth of crime by glorifying the outlaw. As Lyn Pykett points out, "Both the Newgate novel and the Newgate novelist were to a large extent journalistic constructs" defined by the cheap newspaper sources from which they took their characters and plots as well as by the criticism they received in the elite press (21). In 1842, *Punch* published a satirical image of the new "Literary Gentleman" depicting a writer of Newgate fiction whose desk is complete with a tiny gallows, a copy of the *Newgate Calendar*, and an execution speech, among other symbols of crime and sensation (Figure I.1).[2] With the elimination of the English Stamp Tax in 1855, the number of cheap papers and magazines skyrocketed along with an increase in sensational "penny bloods" and "penny dreadfuls" serialized in those periodicals.

According to David S. Reynolds, sensational journalism emerged in America as a popular form of entertainment in the first decades of the nineteenth century (173). In 1807 Philadelphia's suggestively titled *The Tickler* was established, followed by New York's *The American Magazine of Wonders* in 1809. The latter featured stories, so the paper advertised, that were "Miraculous! Queer! Marvelous! Whimsical! Absurd! Out of the Way! Unaccountable!" Similar papers emerged in the 1820s and 1830s, and by 1831 the *New York Genius of Temperance* reported that crimes "now form the '*Domestic News*' of every journal ... [W]hat was once too shocking for recital, now forms a part of the intellectual regalia which the public

---

[2]   We would like to thank our students Adam Thomas-Brashier and Jennifer Fenton for bringing this illustration to our attention.

Fig. I.1   "The Literary Gentleman." *Punch* (February 1842): 68. Courtesy
                 of the LaBudde Department of Special Collections at the
                 University of Missouri–Kansas City.

appetite demands with a gusto that will scarcely brook the disappointment, should the mails bring fewer murders than temperance meetings!" (qtd. in Reynolds 173). Following the advent of modern printing technology in the early 1830s, every major U.S. city had at least one penny press paper. The most famous—Boston's *Daily Times*, Philadelphia's *Public Ledger* and the *New York Herald*—catered to large audiences.

A new source of literary inspiration, cheap papers in the United States were not without their critics, many of whom were across the Atlantic. Charles Dickens, in 1842, denigrates the American penny press with its "pimping and pandering for all degrees of vicious taste, and gorging with coined lies the most voracious maw; [and] imputing to every man in public life the coarsest and vilest motives" (qtd. in Reynolds 173). Echoing Dickens's sentiments, the *London Foreign Quarterly Review* notes the same year that "the more respectable the city in America, the more infamous, the more degrading and disgusting we have found to be its Newspaper Press" (qtd. in Reynolds 172). Such accounts downplayed or willfully ignored the affinities between the sensationalism in the English and American press. However, a decade later a writer for the *Westminister Review* puts it more baldly when comparing the penny papers of the two nations: "Our press is bad enough, but its violence is meekness and even its atrocities are virtues, compared with that system of brutal and ferocious outrage which distinguishes the press of America" (qtd. in Reynolds 172).

Those who derided sensationalism often did so because they feared the corrupting influence that dangerous emotionalism and bodily excitement were thought to have on readers, particularly women and the working classes. The attention devoted to the minute details of sexual, morally corrupt, and criminal activities were disturbing to most critics, though they typically acknowledged that the coverage of such violent and titillating events in the press preceded fictional accounts that were often ripped from the headlines. As *Chambers's Journal* notes in its article on "Sensational Reporting": "The principal object of a newspaper report nowadays would seem to be to present the public with an exciting and dramatic narrative, rather than a calm, unimpassioned statement of the facts; to write, in short, rather for their amusement than information" (151). Such reporting of criminal events and trials is characterized as devoid of "refinement, good taste, or common decency" (152), yet sensationalism in all its forms remained immeasurably popular among every class of society. While the press was reveling in illicit activity, performers, novelists, and everyday folks of all sorts were following suit, much to the dismay of the literary establishment.

Throughout the 1860s and 1870s *Punch* ran a series of articles parodying the public's attraction to all things sensational. They included "Sensation Scribbling" (May 31, 1862), "'Sensation' Suicides" (December 27, 1862), "Sensation Census" (March 5, 1864), "Sensation Sermons" (July 13, 1867), "Sensational Savages" (October 24, 1868), "Sensation Food" (December 19, 1868), "Sensation for the Sea-Side" (September 13,1873), and "Novel Sensations for the Blasé" (May 13, 1876). In "'Sensation' Suicides," "Jack Rattler" (a sort of Jack Sheppard of journalism) warns that popular interest in sensationalism has gotten so out of hand that

> I would suggest to the proprietors of our sensation supper-rooms, that doubtless they might do a tidy stroke of business by engaging a performer to break his neck in public on such and such an evening ... and if by accident the acrobat escaped, and only smashed a leg or so, instead of breaking his backbone or dashing out his brains ... the spirited proprietor might return the entrance money, or issue tickets for the suicide which should take place some other night ... and the spectators, I dare say, would not grumble very much, if they were to see a fellow crippled, say, for life, although he disappointed them by not breaking his neck. (260)

Rattler's wry commentary nicely brings together performance, dining, violence, and suicide—hallmarks of this new genre of journalism. *Appleton's*, across the Atlantic, ran a complementary article, "Hanging as One of the Fine Arts" (1871). Focusing on hanging as a choice form of suicide, the article examines several cases of professional stage performers and children who "played at hanging" and who sometimes inadvertently became its victims (670). *Harper's* the following year printed a short article titled "The Guillotine" (1872), a subject of transatlantic intrigue. Replete with three illustrations of beheadings in progress, the article presents a prehistory of the French physician's invention, discussing earlier uses of a decapitation device employed in Germany from medieval times to the late eighteenth century. It ends with a curious anecdote about German doctors in 1795 who took a prurient interest in the actual, physical sensation of beheadings: "Eminent physicians assiduously attended executions, and by striking at the severed head, shouting in its ear, and divers other ways, endeavored to ascertain whether sensation survived the shock of decapitation" (187). Such a concluding example says as much about contemporary American interests as it does about those of late eighteenth-century Germans.

Sensation, it seemed, was everywhere and out of control. In addition to the popular press, its influence was ever-present in popular literature. "Receipt for a Sensational Novel," a satirical poem printed in *Powder Magazine*, went so far as to provide aspiring sensation writers with a ready-made formula, one that employed a so-called 'low' style and mixed the social classes:

> First take the quintessence of everything bad,
> Dress it up in the language and style of a cad;
> Let your plot upon deeds of rascality hang,
> Add some *double entendre*, and a good deal of slang;
> Take a quart of the liquor that flows in our veins,
> And daub it about in most hideous stains; ..
> Take a modern young lady, well-born and refined,
> With every advantage in person and mind;
> Allow her *carte blanche* to do all that she likes,
> And let her elope with Lord Claude or Bill Sykes ..
> Dish up with the flavour of dissolute lives,
> And serve for the use of our daughters and wives. (267–268)

The focus on women readers here is typical as women were assumed to be the primary audience for all fiction, but particularly for middlebrow sensation novels. Women were also feared to be the most easily harmed readers as *Putnam's* notes in September 1857: Novels "exert a bad influence on growing minds, especially on feminine minds, by nature inclined to an overbalance on the side of feeling. They excite the imagination, arouse morbid emotions and aspirations, and so render them unfit for homely duties and aims of common life, and cause them to feel unsatisfied with its realities'" ("Novel Reading" 384). Sensation novels only amplified this fear of female corruption by way of reading.

The association of novel writing with cooking in "Receipt for a Sensation Novel" is also telling. It not only suggests a "recipe" for success that is written in an undoubtedly feminized form, but provides a list of deleterious ingredients on which a hungry public was eager to feast—either in the privacy of their own homes or in public "sensation supper-rooms" derided by Jack Rattler. In America, working-class novelists such as George Lippard, George Thompson, and Ned Buntline unapologetically drew from such a recipe or "receipt" and found inspiration in innovative French and British precursors and contemporaries, such as Eugene Sue and William Harrison Ainsworth. In fact Lippard, who was often dubbed "the American Sue," records his humble admiration of Ainsworth, "whom all the starch-and-buckram critics have been abusing so heartily for years" in his best-selling novel, *The Quaker City* (1845). Later in *The Quaker City*, Lippard savages such critics in an extended attack on a representative "shallow pated critic," a "sweet-maiden man" whose "innocent and girlish soul would be shocked" by the things described in his and like-minded works (305). "Our taste is different from yours," Lippard asserts, further lampooning the "sweet virgin man," the genteel "Mr. Miss" critic who disapproved of the new wave of popular fiction that featured the macabre, the criminal, the sensational. Emasculating genteel critics and adopting an often used fiction-as-food metaphor[3]—a commonplace,

---

[3]   For an excellent discussion of the reading-as-eating trope, see Steven Mailloux, "The Use and Abuse of Fiction: Readers Eating Books," in *Reception Histories: Rhetoric, Pragmatism and American Cultural Politics* (Ithaca, N.Y.: Cornell University Press, 1998), 129–148. In tracing the trope across various cultural spheres, Mailloux cites a number of salient examples, including the following instructions to readers in Anna Brackett's *The Education of American Girls* (1874): "We must remember that the brain craves thought, as the stomach does food; and where it is not properly supplied it will feed on garbage. Where a Latin, geometry or history lesson would be a healthy tonic, or nourishing food, the trashy, exciting story, the gossiping book of travels, the sentimental poem, or still worse, the coarse humor or thin-vailed [*sic*] vice of the low romance, fills up the hour—and is at best but tea or slops, if not as dangerous as opium or whisky" (qtd. in Mailloux 144). While Mailloux focuses on nineteenth-century American culture, the reader-as-eater figure is not of course, as he points out, limited to the nineteenth century or American culture. Indeed, it has a history stretching back to Plato's *Gorgias* (Mailloux 147). We too draw on the figure's use in the nineteenth century but do so in terms of a transatlantic culture of sensationalism. Moreover, whereas Mailloux emphasizes its gendered dimensions, we primarily stress

as we shall see, in nineteenth-century discussions of literary sensationalism—Lippard concludes his assault as a dainty little letter addressed to a "dear Mister-Miss, surrounded with a border of sugar plumbs, besprinkled with pendent drops of frozen treacle" (306). If this new breed of writers served up what genteel critics dismissed as pub fair, Lippard countered by ridiculing the works privileged by such critics as frivolous treats with little substance. Either way, readers apparently were what they ate, and the public's appetite for sensation deeply troubled vanguards of the literary establishment.

By the 1860s, however, it was middle-class novelists who were taken to task for following the recipe for sensation. An 1866 *Macmillan's Magazine* article on "Penny Novels," reprinted in the U.S. in *Littell's Living Age*, notes that "About a dozen or fifteen years ago ... our lower classes were being entertained with tales of seduction, adultery, forgery, and murder ... But these twelve or fifteen years have wrought a change, and any one who will look at such a periodical as the *London Journal* will be much struck, perhaps a little abashed, by the strong moral tone that pervades the writing" (108). Likewise, Margaret Oliphant defended working-class sensationalism while famously berating middle-class versions of the form. In her 1858 article "The Byways of Literature: Reading for the Million," Oliphant pardons the hard-working "multitude" for liking "amusement better than instruction" (203). She maintains that the penny papers, while filled with tales of adventure, intrigue, and sensation contain "nothing, so far as we could perceive, to offend anybody" (212). Yet, Oliphant vehemently opposed the entry of sensation fiction into the ranks of the middle classes, especially when written by women like Mary Elizabeth Braddon. She famously pronounces Braddon's sensational depiction of an "intense appreciation of flesh and blood" as "the natural sentiment of English girls" as proof that Braddon did not know "how young women of good blood and good training feel" ("Novels" 259–260).

W. Fraser Rae similarly berates Braddon for "making the literature of the kitchen the favourite reading of the Drawing-room" (198). Both Oliphant and Rae articulate the acutely English fear of the leveling of the classes through shared reading practices. Not only were the servants potentially reading the same books as their "betters"—as illustrated by the famous *Punch* cartoon "Sensation Novels" (Figure I.2)—but a working-class genre was infiltrating the middle-class domain of the circulating library frequented by leisured women. Braddon good-naturedly poked fun at her own transgression of gender and class boundaries with the character of Sigismund Smith in *The Doctor's Wife* (1864). Smith writes fiction for "the penny public" who want "plot, and plenty of it; surprises, and plenty of 'em; mystery as thick as a November fog" (45). Smith, who is depicted in a later novel as a respectable three-volume novelist, has a "tendency towards" accumulating dead "bodies" in a "ghastly and melodramatic" style (46–47). Braddon likewise

---

what the trope tells us about reading habits and perceived notions of so-called high/low literature—issues readily apparent in Mailloux's example from Brackett's book and in ours in the body of this introduction.

writes that "on one occasion, after admiring the trim flower-gardens and ivied walls, the low turreted towers and grassy moats, of a dear old place that had once been a grange, he ventured to remark that the spot was so peaceful it reminded him of slow poisoning, and demanded whether there would be any objection to his making the quiet grange the scene of his next fiction" (50). Smith's imagination thus imbues even the most respectable places with sensationalism, thereby embodying the anxieties of critics that an urban, working-class form was invading the bastions of upper-class tranquility.

Americans, by comparison more accepting of the intermingling of the classes, were instead deeply disturbed by the sinful nature of sensational subjects. Popular works by William Gilmore Simms, Catherine Williams, Lippard, and others contained prefatory warnings imploring readers to derive the moral in their tales of murder and seduction. Simms, for instance, makes such a claim in the "Advertisement" to *Martin Faber: The Story of a Criminal*: "The design of this work is purely moral, and the lessons sought to be inculcated are of universal application and importance" (2). Similarly, Williams in the preface to *Fall River: An Authentic Narrative*, notes that her tale of the seduced and murdered Sarah Maria Cornell "may prove useful ... as a salutary and timely warning to young women in the same situation in life, in which the ill fated girl was placed, who is the subject of this narrative" (3). And Lippard concludes his 1849 Preface to *The Quaker City* with the following injunction to the reader:

> Would to God that the evils recorded in these pages, were not based upon facts ... If you discover one word in its pages, that has a tendency to develop one impure thought, I beseech you reject that word. If you discover a chapter, a page, or a line, that conflicts with the great idea of Human Brotherhood, promulgated by the Redeemer, I ask you with all my soul, reject that chapter, that passage, that line. At the same time remember the idea which impelled me to produce the book. Remember that my life from the age of sixteen up to twenty-five was one perpetual battle with hardship and difficulty, such as do not often fall to the lot of a young man such as rarely is recorded in the experience of childhood or manhood. Take the book with all its faults and all its virtues. Judge it as you yourself would wish to be judged. Do not wrest a line from these pages, for the encouragement of a bad thought or a bad deed. (2)

Such themes of warning in mid-nineteenth-century sensation literature hearken back to early American gallows literature, what Daniel A. Cohen rightly identifies as the origins of popular literature in American culture. Cotton Mather's *Pillars of Salt* (1699) provides a case in point. A compilation of famous execution narratives—including titillating accounts of rape, bestiality, and adultery for which the punishment was death—*Pillars of Salt* overtly indulged in lurid crime and sensation but was justified by the pious Mather for its instructional purposes. Such stories, he advises readers in the preface, "might be of singular Use, to Correct and Reform, the *Crimes*, wherein too many do *Live*"(65).

Later American critics from the nineteenth century often drew causal links between sinful or criminal behavior and sensation fiction. Amelie V. Petit, for example, claims in a scientific journal that "[t]he sensational literature of the day is the parent of, at least, one-third of the sin of the day. Directly or indirectly, it is dragging down the pure, the innocent, the beautiful, and the brave into the slime, the degradation, and the corruption of the lowest haunts of infamy. It is as hundred-headed as the Hydra, and, snake-like, glides everywhere" (84). Lydia Maria Child, herself a dabbler in sensation, similarly blamed popular literature for promoting a culture of violence and vengeance in her widely read *Letters from New York* (321), whereas New England Minister Leonard Bacon lambasts "Newgate literature" for the "charms of poetry and the colors of romance" it casts "over robbery and murder and piracy" so that the criminal "becomes immediately an object of special sympathy" (565). But perhaps the strongest indictment against sensation as sin came from neither a woman nor a minister but a doctor in *Confessions and Experiences of a Novel Reader* (1855). Written by "a Chicago physician," the book equates "popular literature" with "popular licentiousness" (vii–viii) and bemoans "the enormous circulation of over 2,500,000 volumes [of novels], exerting their deleterious influence, and diffusing their pernicious principles throughout society" (32). Quoting at one point from an unidentified "celebrated lady author of our country" who remarked that "healthy reading produces the same effect upon the mind that healthy food does upon the body," the book's anonymous author draws the following conclusion: "Now the most obtuse mind will tell you the effect of unhealthy food upon the animal economy. What, then, is the effect of unhealthy reading upon the mind?" (38). For this "celebrated lady" and the representative physician author, literature was likened to food—food for the body and the mind—and readers were analogous to eaters whose moral development depended on healthy reading habits. Thus, whether distressed by the shared reading practices across class lines in England, or obsessed over the transgression of moral codes in the United States, enemies of sensation were fiercely opposed to this protean form that weakened bodies (or the body politic) and poisoned minds.

But not all the literary establishment decried the affects of sensationalism. Some well respected authors and journals came to sensation's defense. In "The Sensational Williams," for instance, Dickens argues that even the bard Shakespeare would be condemned by contemporary critical standards. To illustrate the point, he constructs mock reviews of *Macbeth* and *Hamlet* according to a criteria close to what Lippard dismissed as pretentious starch-and-buckram criticism: "The anti-sensation critic will tell you," declares Dickens,

> that, if you would write a novel or a play that is fit to be read by anyone with tastes superior to those of a butcher-boy, you must confine yourself strictly to the common events of common lives, have nothing whatever to say to any of the extremes of passion or of action, leave murder to the penny papers, be ignorant of suicide, have no idea that there are dark shadows in the world, and shun a mystery as you would the measles ... But why is all art to be restricted to the uniform level of quiet domesticity? ... Why is the literary artist to be shut out from the tragedy of existence, as he sees it going on around him? (14)

In a defense of sensation that resonates with Lippard's attack on genteel criticism of the establishment's Mr. Misses, Dickens highlights the importance of extreme passions and actions in works of high literature.

George Augustus Sala likewise extends both the critique of hyper-sensitive critics and the yoking of literary and culinary consumption in his defense of sensationalism in Braddon's *Belgravia Magazine*:

> If we read the newspapers, if we read the police reports ... we shall take no great harm by reading realistic novels of human passion, weakness, and error ... [We] want novels about that which Is, and not about that which never Was and never Will be. We don't want pap, or spoon meat, or milk-and-water, or curds-and-whey, or Robb's biscuits, or boiled whiting, or cold boiled veal without salt. We want meat; and this is a strong age, and we can digest it. (53–54)

Appropriating the reading-as-eating analogy, Sala likens sensation to "meat"—literature with sustenance for "a strong age" prepared to "digest it." The American journal *The Round-Table*, which often attacked sensationalism, adopts a similar line of argument in "A Good Word for Sensation," an editorial diagnosing the literary phenomenon. "It has become a fashion to abuse Sensation," the article begins, concluding that to "apply the term to a book, a newspaper, a play, or an artist is to suggest a certain form of condemnation" (151). The article explains sensationalism as a "natural reaction from a rather over-wrought tendency to didacticism. The world has grown so weary of being sermonized, so dazed and stupefied by dullness and stupidity ... that it has welcomed the sensation writers much more heartily than they deserve because they were the exact antithesis of those who had been such monstrous bores before" (151). In this way, the magazine reluctantly put in its "good word" by laying blame for sensation's popularity on unsensational writers for being such pontificating, "monstrous bores."

Thus, despite the many commonalities of the sensation phenomenon on both sides of the Atlantic, the Americans and English pointed fingers of blame at each other for the popular form. Perhaps not surprisingly given his unsettling experiences touring the United States in 1842,[4] Dickens argues in a May 1861 *All the Year Round* article that the escalation of sensationalism is rooted in American culture. In the United States, he claims, "sensations are epidemic; they run through the whole community, from abolitionist to slave-dealer ... We at home have our insanities, but I think the Americans run madder, and suffer oftener" ("American Sensations" 132). In July of the same year, *Punch* agreed that America was an inherently sensational nation, whereas England was more naturally sensible in the poem "Sense v. Sensation," a portion of which serves as the epigraph to our introduction. Opposing British "Sense" to American "Sensation," the poem

---

[4]   See Meredith McGill's *American Literature and Culture of Reprinting 1834–1853* (Philadelphia: University of Pennsylvania Press, 2001) for an excellent account of Dickens's American tours and his dissatisfaction with a lack of interest in the United States for an international copyright law.

firmly locates the origins of sensationalism in the United States and its literary traditions: "If the age one of Sense may not be," the poem muses, "The Word's not *Old* England's creation, / But New England's over the sea" (31). Albeit short-sighted and self-interested, the poem's argument does make some sense when read in light of Cohen's provocative claim, as noted earlier, that American popular culture has its origins in early New England crime literature, which included not only the Puritan execution sermon, but dying verses, execution ballads, and the criminal conversion narrative. At the same time, however, *Punch*'s declaration ignores England's own fascination with gallows literature and picaresque criminal narratives that had been widely read since the seventeenth century and that strongly influenced classic eighteenth-century British novels, such as Daniel Defoe's *Moll Flanders* (1722) and Henry Fielding's *Jonathan Wild* (1743) as well as inaugural Gothic novels like Horace Walpole's *The Castle of Otranto* (1764) and Ann Radcliff's *The Mysteries of Udolpho* (1794). In many ways, these earlier canonical works and others like them anticipated the nation's decade of the sensation novel in the 1860s. *Chambers's Journal* joined both *Punch* and *All the Year Round* in holding America responsible for sensationalism, but it more generously saw the phenomenon as a by-product of U.S. democracy: "America, to a greater extent than any other, is a country of sensations. An excitement has wider range and involves a larger proportion of the entire population. The reason of this may be found in the general equality, and the universal diffusion of intelligence. There are fewer persons raised above the influence of popular excitement, and there are also fewer who are sunk below it" ("American Sensations" 353). American magazines, for their part, often associated sensationalism with English or European trends that threatened to invade its more pious shores. Despite embracing some of his foreign influences, Lippard also did his share of nationalistic bashing of English fiction. In "English Novels," he declares that these foreign imports "do more to corrupt the minds of American children than any sort of bad literature that ever cursed the world. They are filled with attacks upon American freedom ... Published by greedy pirates in New York, who will not pay a decent price for a book even from the pen of a Cooper or an Irving, these books are scattered broadcast over the land" (253). Likewise, *The Round-Table* notoriously censured British sensation novelists Braddon and Charles Reade, accusing them of moral corruption as well as plagiarism and deception. The magazine denounces Reade's novel *Griffith Gaunt* as

> one of the worst novels that has appeared during this generation, the worst perhaps, that has ever been produced by the pen of any writer of position. The novels of the day have been tending more and more toward the delineation of adultery and bigamy and seduction and nameless social crimes; but most of them have preserved at least the appearance of reprehending vice, and none have shown such temerity in narrating a story so compact with crime, so replete with insidious illusions even more demoralizing than the sins plainly enough described, or in endeavoring to awaken our sympathizing pity and forgiveness for a man who has sinned unpardonably and vilely. ("An Indecent Publication" 472)

Reade went so far as to sue the journal for slander, accusing it and other American publications of "prurient prudery"; of course, the publicity ensured that the novel became a best-seller (Fantina 29). While U.S. journals braced themselves against a British invasion, American sensation novelists often attributed the most depraved crimes to characters of foreign extraction. Take, for instance, George Thompson's *City Crimes*, in which an ingenious French pickpocket hides a stolen watch in her genitals, a Spanish nobleman attempts to seduce a young boy, and a notorious French criminal who, according to "the French criminal records," not only "brutally murdered" a woman but "outraged the corpse, and afterwards *ate a part of it*" (emphasis original 304). Similarly, in Thompson's *The Gay Girls of New York* (1849) the worst of the novel's assorted criminals are "Monsieur" Louis Michaud from France and Dick Flipper, "an English cockney, a traveling showman, a professional thief, and a graduate of almost every criminal institution in the country" (100). Among the atrocities committed by Monsieur Michaud and Dick Flipper (whose name suggests his sexual deviance) include the rape, commercial exploitation, and eventual murder of a blinded young women, whose voluptuous body and hideously disfigured face make her the star attraction in Michaud and Flipper's freak show. In this way, Thompson and other popular American novelists celebrated sensation and profited from it but often blamed its immorality on European influences and immigrants.

Thus, while sensation may have been, as *Punch*'s "Sense v. Sensation" characterized it, a "pois'nous exotic," it grew and flourished in England and Europe as well as in the United States. Indeed, it cross-pollinated over the long nineteenth century through transatlantic exchanges that gave rise to a new kind of writing, including the century's best-selling sensation novels that found large readerships in Britain, Europe, and the Americas. As Amanda Claybaugh argues, the lack of an international copyright law until 1891 and the rampant reprinting of British works in the United States contributed to a bifurcated Anglo-American publishing system in which each nation had its dominant realm: British authors produced more literary works, while American publishers sold more literary texts. Claybaugh elaborates:

> The U.S. market had stabilized at a lower price than the British; U.S. papers sold many copies of relatively inexpensive editions, whereas British publishers would sell relatively few copies of expensive ones ... Viewed from the perspective of writing, then, the Anglo-American literary marketplace was clearly centered in London. Viewed from the perspective of publishing, however, it was increasingly centered in Boston and New York ... On the one hand, Harper and Brothers had dwarfed its British rivals, publishing two million volumes a year. As a consequence, British authors submitted to the taste of Harpers and its rivals as surely as they submitted to the taste of those circulating libraries, Mudie's and W.H. Smith most prominently, that purchased the expensive British editions of their works. On the other hand, the vast majority of what Harpers published was written by British authors ... To consider publishing alongside writing is, then, to see that neither nation clearly dominated the literary marketplace. (19)

Regardless of this astonishingly interconnected literary relationship, scholars have, until quite recently, neglected the interdependent development of literary trends such as sensationalism. In 2003, Lawrence Buell outlined recent studies in transatlanticism, announcing that "these days ... look like boom-times for transatlantic literary studies" (66). Despite the clear interest in "African-diasporic and trans-Pacific and Hispano-phone America-hemispheric initiatives," however, Buell acknowledges that Anglo-American studies have lagged behind, perhaps because "[t]he leading *dramatis personae* on whom one presumably needs to concentrate in order to render a comparative Anglo-American or 'white Atlantic' analysis are pretty familiar within their respective specializations even if a comparatist focus is not. Nevertheless, this too has been gathering momentum, and to good result" (67). He cites Paul Giles, whose book *Transatlantic Insurrections* the article reviews, as the leader of this movement in Anglo-American literary studies.[5]

Transatlantic Sensations offers the first sustained investigation of the intersections, commerce, and exchange between nineteenth-century British and American sensation literature. This collection reinforces Paul Giles's argument that "British-American culture" is marked less by patterns of dominance and resistance than by "the more discomfiting figures of mirroring and twinning, where mutual identities are not so much independently asserted but sacrilegiously travestied." Giles is "concerned with American literature not as subordinate to an imperial British literature, but rather as something that develops in parallel to it"; his focus, and ours, attends to "points of transnational convergence and interference that arise out of works incorporating their own particular local perspectives" (8–9). Given that for nineteenth-century critics sensation was an obvious point of contention bandied across the Atlantic, it is surprising that few contemporary critics have taken up the subject from a transatlantic perspective. In fact, a brief survey of recent scholarship in British and U.S. sensation literature— not to mention Europe and the Americas more broadly—helps to show what little work in the field has been done from a transatlantic perspective. The time is now ripe for such an intervention.

---

[5]   Scholars who have contributed to this emerging field include Robert Weisbuch (*Atlantic Double-Cross: American Literature and British Influence in the Age of Emerson*, Chicago: University of Chicago Press, 1986); Nancy Armstrong and Leonard Tennenhouse (*The Imaginary Puritan: Literature, Intellectual Labor, and the Origins of Personal Life*, Berkeley: University of California Press, 1992); Meredith McGill (*American Literature and the Culture of Reprinting, 1834–1853*, Philadelphia: University of Pennsylvania Press, 2001, and *The Traffic in Poems: Nineteenth-Century Poetry and Transatlantic Exchange*, New Brunswick, N.J.: Rutgers University Press, 2008); Paul Giles (*Transatlantic Insurrections*, 2001, and *Atlantic Republic: The American Tradition in English Literature*, New York: Oxford University Press, 2006); Leonard Tennenhouse (*The Importance of Feeling English*, 2007); and Kate Flint (*The Transatlantic Indian, 1776–1930*, Princeton, N.J.: Princeton University Press, 2008). Susan Manning and Andrew Taylor have also co-edited *Transatlantic Literary Studies: A Reader*, which helpfully maps out the varying approaches to the field for scholars and students alike.

Bridging the Atlantic: Sensation in scholarship today

In recent years, sensationalism has attracted the attention of scholars of both British and American literature and culture. Over the past decade there has been a surge in critical concern about British Sensation fiction made possible by the foundational work of Ann Cvetkovitch, Winifred Hughes, Lyn Pykett, Elaine Showalter, and others writing in the 1980s and 1990s. Recent books that build on their scholarship include Pamela K Gilbert's *Companion to Sensation Fiction* (2011); Kimberly Harrison and Richard Fantina's *Victorian Sensations: Essays on a Scandalous Genre* (2006); Andrew Maunder and Grace Moore's *Victorian Crime, Madness and Sensation* (2004); Deborah Wynne's *The Sensation Novel and the Victorian Family Magazine* (2001); and Marlene Tromp, Pamela Gilbert, and Aeron Haynie's *Beyond Sensation: Mary Elizabeth Braddon in Context* (2000). These books explore a wide range of topics within the genre including authorship and publishing, gender, domesticity, class, crime, madness, modernity, and imperialism. Add to these studies numerous articles and chapters devoted to sensationalism, books devoted to individual sensation novelists, and Andrew Radford's sweeping and summative "reader's guide" to *Victorian Sensation Fiction* (2009) and one has the making of a booming trend in current literary scholarship.

Interest in American sensationalism is just as keen. Works such as Jane Tompkins' *Sensational Designs: The Cultural Work of American Fiction, 1790–1860* (1986), Michael Denning's *Mechanic Accents: Dime Novels and Working-Class Culture in America* (1987), and especially David S. Reynolds's *Beneath the American Renaissance: The Subversive Imagination in the Age of Emerson and Melville* (1988) laid the groundwork for a critical understanding of sensation literature in the United States, whereas Daniel A. Cohen's *Pillars of Salt, Monuments of Grace: New England Crime Literature and the Origins of American Popular Culture, 1674–1860* (1993) and Karen Haltunnen's *Murder Most Foul: The Killer and the American Gothic Imagination* (1998) have used sensational literature (e.g., execution sermons and broadsides, criminal biographies, and trial reports) as a touchstone for evaluating U.S. cultural history before the Civil War. More recently, Shelley Streeby's *American Sensations: Class, Empire, and the Production of Popular Culture* (2002) has established a transnational context (principally between the United States and Mexico, but Cuba and Nicaragua as well) to explore America's "culture of sensation," while Reynolds continues to produce important scholarship on George Lippard and George Thompson—two of the most popular and radical Sensation novelists in nineteenth-century America.[6]

---

[6]   Reynolds and Denning (in particular) situate their studies in a broader transatlantic context, noting the influence of Samuel Richardson, G.W.M. Reynolds, Eugene Sue, and a number of other British and European authors, but their focus is squarely on U.S. writers and the antebellum context. Drawing explicitly from Denning and Reynolds, Streeby has moved the study of U.S. sensationalism beyond the antebellum period in *American Sensations*. With the Mexican-American and Spanish-American wars as an historic frame (1848–1898), Streeby examines America's "culture of sensation," her term for the period's

Despite the increased interest in sensationalism among scholars of British and American literature, no one has undertaken a thorough investigation of the transatlantic intersections, commerce, and exchange between these two literary traditions. Given that the genre has a complicated and interconnected history on both sides of the Atlantic, this lack of attention is striking. The essays in this collection attempt to build a bridge across the Atlantic by examining the transnational publication system that shaped the development of sensation literature—especially the best-selling genre of the sensation novel—over the course of the nineteenth century. Examining sensation literature in a transatlantic context enables us to redefine the field in both traditions. For, on the one hand, American sensation literature is usually seen as peaking in the 1840s, with the massive popularity of the city-mysteries and urban-Gothic novels of Lippard, Joseph Holt Ingraham, Ned Buntline, and others. The British sensation novel, on the other hand, is said to begin with Wilkie Collins's *The Woman in White*, Braddon's *Lady Audley's Secret*, and Ellen Price Wood's *East Lynne*. Indeed, Richard Fantina proclaims that "sensation fiction was a controversial genre that emerged primarily in England in the mid-nineteenth-century" (*Victorian Sensational Fiction* 11). However, as Andrew Maunder argues, we need to acknowledge that sensation as a genre extends well beyond the decade of the 1860s (*Sensationalism and the Sensational Debate* xiii). We, in turn, argue that placing sensationalism within its transatlantic context also points to the importance of the genre's pre-1860 counterparts. The Gothic novel, the Newgate novel, and American urban crime fiction are all part of sensationalism, which evolved into many individualized forms from the late eighteenth to the late nineteenth century.

By analyzing sensation literature in a transatlantic context, we can see how both traditions developed in a reciprocal relation that defies traditional conceptions of a one-way flow of cultural influence from the "old world" to the "new" while also demonstrating that sensationalism has a long historical line with many branches that emerged at various times on each side of the Atlantic, often responding to or reacting against trends from across the pond. Such a perspective, in fact, enables us to look beyond these two decades (the 1840s in America and the 1860s in England) to a century of sensation, from Gothic fiction to the rise of the sensational press at the turn of the nineteenth century to detective fiction and the popular romances and westerns against which literary realism defined itself at the century's close. Moreover, placing sensational literature within a broader transatlantic context that spans the long nineteenth century provides a

---

popular low-brow literature and related arts and cultural practices (e.g., journalism, music, blackface minstrelsy, and popular theater). Unlike Denning and Reynolds, however, Streeby calls attention to a transnational rather than a transatlantic context for sensationalism, one that situates U.S. literature in relation to the Americas, particularly Mexico, Cuba, and Nicaragua. While acknowledging the importance of Streeby's work, this collection returns to the transatlantic culture of nineteenth-century sensationalism—a culture tentatively sketched by Denning, Reynolds, and other more recent Americanists in the field but one virtually ignored in the scholarship of British sensation literature.

fresh perspective from which to reevaluate other popular literary forms, such as sentimental fiction and Newgate novels. At the same time, the perspective granted us through a transatlantic approach allows us not only to track back to the seduction narratives that gave birth to sensation novels but also to look forward to realistic forms that incorporated elements of the sensational.

A century of sensation: Essays in this volume

Transatlantic Sensations begins with "prehistories" of sensation by looking at the dialogue and debate generated by the publication of William Godwin's, Susanna Rowson's, and Charles Brockden Brown's sentimental and Gothic fiction, even while it engages with the works of some of sensation's "usual suspects," including Louisa May Alcott, Dion Boucicault, Braddon, Collins, Lippard, Reade, and Thompson. The volume closes with a reassessment of the realist and domestic fiction of George Eliot, Charlotte Yonge, and Thomas Hardy in the context of transatlantic sensationalism, whereas the book's final essay further stretches national borders and generic boundaries by examining a sensational turn-of-the-century kidnapping case in the Balkans that played out in both the U.S. and British popular press. Together, these essays study a wide range of sensational topics including sexuality, slavery, crime, literary piracy, mesmerism, and the metaphors of foreign literary invasion and diseased reading. While some of the essays are thematically paired, we have generally arranged them in chronological order to emphasize the evolution of the form throughout the century as well as to map a new transatlantic lineage for sensationalism.

Several of the essays in this volume illustrate how national traditions of sensation were defined against one another, as we have demonstrated was common in discussions of the subject in the popular press. David S. Reynolds points out that Lippard's particular brand of radical working-class sensationalism, while certainly influenced by European writers like Sue, stood on its own as a manifestation of both Jacksonian democracy and American shock-Gothic techniques. Reynolds argues that Lippard rejects European-style "upper-crust" heroes who save the day and refuses to provide clear moral alternatives to readers because "the realities of American life prevent him from doing so" (p. 84). Instead, Lippard offers what he himself describes as a purely American style of sensation. Likewise, Alexander Moudrov argues that Thompson defined his version of working-class American sensation fiction in opposition to the more offensive and self-indulgent spectacle of European forms. According to Moudrov, Thompson "claimed that he indulged in the scandalous for no other reason than to promote traditional American values and to warn his compatriots about the dangers" presented by "the pernicious influence" of European culture (p. 97). Yet Thompson's insistence on a moral message, like Lippard's, was often seen as suspect given the violent and shocking nature of his fiction.

In contrast, other essays in *Transatlantic Sensations* examine how authors incorporated the strategies of their rivals across the Atlantic. Christopher Apap reverses traditional conceptions of the transatlantic flow of literary influence by demonstrating how American writer Brown inspired changes in Godwin's Gothic fiction. Apap argues that "the transmission of ideas back and forth across the Atlantic reveals a dialog about literary responsibility that implicates agents on both sides of the Atlantic, troubling nationalist readings of each individual author and inaugurating a literary sensationalism that was transatlantic at its inception" (p. 25). Similarly, Dorice Williams Elliott looks at the social-activist influence of Harriet Beecher Stowe's *Uncle Tom's Cabin* on Charles Reade's *It's Never Too Late to Mend*. Elliott points out that Stowe's sentimental melodrama was a clear precursor to Reade's socially aware sensation fiction "partly because of the strong emotional responses it provoked ... but also the explicit scenes of violence or physical suffering that it portrayed" (p. 125). However, Stowe and Reade—and sentimental and sensational fiction—differed in their attitudes toward the sanctity of home, family, the purity of women, and the clear distinction between good and evil, with Stowe reinforcing these values and Reade undermining them. Building on this connection between 1850s abolition literature and British sensation fiction, Kimberly S. Manganelli argues that American fictional portrayals of the figure of the tragic mulatta by Stowe, Child, and William Wells Brown influenced the birth of the middle-class sensation novel in England. Manganelli concludes that anti-slavery narratives traditionally categorized as sentimental are disrupted by the "realities of slavery" that introduce "mysterious identities, sexual transgressions, madness, and violence—elements that would later define British sensation fiction" (p. 138). The influence of American works can be seen in Captain Mayne Ried's *The Quadroon* (1856), Boucicault's play *The Octoroon* (1859), and Braddon's *The Octoroon* (1861), ultimately causing us to rethink Collins's *The Woman in White* as the traditional starting point for British sensation fiction.

Some essays in this collection reflect the anxieties of transatlantic culture itself. Holly Blackford examines Rowson's seduction novel, *Charlotte Temple, A Tale of Truth*, as a precursor to sensation fiction that adapts British literary traditions to a new American form. Blackford argues that this truly transatlantic tale, wherein the seduction occurs as the heroine crosses the Atlantic on her way from England to America, embodies fears about the failure of second-generation Americans to live up to the ideal of self-governance. This generational tension calls into question the ability of the adolescent America to come into its own as a successful, independent, and moral generation. Narin Hassan's essay on tea and other exotic objects in Braddon's *Lady Audley's Secret* and Alcott's *Behind a Mask* reveals the ways in which women's engagement with global consumption is represented as a threat to one's home culture. Hassan argues that sensation fiction was, on both sides of the Atlantic, inextricably linked to the activities of Empire. Similarly, Tamara S. Wagner examines the anxieties of transatlantic exchange in Yonge's failed settler narratives, maintaining that it is "indeed no coincidence that her most extensive engagement with literary sensationalism contains her most intricate and far-reaching exploration of foreign space" (p. 221). Wagner analyzes Yonge's depiction of failed emigration schemes in New Zealand and America to illustrate the sensational difficulties of transporting English domesticity to exotic new spaces that hold much utopian promise but also offer the possibility of catastrophic failure. Ana Savic Moturu studies the consolidation of Anglo-American imperial power through sensational journalism covering the kidnapping of Ellen Stone in the Balkans in 1901. While press coverage of the event in the United States was undermined by its preoccupation with covering the lurid elements of the crime, it also shaped the nation as a new world power that was superseding its "mother country" in part by linking its coverage to traditional American forms such as the frontier romance and the captivity narrative. Great Britain, in contrast, allied itself to the American identity in an effort to resist its own declining power.

A final category of essays interrogates the influence transatlantic publishing practices had on the development of sensation fiction. David Bordelon investigates how Dickens escaped the label of sensation novelist despite being closely associated with the genre's American authors when *Oliver Twist* was serialized and discussed by critics in American periodicals. Bordelon demonstrates that while *Oliver* "fed America's ongoing hunger for titillating scenes of crime and violence" and helped establish the genre of "city fiction" in the U.S., it "yoked contradictory strains of American culture, maintaining a delicate balance" between the "sensational and the sacred," thereby upholding Dickens's high cultural status as a British import (p. 73). Susan David Bernstein maps important intersections between the themes and publication contexts of Eliot's "The Lifted Veil" and Alcott's "A Pair of Eyes," demonstrating that "both writers use sensationalism to explore the problems and possibilities of gendered knowledge while hiding behind veils of anonymity" (p. 184). In each story, mesmerism, secret identity, and duplicity work as metaphors for the challenges women faced when writing in the sensational mode for the periodical press. Jennifer Phegley explores Braddon's intervention in the overwrought international copyright law debate by metaphorically illustrating "the plight of British texts as they traveled across the Atlantic" only to be 'enslaved' by American publishing pirates in her novel *The Octoroon* (p. 156). Phegley argues that the dual identity of Cora the Octoroon, a British educated society woman who is "outed" as a slave and returned to the auction block when she visits her father in Louisiana, resonates with Braddon's own dual roles as an anonymous penny press "hack" and highly promoted middle-class sensation novelist whose cheap fiction was being pirated and marketed with her name by American publishers. Kate Mattacks also explores international publishing practices, but she argues that sensation drama was the product of more friendly reciprocal marketing strategies. According to Mattacks, theatrical publishers T.H. Lacy and Samuel French encouraged a culture of dramatic influence that made sensation drama into a distinctly transatlantic form. Indeed, their lucrative practice of exchanging playtexts and permission rights shaped the way in which sensation plays were received. Julia McCord Chavez uses the transatlantic publication context of Hardy's works to make a case for him as a cosmopolitan sensation fiction writer, despite his staunch reputation as an insular realist. As Chavez states, "Looking first at the *Return of the Native* in its original serialized publication in the London magazine *Belgravia* and then at the concurrent serialization of the novel in the American magazine *Harper's New Monthly*" demonstrates "the ways in which the sensational qualities of the novel and its transatlantic context invite a radical reinterpretation" that allows the book to shed its insularity and emerge as "an anti-regionalist text that promotes transatlantic reading communities" (p. 240).

Taken together, the essays in *Transatlantic Sensations* reinforce Leonard Tennenhouse's cautionary statement against "assuming that different national governments mean different national literatures"; like Tennenhouse, we posit that "the separation of American from British literatures is still at issue and was therefore nothing like the clean break we tend to project backward onto" it (1). Today, studies in transatlanticism typically address topics such as travel and exploration, migration and diaspora, slavery, aboriginal culture, revolution, colonialism, and anti-colonial resistance. The essays collected in this volume help to foreground a new set of topics and concerns—such as criminal behavior and punishment, eroticism and sexual exploitation, technological innovations, and transnational publishing practices—issues that captivated large audiences on both sides of the Atlantic during the nineteenth century. A foray into a new field, this volume surveys the transatlantic terrain of sensation literature but is not intended to be a comprehensive study of transatlantic sensationalism. Important figures such as Reynolds, A.J.H. Duganne, Mary Dennison, and E.D.E.N. Southworth, Joseph Holt Ingraham, Ned Buntline, Wood, Rhoda Broughton, and Marie Corelli are not discussed in the essays that follow. In this respect, our collection serves as a call for more scholarship in the field as new works come to light and as we learn more about both well-known authors and then-popular-but-now-forgotten writers and the transatlantic contexts within which their work circulated and thrived.

Works Cited

"American Sensations." *Chambers's Journal of Popular Literature, Science, and Arts* (December 5, 1863): 353–355.

"American 'Sensations.'" *All The Year Round* (May 4, 1861): 131.

"An Indecent Publication." *The Round Table* (July 28, 1866): 472.

Bacon, Leonard. "Shall Punishment Be Abolished?" *The New Englander* (October 1846): 563–588.

Braddon, Mary Elizabeth. *The Doctor's Wife*. Oxford: Oxford University Press, 1998.

Buell, Lawrence. "Rethinking Anglo-American Literary History." *Clio* 33.1 (Fall 2003): 65–71.

Child, Lydia Maria. *Letters from New-York*. Ed. Bruce Mills. Athens: University of Georgia Press, 1998.

Claybaugh, Amanda. *The Novel of Purpose: Literature and Social Reform in the Anglo-American World*. Ithaca, N.Y.: Cornell University Press, 2007.

Cohen, Daniel A. *Pillars of Salt, Monuments of Grace: New England Crime Literature and the Origins of American Popular Culture, 1641–1860*. Oxford: Oxford University of Press, 1993.

Confessions and Experiences of a Novel Reader: By a Physician. Chicago: Wm. Stacy, 1855.

Denning, Michael. *Mechanic Accents: Dime Novels and Working-Class Culture in America*. London: Verso, 1987.

Fantina, Richard. *Victorian Sensational Fiction: The Daring Work of Charles Reade*. New York: Palgrave Macmillan, 2010.

Giles, Paul. *Transatlantic Insurrections: British Culture and the Formation of American Literature, 1730–1860*. Philadelphia: University of Pennsylvania Press, 2001.

"A Good Word for Sensation." *The Round Table* (October 6, 1866): 151–152.

"The Guillotine." *Harper's New Monthly Magazine* (July 1872): 186–187.

Haltunnen, Karen. *Murder Most Foul: The Killer and the American Gothic Imagination*. Cambridge, Mass.: Harvard University Press, 1998.

"Hanging as One of the Fine Arts." *Appletons' Journal of Literature, Science and Art*. (December 3, 1870): 670–671.

Lippard, George. "English Novels." Reprinted in George Lippard, P*rophet of Protest: Writings of an American Radical, 1822–1854*. Ed. David S. Reynolds. New York: Peter Lang, 1986. 253–254.

———. *The Quaker City; or the Monks of Monk Hall*. Ed. David S. Reynolds. Amherst: University of Massachusetts Press, 1995.

"The Literary Gentleman." *Punch* 2.4 (February 1842): 68.

Mailloux, Steven. *Reception Histories: Rhetoric, Pragmatism and American Cultural Politics*. Ithaca, N.Y.: Cornell University Press, 1998.

Maunder, Andrew. *Sensationalism and the Sensational Debate*, Volume I: *Varieties of Women's Sensation Fiction, 1855–1890*. London: Pickering and Chatto, 2004.

McGill, Meredith. *American Literature and Culture of Reprinting 1834–1853*. Philadelphia: University of Pennsylvania Press, 2001

"Novel-Reading." *Putnam's Monthly Magazine* (September 1857): 384–387.

[Oliphant, Margaret]. "The Byways of Literature: Reading for the Million." *Blackwood's Edinburgh Magazine* 84 (August 1858): 200–215.

[———]. "Novels." *Blackwood's Edinburgh Magazine* 102 (September 1867): 257–280.

"Penny Novels." *Littell's Living Age* (July 15, 1866): 108–115.

Petit, Amelie V. "The Pernicious Influence of Sensational Literature." *The Phrenological Journal and Science of Health* (August 1873): 83–85.

Pykett, Lyn. "The Newgate Novel and Sensation Fiction, 1830–1868." *The Cambridge Companion to Crime Fiction*. Ed., Martin Priestman. Cambridge: Cambridge University Press, 2003. 19–40.

[Rae, W. Fraser]. "Sensation Novelists: Miss Braddon." *North British Review* 43 (September 1865): 180–204.

"Receipt for a Sensational Novel." Powder Magazine (October 1869): 267–268.

Reynolds, David S. *Beneath the American Renaissance: The Subversive Imagination in the Age of Emerson and Melville*. Cambridge, Mass.: Harvard University Press, 1988.

Sala, George Augustus. "The Cant of Modern Criticism." *Belgravia; A London Magazine* (November 1867): 45–55.

"Sensation Novels." *Punch* (March 28, 1868): 140.

"'Sensation' Suicides." *Punch* (December 27, 1862): 260.

"The Sensational Williams." *All the Year Round* (February 143, 1864): 14–17.

"Sensational Reporting." *Chambers's Journal of Popular Literature, Science, and Arts* (March 9, 1878): 150–152.

"Sense v. Sensation." *Punch* (July 20, 1861): 31.

Simms, William Gilmore. *Martin Faber: The Story of a Criminal*. Whitefish, MT: Kessinger Publishing, 1996.

Streeby, Shelly. *American Sensations: Class, Empire, and the Production of Popular Culture*. Berkeley: University of California Press, 2002.

Tennenhouse, Leonard. *The Importance of Feeling English: American Literature and the British Diaspora, 1750–1850*. Princeton, N.J.: Princeton University Press, 2007.

Thompson, George. *Venus in Boston and Other Tales of Nineteenth-Century City Life*. Ed. David S. Reynolds and Kimberly R. Gladman. Amherst: University of Massachusetts, 2002.

Tompkins, Jane. *Sensational Designs: The Cultural Work of American Fiction, 1790–1860*. New York: Oxford University Press, 1986.

Williams, Catherine. *Fall River: An Authentic Narrative*. Ed. Patricia Caldwell. New York: Oxford University Press, 1993.

Chapter 1
Irresponsible Acts:
The Transatlantic Dialogues of William Godwin and Charles Brockden Brown

Christopher Apap

William Godwin intended *Caleb Williams* (1794) to be a "book of fictitious adventure" that would literally transform the reader, so "that no one, after he has read it, shall ever be exactly the same man that he was before" (*Caleb Williams* 444, 447). Godwin was fairly prescient; *Caleb Williams*, which outsold Godwin's more philosophically dense and politically radical *Enquiry Concerning Political Justice* (1793), not only affected his readers but inspired a generation of authors, from the rising generation of British romantics to popular novelists portraying sensational crimes.[1] Among Godwin's admirers was Philadelphian novelist Charles Brockden Brown, whom John Neal dubbed the "Godwin of America" (68), and while there is little question that Brown was deeply influenced by Godwin's carefully crafted plot, philosophical underpinnings, and overt didacticism, readers have all too often accepted the accuracy of David Lee Clark's early assessment of Brown as a Godwinian radical.[2] Recent readings have troubled such easy categorizations, downplaying Brown's politics in favor of a fuller contextualization of Brown's

---

[1]   Christopher Apap wishes to thank Bryan Waterman, who urged him to take up this topic and provided key guidance in its early development as a part of the Fales Library Special Exhibit, *Circles and Circulations in the Revolutionary Atlantic World*; the current chapter represents a radically expanded and updated version of the earlier research. The author also gratefully acknowledges the valuable insights of Nancy Ruttenburg, John Barton, Jennifer Phegley, and the anonymous reviewers for Ashgate Press, who all contributed to the chapter's current form. Henry Crabb Robinson noted that Godwin's innovative narrative resulted in a huge proliferation of crime novels, which ran "from one end of Europe to another" (Robinson I: 377).

[2]   Even Jane Tompkins' suggestion that Brown was critiquing Federalism was recast by Pamela Clemit as Brown's failure to fully live up to Godwin's radicalism. Stephen Watts has gone so far as to suggest that the radical early Brown became a conservative in April 1800—a clean break that strictly demarcated Brown's philosophy, politics, and literary output into a Godwinian and a socially conservative phase.

intellectual debts.[3] It is precisely in this spirit that we should call for a re-examination of Brown's and Godwin's novels; though Brown shared with Godwin an interest in sensational plots, Brown's most famous works—*Wieland* (1798), *Edgar Huntly* (1799), *Ormond* (1799), and *Arthur Mervyn* (Vol. I 1799, Vol. II 1800)—used the sensational as a platform from which to launch philosophical musings that rival Godwin's in depth and breadth.

While Brown's dependence on Godwin has at times been overstated, Godwin's interest in Brown's fiction has suffered the opposite fate. Godwin claimed, in the preface to *Mandeville* (1817), to have been partially inspired by *Wieland*, and critics tend to take Godwin's self-assessment at face value.[4] Even Pamela Clemit, who generally sees more important links between the two, misconstrues their relationship. She casts Brown and Godwin as men interested primarily in the role of politics on the individual, claiming that Godwin had begun "to share Brown's skepticism about the possibility of resolving internal conflicts engendered by revolutionary change" (101). If, as recent critics have argued, this understanding of Brown's conservative, Federalist politics is fundamentally flawed, then so too is Clemit's claim here. The critique of Clemit's analysis of Brown's and Godwin's politics does not deny that the two are engaged in an ongoing dialogue, but instead recasts that discourse. Tracing their literary exchanges allows us to follow the transatlantic circulation of intellectual influence and energy in the late eighteenth century and to recover both Brown's and Godwin's connections to popular and high cultural traditions, including the sensation genre.[5] In this light, sensational

---

[3]   In Bryan Waterman's reading, the famous evidence of Brown's interest in Godwin—a letter from Elihu Hubbard Smith that enthused "*Godwin came, and all was light!*" (Smith 171)—is less a rebuke than a recognition that *Caleb Williams* represented a model for didactic prose that directly issued from moral philosophy (Waterman 99–100). W.M. Verhoeven locates a recent "parameter shift" in Brown studies in which Brown's radicalism or political allegiance is a secondary concern; instead, the focus should be on Brown's "negotiations with eighteenth-century philosophical and historical thought, and to his place in the tradition of what has been called 'philosophical history,' or alternatively, 'the philosophical novel'—the narrative rendering of philosophical explorations" ("This blissful period" 29).

[4]   See, for example, B. Sprague Allen.

[5]   Winifred Hughes most clearly defines the genre of sensation as a Victorian genre, the "violent yoking of romance and realism" (16), and subsequent critics of English sensation have followed suit. See, for example, Anna Maria Jones, collections by Marlene Tromp, Pamela Gilbert, and Aeron Haynie, as well as by Kimberly Harrison and Richard Fantina. Among Americanists, David S. Reynolds notes the differences between the sensational literature of a working class and a more bourgeoisie literature (that would eventually become "high culture"). Michael Denning's reading of working-class culture and the dime novel makes similar points. Shelley Streeby extends these arguments while linking sensational literature to the American imperial imagination and the Mexican-American War in the 1840s Though Streeby notes the transnational contexts of later sensational novels, she understands these contexts functioning on a distinctly North-South axis. In the case of Brown and Godwin, that relevant axis is distinctly East-West.

literature's origins are both grounded in the eighteenth century and necessarily transnational. The transmission of ideas back and forth across the Atlantic reveals a dialogue about literary responsibility that connects both New World and Old, troubling nationalist readings of each individual author and inaugurating a literary sensationalism that was transatlantic at its inception.

"A machine over which I had no control"

Caleb Williams was published in Philadelphia in 1795, following closely the publication of Godwin's *Enquiry Concerning Political Justice* in serial form in *New York Monthly*. It is easy to see what appealed to Brown, who had been struggling to find a narrative form that allowed him the best means of exploring issues of human morality.[6] *Caleb Williams* traces the title character's youthful obsession with his patron Falkland's strange behavior, which leads to the revelation of a long past crime. With the recognition of Falkland as a murderer whose silence allowed two innocent men to be executed for his offense, the novel takes a radical new direction. Falkland, hoping to monitor Caleb for signs of betrayal, demands that Caleb remain in his service for life. Caleb, though he had decided not to expose his patron's sins, considers Falkland's domestic tyranny a horrific imposition and absconds, only to find every avenue of escape closed by Falkland's superior foresight, social status, and monetary resources. By the end of the novel, Caleb sees that the aristocratic Falkland's noble disposition was corrupted by "the wilderness of human society" (434), which led Falkland to murder. Yet Falkland's obsession had deprived Caleb "of the sympathy and good-will of mankind ... the very bread by which life must be sustained" (406). Caleb's eventual decision to confront Falkland with a public accusation of murder—which leads to Falkland's confession and execution—has been understood to represent the individual's resistance to institutional power. But if human society is a "wilderness," retreating to the "civilization" of the individual is not a solution. Instead of freeing Caleb, Falkland's declaration imprisons him with feelings of guilt and his self-characterization as Falkland's murderer. Godwin uses the sensational elements of the narrative to suggest that the first step to personal redemption is to take responsibility for one's actions; Falkland's confession, and Caleb's confessional narrative, might thus be seen not merely as solutions for the characters, but the first step towards a civilizing process in readers, encouraging in them a sense of personal and civic responsibility.

The sensational storyline of *Caleb Williams*, while complex, seems bland when compared to Brown's plot twists. *Wieland* follows the cataclysmic confrontation of the melancholic Theodore Wieland, who is predisposed to antinomian and

---

[6]   Waterman's close reading of Smith alongside recent research by Caleb Crain and Peter Kafer suggesting that Brown had likely read Godwin's *Political Justice* as early as 1793—well before Smith read the work in late 1795 or early 1796—upends long held assumptions that Smith introduced Godwin to Brown. The Friendly Club discussed Godwin, Waterman notes, in early April of 1796 (Waterman 280 n21).

Calvinistic ideas about religion, and Carwin, a morally ambiguous ventriloquist. When Carwin, improvising a test of Wieland's rational capabilities, hides and impersonates the voice of God, Wieland descends into an antinomian nightmare in which he murders his family in response to what he claims is the Almighty's behest. Having escaped from prison to murder his sister Clara and to fulfill what he believes is a divine mandate, Wieland is instead faced with the possibility that he had been deluded all along, and kills himself. By the novel's conclusion, Clara has absconded from her inherited property in Pennsylvania and, having married her longtime friend Pleyel, contemplates the past from Montpellier as an expatriate.

As I will discuss shortly, the critical response to the novel's conclusion tends to evince frustration with this final shift in setting. Yet the more global perspectives that Brown inserts into *Wieland* should not be surprising. Beyond his interest in Godwin, Brown was deeply influenced by sensational and Gothic literature from both the English and German traditions. Brown famously rejected certain elements of plot and setting in the English Gothic tradition in his preface to *Edgar Huntly*, claiming that haunted castles and monasteries were absurd in a New World setting. Still, Brown is clearly inspired by key elements within those novels, such as the nature of the rational and irrational mind, or the interest in explaining events that were seemingly supernatural through rational scientific explanation. Wieland's descent into madness or Carwin's explanation of his biloquism (complete in the text with footnotes citing scientific proof of such phenomena) seem key examples of this influence. Brown's use of German horror and pre-romantic sources is reflected not only in the horrific mass murder at the novel's core but also, in his choice to make his title family related to German Enlightenment poet Christoph Martin Wieland. Philip Barnard and Stephen Shapiro usefully suggest that Brown's tripartite title reflects the complexity of his intentions and his sources: *Wieland or The Transformation. An American Tale* thus reflects "a German reference associated with the culture of Absolutist Enlightenment, a noun indicating the politics of counterenlightenment, and finally a regional occurrence of this contradiction" (xxvii).[7] This reading insists on Brown's interest in both English and Germanic traditions, his philosophical underpinnings, and, especially, the transatlantic nature of these elements. In this argument, it becomes clear that the Gothic and the sensational traditions are deeply interconnected. The English Gothic was in some ways transformed by German pre-romantics into a more sensationally violent and emotionally turbulent genre, and Brown successfully builds on both traditions.

Despite its more spectacular and sensational elements, *Wieland* is at bottom a story about morality. Brown argues that the novel "aims at the illustration of some important branches of the moral constitution of man" (3). Yet up until the novel's moral is offered in the final paragraph by Clara, readers are invited to

---

[7]   Barnard and Shapiro provide compelling evidence regarding Brown's use of the Germanic tradition to critique and unsettle English radicals like Godwin and Wollstonecraft (xx–xxvii).

read the narrative not merely as a tragedy, but as a travesty of justice. Brown interrogates the adjudication of blame in the face of an invisible authority. *Wieland* embodies, as Nancy Ruttenburg suggests, a crisis in interpretation: how does an individual interpret the divine will, something that is essentially invisible (210)? Carwin's disembodied voice, in such a reading, represents a fear that ideas will circulate and take hold without an arbiter who can properly rein in the excesses of interpretation symbolized by Wieland's deluded obsession. If not Wieland, then who, we might ask, is responsible for the novel's dramatic events? Laura H. Korobkin, extending Jay Fliegelman's discussion of the late eighteenth-century American preoccupation with responsibility and authorship in relation to *Wieland* (xvii–xxi), argues that a close reading of Brown's textual evidence demands that the reader understand Carwin as both morally and legally culpable.

Carwin confesses to being too curious and not cautious enough with the power of ventriloquism, but refuses to characterize himself as a criminal—whether out of guilt or, as Korobkin suggests, a sincere belief that his intentions exonerate him of what may be construed as criminally reckless behavior (733). Carwin's experimentation with ventriloquism has disastrous results: he ruins Clara's reputation as a virtuous woman with her beloved in an attempt to seduce her himself, and, by playfully voicing several inexplicable commands and scenarios, precipitates Wieland's psychotic break. Yet Carwin argues that "'I am not a villain; I have slain no one; I have prompted no one to slay; I have handled a tool of wonderful efficacy without malignant intentions, but without caution; ample will be the punishment of my temerity, if my conduct has contributed to this evil'" (198). Interestingly, Carwin uses the conditional here. Unsure or perhaps understandably unwilling to acknowledge that he has in fact contributed to Wieland's actions, he will only acknowledge that he has acted "without caution." Admitting to "rashly setting in motion a machine over whose progress [he] had no control" (215–16), Carwin would only take responsibility for his own irresponsibility.

In the finale of *Caleb Williams*, Caleb acknowledges his own accountability in Falkland's eventual demise and Falkland admits his guilt, accepting capital punishment as the consequence of his actions. Their mutual acknowledgements mark Godwin's sense of the beginning of a just system.[8] *Wieland* had no such just conclusion. Despite the fact that Carwin predicted that his punishment would be "ample," justice was not served, and he would finish his days unpunished, Clara reports, as a farmer in "some remote district of Pennsylvania" (239). Moreover, Clara insists that the "innocence and usefulness of his future life may, to some

---

8   It is interesting to note that Godwin's original conclusion to the novel was considerably more pessimistic and disturbing: Caleb was utterly destroyed by the legal system. Though Brown obviously had no access to Godwin's original draft, it is worth asking whether in a close reading of the novel Brown picked up on the philosophical possibilities that Godwin had tried and originally rejected. Interestingly, Mitzi Meyers argues that the revised ending is more morally ambiguous: Caleb, though technically free, is imprisoned by his own psychological guilt. See also Gary Handwerk and A.A. Markley.

degree, atone for the miseries so rashly or so thoughtlessly afflicted" (239). As evidenced by her use of the words "may" and "to some degree," Clara is unsure if Carwin actually could atone—his redemption was partial, provisional, and, like his confession, conditional at best. Yet she refuses to see Carwin as evil, seemingly agreeing with his self-characterization as merely "thoughtless" and irresponsible.

In *Wieland*, as in *Caleb Williams*, the reader might gain moral knowledge, though Brown offered a more troubling account. Unlike Godwin, he did not have "truth" prevail in the end. Justice was not done. The Wieland family excoriated itself, and irresponsibility—embodied in Carwin—still remained at large. Scholars focus not merely on Carwin's admission of carelessness, but on Clara's subsequent self-indictment, in which she blames her brother and herself: "If Wieland had framed juster notions of moral duty, and of the divine attributes; or if I had been gifted with ordinary equanimity or foresight, the double-tongued deceiver would have been baffled or repelled" (244). Some have understood Clara as deeply unsettled by the novel's events, and her self-condemnation as the recognition of her own predisposition for sensuousness and poor moral interpretation.[9] Korobkin's reading downplays Clara's final analysis of the novel's events, however, seeing her "new, limited role of calmly detached wife and ex-American" (743) as an abdication of what up until that point has been a probing and legalistic analysis. Yet Brown's characterization of Clara is more complicated than Korobkin and other critics have suggested; by the novel's end, he advances an argument about radical irresponsibility in dialogue with Godwin that implicated agents on both sides of the Atlantic.

In fact, to make Clara's sense of her own culpability stand in for Brown's conclusion is misleading; his hastily composed concluding chapter was in fact much more compelling. In his first draft, Brown had neglected to resolve the story of Louisa Conway, the ward of Wieland whom he murdered alongside his family; earlier in the novel, Conway's father, Major Stuart, had promised to retrieve her from Mettingen but had never reappeared in the narrative. Alerted to this fact, Brown hastily composed a final chapter.[10] In it, Clara recovered from her grief and shock at the novel's events and moved to Europe, where she encountered

---

[9]   Norman Grabo understands the concluding chapter in general to be Clara's own obsessive need to create a utilitarian moral out of tragedy—his reading sees her self-indictment as a form of social adjustment (29). Bill Christophersen notes that the dramatic core of Wieland is Clara's discovery, in her attraction to Carwin, of her own potential moral weakness (29).

[10]   William Dunlap's diary hints that he, Elihu Hubbard Smith, and William Johnson, upon looking at Brown's final draft in late July, had alerted Brown to the omission (I: 317). A mere ten days later, Dunlap reports perusing Brown's new additions (I: 323). Interestingly, while Dunlap was reading *Wieland* to his wife and children in late July, and speculating on possible revisions with Brown, his diary is dominated by a different story of extreme violence and what Dunlap calls "monstrous error": the story of a murder-suicide of an acquaintance, Monsieur Gardie, who murdered his dancer wife and left behind her nine-year old son (I: 312–317).

Stuart and resolved his plotline. Critical response, when it has turned to this subplot, construes the chapter as an aberration, citing the conclusion as evidence of Brown's hasty composition style and shoddy plotting and, in the case of Clemit, of his final reaffirmation of "inherited values and sources of external authority and control" (137).[11] Korobkin treats it as Clara's rejection of American legal reasoning and sees her circumscribed within her domestic role as wife. This reflects an American-centered reading of the novel that reinscribes Brown as a fundamentally American author.

Such assessments, I argue, completely miss Brown's point. Brown's conclusion is one of the more interesting moments in the novel—and not merely because he almost forgot to include the chapter in his final draft. The conclusion highlights Brown's philosophical roots in transatlantic dialogues about the nature of literature and marks his vital participation in the circumatlantic intellectual dialogues of the late eighteenth century. Moreover, the European murder plot acts to catalyze Clara's final verdict on her own violent history in America, thus marking Brown's interest in sensational crime in both the New World and the Old. Shifting the focus to Brown's conclusion and his transatlantic roots demonstrates that it is altogether necessary that *Wieland* ended not in the utopian American space of Mettingen, but in the European location of Montpellier.[12] An uprooted, expatriate Clara narrates the fate of Major Stuart: in short order, we learn of his reaction to Louisa's murder, his discovery that his wife had been seduced and convinced to flee to the New World with his young daughter, and his realization that the seducer had been a family acquaintance named Maxwell. Stuart tracks Maxwell to Montpellier (where Maxwell had become, coincidentally, an intimate of Clara and her uncle) and challenges him to a duel. Before the duel can occur, Stuart is murdered, and Maxwell, the presumed assassin, disappears.

Clara—perhaps sensing that in making Maxwell "a favorite" (242) she has once again trusted a Carwinian antihero—cannot help but read the Stuart affair in the light of her own biography. It is Stuart's murder that ultimately prompts Clara's self-condemnation. In fact, before blaming herself for falling victim to Carwin's trickery, she makes a set of interesting comparative statements worth quoting in full:

---

[11]   In his introduction to the Kent State edition of *Wieland*, Sidney Krause calls it "the oft-regretted last chapter of *Wieland*" (x). Donald Ringe is more critical, calling the Conway-Stuart subplot "indefensible" (139) and arguing that it was an "extraneous afterthought" that "throws the book off balance" (44). A notable exception is Norman Grabo, who admits that though "everyone agrees" that the chapter was "a disastrous digression," it was not without purpose (23–24). Grabo insists that Clara saw the conventions of sentimental fiction as a way to successfully adjust to the shock of the novel's events and re-integrate herself into society. Clemit's reading ignores the subplot completely and merely focuses on the European locale as the marker of Brown's acceptance of European values and authority.

[12]   A fair amount of scholarship focuses exclusively on the utopian setting of Mettingen, making the American setting a lynchpin of the subsequent analysis. See Larzer Ziff, Nancy Ruttenburg, Hsuan Hsu, and Ezra Tawil.

I leave you to moralize on this tale. That virtue should become the victim of treachery is, no doubt, a mournful consideration; but it will not escape your notice, that the evils of which Carwin and Maxwell were the authors, owed their existence to the errors of the sufferers. All efforts would have been ineffectual to subvert the happiness or shorten the existence of the Stuarts, if their own frailty had not seconded the efforts. If the lady had crushed her disastrous passion in the bud, and driven the seducer from her presence, when the tendency of his artifices was seen; if Stuart had not admitted the spirit of absurd revenge, we should not have had to deplore this catastrophe. If Wieland had framed juster notions of moral duty, and of the divine attributes; or if I had been gifted with ordinary equanimity or foresight, the double-tongued deceiver would have been baffled or repelled. (244)

Thus, to understand *Wieland*, one must understand more than merely the localized American contexts of irresponsibility. Paul Giles's sense of British-American literary production is that of a kind of "mirroring and twinning" (3), in which each national tradition twists the literary image of the other into strange forms; Brown, though not discussed in detail by Giles, anticipates this critique. Clara's comparative reading of "double-tongued deceiver[s]" demonstrates that democratic excesses in the United States reflected the social systems in Europe; or perhaps instead of Giles's metaphor of the distorting funhouse mirror of early transatlantic discourse, we might imagine the relatively restricted social milieu of Europe to be refracted by the Atlantic ocean into a host of unmanageable possibilities in the young republic. Regardless of the metaphor we choose, *Wieland* was clearly *not* just a cautionary Federalist fable, but a transatlantic tale. As Barnard and Shapiro suggested, the complex geographical, philosophical, and political contexts of *Wieland* complicate an exceptionalist reading of Charles Brockden Brown. Lest anyone think that America was the only place where irresponsibility ran rampant, Brown insisted that the issue was both far more difficult to define, and more difficult to contain. If enthusiasm and rationality, embodied in Wieland and Clara, had disastrous potential in the United States that was the forum for Federalist and Jeffersonian debates, then *Wieland* forces us also to attend to the disastrous possibilities and necessary responsibilities inherent in the complex social systems of Europe. It should come as no surprise that duels and subtle social slights, the crux of Falkland's failure in *Caleb Williams*, and the seduction novels that had long been popular in both Europe and the United States, were the means by which Brown expanded his argument beyond the borders of the new republic. Brown linked Old and New World not only in the ways that Clara navigated her narrative, but in the ways that sensationalism helped to demarcate how irresponsibility circulated from Europe to America and back again.

The transatlantic circulation of criminally and sensationally irresponsible acts was not unique to *Wieland*, either—it is a vital element of each of Brown's major fictions. With enough time, we might also trace irresponsibility in *Edgar Huntly*, whose title character's real peril lay not in his sleepwalking, but his Carwinian lack of foresight, of which he does not seem to be finally cured. Irresponsibility circulates too in *Ormand*, which has a European title character who is not only a seducer, a murderer, and a kidnapper, but also a political radical tied, like Carwin, to the Bavarian Illuminati. In *Arthur Mervyn*, the title character's irresponsibility and naiveté take the more humorous form of his neglecting to knock before entering homes. One wonders if in *Arthur Mervyn* irresponsibility might be a kind of contagion—traversing the Atlantic via merchant vessels, much like the yellow fever epidemic that frames the novel; like Clara, Mervyn leaves Philadelphia at the end of the novel, traveling to Europe with his new wife. Even such a cursory reading suggests a productive transatlantic matrix within which Brown worked, one in which the sensational plot could drive a variety of Old World and New World narratives.

"Invisible things are the only realities"

Godwin read each of Brown's major novels, perhaps on the recommendation of his daughter, Mary, or her husband Percy Shelley (who had enjoyed several of Brown's novels in 1814 and 1815). In fact, Godwin devoured five of Brown's works in one five-week glut in 1816 (St. Clair 380). Whatever influence Godwin had transmitted to Brown had made the return trip: one year after encountering Brown's work, Godwin's first novel in a decade, *Mandeville. A Tale of the Seventeenth Century in England* (1817), appeared with the following acknowledgement:

> The impression, that first led me to look with an eye of favour upon the subject here treated, was derived from a story-book, called Wieland, written by a person, certainly of distinguished genius, who I believe was born and died in the province of Pennsylvania in the United States of North America, and who calls himself C.B. Brown (ix).

The posthumous attention of Godwin and his circle, along with William Dunlap's biography of Brown, published in 1815, resulted in a critical re-assessment of Brown's place in American literature and an aggressive campaign for his canonization as the father of American literature. For many critics, the tale of the intellectual dialogue between Brown and Godwin ends there.[13] *Mandeville*'s critics tend to see Joanna Baillie's *De Monfort* (1800), a tragedy that explored the destructive nature of hatred and antipathy, as considerably more influential for Godwin.[14] Yet read within the context of Brown's novels, *Mandeville*'s focus

---

[13]   Even Ian Ward, who argued that as early as 1799 Godwin considered sensibility a viable philosophical option and noted that *Mandeville*'s critique of "institutional religion and its inexorable tendency to foster bigotry" (39), ignores Brown. This omission is especially interesting in the light of Waterman's recent reading, which excavates *Wieland*'s profound criticism of religious enthusiasm.

[14]   Godwin names one of the minor families in the novel the Monforts, likely as an homage to Baillie's novel. For critical interest in Baillie's influence on Godwin, see Allen (368–369).

on jealousy and misanthropy may be seen as a nuanced response to Brown's critique of responsibility—one which developed Brown's argument and reflects it backward into English Commonwealth history. Moreover, the extreme violence of Mandeville's fantasies suggest the influence of elements from the German horror novel—elements he certainly imported from Brown, if not also the German novels that were quite popular in London at the time.[15] In this light, Brown and Godwin's relationship might usefully be reassessed, extending to the ways in which the development of sensational literature owed something to their interactions.

The novel is narrated by Charles Mandeville, an orphan whose English parents are murdered during the 1641 Ulster uprising in Ireland. He subsequently becomes the ward of his scholarly and melancholic uncle, who, with his deserted mansion, morose servants, and the dour Calvinist preacher he hires to tutor the young Mandeville, predisposes the young Mandeville to bitterness and depression—not unlike the way that Brown created a character in Wieland who is predisposed to the religious enthusiasm that would eventually prove his downfall. At school, Mandeville's natural intelligence is overshadowed by the talent and popularity of his school-fellow Lionel Clifford, resulting in an irrational envy that consumes Mandeville. At every turn, he attempts to avoid his avowed "enemy" but is continually thwarted. When he leaves Oxford to join the royal army, his expected advancement is retarded when Clifford is named personal secretary to a royalist general, prompting Mandeville's desertion. This makes him a pariah among his peers, to the point that he believes himself to "have no place in the world of mankind" (II: 107), and, in a scene reminiscent of Brown's *Edgar Huntly*, he rushes into the nearby wilderness and blacks out for several days, only to awaken in a sanitarium with no memory of his actions.[16] Despite the attempts of his sister, Henrietta, to reawaken his potential for human sympathy, Mandeville's frenzied mental state reappears whenever he discusses Clifford or Commonwealth politics. The revelation that his sister is engaged to none other than Clifford completes his final descent into madness. In the ensuing events, Mandeville attempts to kidnap his sister, and Clifford's defense of Henrietta results in a disfiguring injury to Mandeville, who sees the scar as the visible symbol of his own estrangement from the world.

Though Godwin's daughter and her husband responded to *Mandeville* encouragingly, critical and popular response was markedly negative on both sides of the Atlantic, and in some cases was more a target for satire than a model for

---

[15] For more on the popularity of German sensationalism in England, see Mortensen and Skokoe.

[16] This may be an example of playful one-upmanship on the part of Godwin. In Brown's *Edgar Huntly*, the title character claims to have "never conceived a parallel" (158) to his experiences of sleepwalking and blackout—might Godwin, by transplanting his narrative into the seventeenth century, have suggested that such psychological events were unique neither to the late eighteenth century nor to the Americas?

emulation.[17] John Wilson Croker, in the *London Quarterly Review*, called the book and its eponymous narrator "intolerably tedious and disgusting" (177). An obsessive villain was an effective plot device, though its success in *Caleb Williams* was due to the fact that Falkland's obsession was filtered through his innocent victim. "But when Mr. Godwin makes the Bedlamite not only the hero but the relater of the tale, it is evident that all contrast is lost, all interest vanishes," Croker argued, and of the other characters, "nobody feels about them any thing but that they are the inventions and colourings of a madman's brain" (177).[18] Croker's critical distaste for the madman perhaps adds more evidence that Godwin has, in *Mandeville*, immersed himself in the sensational.[19] Yet Croker misses completely Godwin's largest innovation and contribution to the genre of crime fiction. Godwin constructs a narrator who seems rational, even self-critical at times. Early in the work, Mandeville presents himself as a reasonable narrator; he admits that he could be prone to bias with regard to Clifford, and freely acknowledges the possibility that he is wrong on several counts. Indeed, Mandeville actually admits that he has made poor decisions due to his envy or his melancholy. However, by the third volume, Godwin reveals Mandeville to be fundamentally unreliable.

The problem for Mandeville becomes one of interpreting the world, not unlike the problem of Theodore Wieland. Early in the third volume, after discovering Clifford's apostasy to Catholicism, Mandeville expounds on religion in a long passage that many take to represent Godwin's own mature attitude toward and acceptance of theology.[20] The most interesting moment in this scene is the one in which Mandeville argues that "Invisible things are the only realities; invisible things alone are the things that shall remain" (III: 48). This statement resonates with Brown's problematization of the invisible in *Wieland*, in which he asks how, in the face of an invisible authority, we can even interpret the world, much less assign any real responsibility for events. In *Mandeville*, Godwin amplifies this question. When the senses cannot be trusted—as Mandeville maintains—in *which* invisible things can we trust? Godwin seems to pick up on Brown's critique of

---

[17]   In a review for *The Examiner*, Shelley called Henrietta's moral pleading with her brother "the most perfect and beautiful piece of writing of modern times" (827). For a discussion of the satire of Godwin and sensational fiction contained in Thomas Love Peacock's *Nightmare Abbey* (1818), see John Colmer.

[18]   For a similar view from the United States, see the May 1818 edition of *The North American Review*.

[19]   On one level, this complicates the question of the lukewarm public reception of *Mandeville* since crime literature often sold so well. Peacock's satire of *Mandeville* suggests that it was not the sensationalism of the novel that turned away readers but the narrator's extended and morbidly philosophical rantings.

[20]   For example, see Peter H. Marshall's suggestion that Mandeville's argument that religion is "the most important of all things" (III, 48) represents Godwin's respect for religion (338). However, such a statement—in the middle of one of Mandeville's "phrenzies"—ignores Mandeville's often flawed interpretation and rationalizing. I argue that Godwin's representation of religion is profoundly more complicated.

religion and human psychology and, through the lens of a narrator who sees only the invisible things as trustworthy, makes a mockery of rational interpretation. Moreover, this framing of Mandeville's madness as a problem with the senses might be understood as a prescient evaluation of the genre of shocking crime, which will be characterized as "sensational" in the middle of the nineteenth century. Sensational literature is so named, after all, because of its violently exciting affect on its readers' senses.

Henrietta's own reaction to her brother's melancholy and prejudice reflects the experience of the reader; dismayed by Mandeville's actions but still loyal to him, Henrietta prays for guidance. As if by providential design, Mandeville suddenly appears to convince Henrietta of her error in attaching herself to Clifford. It is at this crucial moment that the problem becomes clear. Mandeville calmly outlines a series of rational arguments against Clifford, all but winning Henrietta to his side, until his rationality descends into a frenzied and violent rampage that horrifies his sister and confirms that he is in fact a madman. Like Henrietta, the reader might have proceeded through the early novel under the impression that the narrator was a reasonable, rational being. Mandeville views Henrietta and Clifford's affair as monstrous, but it is his own reaction that is in fact grotesque. Imagining his sister and Clifford's future children, Mandeville fantasizes about kidnapping them in order to turn them against their parents: "I will make them the instruments of my vengeance. How it will delight me, what mitigation it will bring to the fire that burns within me, to see their infant fingers stream with their parents' blood!" (III: 325). Virulent passages such as this, which often proceed for pages at a time, suggest the evidence for Croker's objection to the "disgusting" novel, and simultaneously suggests that Godwin was laying the roots for the later flourishing of sensational plots of crime, murder, and madness. Yet part of the novel's effect comes from the realization that he who had seemed through the first two thirds of the narrative to be a lucid and reflective guide, though flawed by bias, was in fact not rational at all. Mandeville was insane.

By the final chapter, Mandeville's early admission that his hatred was possibly in error disappears, replaced by a deranged certainty. The scar from the final conflict is "a deep and perilous gash, the broad brand of which I shall not fail to carry with me to my grave. The sight of my left eye is gone; the cheek beneath is severed, with a deep trench between" (III: 365). Clifford had "given a perpetual grimace, a sort of preternatural and unvarying distorted smile, or deadly grin, to my countenance" (III: 366). The scar has been interpreted variously. It is certainly a mark of Cain, indicating Mandeville's estrangement from humanity. Jarrells has called it the visible reminder of the violence of history (28). I read it also as the symbol of the form of Mandeville's error. Just as Brown fictionalizes terrifying misinterpretations in *Wieland*, Godwin creates a narrator who is, from childhood, unable properly to interpret the world. Though Mandeville explains that his worldview is obscured by his anti-Catholic prejudice and the misanthropy of his upbringing, neither fully accounts for his increasingly paranoid hatred of Clifford. Mandeville is, in the end, irredeemable, and, as Jarrells argues, the scar mars the portrait of a rational individual that the rest of the narrative builds (31). Yet Jarrells fundamentally misunderstands the character of Mandeville—it is only the scar, for Jarrells, which mars the portrait. I argue, by contrast, that the scar merely comes to symbolize the distorted portrait that Godwin has been painting all along. It is fitting, then, that Mandeville's myopic worldview is reflected in his loss of an eye. When Mandeville looks with his one good eye in a mirror, he sees reflected his narrowed and bigoted interpretive framework. Mandeville finally recognizes visually what his friends, his sister and even the reader have already acknowledged: that he is "monstrous" (III: 366) and his name, properly seen as "Man Devil," is profoundly apt.

If Mandeville recognizes himself as a madman and a fiend, what he fails to accept is the possibility that he is in any way responsible for that monstrosity. His prejudice against Catholics is the result of his parents' demise; his saturnine attitude the consequence of his upbringing in Mandeville Mansion; his misanthropy the result of being cut off from human friendships by the actions (though inadvertent) of Clifford. Readers tend to understand Godwin as creating a portrait of the extreme dangers of a life bereft of human companionship—a theme that he explored in each of his previous novels. What makes *Mandeville* different from *Caleb Williams*, however, is the narrator's culpability in that estrangement. When characters in the novel reach out to connect with Mandeville, he more often than not rejects them. The reader comes to see Charles Mandeville as monstrous, and understands his hatred for Clifford as a paranoid and self-deluding error. Godwin does not provide a traditional ending—as William St. Clair says, Mandeville "comes to a stop rather than to an end" (439–40). This is less a failure of Godwin's intellectual energy than a calculated authorial move that leaves Mandeville simmering in his own hatred and bitterness. No longer does Godwin trace a narrative in which justice is tied to accountability; as in *Wieland*, there is a distinct sense in *Mandeville* that justice will not be done.

Moreover, I would argue that Godwin, even in a novel set in the seventeenth century, gestures toward a larger theater for the narrative of sensation. The final line of *Mandeville* hints at this development: "Even as certain tyrannical planters in the West Indies have set a brand with a red-hot iron upon the negroes they have purchased, to denote that they are irremediably a property, so Clifford had set his mark upon me, as a token that I was his for ever" (III: 367). Mandeville represents himself as enslaved—a branded victim of a tyrant intent on trampling on his rights and happiness.[21] Using the West Indies as Mandeville's context is a compelling move. Though it has been argued that one of Godwin's targets is Scott's triumphant nationalism in *Waverley*,[22] the problem is not merely that Scott's fictions obscured the violence of the nation's past—they obscured the broader global repercussions

---

[21]   It is important to resist an obvious critique of Godwin's racial context here—there is no evidence that Godwin is implying that the condition of the enslaved is a kind of pathology, or attempting to racialize Mandeville's "monstrosity."

[22]   See Jarrells.

of that past. By alluding to the horrors of colonization, African slavery, and the beginnings of English empire in the Americas, Godwin tied specific moments of political, religious, and social unrest in seventeenth-century England to the history of oppression and victimization in the Atlantic world.

Godwin provides an urgent counterpoint to Brown's claim that irresponsibility is a human condition that merely exists differently within the different specific social and cultural contexts of Europe and the United States. At the end of *Wieland*, Clara offers her reader a moral: a set of suggestions that, though conditional, offered some guidance through the labyrinthine events of the plot and through the intellectual and political possibilities present for Americans and Europeans at the dawn of the nineteenth century. With an unbalanced and unrepentant Mandeville closing out the novel by suggesting that he, like a slave, was tied to Clifford until death, Godwin provocatively refuses to provide any sense of moral closure, conditional or otherwise. He leaves his reader with the possibility that, for all of humanity's interest in rationality and even sensibility (both topics that Henrietta favorably expounds upon and Mandeville claims to agree with), it is possible that *all* one is left with in the end is a prejudicial and myopic view of one's relation to the world.

The exploration of irresponsibility through sensational genres allowed both Godwin and Brown to extend their fictional examinations into human psychology and morality; one could argue, moreover, that their exchanges also inspired a distinct genealogy of authors who recognized the dramatic, creative possibility in the way that irresponsible characters could push a radical narrative line forward. Though an exhaustive list would be impossible in the space provided here, one thinks immediately of Godwin's daughter, Mary Shelley, whose *Frankenstein* (1818) —the action of which proceeded from the title character's moment of intellectual pique and moral capriciousness—investigated the relationship of moral responsibility and science by way of a sensational and Gothic plot.[23] In the United States, Edgar Allan Poe marks an especially interesting case, since he too claimed both Brown and Godwin as inspiration.[24] George Lippard may be understood as extending the literary debate about responsibility in *The Quaker City or, The Monks of Monk Hall, A Romance of Philadelphia Life, Mystery, and Crime* (1845). Though some protested that his sensational depictions of seduction and

---

[23]   Clemit notes that Shelley's perspective perhaps has more to do with her husband's radical internationalism than might be suspected (145). We might wonder, in the light of what I read as a broader intellectual context for Brown's thinking, if this concern is what makes Brown such a favorite of the Shelleys.

[24]   One need look no further than Poe's story, "Loss of Breath" (1835) to find a narrative deeply influenced by Godwin's *Mandeville*: the narrator, after having lost his voice while seemingly strangling his wife of less than a day, approvingly quotes Mandeville's statement that "Invisible things are the only realities" (154). Poe established the rational derangement of his narrator from the tale's first lines and reveled in the subsequent dramatic depths to which an irresponsible and disturbed narrator gave license. For a further discussion of both Brown and especially Godwin's relationship to Poe, see Burton R. Pollin.

crime bordered on moral negligence, Lippard, who dedicated *The Quaker City* to Brown's memory, claimed to model responsibility (and excoriate irresponsibility) for an engaged readership.[25]

By focusing on the philosophical-historical content of Godwin and Brown's literary debates, we might also uncover a different genealogy: each author's ideas circulate so powerfully because of the dramatic possibilities that irresponsibility provided. It is also here that we might generally extend their influence to a figure like Herman Melville, who had crowed to Nathaniel Hawthorne in 1851 that his latest novel about whaling was a "wicked" book (Melville 212). While ostensibly about the United States, *Moby-Dick; or, The Whale* (1851) featured a truly international cast of characters, implying that the philosophical questions of the novel operated globally and were too large for national narratives to possibly contain. Moreover, Melville's follow-up to *Moby-Dick*, *Pierre; or, The Ambiguities* (1852) features not merely the theme of irresponsibility, but elements of sensation such as incest, murder, and suicide. Looking at such sensational irresponsibility through the lens of a figure like Melville recalls David S. Reynolds's arguments that canonical American authors were as much enmeshed in the culture of crime and sensation as they were in the aesthetics of democracy. In some ways, my reading of Brown and Godwin enables a similar and necessary re-framing of each author as a part of the growing culture of sensation at the end of the eighteenth and beginning of the nineteenth centuries.

What results from an increased awareness of such connections is a more complicated portrait of the legacies of both Brown and Godwin, and the ways in which those legacies intertwine. An anonymous reviewer once argued that Brown was deeply influenced by Godwin but "not his slave" ("*The Life of Charles Brockden Brown*" 77)—a compelling choice of terms in light of *Mandeville*'s closing metaphor. Yet neither was Godwin shackled to Brown's philosophical rejoinders. Rather than see the two as inexorably bound like Mandeville and Clifford, allow me to suggest a model inspired by *Wieland*. Each serves as a Carwin of sorts to the other—"setting in motion a machine over whose progress [he] had no control" (199). I am less interested in reading Carwin as an authorial figure here than in recognizing that Carwin's at times careless examinations of others' philosophies might be understood as a model for the power and danger of intellectual transmission.[26] Brown experienced Godwin's ideas through his own reading and subsequent debate with members of the Friendly Club, and created some of the most original and compelling early commentaries on the new republic; Godwin, through the advocacy of his daughter and Percy Shelly,

---

[25] Dana Luciano has traced the links between Brown and American sensational writers like Poe and Lippard, as well as E.D.E.N. Southworth.

[26] Robert Ferguson reads in Carwin the symbol of an individual who, not unlike Brown, considered laws a form of tyranny and authorial control an alternative outlet. For a discussion of Carwin's possible authorial function—and the transmission of that function to Clara Wieland—see Nancy Ruttenburg (210–258).

was introduced to Brown's works, which at least in part inspired Godwin's return to fiction. Though both tended to use more caution in their experiments than Carwin, each writer's fictional investigations of responsibility challenged the other, helping to inspire a generation of authors and extend the often intertwined genres of Gothic and sensational fiction on both sides of the Atlantic. Their tales of murderers and madmen unveil a dialogue about irresponsible characters, actions, and interpretations that reminds us that the transnational trajectories of fiction— and sensation—have long been the rule rather than the exception.

Works Cited

Allen, B. Sprague. "William Godwin and the Stage." *PMLA* 35. 3 (1920): 358–374.

Barnard, Philip, and Shapiro Stephen. Introduction. *Wieland; or The Transformation. An American Tale.* By Charles Brockden Brown. Indianapolis: Hackett Publishing Company, 2009: ix–xlvi.

Brown, Charles Brockden. *Wieland: or, the Transformation, an American Tale; Memoirs of Carwin the Biloquist.* Ed. Sydney J. Krause and S.W. Reid. Kent, OH: Kent State University Press, 1977.

———. *Edgar Huntly, or, Memoirs of a Sleep-walker.* Ed. Sydney J. Krause and S.W. Reid. Kent, Ohio: Kent State University Press, 1977.

Christophersen, Bill. *The Apparition in the Glass: Charles Brockden Brown's American Gothic.* Athens: The University of Georgia Press, 1993.

Clark, David Lee. *Charles Brockden Brown: Pioneer Voice of America.* Durham, N.C.: Duke University Press, 1952.

Clemit, Pamela. *The Godwinian Novel: The Rational Fictions of Godwin, Brockden Brown, Mary Shelley.* New York: Oxford University Press, 1993.

Colmer, John. "Godwin's Mandeville and Peacock's Nightmare Abbey." *The Review of English Studies* 83 (August 1970): 331–336.

Croker, John Wilson. "Review of Godwin, Mandeville." *London Quarterly Review* 18 (October 1818): 176–177.

Denning, Michael. *Mechanic Accents: Dime Novels and Working Class Culture in America.* New York: Verso, 1998.

Dunlap, William. *Diary of William Dunlap (1776–1839).* 3 vols. New York: The New York Historical Society, 1930.

Fliegelman, Jay. Introduction. *Wieland and Memoirs of Carwin the Biloquist.* By Charles Brockden Brown. New York: Penguin, 1991. vii–xlii.

Ferguson, Robert. "Literature and Vocation in the Early Republic: The Example of Charles Brockden Brown." *Modern Philology* 78.2 (Nov. 1980): 139–152.

Giles, Paul. *Transatlantic Insurrections: British Culture and the Formation of American Literature 1730–1860.* Philadelphia: University of Pennsylvania Press, 2001.

Godwin, William. *Caleb Williams.* Ed. Gary Handwerk and A.A. Markley. Peterborough, Ontario: Broadview Literary Texts, 2000.

————. *Mandeville. A Tale of the Seventeenth Century in England.* London: Longman, Hurst, Rees, Orme, and Brown, 1817.

"Godwin's Mandeville." *The North American Review* 7:19 (May 1818): 92–106. Print.

Grabo, Norman. *The Coincidental Art of Charles Brockden Brown.* Chapel Hill: The University of North Carolina Press, 1981.

Handwerk, Gary and A.A. Markley. Introduction. *Caleb Williams.* By William Godwin. Peterborough, Ontario: Broadview Literary Texts, 2000. 9–46.

Harrison, Kimberly and Richard Fantina, eds. *Victorian Sensations: Essays on a Scandalous Genre.* Columbus: Ohio State University Press, 2006.

Hsu, Hsuan. "Democratic Expansionism in 'Memoirs of Carwin.'" *Early American Literature* 35:2 (Fall 2000): 137–156.

Hughes, Winifred. *The Maniac in the Cellar: Sensation Novels of the 1860s.* Princeton, N.J.: Princeton University Press, 1980.

Jarrells, Anthony. "Bloodless Revolution and the Form of the Novel." *Novel* 37:1/2 (Fall 2003): 24–44.

Jones, Anna Maria. *Problem Novels: Victorian Fiction Theorizes the Sensational Self.* Columbus: Ohio State University Press, 2007.

Kafer, Peter. *Charles Brockden Brown's Revolution and the Birth of American Gothic.* Philadelphia: University of Pennsylvania Press, 2004.

Korobkin, Laura H. "Murder by Madman: Criminal Responsibility, Law, and Judgment in *Wieland.*" *American Literature* 70.4 (December 2000): 721–750.

Krause, Sydney J., and S.W. Reid. Introduction. *Wieland: or, the Transformation, an American Tale; Memoirs of Carwin the Biloquist.* By Charles Brockden Brown. Kent, OH: Kent State University Press, 1978. vii–xxv.

Luciano, Dana. "The Gothic Meets Sensation: Charles Brockden Brown, Edgar Allen Poe, George Lippard and E.D.E.N. Southworth." *A Companion to American Fiction: 1780–1865.* Ed. Shirley Samuels. Oxford: Blackwell, 2006. 314–329.

Marshall, Peter H. *William Godwin.* New Haven, Conn.: Yale University Press, 1984.

Melville, Herman. *Correspondence. The Writings of Herman Melville.* Ed. Lynn Horth. Vol. XIV. Evanston, Ill.: Northwestern University Press, 1993.

Meyers, Mitzi. "Godwin's Changing Conception of *Caleb Williams.*" *Studies in English Literature* 12 (1972): 591–628.

Mortensen, Peter. *British Romanticism and Its Continental Influences: Writing in an Age of Europhobia.* New York: Palgrave Macmillan, 2004.

Neal, John. *American Writers: A Series of Papers Contributed to Blackwoods Magazine (1824–1825).* Ed. Fred Lewis Pattee. Durham, N.C.: Duke University Press, 1937.

Poe, Edgar Allan. *The Complete Works of Edgar Allan Poe.* Ed. James A. Harrison. Volume II. New York: AMS Press, Inc., 1965.

Pollin, Burton R. "Poe and Godwin." *Nineteenth-Century Fiction* 20.3 (Dec. 1965): 237–253.

Reynolds, David S. *Beneath the American Renaissance: The Subversive Imagination in the Age of Emerson and Whitman.* Cambridge, Mass.: Harvard University Press, 1989.

Ringe, Donald A. *American Gothic: Imagination and Reason in Nineteenth-Century Fiction.* Lexington: University Press of Kentucky, 1982.

Robinson, Henry Crabb. *Henry Crabb Robinson on Books and Their Writers.* Ed. Edith Morley. Vol. I. London: Dent, 1938.

Ruttenburg, Nancy. *Democratic Personality: Popular Voice and the Trial of American Authorship.* Stanford, CA: Stanford University Press, 1998.

Shelley, Percy Bysshe. "Review of *Mandeville.*" *The Examiner* (December 28, 1817): 826–827.

Skokoe, Frank Woodyer. *German Influence in the English Romantic Period, 1788–1818.* Cambridge: Cambridge University Press, 1926.

Smith, Elihu Hubbard. *The Diary of Elihu Hubbard Smith (1771–1798).* Ed. James E. Cronin. Philadelphia: American Philosophical Society, 1973.

St. Clair, William. *The Godwins and the Shelleys: A Biography of a Family.* Baltimore, Md.: The Johns Hopkins University Press, 1991.

Streeby, Shelley. *American Sensations: Class, Empire, and the Production of Popular Culture.* Berkeley, CA: University of California Press, 2002.

Tawil, Ezra. "New Forms of Sublimity": *Edgar Huntly* and the European Origins of American Exceptionalism." *Novel* 40: 1/2 (Fall 2006): 104–124.

"*The Life of Charles Brockden Brown: Together with Selections from the Rarest of His Printed Works, from His Original Letters, and from His Manuscripts before Unpublished* by William Dunlap." *The North-American Review and Miscellaneous Journal* 9: 24 (June 1819): 58–77.

Tompkins, Jane. *Sensational Designs: The Cultural Work of American Fiction, 1790–1860.* New York: Oxford University Press, 1985.

Tromp, Marlene, Pamela Gilbert, and Aeron Haynie, eds. *Beyond Sensation: Mary Elizabeth Braddon in Context.* Albany, N.Y.: SUNY Press, 2000.

Verhoeve, W.M. "'This blissful period of intellectual liberty': Transatlantic Radicalism and Enlightened Conservatism in Brown's Early Writings." *Revising Charles Brockden Brown: Culture, Politics, and Sexuality in the Early Republic.* Ed. Philip Barnard, Mark L. Kamrath, and Stephen Shapiro. Knoxville: The University of Tennessee Press, 2004. 7–40.

Ward, Ian. "A Man of Feelings: William Godwin's Romantic Embrace." *Law and Literature* 17:1 (Spring 2005): 21–46.

Waterman, Bryan. *Republic of Intellect: The Friendly Club of New York City and the Making of American Literature.* Baltimore, Md.: The Johns Hopkins University Press, 2007.

Watts, Steven. *The Romance of Real Life: Charles Brockden Brown and the Origins of American Culture.* Baltimore, Md.: The Johns Hopkins University Press, 1994.

Ziff, Larzer. "A Reading of *Wieland.*" *PMLA* 77.1 (Mar. 1962): 51–57.

Chapter 2
Daughters of the American Revolution: Sensational Pedagogy in Susanna Rowson's *Charlotte Temple*

Holly Blackford

"Democracy is Lovelace and the people are Clarissa ... The artful villain will pursue the innocent lovely girl to her ruin and her death."

—John Adams, 1804

As John Adams observed, the framework of the popular eighteenth-century seduction novel glossed the question of whether liberal governance could sustain virtue. The question of sustaining virtue in an environment of ungoverned passions prefigures later debates about sensational literature, debates that took root in earlier authors who offered sensational subjects to attract and instruct the broadest audiences. Fearful of unbridled democracy, Adams voiced the concern that the character of America would be sacrificed as it came of age after shedding its tyrannical parent, just as Samuel Richardson's Clarissa shed the unreasonable tyranny of her parents only to succumb to the villainy of the artful seducer Lovelace. Adams presages Joseph Fichtelberg's recent argument that sentimental writing, "the language of feeling," "provided the imagery through which Americans sought to explain and shape the market," thereby symbolizing "the mechanisms of exchange" (1). Viewing the seduction novel as a representation of an unbridled marketplace, Fichtelberg opposes dominant critics, such as Ann Douglas, Julia Stern, Nina Baym, Jane Tompkins, and Cathy Davidson, who in various ways "treat sentimental writing as a refuge, a protest, or an occult expression of the market and its consequences" (Fichtelberg 2).

John Adams exchanged lively letters with his wife and later with Thomas Jefferson on the intersections among character, familial relations, and politics. In the eighteenth century, both parent-child relations and marriage were understood as analogous to public governance, which explains the prominence of seduction fiction, argues Elizabeth Barnes (14). *Clarissa* had crystallized British concerns about the consequences of questioning absolute patriarchal authority: "in the wake of the English Revolution of 1688, when absolute monarchy fell out of favor, domestic patriarchy was also open to assault" (Woloch 56). Given the political meaning of novels depicting women in the marriage market who fall prey to men with low intentions, it makes perfect sense that the first bestselling novel in America would be a condensed and melodramatic version of *Clarissa*, refashioned with a younger adolescent protagonist named Charlotte Temple. In contrast to the vulnerable teen, a hovering, maternal narrator emerges to put forth a theory of "the talking book" as democratic parent, protector, and teacher. The narrator foregrounds the dangers of sensational, scandalous subjects with her self-conscious apologies, blushes, and shaming devices. Yet she simultaneously offers the theory that the narrator's control of the reading experience models and dominates emotional excess so that a widely popular and emotional reading experience can be a vehicle of teaching as much as titillation.

As Suzanne Keen demonstrates, a novel arousing the reader's sensibility had the support of such eighteenth-century theorists as David Hume (*A Treatise of Human Nature* 1739), Adam Smith (*Theory of Moral Sentiments* 1759), and Henry Lord Kames (*Elements of Criticism* 1762), yet, "[b]y the late eighteenth century, cultural watchdogs had begun to worry about the kinds of fictional representations that excited readers' sensations" (45). Critics such as Henry Mackenzie worried about the effects of sentimental literature on young people, and Anna Laetitia Aiken in 1773 expressed concern about the dangers of strong impressions that may not achieve in readers proper effect (Keen 45–47). Modern critics share the viewpoint that scenes of suffering encourage the reader's vampirism, "as if the person of sensibility feeds on the pain of others" (Keen 47). Later readers pointed to the sensationalism of Rowson's tale both to deplore and to explain the novel's success (Brandt 66, Parker, preface). At the time of publication the novel was understood as a *roman-à-clef*, "documenting in loosely-disguised form a notorious scandal of the Revolutionary era" involving John Montresor and Charlotte Stanley (Brandt 60, Parker 51). It tantalized with its aura of sensational truth.

Anxieties about the respectability of her work permeate every page of Rowson's novel. Attempting to balance sensational thrill and moral voice so she could enjoy broad appeal, Rowson foregrounds her narrator's heart-felt responses, blushes, and shame, thereby encouraging the reader to mirror her feelings. The narrator ironically signposts the illicit pleasure of voyeurism, Marion Rust argues, when she calls attention to her own blushes (76). But this voyeurism is always tinged with shame as Rowson's narrator apologizes for her characters and scandalous subjects. Rowson's inconsistent narrative address reveals her reasons for engaging with the tension between pleasure and profit. Although she more than once claims to be writing for young girls "only," she also addresses sober matrons, fathers, and older men who might enjoy mourning innocence. Rust argues that the numerous narrative asides actually gesture toward self-doubt and that the narrative voice "shifts between monitorial didacticism and an almost ecstatic celebration of submission to benevolent impulse" (75). Rowson's scenes of female submission become, Rust argues, intensely erotic (25). Rowson indeed wishes to involve and arouse her reader, and she uses both her apologetic stance and her pleas for forgiveness to prove that she understands the risk. She ultimately controls improper and proper reading by showcasing in the novel bad readers (Montraville) and good readers (Mrs. Beauchamp) as well as blaming Charlotte's fall as much on scandalous reading practices as on Charlotte's character. Further, the narrator's blushes add up to a very human mother advocating for the ruined child, modeling proper parental feeling.

From its very birth, America was a country deeply identified with the adolescent character who was forging an identity independent from the parent, legitimately or not. Susanna Rowson's *Charlotte, A Tale of Truth* (1791) was written and first published in England, but received little attention until it was published in America in 1794 (Stern 31–32). Instantly and overwhelmingly popular in the early republic, it would be one of the nation's biggest bestsellers until it was displaced by mid-nineteenth-century novels such as George Lippard's *The Quaker City* (1845) and Harriet Beecher Stowe's *Uncle Tom's Cabin* in 1852; *Charlotte Temple* went through 200 editions and continued to sell well into the early twentieth century (Douglas viii).. The story is simple. A British girl (Charlotte Temple) at a boarding school is seduced by a soldier named Montraville, whose attentions and clandestine letters are encouraged by Charlotte's duplicitous teacher, Mademoiselle La Rue, and Montraville's depraved "friend," Belcour. La Rue accepts Montraville's money in exchange for facilitating the budding relationship between Charlotte and Montraville. Although Montraville is shortly to depart for America, he does not give much thought to what he is doing and subsequently carries Charlotte to America on the promise of marriage. Charlotte loses her virtue in the crossing and is eventually abandoned outside New York, left to die shortly after giving birth.

For La Rue and for Montraville, who will meet an independent and spirited American girl named Julia Franklin once in New York, America is a land of opportunity and self-making. For Charlotte, America is a paralyzing wilderness where only the trickiest are fit to survive. Although she repeatedly throws herself on the mercy of others, hopelessly seeking replacements for the mother she abandoned in England (Lucy Temple), she finds only people with short attention spans (Montraville); people who lie (Belcour, La Rue); and people who demand rent (her worldly landlady, who expels her into the streets). The novel is an early instance of a feminist tradition arguing for better treatment of fallen women, improved laws protecting women, and education that would prevent girls "from the error which ruined poor Charlotte" (Rowson 1). *Charlotte Temple* is definitely not a declaration of adolescent independence, something we see in *Clarissa* and in Hannah Foster's epistolary seduction novel *The Coquette*, in which Eliza Wharton declares her rights to liberty and the pursuit of happiness. Unlike Eliza, whom Barbara White identifies as a prototype of the feisty and rebellious teen girl (30–32), Charlotte is frustratingly not a character with intellectual resources or interior subjectivity. She spends much of the novel unconscious or asleep, melodramatically wailing or voicing pitiful regret at deserting her parents.

In short, as Julia Stern argues, Charlotte remains a child who continually selects surrogates for her lost maternal object (56–58). Her stunted development is best revealed when she finally gives birth but does not recognize the infant as hers:

> "Oh," said she one day, starting up on hearing the infant cry, "why, why will you keep that child here; I am sure you would not if you knew how hard it was for a mother to be parted from her infant: it is like tearing the cords of life asunder. Oh could you see the horrid sight which I now behold—there—there stands my dear mother, her poor bosom bleeding at every vein, her gentle, affectionate

heart torn in a thousand pieces, and all for the loss of a ruined, ungrateful child. Save me—save me—from her frown. I dare not—indeed I dare not speak to her." (122)

Charlotte's pathological inability to deal with her mother's disapproval, and the awe with which she regards her mother, parallel a developmental theme we see in countless later texts of female development, in which daughters rarely equal the perfection of their introjected mothers. But Rowson's exploration of generational dynamics has further political implications. Like Benjamin Franklin's son, to whom Franklin addressed the first part of his autobiography but who turned out to be loyal to the British crown, Charlotte is an embodiment of anxieties about the next generation of Americans—anxieties about whether sons and daughters of the revolution can equal the greatness of parents who have forged independence and ideals of self-governance.

Rowson's didactic message to America seems to amount to a warning about how founding parents might actually stunt child development. How can a nation identified as adolescents coming-of-age also stand as parents? In her 1824 tale of American settlement, *Hobomok: A Tale of Early Times*, Lydia Maria Child would glorify the nation as a budding daughter: "Who would have believed that in two hundred years from that dismal period, the matured, majestic, and unrivalled beauty of England, would be nearly equaled by a daughter, blushing into life with all the impetuosity of youthful vigor?" (100) What kind of daughter "the next generation" of America would be was deeply in question in the 1790s. In letters to her husband, Abigail Adams deplored the backward state of female learning (Davidson 61) and argued that only a well-informed woman could discern and retain the affection of a worthy partner (Woloch 59). In 1776 she had written to her husband, "Emancipating all nations, you insist upon retaining absolute power over Wives ... Do not put such unlimited powers into the hands of husbands. Remember all men would be tyrants if they could" (qtd. in Woloch 56).

Worried about the implications for the new republic if the rights and minds of women were not improved, she, along with other public figures such as Caleb Bingham in 1791, argued that only improved education for daughters would result in better fulfillment of women's future roles as mothers (Davidson 63). Similarly, Benjamin Rush, in his 1787 "Thoughts upon Female Education," argued that "our ladies should be qualified to a certain degree, by a peculiar and suitable education, to concur in instructing their sons in principles of liberty and government" (qtd. in Davidson 62). The ideal of what Linda Kerber has termed "the republican mother" clashed with the reality of the dying Charlotte, who acted as a post-revolutionary counterpart to today's "Reviving Ophelia," the recent rallying cry of psychologist Mary Pipher. And rally around the drowning Charlotte, the nation did, even so far as to devote a fictitious grave to her, which would be visited by weeping audiences throughout the nineteenth century. The first instance of a truly popular American novel, *Charlotte Temple* would forge a democratic readership even as it expressed anxiety that the new nation's children would not fulfill the republican mission of independence and critical literacy.

Rowson depicts Charlotte as an object of utter pity and surrounds her with strong women, especially a narrator who puts forth her pedagogical agenda, advancing a new role for novels as tools for readers' self-education. Novels had previously been viewed with suspicion by Benjamin Rush and various educational theorists (Nichols 1–5), yet in the new republic a thriving book market had been launched because of the demand for materials designed to assist citizens with improving reading and writing skills (Davidson 65). Early novelists defended their form by claiming the validity and pedagogical value of their tales, inspiring a democratic practice of readers seeking self-improvement and pleasure through books. As Davidson demonstrates through analyzing marginalia of various editions of *Charlotte Temple*, Rowson's novel became a beloved object passed down through families and even commented upon by working-class girls who interacted with the story as well as used the novel to improve vocabulary.

Rowson essentially popularized the British *Clarissa* by drawing upon her experience in the theater, her personal views of America, and her feminist views of education and self-reliance. A truly transatlantic figure, Rowson was born in England but immigrated to New England as a child; her father was a collector of the Royal Customs and he tried to maintain a platform of neutrality during the Revolution, which only brought his family into impoverished imprisonment (Brandt 9–13). Rowson was an industrious actress, writer, playwright, song lyricist, teacher, and breadwinner. Rowson's family was eventually allowed to leave again for England, where she married and began writing even while acting in numerous plays.

The energy of the stage infuses the dramatic *Charlotte Temple* (Parker 52). In it, Rowson eliminated the sorts of sub-plots that vex her other novels and wrote direct, emotionally charged scenes and dialogue. In contrast to the overtly novelistic flavor of the epistolary *Clarissa*, *Charlotte Temple* conveys the moving power of the stage from an omniscient yet embodied narrator who watches events unfold and comments on tragic meaning, like a univocal chorus. Rowson probably adapted the novel to play form around 1799 or 1800, in which "the melodramatic possibilities inherent in the story are utilized to the hilt. There is an intensification of character types. LaRue becomes the blackest stock villainess, and Belcour is the decadent, mustache-stroking 'heavy' of the popular theater ... and Charlotte is melodrama's darling, the 'delicate flower,' a phrase consistently used to describe her" (Brandt 69). However, the strongest and most interesting character in the novel is actually the narrator, who transforms the theatrical tableaux and emotions into pedagogical commentary and thereby offers a democratic tool for reader improvement. Her blushing reactions and pleas for sympathy both humanize the narrator and model for readers (or watchers of the "play") the appropriate sympathetic response. It is the narrator that invites readers into a democratic community "watching over" Charlotte, as opposed to readers peering into private letters in *Clarissa*.

Perhaps the most telling difference between *Clarissa* and *Charlotte Temple* is the contrast between "the steadiness of [Clarissa's] mind" (Sill 179) and Charlotte as "young lady of intense sensibility" rather than sense (Weil 119). While the steadfast Clarissa makes only the one false step of meeting Lovelace in her garden, where ironically "it is her passion, and not he, that makes her run" (Sill 180), the continually victimized, swooning Charlotte remains an innocent child. In her transparency and innocence, she is vulnerable to the dissimulating, sensational stories Belcour tells Montraville about her. Even her initial seduction pits her natural subliterate emotions against machinations of text; she is doomed the moment La Rue convinces Charlotte to read Montraville's letter. Charlotte spills her "tale of truth" to everyone she meets, but her truth goes nowhere. Without the tact to manipulate words strategically, she spills out her story to her landlady and receives a cold reader response. Her letters to her parents are intercepted, her letter to La Rue is unacknowledged, and she becomes more and more a victim of sensational accounts of her reputation. Only her dead body has the power of story. Literally a tale of transatlantic cross-pollination, the story of the naïve Charlotte presents a vexed vision of the new world and how precarious is one's dependence on reputation, once separated from one's parents or one's mother country. The new-world girl is stalked by sensational European villains, her awakening sensations and blushes opening her up to old-world penetration. La Rue and Belcour could have marched off the melodramatic stage of Guilbert de Pixerécourt or the Gothic novels of Ann Radcliffe, generic influences that, Walter C. Phillips (6–7) and Lyn Pykett (6) demonstrate, coalesce in the later sensationalist writing of the nineteenth-century marketplace. Charlotte's increasing incarceration functions as a muted gothic, and Belcour, who in one particularly over-the-top scene stages Charlotte's unfaithfulness, is nothing if not the unregenerate villain of standard melodrama, with a healthy infusion of Shakespeare's Iago. Charlotte has placed herself "under the protection" of Montraville but ironically he is, more than Charlotte, vulnerable to malicious rumors. Rowson represents the transatlantic crossing of Belcour and La Rue, who care nothing for truth, as the corruption of naturally felt emotion. Their talents become magnified in New York when all the (new) world becomes their stage.

Charlotte goes mad and is reduced to the simple text of a grave because her transparent nature is occluded by the circulation of stories "between men." Charlotte's character is compromised more by the circulation of sensational reports about her sexuality than by sexuality itself. The moment Charlotte takes her misstep, she becomes an unconscious, open text that can be read by a male marketplace: "every libertine will think he has a right to insult her with his licentious passion" (62). Scandalous stories are more powerful seducers than young men like Montraville, who gullibly believes Belcour's crude reports of her unfaithfulness, which is astonishing given her reclusive life and "visible situation" of late pregnancy (81).

This "visible situation" underlines her transparency when she meets Mrs. Beauchamp, tellingly the only character who represents an ideal reader because she ignores stories about Charlotte, becomes a direct "witness to the solitary life Charlotte led," and wishes to meet her without mediating opinions (77). Mrs.

Beauchamp witnesses Charlotte's death as well. Once this ideal reader abandons Charlotte—called away to Rhode Island—Charlotte's vulnerability to stage artists like Belcour is inevitable. In an emotionally climactic scene that seals her doom, Belcour is visiting Charlotte, who has fallen sleep, and sees Montraville coming so he stages the scene by lying down next to Charlotte and thereby implying the unbelievable idea that he has just had sex with her. Montraville believes this even though Charlotte has to be in her final trimester of pregnancy. Belcour is a sensationalist writer and Montraville a duped reader. The false writer and reader rage out of control and occlude the female voice, explaining the "fight fire with fire" strategy of the strong narrator, who reveals *her* skills at staging correct and incorrect readings of Charlotte and, by extension, her seduction novel.

However much Rowson deplores the sensational marketplace that ruins Charlotte, she imagines maternal forces that could transform the early novel into a popular, theatrical tool for pedagogy and self-help. She creates a maternal, feminist narrator to compensate for well-meaning but essentially weak and out-of-touch, ineffectual parents, who represent the generation relatively immune to the new environment of text. For example, the day of Charlotte's elopement is melodramatically the very day her mother has planned Charlotte's sixteenth birthday party, symbolic of a series of births and re-births that accompany the narrator's maternal stance in addressing the "young and unprotected woman in her first entrance into life":

> While the tear of compassion still trembled in my eye for the fate of the unhappy Charlotte, I may have children of my own, said I, to whom this recital may be of use, and if to your own children, said Benevolence, why not to the many daughters of Misfortune who, deprived of natural friends, or spoilt by a mistaken education, are thrown on an unfeeling world without the least power to defend themselves from the snares not only of the other sex, but from the more dangerous arts of the profligate of their own. (Rowson, Author's Preface, xlix–l)

The author's preface clarifies her Wollstonecraft-like position that the real villainy against young girls lies with poor female teachers and role models as well as with "mistaken education," which it is the duty of the narrator's own maternal voice to correct or "rebirth." Perhaps the most atrocious character in the novel is Charlotte's teacher La Rue, who elopes with Belcour but subsequently makes an even better match on the ship. Clearly considering La Rue the major villain, Rowson gives her a prominent position in the concluding chapter of the novel, where La Rue appears as an ill wretch unable to eat, preparing to die, and repentant of her choice to refuse Charlotte shelter in childbirth.

Rowson's novel aspires to a pedagogical and parenting platform that was simultaneously being modeled by Benjamin Franklin's autobiography, overtly addressed to his son, an address he would desert after their painful political differences would forever divide them. Part one of the autobiography was translated into French in 1791 but not available in English until 1793; nevertheless the contemporaneous publication of Rowson's novel and Franklin's memoir gives us insight into how the new nation was seeking to develop a parental viewpoint and advocate a model of democratic character—helping younger readers with how to think rather than telling them what to think. Franklin discusses how he exchanged a series of opinion papers with someone opposed to female learning and his father chanced to read them:

> Without entering into the discussion, he took occasion to talk to me about the manner of my writing; observed that, though I had the advantage of my antagonist in correct spelling and pointing ... I fell far short in elegance of expression, in method and in perspicuity ... I saw the justice of his remarks and thence grew more attentive to the manner in writing, and determined to endeavor at improvement. (14)

His father critiques Franklin's composition rather than his actual content, a key component of critical pedagogy. Immediately afterward, Franklin begins the practice of imitating excellent writing that he encounters in books on his own. Eager to increase his dexterity with words, Franklin uses the *Spectator* to practice turning prose to verse and verse to prose, learning how to vary words, sentence length, measure and rhyme, variety, and order of thought, "to teach me method in the arrangement of thoughts" (15). In comparing his own writing with the book's, he "discovered some of my faults, and corrected them" (15). He moves on to the study of other subjects through books as models, learning the method of "humble inquirer and doubter" from Xenophon's *Memorable Things of Socrates* (16). Franklin takes pains to model democratic self-teaching as the legacy bequeathed to him by his father, which is precisely what he wants his son to learn—to self-scrutinize, detect his own errors, and correct his own faults.

The post-revolutionary period saw a general increase in interest in families (Calvert 67) and in educating children "so that they would become virtuous citizens" (Chudacoff 39). Books for young Americans were part and parcel of that vision. Most of the early post-revolutionary novelists also wrote essays on education, and the issue of characters' capability for reading and writing was usually a dominant theme of the early novels (Davidson 66). Not only do characters overtly address the need for education, but they also comment upon the reading and writing skills of other characters. A pioneer of female education and a writer of textbooks for girls that promoted critical thinking and that ranged from geography to history, spelling to Bible studies, Rowson was part of the movement for more ladies' academies in the 1780s and 1790s, when female literacy generally improved (Parker 103–115, Bontatibus 19, 24, Eldred and Mortensen). Rowson's academy was "particularly revolutionary in that it included and encouraged public speaking" (Bontatibus 54) as well as art, music, dancing, and literature. In her teaching methodology and in her annual student performances, which were well attended and which featured dialogue as well as pantomime, she drew upon "her theatrical experience [that] had taught her to entertain as well as instruct" (Parker 19). *Charlotte Temple* must be understood in the spirit of a teaching philosophy: everyone is imperfect—"but surely, when we reflect how many errors we are ourselves subject to ... we surely may pity the faults of others" (69–70). What Franklin calls our "errata" is what binds a community together in a continual mission for self-improvement. It is therefore crucial to expose errata, even erotic errata. We must blush to bloom.

In a period with national and particularly female education on the mind (Weil 32–34), it is important for us to know that Charlotte's parents made a critical mistake and "permitted [Charlotte] to finish the education her mother had begun, at Madame Du Pont's school" (22). This is crucial information because Lucy Temple, Charlotte's mother, is offered as a model of perfection and virtue, largely *because* she *did not* finish that type of French finishing-school education. Lucy Temple chose to marry and set up a dairy and poultry farm rather than court an aristocratic lifestyle. In fact, while the life of Lucy Temple resembles the ideal life sketched in John de Crevecoeur's 1782 *Letters From an American Farmer*, or even the self-made ideal of Franklin's autobiography, the fallen life of Charlotte who "returns" to a European sensibility embodies a parental mistake. Franklin was not above reproaching himself as a parent; he devotes a touching passage to his mistake in not inoculating his younger child against smallpox, which cost him the child's life. Importantly, Franklin, immediately after invoking William as an occasion to write his life, puts forth the idea that life is like a rough draft of text, full of errata and never perfect, but always in need of a printer's correction. He says that were he to repeat his life, he would only ask "the advantages authors have in a second edition to correct some faults of the first" (3). The metaphor of life as a first edition, which both writer and new generation can perhaps correct, aptly characterizes Rowson's intent in offering Charlotte as an example of an erring girl whom parents and children can transform into a second edition. Even in the novel itself, Charlotte's daughter is christened Lucy Temple and brought back to Charlotte's mother, making the mother "almost fancy she again possessed her Charlotte" (131). Errata are exposed so they can be erased.

Just as Franklin cleverly uses an address to his son as a ruse to reach a wider audience with a paternal stance, Rowson uses her address to "my dear girls" (24) and their mothers ("My dear Madam" 25) to distract us from the larger audiences she has in mind, including men, "Any reader who has the least knowledge of the world, will easily imagine [Montraville's] letter was made up of encomiums on [Charlotte's] beauty ... nor will he be surprised that a heart open to every gentle, generous sentiment, should feel itself warmed by gratitude for a man who professed to feel so much for her" (25–26). The narrator even expostulates how the doting male parent must feel "when he sees the darling of his age at first seduced from his protection ... when fancy paints to me the good old man stooping to raise the weeping penitent" (25). Rowson's narrator vacillates between presuming a worldly reader—"The reader no doubt has already developed the character of La Rue" (60)—and an innocent one that cannot possibly understand Charlotte's story, perhaps growing impatient with it:

> "Bless my heart," cries my young, volatile reader, "I shall never have patience
> to get through these volumes, there are so many ahs! And ohs! So much fainting,

tears, and distress, I am sick to death of the subject." My dear, chearful [*sic*], innocent girl, for innocent I will suppose you to be, or you would acutely feel the woes of Charlotte, did conscience say, thus might it have been with me. (108)

Rowson's narrator then engages in a long, sustained dialogue with her reader as she encodes possible reader responses of the impatient, the ones who suspect her moral intent, the unfeeling, and even the sarcastic. The imagined dialogue with this dizzying array of readers inculcates a broad classroom, but it also telegraphs the narrator's knowledge that some are reading for titillation and some to learn. She challenges everyone to work very hard at actually understanding Charlotte, "Who can form an adequate idea of the sorrow that preyed upon the mind of Charlotte?" (68)

While the oscillation between "sympathetic identification" and "disciplined detachment" gives the reader a disparate feeling of mixed genres and conveys uncertainty about the relationship between pedagogy and pleasure, it also reveals Rowson's "canny employment of sentimentalism's sensationalist and didactic registers" (Rust 75, 38). She wants us to feel alternatively aroused and detached as we consider and forgive our blushes. Later female writers protesting seduction would handle the subject in similar ways. Harriet Jacobs, in her *Incidents in the Life of a Slave Girl*, alternatively apologizes and asserts without apology her strong maternal voice. Harriet Beecher Stowe in *Uncle Tom's Cabin* continually features in characters (especially Cassy) and in her narrator a rhetoric of shame and apology for needing to represent unseemly subjects. The stance acknowledges, forestalls, and forgives readers for having improper feelings.

Rowson's strategy of addressing young girls only to "slip" and demonstrate her awareness of other voyeurs, ultimately to suggest that no one can grasp her story although all must aspire to feeling it, becomes an instantiation of a democratic readership. She literally built a large reading community by challenging everyone to feel for the most pitiful citizen. An 1870 commentary on the popularity of *Charlotte Temple*, published by Elias Nason in *Memoir of Mrs. Susanna Rowson*, vividly depicts the diversity of audiences captivated by the accessible, melodramatic novel:

It has stolen its way alike into the study of the divine and the workshop of the mechanic; into the parlor of the accomplished lady and into the bedchamber of her waiting maid; into the log-hut on the extreme border of modern civilization and into the forecastle of the whale ship on the lonely ocean. It has been read by the grey-bearded professor after his "divine Plato"; by the beardless clerk after balancing his accounts at night; by the traveler waiting for the next conveyance at the village inn; by the school girl stealthfully in her seat at school. It has beguiled the woodman in his hut at night in the deep solitudes of the silent forest; it has cheated the farmer's son of many an hour while poring over its fascinating pages, seated on broken spinning wheel in the attic; it has drawn tears from the miner's eye in the dim twilight of his subterranean dwelling; it has unlocked the secret sympathies of the veteran soldier in his tent before the day of battle. (Nason 50–51)

At the birth of the novel in America, then, is the birth of the idea that democracy means popular culture. The mechanic, the lady and her maid, the professor and clerk, the school girl and woodman share this popular text. One of the ways in which the novel gives readers this power and narrative authority is by virtue of its melodrama; rather than interrogate the complexity of character, it sketches sparse tableaux and consistent characters who can be easily classified in variable degrees of good and evil. The relationship between the narrator and implied reader(s) is far more complex than any of the actual characters in the novel. It is "the talking book" itself whom we most get to know.

The plea to feel for Charlotte cuts across all levels of education and class, empowering readers to come together and mother a lost child. Ann Douglas argues that the melodramatic mode gives power to the viewer and is thus inherently anti-authority. Because melodrama excites readers by dealing with "'subliterate myths' marketed to that 'feeling heart' ... melodrama gave its audience precedence, top billing, so to speak, over the author—indeed, over all established authority" (xiii). As Douglas points out, the quintessentially melodramatic moment of Charlotte fleeing into the icy winter night, essentially to be cast out and die in childbirth, is re-imagined by Stowe through Eliza, who flees across the icy floes of the Ohio to save her child from slavery (xlii). Charlotte's flight can be recast as Eliza's flight because the angry maternal voice of the novel becomes a social protest that transfers parental authority to the reader. It is not an accident that Rowson begins to address parents, especially sober matrons, when the going gets tough, eager to broaden the responsibility of mothering to the republic. Even the young learn to self-parent and internalize a moral barometer. As Stern points out, a collective mourning for Charlotte was inevitable, just as the dying Eva or the drowning Ophelia later became rallying cries to save the nation's daughters. Charlotte has left a mother who already meets the qualifications for American republican mother, but Charlotte was not taught her skills.

Lucy Temple is offered as a complete pillar of virtue throughout the novel. In fact, the glorification of Lucy Temple is given a lot of narrative space in the novel, in complete contrast to other novels of seduction that marginalize mothers. Lucy Temple is a decisive mother who rules her household and speaks with a firmness other female characters lack, who withstood her own trials of seduction when young, who forged an independent life on a dairy rather than marry for money, who stands tall even upon the death of her mother and brother, who supports her father in prison, and who deliberately puts away her grief for Charlotte to maintain her duties as wife and daughter. Charlotte was never destined to compete with her mother, who, although perceived by most critics as an allegorical representation of England, could equally be understood as the republican mother espoused as a female ideal among American writers and leaders who were seeking a new role for female leadership and patriotism.

Critics have traditionally understood Charlotte as the fallen child America, who made the mistake of breaking away from overindulgent English parents. In many early American works, such as William Hill Brown's *The Power of*

Sympathy, Hannah Foster's *The Coquette*, and numerous short stories, America was symbolized as "a fallen woman, not because she was seduced and abandoned by the hope of democracy, but because she expressed filial disobedience in a war for independence" (Bontatibus 3). However, Charlotte is notably not a victim of parental persecution and thus she has been considered a mistaken revolutionary. The view of Lucy as "the English motherland mourning its erring colonial child" (Stern 35–36) can be reconsidered if we also analyze Rowson's emphasis on the Temples as themselves children who threw off tyrannical parents and aristocratic expectations to live independently. In *Charlotte Temple*, we learn a significant amount of backstory about Lucy Temple, whom Mr. Temple first meets when she is dutifully supporting her father in debtor's prison. Lucy's family had been wronged by an associate who had lent them money and wanted Lucy as mistress in return. The seduction plot thus cycles through both generations. Temple rejects his father's requirements for a better match and marries Lucy, rejecting "splendor, profusion, and dissipation" (19) for the simplicity of an Edenic cottage with cows, poultry, and garden, where Lucy is Queen. Their modest living on "three hundred a year" (21) is reminiscent of Crevecoeur's pride in his 371 acres of farm, epitomizing freedom of thought and action as well as domestic bliss.

The Temples embody the willful forging of independence, a theme that shifts the political meaning of the story from America as erring child to America as ideal parents without the skills to properly educate children. Charlotte is "the only pledge of their mutual love" (22), a marital ideal that matches what in the eighteenth century was called companionate marriage. Even the fact that the Temples have only one child matches Crevecoeur's model of the ideal life. The idea of companionate marriage was merely one of many post-Revolutionary changes in women's status, also including "the new legitimacy of women's education, a new rhetoric of female self-esteem, and an enhanced regard for motherhood" (Woloch 63). A new ideal of egalitarian marriage, requiring "mutual esteem, mutual friendship, mutual confidence, begirt about by mutual forbearance," would alter how marital choices would be made (Woloch 56). There was some rise in the divorce rate, as loss of affection became an acceptable reason to separate, and children became significant factors in choosing a match. For daughters, this meant, too, that parents were not acting in their behalf and thus "emphasis fell on the personal qualifications and discretion of the candidate herself" (Woloch 57–59). Companionate marriage meant that even greater importance would be placed on girls' critical thinking skills.

Lucy Temple's vow of independence, companionate marriage, and simple farm life are antithetical to the French school of Charlotte's undoing. In other words, Charlotte's education and upbringing do not match the values of her founding mother and father. Not only does the backstory of Lucy Temple make Rowson's novel stand out from other seduction novels, but it also seems to have the added significance of positing Charlotte as a next-generation American who cannot equal the republican motherhood Lucy has established with her sense of virtue and goodness. Chapter 8, titled "Domestic Pleasures Planned," is entirely devoted to apostrophizing the goodness of Lucy Temple, who is worshipped in both a spiritual and secular manner:

> Look, my dear friends, at yonder lovely Virgin, arrayed in a white robe devoid of ornament; behold the meekness of her countenance, the modesty of her gait; her handmaids are *Humility, Filial Piety, Conjugal Affection, Industry,* and *Benevolence*; her name is *Content*; she holds in her hand the cup of true felicity, and when once you have formed an intimate acquaintance with these her attendants, nay you must admit them as your bosom friends and chief counselors, then, whatever may be your situation in life, the meek eyed Virgin will immediately take up her abode with you ... She will dwell in the humblest cottage; she will attend you even to a prison. Her parent is Religion; her sisters, Patience and Hope. (33)

The strong mother-worship of the narrator presages works of sentiment that would rise in the nineteenth century, such as *Little Women* and *Uncle Tom's Cabin*, in which worship of mothers and their economies (Rachel Halliday's kitchen, for example) embody democratic order and republican virtue.

Mothers and private spheres come to compensate for unbridled public voyeurisms. Lucy Temple is so virtuous that when Charlotte deserts her, importantly on her birthday as if to imply that Charlotte is betraying her democratic birth in the purity of a poultry farm, she resolves to appear cheerful and continue her duty as wife and daughter. Resolving to bow to God's will and not let the "'duty of a wife be totally absorbed in the feelings of the mother,'" Lucy vows to conquer "'selfish indulgence of my own grief'" and therefore "'alleviate the sufferings of my husband'" (59). Like Alcott's Marmee, who conceals her true feelings, Lucy resolves to "'wear a smile on my face, though the thorn rankles in my heart'" (59), and the narrator expostulates the reader to consider the pain of a deserted mother as "your maker" and "reflect that you may yourselves one day be mothers" (55). This internalization of motherhood is precisely her point. Seduction becomes a betrayal not of self or patriarchy, but of this dispassionate maternal ideal. Stern argues that the narrator takes on a tone of rage and mourning for the girl dispossessed from the American dream, but it could also be argued that the narrator glorifies Lucy so that she can radically transform a nation from a democratic fraternity (Montraville and Belcour "sharing" Charlotte) to a pedagogically minded and self-governing matriarchy. Such a stance, as Jane Tompkins has argued, is precisely the kind that later nineteenth-century sentimental writers would take.

Unlike in other seduction novels, women are important agents in Charlotte's plight: Lucy Temple, La Rue, Mrs. Beauchamp (the landlady who is thoroughly American in her business outlook), and Julia Franklin (a proto-type of an American girl with the spirit and independence Charlotte lacks). Julia is also mourning for her lost mother, but she has arisen with a newfound independence and thus attracts Montraville. In contrast to the power of women and the maternal narrative voice in *Charlotte Temple*, the seducer is actually quite weak and therefore not at all a Lovelace. The first words of the novel are Montraville's, but he is asking his friend

Belcour what he would like to do, typical of the indecisive Montraville. When the men see the school-girls, they "involuntarily pulled off their hats" (3), again lacking agency, and when Montraville decides not to pursue Charlotte, he changes his mind because "as he turned, he saw the gate which led to the pleasure grounds open" (5). Julia Franklin literally falls into his lap; during a house fire, someone thrusts her jewels into his hands for safe-keeping, after which he has to find the owner. Montraville's flaw is that he is "good-natured almost to a fault" and "staid not to reflect on the consequence which might follow the attainment of his wishes" (36). Like Charlotte, Montraville could have been saved by a humane friend, but instead had chosen a villainous friend who is inexplicably bent on ruining Charlotte. Montraville presages the sort of character we find in later novels such as Edith Wharton's Newland, who makes decisions by accident or arbitrariness: "'If [the Countess] doesn't turn before that sail crosses the Lime Rock light I'll go back'" (43), Newland thinks. A passive villain in a post-revolutionary American novel, Montraville is rather weak and pathetic.

In my reading of *Charlotte Temple*, the crime against Charlotte is the inconsistency between her education and her founding parents, a reading that corresponds with other evidence of Rowson's interest in the education of girls. In fact, the problem with both Montraville and Charlotte is their suggestibility—their very nature as potential, openness, virgin land. Unlike the founding parents in the novel, the young are subject to peer pressure: "The mind of youth eagerly catches at promised pleasure: pure and innocent by nature, it thinks not of the dangers lurking beneath those pleasures" (24). A young country can hardly help finding pleasurable promise itself. Rowson claims to be writing for young girls, but in the course of doing so she seems to be chastising readers as ineffectual parents who have failed to inculcate in the young self-governance of passions. In her viewpoint, the ideal American mother would be a teacher, a novel writer, and an icon of virtue. The narrator becomes the republican mother Lucy Temple was but could not reproduce, and she begets a nation of readers invested in nurturing drowning, stunted children who act without thought. As Barnes notes, early sentimental writing feminized men, too, transforming them into agents of sympathy and into fathers against whom there would be no need to rebel (43). Charlotte's father becomes a sort of midwife to Charlotte, finding her in America just in time to bring her child, named Lucy Temple, back to the mother, as if printing a second edition and erasing his errata. In doing so, he is asking men to mother, complicit with Rowson's broad goal for transforming all sorts of voyeuristic readers into parents, roles that would greatly expand the ideology of independence to include dependence and nurture.

Even as she pioneered the bestselling novel's penchant for sensational elements, Rowson paved the way for nineteenth-century concerns with pedagogy and the shift to teaching self-regulation through "loving" discipline, as explored by G.M. Goshgarian. In *Charlotte Temple*, learning occurs through recognition of our common imperfection and shame—the need for all of us to err and revise the editions of our lives. With her worldly narrator and her matron Mrs. Beauchamp, both of whom become witnesses and editors of errant youth, Rowson sought to draw a line between voyeurism and sympathy, both of which appeal to the body, heart, and nerves more than to the intellect. Luckily her rhetoric of apology and forgiveness enables any reader, with any purpose, to experience catharsis and regeneration through tears.

In Rowson's agenda, the pedagogical novel would deploy sensational elements to involve every reader, whose awakening sensations would thereby open the reader to the novel's social message. Rowson thus opened a can of stylistic worms that would burst into two very divergent paths: on the one hand, her socially persuasive use of sensationalism presages the work of George Lippard, whose gratuitous sensationalist elements soon eclipsed his messages (Reynolds 207); on the other hand, she bequeathed a legacy to later sentimental writers, who similarly used a multi-voiced maternal narrator to reign in subjects that might titillate as much as teach. While her theory of the book as entertaining and particularly democratic pedagogy blossomed in American schools—and in the mid-nineteenth century's increasing concern with active parenting—she also inadvertently spawned illegitimate literary progeny. An author can hardly control a story that migrates into popular culture, where books take on a life of their own. For example, Stowe never gave permission for the Uncle Tom melodramas that became what Sarah Meer calls Uncle Tom mania on both sides of the Atlantic. As early as 1852, in a British version of *Uncle Tom's Cabin* titled *Pictures of Slavery in the United States*, illustrations embedded voyeurism and conveyed the erotic potential in scenes of whipped, naked slaves (Morgan 13). The awakening sensations of Rowson's mass-market readers turned into a hunger for more and more shocking sensations. But as David S. Reynolds demonstrates, *Beneath the American Renaissance*, the lively mix of oratories and sensationalist stories inevitably comprises democracy and mass readership, something Rowson's canny narrator already seems to know. Rowson was the first to bring her experience with the English theater to the novel that crossed into American popular culture. Her "talking book" became the mother of a very American idea: the idea that scandals must receive press because reading about them is instructional. We might say, ironically, that she was the first to cross the line between sensational and didactic—a line that her narrator drew and then blurred with blushes and tears.

Works Cited

Barnes, Elizabeth. *States of Sympathy: Seduction and Democracy in the American Novel*. New York: Columbia University Press, 1997.

Bontatibus, Donna R. *The Seduction Novel of the Early Nation: A Call for Socio-Political Reform*. East Lansing: Michigan State University Press, 1999.

Brandt, Ellen B. *Susanna Haswell Rowson: America's First Best-selling Novelist*. Chicago: Serbra, 1975.

Calvert, Karin. "Patterns of Childrearing in America." *Beyond the Century of the Child: Cultural History and Developmental Psychology*. Ed. William Koops and Michael Zuckerman. Philadelphia: University of Pennsylvania Press, 2003. 62–81.

Child, Lydia Maria. *Hobomok and other writings on Indians*. Ed. Carolyn L. Harcher. New Brunswick: Rutgers University Press, 1986.

Chudacoff, Howard P. *Children at Play: An American History*. New York: New York University Press, 2007.

Davidson, Cathy N. *Revolution and the Word: The Rise of the Novel in America*. New York: Oxford University Press, 1986.

Douglas, Ann. Introduction. *Charlotte Temple and Lucy Temple*. New York: Penguin, 1991. vii–xliii.

Eldred, Janet Carey, and Peter Mortensen. "'A Few Patchwork Opinions': Piecing Together Narratives of U. S. Girls' Early National Schooling." *Girls and Literacy in America: Historical Perspectives to the Present*. Ed. Jane Greer. Santa Barbara: ABC-CLIO, 2003. 23–50.

Fichtelberg, Joseph. *Critical Fictions: Sentiment and the American Market, 1780–1870*. Athens: University of Georgia Press, 2003.

Foster, Hannah Webster. *The Coquette*. New York: Oxford University Press, 1986.

Franklin, Benjamin. *The Autobiography & Other Writings*. Ed. Peter Shaw. New York: Bantam, 1982.

Goshgarian, G.M. *To Kiss the Chastening Rod: Domestic Fiction and Sexual Ideology in the American Renaissance*. Ithaca: Cornell University Press, 1992.

Jacobs, Harriet. *Incidents in the Life of a Slave Girl*. New York: The Modern Library, 2004.

Keen, Suzanne. *Empathy and the Novel*. New York: Oxford University Press, 2007.

Kerber, Linda K. "The Republican Mother: Women and the Enlightenment, An American Perspective." *American Quarterly* 28 (Summer 1976): 187–205.

Meer, Sarah. *Uncle Tom Mania: Slavery, Minstrelsy, and Transatlantic Culture in the 1850s*. Athens: University of Georgia Press, 2005.

Morgan, Jo-Ann. "Picturing Uncle Tom with Little Eva-Reproduction as Legacy." *Journal of American Culture* 27.1 (March 2004): 1–24.

Nason, Elias. *Memoir of Mrs. Susanna Rowson*. Albany: Joel Munsell, 1870. http://etext.lib.virginia.edu/railton/enam854/ctemple.html . 9 October 2007.

Nichols, Elisabeth B. "'Blunted Hearts': Female Readers and Printed Authority in the Early Republic." *Reading Acts: U. S. Readers' Interactions with Literature, 1800–1950*. Ed. Barbara Ryan and Amy M. Thomas. Knoxville: University of Tennessee Press, 2002. 1–28.

Parker, Patricia. *Susanna Rowson*. Boston: Twayne, 1986.

Phillips, Walter C. *Dickens, Reade, and Collins, Sensational Novelists: A Study in the Conditions and Theories of Novel Writing in Victorian England*. New York: Russell & Russell, 1962.

Pipher, Mary. *Reviving Ophelia: Saving the Selves of Adolescent Girls*. New York: Riverhead, 2005.

Pykett, Lyn. *The 'Improper' Feminine: The Women's Sensation Novel and the New Woman Writing*. New York: Routledge, 1992.

Reynolds, David S. *Beneath the American Renaissance: The Subversive Imagination in the Age of Emerson and Melville*. New York: Alfred A. Knopf, 1988.

Richardson, Samuel. *Clarissa*. Boston: Houghton Mifflin, 1962.

Rowson, Susanna. *Charlotte Temple*. New York: Penguin, 1991.

Rust, Marion. *Prodigal Daughters: Susanna Rowson's Early American Women*. Chapel Hill: University of North Carolina Press, 2008.

Sill, Geoffrey. *The Cure of the Passions and the Origins of the English Novel*. New York: Cambridge University Press, 2001.

Stern, Julia. *The Plight of Feeling: Sympathy and Dissent in the Early American Novel*. Chicago: University of Chicago Press, 1997.

Tompkins, Jane. *Sensational Designs: The Cultural Work of American Fiction: 1790–1860*. New York: Oxford University Press, 1985.

Weil, Dorothy. *In Defense of Women: Susanna Rowson (1762–1824)*. University Park: Pennsylvania State University Press, 1976.

Wharton, Edith. *The Age of Innocence*. New York: Appleton, 1920. http://www.bartleby.com/1005/21.html. 29 February 2008.

White, Barbara. *Growing Up Female: Adolescent Girlhood in American Fiction*. Westport: Greenwood, 1985.

Woloch, Nancy. *Women and the American Experience: A Concise History*. 2nd ed. Boston: McGraw Hill, 2002.

Chapter 3

"Raw Pork Steaks with Treacle": Nineteenth-Century American Sensationalism and *Oliver Twist*

David Bordelon

In an 1842 editorial, the New York monthly *Arcturus* lamented the American appetite for literature steeped in violence. It yearned for more uplifting stories and looked forward to "the time ... when the readers will no more devour, with ghoul-like appetite, the blood and murder of Jack Sheppard, than they will eat raw pork steaks with treacle; and ... Harrison Ainsworth will go out of fashion" ("Criticism" 402). Unfortunately for the editors, it seems that time never came. More than forty years later, there was still concern about the influence of such fiction—and the metaphors had shifted ominously from food to disease. The Presbyterian preacher and social reformer Thomas Talmage, in *Social Dynamite; or, The Wickedness of Modern Society* (1888), declared that sensational literature "has helped to fill insane asylums and penitentiaries and almshouses and dens of shame. The bodies of this infection lie in the hospitals and in the graves, while their souls are being tossed over into a lost eternity" (172). The exaggerated tone of this jeremiad lends it a ridiculous air, but Talmage's conflation of sickness and sin makes it a potent warning, linking the objectivity of science to the stern morality of religion. According to him, such literature deals a death blow to society, leading inexorably to moral degradation and death.

Given this abhorrence for lurid descriptions of vice, what would the *Arcturus* critic and Talmage make of a novel dealing with prostitution, burglary, kidnapping, and the brutal murder—by pistol-whipping and clubbing—of a defenseless woman? In short, what would they make of Charles Dickens's *Oliver Twist* (1838–39)? The answer is not as simple as it seems, given America's love-hate relationship with sensationalism, a predominant topic in the essays collected in this volume. For instance, one year after the *Arcturus* article, a reviewer in the *Southern Monthly* argued that while Dickens did indeed "paint the horrors of custom and the deformities of moral aberration," he did so for a salutatory purpose: "to bring the tale home to the ears of generous philanthropy, and ensure a hearing for the voice of obscure misery, from those who seldom turn from themselves, to consider, for a moment, the sufferings of the distressed" ("Dickens's Novels" 441). And even Talmage, after his excoriating blast against sensational fiction, offers Dickens as a novelist who creates "ennobling and purifying" works (174).

While many of Dickens's novels feature sensational elements, *Oliver Twist*'s best-selling mixture of virtue and vice make it a central text for examining sensationalism in the United States. As the targets of the *Arcturus* editorial—the popular English writer Harrison Ainsworth and his outlaw protagonist Jack Sheppard—make clear, an ocean could not separate such fiction from American readers. And for many of these readers, *Oliver* fit the bill. This is borne out by the cultural resonance of the novel: while often remembered as the story of an orphan boy who made good (and who had the temerity to "ask for more"), the many casual references in articles, books, and letters throughout the century to "Fagin" and "Sikes" as shorthand for criminality and vice, and its popular transformation into a play with Oliver as a secondary character to Nancy, ground the novel firmly in the sensational.

First published in the United States in 1838 as a serial in the *Museum of Foreign Literature* and in the American edition of *Bentley's Miscellany*, with book editions appearing in 1839, it remained, like all of Dickens's work, popular in various formats including drama, children's books, and even as part of a card game, throughout the nineteenth century. Indeed, thirty years after its initial publication, a flood of inexpensive "Collected Editions" of Dickens by various publishers ensured its ubiquity throughout the country (Mott 85–88). Initially appearing amid a wave of native sensationalistic texts, its continued availability, coinciding with the rise of Dime novels and story papers in the latter half of the nineteenth century, make the novel a part of the library of American sensationalism, a library readers stocked with both foreign and native writers.

Divided into three sections, this essay traces *Oliver*'s position as an American sensational text, first illustrating the extent to which *Oliver* fed America's ongoing hunger for titillating scenes of crime and violence. The second section focuses more narrowly on the novel's role in the rise of literature associated with the city; appearing right before the vogue of "city fiction," *Oliver* helped establish the genre's forms and themes, including descriptions of squalor and the country as refuge. The final section explores the mixed reception of sensationalism in America, explaining how Dickens largely escaped the stigma of exploitationism attached to other writers. More broadly, situating *Oliver* within the larger frame of nineteenth-century American sensationalism blurs the line of demarcation between American literature and British literature, revealing a cross-fertilization between two ostensibly "national" discourses.

The general topic here—Dickens and sensationalism—does not break new critical ground. What is new is the transatlantic focus. While critics have long identified *Oliver*'s sensational elements,[1] and have examined America's sensational

---

[1]   Investigations of Dickens and sensation include Walter Phillips's *Dickens, Reade, and Collins: Sensation Novelists* (1919); Philip Collins's *Dickens and Crime* (1962); Keith Hollingsworth's *The Newgate Novel 1830–1847* (1963); John Cawelti's *Adventure, Mystery, and Romance: Formula Stories as Art and Popular Culture* (1976); and Winifred Hughes' *The Maniac in the Cellar: Sensation Novels of the 1860s* (1980). More recent

and urban literature, there have been no sustained attempts to connect these two roughly contemporaneous developments. The lack of criticism on Dickens and American popular literature is all the more surprising given his popularity. Nina Baym, alone among recent critics, notes Dickens's influence as a progenitor of a class of American texts she labels "Metropolitan Novels" (209–213). But her examination, given her overall focus on general responses to fiction, is cursory, and its emphasis on urban novels ignores the way his fiction fit into earlier American works that emphasized frontier violence.

Scholarly examinations of American sensationalism include works such as Richard Slotkin's classic *Regeneration Through Violence* (1972), which traces the long cultural history of violence in American colonial and antebellum culture. Janis Stout's *Sodoms in Eden* (1976) and Adrienne Siegel's *The Image of the City in Popular Literature* (1981), two seldom cited but important works on sensationalism, focus primarily on nineteenth-century American popular fiction. Michael Denning's exploration of the class dimensions of American sensational literature throughout the nineteenth century in *Mechanic Accents*, first published in 1987, remains relevant and insightful. David S. Reynolds' discussion and categorization of different forms of antebellum sensational literature in *Beneath the American Renaissance* (1989) provides a broader theoretical framework to discuss differences among sensational texts. More recently, Shelley Streeby reveals the political and gendered aspects of Dime novels and story-paper literature in *American Sensations: Class, Empire, and the Production of Popular Culture* (2002). Yet while these works make occasional nods to foreign influences, their emphasis on the work of American writers results in a focus on native literature. This essay acknowledges a textual reality: nineteenth-century readers did not respect national boundaries when looking for entertainment or enlightenment. And the mass reprinting of Dickens's texts show that nineteenth-century American publishers, in their search for inexpensive and popular literature, adopted a decidedly open door policy when it came to authors and titles.[2]

I

The reasons behind *Oliver*'s popularity in America and its connection to sensationalism become clear when it is placed against the backdrop of popular literature preceding and concurrent with its appearance. Sensational literature, both non-fiction and fiction, constitutes a majority of the texts printed in America from 1820 to 1850 (Reynolds *Beneath* 8, Siegel 6). In the years before *Oliver*'s publication, readers could peruse the latest novel by Edward Bulwer-Lytton,

---

essay length works include Mirella Billi's "Dickens as a Sensation Novelist" (2000) and Diana Archibald's "'Of All the Horrors ... the Foulest and Most Cruel': Sensation and Dickens's Oliver Twist" (2006).

[2] Meredith McGill's *American Literature and the Culture of Reprinting, 1834–1853* (2003) offers an overview of Dickens's role in antebellum American publishing.

whose *Paul Clifford* (1830) casts a romantic light over its criminal hero, or be regaled by the exploits of an American outlaw in Joseph Holt Ingraham's *Lafitte; or The Pirate of the Gulf* (1836). This popular novel, purporting to offer the "true" life of Lafitte, includes scenes of rape, torture, murder, and fratricide all described in rococo language to heighten the effect of the sensational events.

Readers looked for these same thrilling narratives not only in the pages of books but in the columns of newspapers. James Gordon Bennet, publisher of the penny tabloid *New York Herald*, realizing that Americans were interested in "the details of brutal murder, or the testimony of a divorce case, or the trial of a divine for improprieties of conduct" (qtd. in Reynolds *Beneath* 174), put his editorial philosophy into practice in his 1836 coverage of the Helen Jewett scandal, involving the ax murder of a prostitute by a wealthy customer. He followed the sordid story, from the initial discovery of Jewett's body through the acquittal of the accused murderer—and watched his circulation increase "three-fold" (Davis *Homicide* 161–162). Given this context, Sikes' savage clubbing and murder of his girlfriend Nancy a year later would seem a mere extension of reality, a fictional representation of a sensational trope—the murder of a fallen woman—which had already proved popular in America. More generally, the prevalence and popularity of these literatures, both non-fiction and fiction, meant that in the years before *Oliver Twist* was published, American readers had consumed a steady diet of sensational literature.

And if the adage of judging by the company one keeps is any indication, at least one American bookseller felt *Oliver* was a perfect companion to sensational texts. On September 14, 1844, Stanwood & Co's, of Bangor Maine, placed *Oliver* under the headline "WEEKLY LIST OF CHEAP PUBLICATIONS": other titles included J.H. Green's *Gambling Unmasked* and Harry Hazel's *The Burglers* ("Advertisement" 1). On October 28 of the same year, *Oliver* appeared again, this time in the company of William B. English's *Rosina Meadows, The Village Maid: or, Temptations Revealed*, and Ingraham's *The Miseries of New York* ("Advertisement" 1). Apparently, Stanwood & Co's customers craved tales and stories rich, as the titles show, in dissolution, vice, criminality, and violence. This mixture of books points to *Oliver*'s centrality as a sensational text for American readers. In the midst of a revolving crop of sensationalist fiction, it remains a constant, the only work appearing in both advertisements. The proprietors may have felt that readers familiar with the pick pocketing, kidnapping, burglary, murder, and hanging in *Oliver* would expect the same in the unfamiliar.[3] *Oliver* acts as a draw, the best seller the proprietors hoped would bring in customers.

One of the books offered along with *Oliver* in the October 28 advertisement, Ingraham's *Frank Rivers* (1843), limns the outlines of American sensationalism. A fictionalized version of the Helen Jewett murder case referred to earlier, it traces the short life of an orphaned "maiden" (4), Ellen (Helen was often referred to as

---

[3]   For instance, the preface to *Rosina Meadows* promises to show "*Vice*, in its most 'hideous mien'" (English n.p.).

Ellen by the press), through her seduction and desertion by Hart Granger, love for the morally pure Frank Rivers (pseudonym used by Richard Robinson, the man charged with the murder of Helen Jewett), ending with Ellen's attempt to blackmail Granger—and subsequent murder at his hands. In this "true crime" story the twinned strands of American sensationalism, sex and violence, are combined.

Given *Frank*'s and *Oliver*'s placement in the advertisement, readers might expect both novels to deliver, in the climatic murder scene, equally thrilling descriptions of gore and violence. And given Ingraham's reputation as a sensationalist writer— according to one antebellum critic he was responsible for "a large number of the vilest yellow-covered novels ever printed in this country" ("Authors and Books" 178)—the bar is set rather high. Oddly, Ingraham's description of the murder of Ellen is rather circumspect: Granger "struck her a violent blow with the hatchet upon her head, and laid her insensible upon the pillow ... Again and again fell the hatchet, and then going to the window he cast it far away" (46). While the act itself is depicted, there is no "word picture" to put the reader in the room with Granger, no lingering over the gory aftermath.

Contrast this terse and literally bloodless description with Dickens's set piece: confronted with Nancy's "upturned face," Sikes

> beat it twice with all the force he could summon ... She staggered and fell: nearly blinded with the blood that rained down from a deep gash in her forehead; ... [her face] was a ghastly figure to look upon. The murderer staggering backward to the wall, and shutting out the sight with his hand, seized a heavy club and struck her down. (186)

Even after the murder, Dickens continues his description into the next chapter; the narrator reports that sometime during the night, after his initial attack, "there had been a moan and motion of the hand" from Nancy and he had "struck and struck again" (187). Unlike *Frank*'s readers, *Oliver*'s get to "see" both the deed and its bloody effects. In horror, repulsed at his own brutality, Sikes watches Nancy's eye "glaring upward, as if watching the reflection of the pool of gore that quivered and danced in the sunlight on the ceiling" (187). This description, along with the spots of blood on his clothes and hat—and even on his dog's feet ("*such* flesh, and so much blood" [187])—cast a lurid air over the murder, turning their apartment into a charnel house and providing readers with the "gore" they desired. While other American sensationalist writers did, indeed, indulge the reader's taste for blood and violence, in this instance Dickens out-Herods the Herod of "the vilest yellow-covered novels," effectively elbowing aside Ingraham, one of the acknowledged American masters of sensationalism.

An American focus on Nancy is aptly illustrated in dramatic versions of the play. Indeed, to meet the demands of native audiences, Joseph Jefferson's retelling of the play (c. 1860), one of the more popular versions, "focuses more on Fagin, Bill, and Nancy than on Oliver," thus emphasizing the sensational aspects of the story at the expense of the moral (Lazenby 67). These dramatic versions constitute an important part of the American reception of *Oliver* because for many it was their first exposure to the story (Granqvist 154). Adapted into a play by George Almar before the book was even completed and performed as early as January 1839 at the Franklin Theater in New York (Winter 512), the play remained in constant circulation throughout the century. Transformed from the story of an orphan boy who makes good to a vehicle for histrionic excess, the play revels in the violence and melodramatic dialogue that are the stock and trade of sensationalism. And the excess was not confined to the words in the script. In a mid-century Boston performance, Lucille Western, in the role of Nancy, "glued a thin slice of raw beef to one side of her face" to heighten the visual effect of her beating at the hands of Sikes (Granqvist 156).

Yet violence in *Oliver* is not limited to the murder of Nancy. A central trope of sensationalism, it ripples through the text, from the opening chapters where the gentleman in the white coat repeatedly asserts Oliver will end up in the gallows, to the final scenes with Fagin in his cell. Since violence as freedom is woven into American culture,[4] the bloodshed in *Oliver* makes it especially suited to American tastes. *Oliver*'s final scenes, with the crowds tearing at Fagin, and the gruesome spectacle of Sikes's own death, offered a surfeit of blood and brutality. Yet to understand the cultural resonance of these scenes, they need to be removed from their English setting and read against the backdrop of violence—particularly mob violence—of American life during the 1830s. For instance, the historian David Brion Davis notes that many believed the nation was in the midst of a period of misrule, when "respected men led lynching mobs, [and when] legislators 'disagreed' with bowie knives and smooth-bore pistols" (244). The threat of mob violence is explicit during the arrest of Fagin. When Chitlin, part of Fagin's gang of child thieves, describes the capture of his boss, it reads more like a scene from the American wild west than a description of an arrest on the staid streets of London:

> the officers fought like devils or they'd have torn him [Fagin] away ... I can see the people jumping up, one behind another, and snarling with their teeth and making at him like wild beasts; I can see the blood upon his hair and beard, and hear the cries with which the women worked themselves into the centre of the crowd at the street corner, and swore they'd tear his heart out! (197)

Such a mob, less interested in seeing Fagin brought to justice than in satisfying their own desires for revenge, could find many correlatives in America. For many American readers, the pulsing crowds surrounding Fagin would be viewed with favor, supplying a visceral thrill at seeing a devil receive his due.

Like Dickens, American authors also understood the sensationalist potential of a mob. George Lippard, author of the classic American sensationalist novel *The Quaker City; or, The Monks of Monk Hall* (1845), includes a scene illustrating its power. Describing the aftermath of an execution, Lippard's antic character Devil-

---

4   In Richard Slotkin's view, the "American mythogenesis" is based on the perception that our nation was created by those who "tore [land] violently away from the implacable and opulent wilderness" (4).

Bug reports, "For thirty minutes we kept him hanging, for thirty minutes the mob yelled and cursed and swore and hurrahed" (509). The mob ends up "tearing the gibbet to pieces, and bearin' splinters away in their fingers, that they might take 'em home to their families, and brag of seein' a man hung!" (509). Both writers recognize the sensational trope of the mob, a trope that can be used for subverting or reinforcing cultural norms.

These sensational tropes were not confined to the boundaries of the page. While Oliver's "asking for more" quickly became a stock phrase in America, a more sinister allusion emerged from the novel as well. The term "Fagin" entered the lexicon as shorthand for a crime boss. This adoption of a fictional character into the vernacular of American English is a powerful example of Dickens's influence on the culture. The socio-linguist Herbert Clark relates the ability of a phrase to enter the currency of everyday language to "Common Ground" theory, which suggests that "there are things *everyone* in a community knows and assumes that everyone else in that community knows, too" (36). With such knowledge, a nineteenth-century writer or speaker could refer to a specific person as a "Fagin," confident that the reader or listener would understand it as an allusion to Fagin in *Oliver*. What allows this term to assume cultural dimensions is Clark's definition of "community," which is not proscribed by physical boundaries, but limited only by the extent of the vernacular itself. Thus, a "community" encompasses anyone who references a particular term or understands the reference. Dickens's work was especially influential because a wide range of communities could recognize allusions to his work. Some of his characters, like Oliver and Fagin, could be recognized even when a person had not necessarily read the book. They had become part of a larger linguistic community, with their expressions—or in the case of Fagin, the name itself—converted from words on a page to figures of speech. In particular, Fagin, in a number of texts including short satirical pieces, descriptive books on city life, and even sermons, was used in various ways to denote a crime or outcast figure that all could recognize—and hate.[5]

Fagin acquired this meaning, in part, through the book's description of his criminal activities. The seemingly minor details on the workings of crime were part of the attractions of the novel, which Dickens enhances by adopting a flat, objective tone when describing the gang's actions. Such details lend an aura of authenticity to the narrative, transforming it into a kind of crime reportage that engages readers in an ironic complicity: the reader experiences the thrill of recognizing the criminal act and, imaginatively placed at the scene of the crime, vicariously participate in it. Thus when the narrator, in a *faux* innocent tone, describes Fagin and his child accomplices Charley and the Artful Dodger playing a "very curious and uncommon game" (56) involving handkerchiefs, readers recognize it for what it is—a lesson in pick pocketing—and can shake their heads in knowing disgust while enjoying the thrill of figuratively participating in crime.

---

[5]   Cf. "The Amorphous" (282) in Junius Henri Browne *Great Metropolis; a Mirror of New York* (353), and "The Curse" (399) in *The Catholic World*.

Similarly, realistic details such as Dickens's use of thieves' argot, including listing the tools used by Sikes and his partners in crime for a robbery, "barkers ... Crape, keys, centre-bit, darkies ... small crowbar" (135–136), and the description of the break in itself, give the reader an inside look at an exotic world—but at a safe remove, without fear of the loss of even a handkerchief. Hallmarks of sensational literature, these explicit descriptions of pick pocketing and burglary helped satisfy the desires of readers who wished to see the inner-workings of crime, a desire that lay, David Stewart argues, in their depiction of culturally transgressive behaviors. He writes,

> Crime was sensationalized in the popular press, not as something to be explained and eliminated from city life, but as a source of mystification and intrigue that overflowed the pages of the exposé, pamphlet novel, or cheap paper and eroticized urban experience that was, for the vast majority of city dwellers, constraining, confining, and mind-numbingly dull. (684)

The scenes of crime in *Oliver* show that readers did not have to resort to "underground" literature to receive their literary stimulation; they could find it in the pages of books published by the most respectable publishers in the land. Ticknor and Fields, the Boston firm under whose imprint the most respected writers of the day, including Emerson, Longfellow, and Hawthorne, were published, reprinted *Oliver* as early as 1859.

II

While Dickens's incorporation of sensationalized images and descriptions of crime and violence fit into previously established and popular modes of American literature, the urban setting of his novel marked a new territory, one that American writers were quick to exploit in both fiction and non-fiction. Some American critics mark Eugene Sue's *Mysteries of Paris* (1842) as the progenitor of the wave of "City Fiction" which swept America in the 1840s and 1850s.[6] But the dates here are important because, while sensational literature existed prior to *Oliver Twist*, it was only after the novel's publication in 1838 and its ensuing popularity that most American sensational texts shifted their settings from the past to the present and from the backwoods and frontier to the city. For example, frontier violence was central in the early work of the Southern writer William Gilmore Simms. In one of his most popular novels, *The Yemmassee*, first published three years before *Oliver* appeared, he describes the fate of a white prisoner trying to escape from a band of Indians in language remarkably similar to Dickens's description of

---

[6]   See Zboray and Zboray "The Mysteries of New England: Eugene Sue's American 'Imitators,'" 1844; David Stewart, "Cultural Work, City Crime, Reading, Pleasure" (680); Reynolds, *Beneath the American Renaissance* (82); Michael Denning, *Mechanic Accents: Dime Novels and Working-Class Culture in America* (85–86); and Frank Luther Mott, *Golden Multitudes: The Story of Best Sellers in the United States* (247).

Nancy's death. After undergoing torture at the hands of his captives, the prisoner manages to break free. However, during his flight, he falls over the roots of a tree and is brutally clubbed. The narrator describes his murder in graphic detail: "a tall chief of the Seratees, with a huge club, dashed the now visible skull down upon the trunk ... the spattering brains were driven wide" (263). Important here is both the sensationalized description and its setting. By exposing body parts which are usually hidden (the skull and brains), the killing becomes a violation of the sanctity of the body, transforming a murder into a sensationalized word-picture. Its backwoods setting illustrates a popular sensational convention: danger still lurked in the dark woods of the border states.

But the dangerous city of *Oliver* marks a shift in the setting of American sensationalist literature. Through a variety of literary influences, including English and American romanticism and gradual urbanization,[7] the American Frontier was transformed from a land of darkness into a locus for individualist democracy, from a place where native Americans wielded clubs (Georgia), to a place where men could find freedom (Walden Pond). Yet sensational writers still needed a setting where riot and degradation could seem the order of the day. So instead of the backwoods brawling and savagery of Simms' border adventures, these authors turned to the teeming metropolises of the eastern coast, and, reflecting Dickensian conventions, saw a mirror image of the slums of London.

One such American city was New York, where Joseph Holt Ingraham's 1850 novelization of the murder of Mary Rogers, *The Beautiful Cigar Girl or, the Mysteries of Broadway*, opens with a description calculated to evoke the degradation of Dickens's view of London:

> There is a crooked, narrow and very miserable street, if street it deserves to be called, leading out from Chatham Square on the west, towards those unknown mazes and partially explored region of the city proper, which lie between Bowery and Broadway. It is not only narrow, but remarkably filthy and lined with old houses that have known no repairs for many years ... The dwellers in this dark alley are chiefly such as the dilapidated character of the buildings would lead one to suppose. They are principally from the dregs of the population. (7)

New York, the bustling capital of American commerce, is cast in a sinister light, with an emphasis on the criminal character—"dregs of the population"—of its inhabitants. Instead of a place to seek a fortune, it, like London, becomes a place of decay and loss, where the environment itself exudes amorality.

---

[7]   Adrienne Siegel reports that "In the four decades which preceded the Civil War, cities with over 2,500 inhabitants swelled in population ninefold, and those over 5,000 rocketed more than twelvefold. Most startling, the decade of the 1840s witnessed the unprecedented increase in urban population of over 92 percent, a rate of growth three times as high as population increments for rural areas" (3). See Richard Slotkin's reading of James Fenimore Cooper's "Leatherstocking Myth" (468–508) for a detailed discussion of the changing views of wilderness in American literature and myth.

Fourteen years before Ingraham's novel, the filth of the slum and its inhabitants formed the main descriptive note in *Oliver*. As Oliver near Fagin's den, he thinks

> a dirtier or more wretched place he had never seen. The street was very narrow and muddy; and the air was impregnated with filthy odors ... The sole places that seemed to prosper, amid the general blight of the place, were the public-houses ... Covered ways and yards, which here and there diverged from the main street, disclosed little knots of houses, where drunken men and women were positively wallowing in the filth. (39)

Using descriptions Ingraham later replicated, Dickens associates the city with poverty and squalor. And given the connection between environment and character such descriptions evoked, readers knew their desire for scenes depicting immoral behavior would be satiated.

To offset these descriptions of city squalor, urban fiction embraced the tradition of a bucolic rural life. Unlike earlier sensationalist writers who often depicted the backwoods and frontier as a place rife with violence and crime, many urban writers, beginning in the early 1840s, contrasted the Eden of the country with the Gomorrah of the cities. While this is a stock literary device with antecedents going back through Virgil's *Eclogues*, the contrasts made by sensationalist writers between an urban reality and a rural ideal seemed to capture the popular imagination. As Siegel argues, "many mid-nineteenth-century urban writers, perplexed by the complexities of life in America's adolescent cities, beat a retreat to the supposedly simple village green" (33–34).[8]

One example of such a retreat takes place in Lippard's *New York: Its Upper Ten and Lower Million* (1854), which ends with a band of "three hundred serfs of the Atlantic cities, rescued from poverty, from wages-slavery, from the war of competition, from the grip of the landlord!" headed toward the Rocky Mountains "far, far in the west." Lippard contrasts "the savage civilization of the Atlantic cities" with the "Promised Land" of the frontier. For Lippard, cities are associated with all the ills of contemporary life, and nature becomes not only a land of freedom but a place of regeneration and growth, where the corruption of urban life is cleansed by the rolling greensward of the "vast prairies" (283–284).

A similar trait, as many critics have noted,[9] is a central theme in *Oliver*, where nature calls up visions of healing and purification, a movement away from the

---

[8]   For extended discussion of this trait, see chapter two of Janis Stout's *Sodoms in Eden* (1976). In *Pastoral Cities*, James Machor problematizes this literary stereotype, suggesting, as his title indicates, that the American mythos also embraced urban settings. Yet Machor admits the tenacity of this urban/rural dichotomy, noting that "many native writers [...] directed their censure against a particular type of city; the overcrowded, hypercivilized urban monster that crushes bucolic hopes" (15). It is this idea of city as "monster" that sensationalist writers exploited.

[9]   See, for example, Joseph Duffy's "Another Version of Pastoral: Oliver Twist" (1968); S.J. Newman's *Dickens at Play* (1981); and Rosemarie Bodenheimer's *The Politics of the Story in Victorian Social Fiction* (1988).

vice and squalor of the city. In the novel, the narrator *cum* Dickens, explaining the benefits Oliver will derive from staying at the Maylie's country cottage, extemporizes on the "gentle influence" of rural greenery, which "may purify our thoughts, and bear down before it old enmity and hatred" and call "up solemn thoughts of distant times to come ... bend[ing] down pride and worldliness beneath it" (126). This interlude in Oliver's life centers around a humble cottage, where "rose and honeysuckle clung to the ... walls; the ivy crept round the trunks of the trees; and the garden-flowers perfumed the air with delicious odors" (126–127). Significantly, it is in this rural idyll that Oliver is accepted into society: the narrator observes that "it is no wonder that, by the end of that short time, Oliver Twist had become completely domesticated with the old lady and her niece" (127). Nature's influence is so powerful that it transforms Oliver, "domesticat[ing]" him, managing in three short months to smooth the rough edges left from his upbringing and the taint of urbanity and transform him into an idealized child. The novel is structured so that he can assume the middle-class virtues valued by nineteenth-century culture only after he is taken out of the harsh environs of the city and settled into a home surrounded by a verdant landscape.

This transformation is best represented in the novel's ending—which anticipates the ending of Lippard's *New York* and many later American urban novels—by its depiction of an escape from the dangers and terrors of the city through a retreat to the safety and community of the country. Oliver and all who love him are safe from the evil contagion of London, ensconced in a quiet, bucolic village. Such an ending would be particularly satisfying to American readers as it fit well with the myth of a rural, Edenic nation. The polyphonic themes of *Oliver*, with the sentimentalism of Oliver coexisting with the sensationalism of Nancy's murder, illustrate that transatlantic influences are not limited to scenes of horror; they include scenes of the hearth.

III

While it is clear that the novel supplied the sensation so desired by American audiences and offered by other native authors, the question remains—given the novel's exposed brain quotient (dashed brains are mentioned at least five times) and the critical condemnation of other sensationalistic novels ("Evil, and evil, and evil again" read one 1880 article [Sweetser 12])—how did it escape the censure of American critics and readers? Why wasn't *Oliver* considered one of the poisons warned against by social critics such as Talmage?

First, while American reviewers often acknowledged Dickens's sensationalism, because the novel fit into an existing ethos of reform it was excused. Dickens and many American urban novelists believed that a reformative impulse lent their books a utilitarian air which should excuse them from censure. In his preface to the third edition of the novel, Dickens stressed that his goal was to "shew [criminals] as they really are" which would therefore "be a service to society" (xxvi). American urban novelists also argued that their fictional forays into dens of iniquity were merely to expose the guilty. For example, Lippard argued in *Quaker City* that only by "show[ing] the festering corruption" of the city could change be affected (4).

This use of sensationalism to instigate reform is a cornerstone of contemporary criticism on Dickens's novels.[10] A reviewer in 1843 made a specific connection between Dickens's descriptions of the poor and reform, commenting that "by mingling a faithful representation of the evils which cry out in bitter curses for correction with the beautiful conceptions of romance, Mr. Dickens has done more towards amelioration than any other novelist" ("Dickens's Novels" 435). At the turn of the century, the Reverend Washington Gladden, an early exponent of the Social Gospel movement, explicitly separated Dickens from mere sensationalists; he noted that "Others, since his day, have reveled in the slums" but avers that Dickens had a "higher motive." The preponderance of quotations such as these, often excusing Dickens from sensationalism while tarring others with its brush, suggests that readers found in his portraits of urban slums scenes designed not merely to shock readers but to portray life "as it is," provoking feelings of disgust and thus a desire for change. Karen Halttunen offers a modern (and psychologically convincing) reading of these appeals for moral absolution. She writes that claims of "higher moral purposes" in exposing various illicit deeds, "actually heightened the illicit qualities of popular murder literature—the titillating prurience of its treatment of violence, pain and death. The dreadful pleasure was a prurient pleasure, which rested on the knowledge, shared between author and reader, that tales of murder dealt with matters of questionable taste" (81). A form of publicity, these claims act as a draw, an advertisement of the very corruption they were trying to limit.[11]

While protestations of reform provided some protection from charges of exploitation, Dickens's careful control of the prevailing discourse of sensationalism provided another buffer, a linguistic *cordon sanitaire*, separating him from other sensation novelists. In particular, Dickens's discreet presentation of sexuality contrasts with the explicitness of some American sensationalists. It is possible, particularly for modern readers not versed in the coded language of Victorian

---

[10]   Amanda Claybaugh's *The Novel of Purpose: Literature and Social Reform in the Anglo-American World* is a modern exposition of this connection between nineteenth-century literature and reform. Claybaugh connects Dickens and other Victorian reformers (in both fictional and non-fictional works) with their American counterparts, asserting the importance of studying the "transatlantic circulation of texts" in understanding the various reform movements of the period (3).

[11]   Some contemporary readers refused to take the bait. Harriet Beecher Stowe, commenting on Dickens's value as an instructor of morals, notes that while his fiction instigated reform in England, "a careful mother might be pardoned for not wishing her young son to follow out the adventures of Oliver Twist, to be domesticated in the den of Old Fagin, the Jew, and to learn the arts and devices of Charley Bates and the Artful Dodger, and to become familiar with all the cant phraseology and dialect of Old Bailey and the gallows" ("Literary" 109). For Stowe, Oliver's virtue is no match against the seedy glamour of Fagin *et al.*; she believes the attractions of crime, and particularly Dickens's description of it, can overcome the moral defenses of young readers.

Granqvist, Raoul. *Imitation as Resistance: Appropriations of English Literature in Nineteenth-Century America*. Teaneck, N.J.: Fairleigh Dickinson University Press, 1995.

Halttunen, Karen. *Murder Most Foul: The Killer and the American Gothic Imagination*. Cambridge, Mass.: Harvard University Press, 1998.

Harrison, Frederic. "Dickens's Place in Literature." *The Forum* Jan. 1895: 543–553.

Hollingsworth, Keith. *The Newgate Novel*. Detroit, Mich.: Wayne State University Press, 1963.

Hughes, Winifred. *The Maniac in the Cellar: Sensation Novels of the 1860s*. Princeton, N.J.: Princeton University Press, 1980.

Ingraham, Joseph Holt. *The Beautiful Cigar Girl; or, the Mysteries of Broadway*. New York: Robert M. Dewitt, Publisher, 1850.

———. *Frank Rivers, Or, The Dangers Of The Town*. Boston, Mass.: Published at the 'Yankee' Office, 22 Congress St., 1845.

Lazenby, Walter. "Stage Versions of Dickens's Novels In America to 1900." Diss., Indiana University, 1962.

Lippard, George. *Quaker City; or, The Monks of Monk Hall. A Romance of Philadelphia Life, Mystery, and Crime*. 1845. Ed. David S. Reynolds. Amherst: University of Massachusetts Press, 1995.

———. *New York: Its Upper Ten and Lower Million*. Cincinnati, Ohio: H.M. Rulison, 1854.

Machor, James L. *Pastoral Cities: Urban Ideals and the Symbolic Landscape of America*. Madison: University of Wisconsin Press, 1987.

McGill, Meredith L. *American Literature and the Culture of Reprinting, 1834–1853*. Philadelphia: University of Pennsylvania Press, 2003.

Morison, J.H. "Charles Dickens." *The Religious Magazine and Monthly Review* August 1870: 129–128.

Mott, Frank Luther. *Golden Multitudes*. New York: R.R. Bowker Co., 1947.

Newman, S.J. *Dickens at Play*. New York: St. Martin's Press, 1981.

Phillips, Walter. *Dickens, Reade, and Collins Sensation Novelists: A Study in the Conditions and Theories of Novel Writing In Victorian England*. New York: Russell & Russell, 1962.

Reynolds, David S. *Beneath the American Renaissance: The Subversive Imagination in the Age of Emerson and Melville*. Cambridge, Mass.: Harvard University Press, 1989.

———. Introduction. *Quaker City; or, The Monks of Monk Hall. A Romance of Philadelphia Life, Mystery, and Crime*. 1845. Ed. David S. Reynolds. Amherst: University of Massachusetts Press, 1995. vii–xli.

Siegel, Adrienne. *The Image of the City in Popular Literature*. Port Washington, N.Y.: Kennikat Press, 1981.

Simms, William Gilmore. *The Yemmassee*. 1835. Ed. Alexander Cowie. New York: Hafner Publishing Co., 1962.

Slotkin, Richard. *Regeneration Through Violence; the Mythology of the American frontier, 1600–1860*. Middletown, Conn.: Wesleyan University Press, 1973.

Stewart, David. "Cultural Work, City Crime, Reading, Pleasure." *American Literary History* 9 (Winter, 1997): 676–701.

Stout, Janis. *Sodoms in Eden: The City in American Fiction Before 1860*. Westport, Conn.: Greenwood Press, 1976.

Stowe, Harriet Beecher. "Literary Epidemics—No. 2" *New York Evangelist* July 13, 1843: 109.

Streeby, Shelley. *American Sensations: Class, Empire, and the Production of Popular Culture*. Berkeley: University of California Press, 2002.

Strong, Templeton George. *The Diary of George Templeton Strong: The Civil War 1860–1865*. Ed. Allan Nevins and Milton Halsey Thomas. New York: Macmillan Company, 1952.

Sweetser, M.F. "What the People Read." *Hints for Home Reading: a Series of Chapters on Books and Their Use*. Ed. Lyman Abbott. New York: G.P. Putnam's Sons, 1880. 5–14.

Talmage, Thomas De Witt. *Social Dynamite; or, The Wickedness of Modern Society*. Chicago, 1889. Rpt. in *The Land of Contrasts 1880–1901*. Ed. Neil Harris. New York: George Braziller, 1970. 272–279.

"The Amorphous." *Vanity Fair*. December 8, 1860: 282.

"The Curse of Print—a Lay Sermon." *Catholic World* June 1885: 395–408.

Winter, William. *The Wallet of Time*. Vol. 2. New York: Moffat, Yard and Company, 1915.

Zboray, Ronald, and Mary Saracino Zboray. "The Mysteries of New England: Eugene Sue's American 'Imitators,' 1844." *Nineteenth-Century Contexts* 22 (2000): 457–492.

Chapter 4
Radical Sensationalism: George Lippard in His Transatlantic Contexts

David S. Reynolds

George Lippard, the prolific Philadelphia author and reformer whose *The Quaker City; or, The Monks of Monk Hall* (1845) was America's best-selling novel before the appearance of Harriet Beecher Stowe's *Uncle Tom's Cabin* (1852), redirected themes and devices from European sensational writings in such a way that they became both more extreme and more politically radical. Borrowing as well from a number of American writers—Charles Brockden Brown, Edgar Allan Poe, and penny-press journalists in particular—Lippard created a new kind of literary discourse that can be called radical sensationalism. This discourse, utilized by some other revolutionary writers of the era, notably Karl Marx, generated many zestful, subversive images of the sort that enlivened certain works by major authors of the American Renaissance such as Herman Melville, Nathaniel Hawthorne, and Walt Whitman.[1] Despite his connections with such figures, George Lippard was *sui generis*. One can look far and wide in the literary annals without finding another writer who combined sensationalism and working-class radicalism with his fiery intensity.

Lippard was immersed in transatlantic sensationalism from the start. His first major novel, *The Ladye Annabel* (1842), is a dynamic meeting place of foreign sensational genres. The very breadth of the novel's transatlantic associations is part of what makes it identifiably American. Just as America was made up of different nationalities, so *The Ladye Annabel* had many European roots. Its transatlantic hybridity was captured by a reviewer who, in an effort to identify "the exciting constituents of this most exciting romance," called the novel "a perfect 'infernal machine' of terror and mystery" written "in the rage of French literary leprosy" and drawing from "the immortal 'Zanoni' draught, the secret societies of German

---

[1]   For a discussion of the way in which major writers of the antebellum period—particularly Hawthorne, Melville, Poe, Whitman, and Dickinson—adopted Lippardian themes and images, see David S. Reynolds, *Beneath the American Renaissance: The Subversive Imagination in the Age of Emerson and Melville* (New York: Oxford University Press, 2011). Shelley Streeby links Lippard with Hawthorne in "Haunted Houses: George Lippard, Nathaniel Hawthorne, and Middle-Class America," *Criticism: A Quarterly for Literature and the Arts* 38 (1996): 443–472.

legends, phantoms, mysterious strangers, subterranean marvels, *a la* Cornelius Agrippa, Castle of Otranto, Three Spaniards, and a dozen other tales of *diablerie*," with enough horror "to make the fortune of a race of a dozen small-fry Monk Lewises" (Manners 422).

Indeed, *The Ladye Annabel*, a bloody narrative of political intrigue and revolution in medieval Florence, owes much to several kinds of European sensationalism. The *Schauerromantik* of Tieck and Schiller; the crime fiction of French feuilletonists; the shock-Gothic of Monk Lewis and Edward Maturin; the bloodiest examples of Newgate fiction and nonfiction—these and other transatlantic modes fed into *The Ladye Annabel*. If, as St. Jean de Crèvecoeur had said, America was the place where "individuals of all nations are *melted* into a new race of men," *The Ladye Annabel* was a text where many molten streams of European sensationalism joined in a blazing river of literary lava (de Crèvecour 55).

In its excessiveness, *The Ladye Annabel* was part and parcel of Jacksonian America, which, as I have noted elsewhere, was energized by the "—est" factor.[2] The exuberance and brashness of the young republic created a fascination with the largest, the smallest, the thinnest, the fattest, the most outrageous, and so forth. American penny newspapers, which rose to prominence in the 1830s by reporting lurid crimes and scandals, were commonly seen as the world's most sensational brand of journalism.[3] It is no coincidence that Phineas T. Barnum opened his museum on Broadway in New York in 1842, the year that *The Ladye Annabel* was published. If Barnum capitalized on the —est factor with his gallery of curiosities and freaks—dwarves, giants, a mermaid, albino Indians, a bearded lady, a man-monkey, and so on—so Lippard catered to it by producing what is arguably the most sensational novel of the nineteenth century. *The Ladye Annabel* features live burials, vivid dreams of hell, a host of murders, decomposing corpses, spouting

---

[2]   David S. Reynolds, *Waking Giant: America in the Age of Jackson* (New York: HarperCollins, 2008), 296–298. For the freakishness and sensationalism of Lippard's fiction, see David S. Reynolds, *George Lippard* (Boston: G.K. Hall and Co., 1982). Other perspectives on the topic include Cynthia Hall, "'Colossal Vices' and 'Terrible Deformities' in George Lippard's Gothic Nightmare," in *Demons of the Body and Mind: Essays on Disability in Gothic Literature*, ed. Ruth Bienstock Anolik (Jefferson, N.C.: McFarland & Co., 2010), 35–46; Geoff Ward, *The Writing of America: Literature and Cultural Identity from the Puritans to the Present* (Cambridge: Blackwell, 2002), 95–101; Gavin Callaghan, "George Lippard: Revolutionary Horror Writer," *Studies in Weird Fiction* 23 (1998): 1–15; and Dawn Keetley, "Victim and Victimizer: Female Fiends and Unease over Marriage in Antebellum Sensational Fiction," *American Quarterly*, 5 (June 1999): 344–384.

[3]   See Reynolds, *Beneath the American Renaissance*, especially ch. 6; and David M. Stewart, "Cultural Work, City Crime, Reading, Pleasure," *American Literary History* 9 (Winter 1997): 676–701. Crime reportage in American newspapers reached back to colonial times, but the inexpensive penny papers brought such reportage to the masses; see William David Sloan and Lisa Mullikin Parcell, eds., *American Journalism: History, Principles, Practices* (Jefferson, N.C.: Mcfarland & Co., 2002), 189–190, and Stephen L. Vaughan, ed., *Encyclopedia of American Journalism* (New York: Routledge, 2008), 156.

blood, and the quivering torso of a man quartered by horses. The Doomsman, a mad executioner who hovers in and out of the action, at one point has a "merry fantasy," described in gruesome detail, of watching a criminal die on the rack. The victim's bones crack and tear through the skin as the rock tightens; the victim screams as the Doomsman scoops out the eyeballs and pours molten lead into the sockets; then the Doomsman breaks open the victim's chest with a jagged club, rips out the heart and holds it "still quivering on high" as the "warm blood-drops fall, pattering on the face of the felon" (51).[4]

This is shock-Gothic with a vengeance—sensationalism infused with the American —est factor. Submerged in *The Ladye Annabel* is a theme that would become prominent in Lippard's later writings: revolutionary protest against social oppression. Another of Lippard's 1842 pieces, the short story "Philippe de Agramont," took up this theme in its fictionalized portrait of the Wat Tyler rebellion of 1381, in which British peasants rebelled against Richard II because of his unfair taxation of the poor. A subplot of *The Ladye Annabel* involves the Monks of Steel, a secret society that vows to avenge crimes against the poor committed by Florentine rulers.

Just after *The Ladye Annabel* and "Philippe de Agramont" appeared, a prominent Parisian feuilleton, the *Journal de debats*, began publishing in serial installments *The Mysteries of Paris* by Eugène Sue. Public excitement over Sue's novel grew as successive installments of the novel appeared in the paper between June 1842 and October 1843. When the novel was published in book form—first in France and soon in other countries, including America, where two translations quickly appeared—it created an international sensation. *The Mysteries of Paris* was the first novel that graphically revealed the gloomy underside of nineteenth-century urban life. To be sure, a few previous books, notably Pierce Egan's *Life in London* (1821) and Charles Dickens's *Oliver Twist* (1837), had depicted urban criminality. But Sue summoned up an entire subterranean world of street urchins, prostitutes, thieves, and murderers. For Sue, the city was a place of awesome "mysteries," of labyrinthine sewers, dark dens of vice, and backstreet saloons run by ghoulish bartenders—in short, an updated version of that former locus of terror, the Gothic castle. Full of horrific scenes, *The Mysteries of Paris* was often criticized as immoral and pernicious. Nonetheless, Sue not only plumbed new depths of urban life but did so with fresh perceptions of both the poor, whom he depicted as largely the victims of circumstance, and the rich, whom he portrayed as frequently corrupt and deceptive. Sue was influenced by the rising tide of socialism in France, and *The Mysteries of Paris* helped ignite the proletarian passions that lay behind the European revolutions of 1848. As an American reviewer noted, "[Sue] invented the *philanthropic* novel,—the *socialist* novel,—the novel to depict the sufferings of the populace and cure them" (*New Mirror*). Sue's novel spawned a host of imitations in England and on the Continent between 1843 and 1860.

---

4   An analysis of sensationalism in *The Ladye Annabel* and Lippard's other fiction can be found in Reynolds, *George Lippard*, especially ch. 1.

Lippard's *The Quaker City* was chiefly responsible for a fifteen-year city-mysteries craze in America.[5] Lippard admired Sue and closely identified with him but did not want to be seen as imitating him. The back wrapper of each of the ten serial installments of *The Quaker City* that appeared successively from fall 1844 through spring 1845 included the ambiguous statement: "Commenced before the 'Mysteries of Paris' appeared, the Romance, in some respects, bears the same relation to Paris that the 'Mysteries' do to Philadelphia" (Reynolds 29). The first segment of Lippard's novel was greeted with a one-line blurb (probably planted by Lippard himself) in the Philadelphia *Public Ledger* that announced, "EUGENE SUE ECLIPSED! Thrilling novel of Real Life" (October 5, 1844). Lippard devoted several passages in his fiction and essays to defending Sue against his numerous American detractors, and in *The Quaker City Weekly* he brandished his sobriquet "The Eugene Sue of America" (January 6, 1849).[6]

But there was good reason why Lippard took care to emphasize that he was no mere imitator of Sue or other foreign sensational writers. Sue approached working-class themes from a very different perspective from Lippard's. The descendant of a long line of French surgeons, Sue was born into a wealthy Parisian family in 1801.[7] Reportedly, his godparents were the Empress Josephine and her son Eugène Beauharnois. He pursued medical training and served in the navy as a doctor before abandoning medicine. For a time, he led a leisurely Parisian life on his family's money. When a friend dared him to challenge James Fenimore Cooper as an adventure novelist, he took up writing as a profession. He wrote sensational maritime novels, notably *Kenock, the Pirate* and *The Salamander*, as well as historical novels, romances about upper-class Parisians, and a five-volume history of the French navy.

---

[5]   See Reynolds, *George Lippard*, 12–13, 28–29, and 111–112; Reynolds, *Beneath the American Renaissance*, 82–84; Ronald J. Zboray and Mary Saracino Zboray, "The Mysteries of New England: Eugene Sue's 'Imitators,' 1844," *Nineteenth-Century Contexts* 22 (September 2000), 457–492 ; Heyward Ehrlich, "The 'Mysteries' of Philadelphia: Lippard's *Quaker City* and 'Urban' Gothic," *ESQ: A Journal of the American Renaissance* 18 (1972): 50–65; Paul Joseph Erickson, "Welcome to Sodom: The Cultural Work of City-Mysteries Fiction in Antebellum America" (Diss., University of Texas–Austin, 2005): Leslie Fiedler, "The Male Novel," *Partisan Review* 37 (1970): 74–89; and J.V. Ridgely, "George Lippard's *The Quaker City*: The World of the American Porno-Gothic," *Studies in the Literary Imagination* 7 (Spring 1974): 77–94. Of course, Lippard put such an original spin on the city-mysteries genre, drawing from many sources unrelated to it, that he resists simple classification as a city-mysteries writer: see Carl Ostrowski, "Inside the Temple of Ravoni: George Lippard's Anti-Exposé," *ESQ: A Journal of the American Renaissance*, 55 (2009): 1–26.

[6]   Lippard's weekly newspaper; hereafter cited as *QCW*.

[7]   Biographical information about Eugène Sue is gleaned from a variety of contemporary sources, including *The Northern Star, and National Trades' Journal* (Leeds: February 1, 1845); *The Expositor* 1 (December 1, 1843): 41; *The New World* (December 16, 1843); and *The New Mirror* 2 (November 18, 1843): 102.

A leftist, Sue saw Paris's masses as interesting fodder for an adventure novel. To do research for *The Mysteries of Paris*, he hired a bodyguard and toured the city's lowest haunts. In this sense, he was much like a number of other European sensation novelists, most of whom came from privileged backgrounds and performed various kinds of slumming to overcome their distance from the social outcasts they described in their novels.[8] In Sue's case, an interest in the lower classes was linked with socialist politics. In 1848, having defended the poor in his fiction, Sue was elected as a deputy to France's National Assembly in the wake of the working-class revolutions, which his *Mysteries of Paris* had helped spark. Working-class reformers in other nations saw him as a like-minded champion of the oppressed. *The Mysteries of Paris* came to be known as the *Uncle Tom's Cabin* of socialism, and *The Wandering Jew*, in which Sue took on the established church, as the *Uncle Tom's Cabin* of anticlericalism.[9]

There was, however, an undeniably paternalistic side to Sue, an atheistic dandy who had vests of every color of the rainbow, always wore gloves (never the same pair twice), changed his clothes three times a day, and ate only at the most fashionable restaurants. His mansion in the Faubourg Saint-Honoré had the amenities of wealth: a lush garden, a long gallery, crimson furniture, massive drapery, and an art collection that included masterpieces by Delacroix and others. His lifestyle contrasted so sharply with his working-class fiction that he was sometimes called a hypocrite. The *New-York Tribune* said of Sue, "Devoted to the cause of the people, his habits [are] those of an aristocrat and a voluptuary" (qtd. in *American Phrenological Journal* 1). The *Leader* (London) branded him as a "charlatan" whose "socialism and democracy are transparent artifices" and who happened to possess a crowd-pleasing "brutal melodramatic power of startling contrasts and rapid changes of scenes" as well as a skill for "fastening upon some hideous subject having in itself the fascination of horror" (*Leader* 65).

In Lippard's eyes, however, Sue's luxurious habits did not negate his contributions to literature and working-class reform. Lippard described Sue as a "gaily dressed … man of fashion and pleasure" but noted that "the voice of the People's woe had pierced the twilight of his voluptuous chamber, and he had obeyed that voice, and arisen, and said to the Rich Men, 'Ye must have a care for these starving ones, or they will have a care for your throats'" (*Adonai* 37). Lippard often highlighted Sue when assessing foreign sensational novelists. While Lippard dismissed the racy fiction of Sue's countryman Paul de Kock as "filth, leprosy, and rags" and lambasted "the thousand and one literary Lazaroni

---

[8]   For example, when the British Newgate novelist William Harrison Ainsworth, the son of a rich lawyer, was asked about his skillful rendering of the language of criminals, he remarked, "Never had anything to do with the scoundrels in my life," explaining that he picked up their "flash patter" by reading a slang glossary at the end of a trial pamphlet (qtd. in Stephen James Carver, *The Life and Works of the Lancashire Novelist William Harrison Ainsworth, 1805–1882* (Lewiston: Edwin Mellen Press, 2003), 9).

[9]   See *The Living Age* 240 (March 26, 1904): 793.

who swelter in the gutters of London, Paris, Vienna, and Leipzig," he heartily applauded a number of European sensationalists and put Sue at the top of the list. In his ranking, Charles Dickens produced "solid iron," William Harrison Ainsworth "polished steel," Edward Bulwer-Lytton "good gold," and Eugene Sue "solid gold" (*Daily Chronicle*).

Despite Lippard's admiration for Sue, it is understandable that he took care to distinguish *The Quaker City* from *The Mysteries of Paris*. Unlike Sue, Lippard approached social issues from a radically democratic, American working-class vantage point. Lippard had known poverty, social upheaval, and severe misfortune long before he began writing fiction.[10] Abandoned at a young age by sickly parents and raised in Germantown and Philadelphia by maiden aunts who slowly sold off the family property, Lippard became impoverished as a teenager when in 1835 his father died and left him no share of his modest estate. Lippard witnessed first-hand the pain and deprivation experienced by working-class Americans during the five-year depression that followed the Panic of 1837. During these years, he lived like a bohemian, drifting through Philadelphia and staying in the studios of artist friends or living in vacant buildings. He saw at street level the grim side of Philadelphia life: the bank closures, the dockworkers' and weavers' strikes, and religious and racial riots during what was one of the most turbulent periods in that city's history.[11] And he saw the suffering of the masses from a radical Jacksonian perspective. For Lippard, as for many others in the Democratic Party, Andrew Jackson was a symbol of the common man who battled mightily against banks and other institutions associated with the moneyed elite. "HE WAS A MAN," Lippard wrote in a fictionalized sketch of Jackson, whom he described as a plebian warrior who boldly confronted wealthy supporters of the Bank of the United States and declared, "I am ready for you all!—By the Eternal—with the people at my back, whom your gold can neither buy nor awe—I will swing you up around the capital, (each rebel of you,) on a gibbet, high as Haman" (*School Friend* 132).

The ferocious anti-elitism that Lippard associated with Jackson as well as the misery Lippard saw among depression-ravaged Philadelphians and his crime reportage for penny newspapers in his pre-novelist phase help explain the extreme radical sensationalism of *The Quaker City*. Though Lippard shared Sue's interest in urban mysteries, *The Quaker City* and *The Mysteries of Paris* are actually dissimilar. The protagonist of Sue's novel, Rodolphe, is a wealthy duke who disguises himself as a poor man and descends into the Parisian underworld, always

---

[10]   Biographical details can be found in Reynolds, *George Lippard*, especially ch. 1, and Emilio DeGrazia, "The Life and Works of George Lippard" (Diss., Ohio State University, 1969).

[11]   For a discussion of Lippard in relation to the turbulence of antebellum Philadelphia, see especially Samuel Otter, *Philadelphia Stories: America's Literature of Race and Freedom* (New York: Oxford University Press, 2010), ch. 3. See also Gary B. Nash, *First City: Philadelphia and the Forging of Historical Memory* (Philadelphia: University of Pennsylvania Press, 2006), 165–167; and Robert Zecker, *Metropolis: The American City in Popular Culture* (Westport, Conn.: Greenwood Press, 2008), chh. 1 and 2.

protecting or rewarding virtue while punishing wickedness like an angel from above. He is the ancestor of many disguised do-gooders and caped crusaders, from Cyrano de Bergerac to Zorro, Superman, Spider Man, and the like.

There is no such hero in Lippard's novel, whose wealthy characters are unregenerate figures that cheat the poor instead of aiding them, while the workers they victimize often resort to crime or suicide not because of inherent sinfulness but because of oppression from above. Lippard, like his idol Jackson, had a special animus against bankers. The depression of 1837–44 put nearly one-third of Americans out of work at a time when hundreds of banks were failing and when some leading bankers were being tried for criminal activity. In 1842 the prominent Philadelphia banker Nicholas Biddle, Jackson's arch-foe, and several assistants were brought to trial in a two-million-dollar fraud case. The trial provoked a storm of protest against Biddle. Even one of Biddle's rich friends, Sidney George Fisher, admitted of the frauds, "Indeed it is villainy on a most enormous scale ... I believe there has been more corruption and fraud in this country for the last five years than in all England for the last five hundred" (Wainwright 120). Lippard also held Biddle responsible for his bank's mishandling of the legacy of the philanthropist Stephen Girard. At his death in 1831, Girard had left some six million dollars to fund a college for poor orphans, but the money languished in Biddle's bank for many years because of Biddle's indifference to the poor. Lippard lamented the plight of the thousands of orphans deprived of an education because of Biddle's complacency.

The Quaker City directs many barbs at bankers, as when one character sees "Old Grab-and-Snatch, the President of the ——— Bank" or when another character says of wealthy Americans, "ain't nothin' but a pack of swindlin' Bank d'rectors" (25, 374). Especially memorable is Lippard's portrait of the bank director Job Joneson—"one of your good citizens, who subscribe large sums to tract societies, and sport velvet-cushioned pews in the church"—who refuses to give a cent to the indigent John Davis, who had deposited a small sum in Joneson's bank before it failed (406). Davis returns home only to find his wife and daughter dead of starvation, at which the poor man kills himself.[12]

Though rooted in Jacksonian democracy, Lippard uses transatlantic imagery throughout *The Quaker City*. Much of the novel's symbolism relates to England or the Continent. The ruling-class Philadelphians who carry on nefarious activities in a pleasure club (the "monks" of the novel's subtitle) are updated versions of the evil monks in castles who had long populated European Gothic novels. Monk Hall—multilayered, full of trap doors and sliding panels, surrounded by ghostly legends, and towering over a deep, skeleton-littered basement known as the Dead Vault—is as mysterious and treacherous as any castle of Gothic fiction. Its keeper,

---

[12]   For a perceptive discussion of the Joneson-Davis episode in relation to antebellum attitudes toward masculinity and affect, see David Anthony, "Banking on Emotion: Financial Panic and the Logic of Male Submission in the Jacksonian Gothic," *American Literature* 76 (December 2004): 719–747.

Devil-Bug, outdoes Gothic or Newgate villains in sheer cruelty. Described as "a wild beast, a snake, a reptile, or a devil incarnate—any thing but—a man," he loves to "watch the blood of his victim fall, drop by drop" (91). The "monks" he hosts in his club are neither medieval evildoers nor modern criminals but outwardly respectable urban dwellers—merchants, judges, editors, men of leisure, and clergymen—whose rottenness the novel exposes.

Lippard uses images of European class distinctions to vilify such ruling-class types, whom he sees as a threat to America's democratic system. He suggests that American capitalism is an altered version of long-entrenched European oligarchy and tyranny. The beautiful, depraved Dora Livingstone, a social riser, plots the murder of her husband, the wealthy "Merchant Prince" Albert Livingstone, when the con man Algernon Fitzcowles dupes her into believing that he is a European nobleman who will make her the Countess of Lyndeswold. (Ironically, Dora discovers too late—as she is dying when poisoned by Livingstone—that her husband is actually an heir to a large British estate.) By pursuing a British title, Dora exhibits the same self-seeking venality that had driven her to choose the rich Livingstone over the poor, younger Luke Harvey. Both a critic of and a willing participant in the corruption around her, the amoral Dora sneers that whereas England boasts an aristocracy based on "long bloodlines," "the Aristocracy of this land" is founded on the "high deeds" of bank directors, businessmen, profit-driven doctors, and other capitalists whose motives are "all jumbled together in a ridiculous mass of absurdities" (Lippard, *Quaker* 183).

The identification of capitalist America with aristocratic Europe is dramatically enacted in Devil-Bug's dream of the future, in which he envisages Philadelphia in 1950. Lippard summons up a dystopia of triumphant tyranny and crushed freedom. Independence Hall lies in ruins, and the American flag lies in tatters in the mud. A haughty king is being carried in a royal procession, surrounded by fawning, well-dressed capitalists and, beyond them, masses of pleading poor people whom the king loathes. This crowd is made up of "the slaves of the city, white and black, marching along one mass of rags and sores and misery, ... slaves of the cotton Lord, and factory Prince, ... the slaves of Capital and Trade" (389). Devil-Bug laughs with glee as he sees the worm-ridden corpses of those who have been crushed by American capitalism rise from their graves and stand near the king and his wealthy acolytes. The scene turns into a cataclysmic picture of the collapse of America, as the city erupts, marble palaces crumble, and a supernatural voice thunders: "The wrongs of the ages are avenged at last ... WO UNTO SODOM" (393).

If Devil-Bug's dream signals Lippard's fears for the future, the Philadelphia of the 1840s, as seen from Lippard's egalitarian standpoint, is the nightmarish present. Lippard does not give us a heroic upper-crust hero like Sue's Rodolphe who dives into crime-ridden sink-holes, assists the worthy, and punishes the vicious. Nor does he offer sharp moral alternatives, as Dickens does in *Oliver Twist*, in which Fagin's criminality contrasts with Oliver's virtue. Lippard provides no clear moral center, for, he believes, the realities of American life prevent him from doing so. Seeing no place where virtue can establish secure footing, he structures the main plots of

The Quaker City in order to emphasize complexity and mixed motives. Take the story of Byrnewood Arlington, who murders the seducer of his sister, Mary. This plot was based on an actual case, played up in the popular press, about a twenty-year-old Philadelphian, Singleton Mercer, who was acquitted for the murder of Mahlon Heberton, a libertine who had lured Mercer's sixteen-year-old sister Sarah into a house of assignation and induced her to have sex by promising to marry her. Mercer's acquittal was based on the principle that he was understandably driven to insane vindictiveness by Heberton's heartless treatment of Sarah. As complicated as this case was, Lippard made it even more so by portraying all the participants involved ironically. Arlington, despite his eventual disgust over the seduction of his sister, had actually facilitated that act by placing a wager on the planned sexual escapade that Gus Lorrimer boasted about in the oyster house. Also ironic is the fact that Byrnewood is a seducer in his own right; Annie, the young servant he impregnated, haunts his mind even as he tracks down and kills his sister's seducer. The sister, meanwhile, at first seems like the innocent heroine of sentimental-domestic literature but comes close to being the opposite. She lies to her parents, she willingly responds to a procuress's enticements, she gullibly swallows Lorrimer's saccharine promise of a Wyoming home, and at the end she croons longingly for her lost "Lorraine," even after he has been exposed as a fraud.

Lippard's ironic treatment of Mary is part of his larger strategy in *The Quaker City* of satirizing the sentimental-domestic genre. The satire is most obvious in his portrait of Sylvester Petriken, editor of the *Ladies' Western Hemisphere*, filled with cloying poetry and prose that typifies what Lippard calls the literature of "Lollipop-itude" (259). Devil-Bug, the keeper of Monk Hall, uses all the terminology of domesticity. He talks of his "purty quiet life" in "the comfortable retiracy o' domestic fellicity" (221). He holds what he calls "a wery respectable family party" in his basement and furnishes a room in Monk Hall "as housewives do for domestic purposes" so that it gives the appearance of "fireside joys and comforts" (109, 120). Such language is savagely parodic, since Devil-Bug is one of the most evil characters in American literature. His female cohort Mother Nancy is also a walking parody of domesticity. "Mother Nancy," Lippard writes, "looked, for all the world, like a quiet old lady" who serves tea in her "fine old room" in Monk Hall (76). Actually, though, she loves to undermine the virtue of pliable girls like Mary Arlington and, we learn, has drawn hundreds of women into prostitution. One of her early victims, now her assistant, is Long-haired Bess, who also uses the appurtenances of domesticity to entrap women, as when she lures Marty to a sham wedding ceremony by posing as a kindly older lady.

While making fun of sentimental-domestic literature, Lippard also reveals his exasperation with an opposing genre: the sensational penny newspaper. Editors of penny newspapers were known to report crimes and disasters with a cold eye for profit, and many took bribes in exchange for praising books, plays, or individuals. Lippard caricatures what he sees as the opportunism and moral laxness of the penny press. Buzby Poodle, editor of the *Daily Black Mail*, seems polite but in fact is amoral and degraded. When he needs cash, he publishes a piece "charging some well-known citizen with theft, or seduction, or some more delightful crime" until the person pays for a contradiction in the next day's paper (163). Known as Count Common Sewer, Poodle feasts on the nefarious activities in Monk Hall like a vulture devouring decaying flesh.

Whereas most novelists of the period emphasized either the sentimental or the sensational, Lippard showed how the two were conjoined in the commercialized environment of urban America. The domestic and religious images of Petriken's sentimental magazine are, in Lippard's view, as manipulated and constructed as is the scandal-mongering and sensationalism of Poodle's *Daily Black Mail*. That the antebellum public was attracted to the sentimental is proven by the success of *Godey's Lady's Book*, religious tracts, and domestic novels. That it was also voracious for crime, horror, and tales of illicit sex is demonstrated by the popularity of penny papers, crime pamphlets, and yellow-covered pulp novels. In *The Quaker City*, sentimentality and sensationalism come together in a swirling, demonic center.

Which means, of course, that sensationalism wins out. Seven years after *The Quaker City* appeared, Harriet Beecher Stowe in *Uncle Tom's Cabin* showed how a novel could be both divertingly sensational and genuinely pious. But Lippard was too steeped in literary sensationalism and too bitter about the social inequities around him to repose comfortably in the moral certainty of the sentimental-domestic genre. The quintessential example of the —est factor, *The Quaker City* takes sensationalism to new limits. It runs with blood and reeks of murder and madness. Its characters swing between scheming rationality and unleashed passion. The novel registers a cacophony of languages and slang words reflective of an increasingly diverse America. It contains a dizzying range of accents and inflections, including the "flash" language of the urban libertine (Lorrimer), gutter slang (Luke Garvey described as Brick-Top and other lowly characters), the slick new American sermon style (Rev. F.A.T. Pyne), Southern dialect (Easy Larkspur disguised as a South Carolina plantation owner), Irish brogue (the servant Peggy Grud and the bootmaker Michael O'Flanagan), African-American speech (Musquito, Glow-worm, and Endymion), and Hebrew inflections (Gabriel von Pelt). Devil-Bug, born in a brothel and surrounded by thugs and prostitutes, has a language all his own, a medley of indigenous and foreign patterns.

In addition to absorbing these and other dialects into his hypersensational novel, Lippard often reaches a stylistic level of premodern distortion. He juxtaposes widely disparate images in presurrealistic fashion. The drunken Lorrimer describes a watch box walking across the street and punching a lamppost. One of his companions rides a fireplug as though it were a galloping horse, and another has a face like "a dissipated full moon, with a large red pear stuck in the centre for a nose, while the two small beads, placed in corresponding circles of crimson tape, supply the place of eyes" (7). In a Philadelphia working-class district, "a mass of miserable frame houses [seem] about to commit suicide and fling themselves madly into the gutter," and distant factories and office buildings look "as if they wanted to shake hands across the narrow street" (48). Inside Monk Hall, where normal folk become "entangled in the mazes of some horrible dream," revelers reach "that state of brutal inebriety, when strange-looking stars shine in the place of lamps, when the bottles dance and even the tables perform the cracovienne, while all sorts of beehives, create a buzz-like murmur in the air" (Lippard, *Quaker* 316, 55).

In this disorienting novel, reality itself is elusive and impenetrable, as captured in Lorrimer's summary of life: "Everything fleeting and nothing stable, everything shifting and changing, and nothing substantial" (23). Lippard conjures up an urban world of mass deceit. His primary confidence man—an identifiably American incarnation of that stock sensational character, the engaging criminal—is Algernon Fitz-Cowles, who has so many disguises that when he asks his servant, "*Who are we?*" he gets the reply, "We is so many tings, dat de debbil hisself couldn't count 'em" (155). But almost every character in the novel becomes a confidence man or woman who presents a false front to others.

Although none of the fiction that Lippard wrote after *The Quaker City* possessed the richness of that landmark novel, Lippard never surrendered his discourse of radical sensationalism, which to the end retained its bizarre, distinctly American quality. America's struggles for independence and expansion took center stage in works such as *Legends of the American Revolution* and *Legends of Mexico*, which mingle idealistic jingoism with intense sensationalism, particularly in gory battle scenes.[13] While Lippard never got rich from his writings because of shoddy treatment by publishers and foreign piracy of his works (*The Quaker City*, for instance, was stolen and issued under different titles in England and Germany), he remained very popular. *The Quaker City* sold an unprecedented sixty thousand copies in its first year and continued to be a hit, and his other writings were so widely read that *Godey's Lady's Book* conceded that Lippard "stands isolated on a point inaccessible to the mass of writers of the present day…. He is unquestionably the most popular writer of the day, and his books are sold, edition after edition, while those of others accumulate like useless lumber on the shelves of publishers" (67).

This statement, appearing in the era's leading sentimental-domestic magazine, attested to the escalating popularity of sensational novels, fueled by Lippard and enhanced by the city-mysteries and adventure fiction produced by many other American writers, including A.J.H. Duganne, Ned Buntline, George Thompson, and Sylvanus Cobb. Rightly, Lippard is often grouped with these and other best-selling sensationalists.[14] But it is important to note that his sensationalism was

---

[13] Useful insights into Lippard's politics of expansion in his Mexican War fiction can be found in Shelley Streeby, *American Sensations: Class, Empire, and the Production of Popular Culture* (Berkeley: University of California Press, 2002); Shelley Streeby, "American Sensations: Empire, Amnesia, and the US-Mexican War," *American Literary History* 13 (Spring 2001): 1–40; and Jesse Alemán and Shelley Streeby, eds., *Empire and the Literature of Sensation: An Anthology of Nineteenth-Century Popular Fiction* (New Brunswick, N.J.: Rutgers University Press, 2007), 107–199.

[14] See, for example, Michael C. Denning, *Mechanic Accents, Dime Novels and Working-Class Culture in America* (London: Verso, 1987); Streeby, *American Sensations*, ch. 2; Shelley Streeby, "Sensational Fiction," in *A Companion to American Fiction, 1780–*

unique in several ways: it infused the terror, thrills, and gore with a psychological depth that Lippard saw in his two favorite American writers, Charles Brocken Brown (who is acknowledged in the dedication of *The Quaker City* and whom Lippard praised highly in newspaper articles) and Edgar Allan Poe (Lippard's close friend and literary comrade in Philadelphia); it became more and more politicized, reflecting Lippard's strengthening agenda of social reform; and its transatlantic dimension became increasingly pronounced, as Lippard meditated on the relationship between America and leading European historical figures and events, both past and present.[15]

This transatlantic tendency is visible in *Paul Ardenheim* (1848), a novel so sensational that one astonished reviewer wrote, with justification, "Such a fathomless, endless whirlpool of incidents, catastrophes, and all kind of stratagems, was never before invented by mortal brain" (*The Nineteenth Century* 157). The book's characters include a demon-woman, a four-foot-tall hunchback with a horselike face, a hundred-year-old Indian who guzzles deer's blood, a three-hundred-year old mad wizard, and other strange figures worthy of Barnum, all involved in a frenzied plot that involves every kind of sensational effect. Lippard knew that some readers would be shocked by his excessive sensationalism. In the novel, he boasts that he has produced "*the most improbable book in the world*," one that "out herods—herod; out-horrors—horror." He even included in the book a mock self-review, which he dared others to print, in which he said of himself: "He crowds his pages with horror; skeletons; corpses; daggers; Monk Lewis is a fool to him in the horrible; and he distances poor Mrs. Radcliffe in the way of the monstrous. Besides, his works smack of the French school; a school made infamous by the licentious George Sand, the profligate Sue, and the unnatural Dumas" (*Paul Ardenheim* 534–535).

As this passage suggests, Lippard was no longer simply competing with European sensationalists; he felt that he was outdistancing them by multiplying their sensational images. But there is a deeper transatlantic element at work in *Paul Ardenheim* than one-upsmanship. The novel communicates a revolutionary political message by going back in time and traversing history up to the American and French revolutions. Drawing from legends about the Rosicrucians and other secret societies, Lippard portrays a ritualistic brotherhood, the B.G.C., that uses certain symbols venerated by many peoples—including the ancient Egyptians, Greeks, Romans, and Druids—and that has been always dedicated to the overthrow of oppression and tyranny. The B.G.C.'s motto, chanted by its members, is "Death to

---

1865, ed. Shirley Samuels (Oxford: Blackwell, 2004), 179–190; Anne C. Rose *Voices of the Marketplace: American Thought and Culture, 1830–1860* (Lanham: Rowman & Littlefield, 2004), 160–161; and Robert M. Dowling, *Slumming in New York: From the Waterfront to Mythic Harlem* (Urbana: University of Illinois Press, 2007).

[15] For Lippard and Brown, see David S. Reynolds, ed., *George Lippard, Prophet of Protest, Writings of an American Radical, 1822–1854* (New York: Peter Lang, 1986), 267–273; for Lippard and Poe, see *George Lippard, Prophet of Protest*, 256–267, and Reynolds, *George Lippard*, 102–110.

the Rich—Life to the Poor!" (*Paul Ardenheim* 107). Over time, the novel suggests, this society spread geographically to Europe, where it appeared as masonry, and America, where it was originally brought from Germany by pietists led by Johannes Kelpius, who established the community of Ephrata on the Wissahickon Creek, outside of Philadelphia near Germantown, Lippard's birthplace. In *Paul Ardenheim*, Lippard presents this society, with its transatlantic branches, as having been an enduring force for good in history, always championing the oppressed while preserving what Lippard believed was Christianity's core message: "Love to Man is Love to God" (*Paul Ardenheim* 185). The B.G.C. resorted to secrecy because this simple principle, taught by the Carpenter of Nazareth, came to be considered heretical when it was abandoned on behalf of sectarian dogmas that bred endless persecution and war. The B.G.C. kept alive an ongoing struggle for social change that periodically exploded at key moments, such as the American and French revolutions.

Paul Ardenheim reveals Lippard's growing interest in the transatlantic roots of radical reform. By the time he wrote his historical allegory *Adonai: The Pilgrim of Eternity* (1851) he had arrived at a thoroughgoing fusion of transnationalism and sensationalism as well as commitment to radical causes. *Adonai*, a novella about time travel, portrays Lucius the Sybarite, a Roman nobleman of Nero's time who embraces Christianity and is about to be executed for heresy when he falls into a trance that takes him into the future. Lucius, renamed Adonai, reenters the world at key points in history: the Inquisition; the Protestant Reformation; the French Revolution; the post-Napoleonic era, which saw the working-class uprisings of 1830 and 1848; the early 1850s, after the Europeans revolutions had been crushed; and, finally, mid-nineteenth-century America. Adonai is accompanied on the journey by the Executioner, a satanic figure who takes wicked satisfaction in the ruling class's unrelenting cruelty.

Before *Adonai*, Lippard had written many sensational novels, several of them full of historical references. In *Adonai* he shows that history itself is an extended sensational narrative, drenched in blood and littered with the corpses of the humble classes. Lippard writes, "Let us with a seriousness worthy of the subject survey the history of the world for eighteen centuries. It is the history of the drinkers of human blood.... Kings raise themselves upon the skulls of the People. Popes build their power upon the sepulchre of Christ" (127). Lippard emphasizes that this "record of successful swindlers and laurelled cutthroats" is "so black, so steeped in hell" that he sometimes verges on losing faith in God and Christ (26). But history also contains "here and there gleams of humanity" that offer hope for the future. With fresh urgency—prompted by his despair over the failed European revolutions, the Fugitive Slave Law of 1850, and, doubtless, symptoms of the tuberculosis that would kill him in 1854, shortly before his thirty-second birthday—Lippard in *Adonai* surveyed the transatlantic scene, highlighting both the horrible injustices and the occasional goodness he found in history. The main source of his vision was Jesus, whom he called the Carpenter of Nazareth, the friend of the meek and the despiser of moneychangers. Following European history through the ages, Lippard finds that Jesus's simple message of love was forgotten, as warring creeds begot endless religious wars, persecution of heretics, and disregard of the practical needs of the poor. Through much of Europe's past, Lippard writes, "Popes, Priests, and Kings were elevated into a horrible Godhead, while the great mass of mankind were brutalized into Devils" (*Adonai* 133). Adonai witnesses Catholic armies going into different nations and slaughtering thousands. The Reformation, he finds, challenged Rome's tyranny but also brought its own forms of persecution and hypocrisy, as when the Trinitarian John Calvin ordered that Servetus, a Socinian, be burned at the stake, or when the power-hungry Henry VIII fashioned a "gross and beastly" Protestantism, or when Martin Luther stood by when hundreds of thousands who had risen up in the German Peasants' War were savagely crushed by a feudal army.

As Adonai goes forward in time, he learns that the vicious pattern of rebellion and reaction continued. France and other European nations were caught in a cycle of revolutions followed by repressive authoritarianism. America offered new democratic promise in its Revolution, but that promise was betrayed in the nineteenth century by chattel slavery in the South and what Lippard depicts as Northern wage slavery, represented by wretched, underpaid seamstresses and factory workers.

Lippard's reform agenda was unusually broad for its era. Most reformers of the day focused on either abolitionism, aimed at freeing enslaved blacks, or labor reform, directed at improving the condition of Northern white workers. Although Lippard emphasized the latter, he embraced both reform impulses. He lamented the plight of "millions of slaves—some toiling in the living death of a Southern plantation, some sweltering in the hot air of the factory, getting a cent in exchange for their hopeless toil, a grave in barter for their *lives*" (*QCW* September 30, 1848).[16] His inclusiveness made him profoundly sensitive to suffering in foreign nations as well. In a remarkable scene in *Adonai*, the protagonist, now accompanied by both the Executioner and the Arisen Washington, looks out from a mountaintop upon far-reaching swarms of ragged, hopeless people of various nations and ethnicities: "famine-wasted Irishmen; kneeling Frenchmen; Russians in chains; Hungarians bathed in the blood of their murdered kindred; Romans with their hands tied behind them to an iron cross that makes them bleed; Negroes, Caffirs, Indians, the men of China, India, Japan, and the Islands of the sea" (84). Lippard writes, "It was as though all the poor of the World had been gathered together by the fiat of God" (84). In a cataclysmic scene analogous to Karl Marx's prophesy of world-

---

[16]   Explorations of Lippard's views on race, abolition, and slavery include Russ Castronovo, *Fathering the Nation: American Genealogies of Slavery and Freedom* (Berkeley: University of California Press, 1995), 172–174 and 181–182; Timothy Helwig, "Denying the Wages of Whiteness: The Racial Politics of *George Lippard's* Working-Class Protest," *American Studies* 47 (Fall-Winter 2006): 87–111; and Carl Ostrowski, "Slavery, Labor Reform, and Intertextuality in Antebellum Print Culture: The Slave Narrative and the City-Mysteries Novel," *African American Review* 40 (Fall 2006): 493–506.

wide proletarian revolt, these miserable masses suddenly wage a bloody revolt against their oppressors, as a supernatural voice cries, "Rise, men of all lands, people of all nations, rise! ... Tremble not, Brothers, tremble not! For the Red Sea is before us. Pharaoh's hour is come!" (95). Adonai and Washington marvel at the scene: "The People were seen doing fierce judgment upon their Oppressors. O, it was an awful sight—the People in arms, and Pope and King and Lord on their knees, before the uplifted steel! And that steel flashed beautifully" (95).

Lippard's rhetoric and message was similar in some respects to those of the German revolutionary Karl Marx and the American poet Walt Whitman. All three writers envisaged an international revolution that they described in sensational terms. Sounding much like Lippard, Marx wrote that capital comes into the world "dripping from head to foot, from every pore, with blood and dirt" and "vampire-like, only lives by sucking living labor," exhibiting "the were-wolf's hunger for surplus-labor" (Marx 834, 257, 268). Marx predicted that workers would rise in bloody rebellion against the bourgeoisie. Whitman in the early 1850s, just before his major phase, used Lippardian images in poems like "Resurgemus," "Blood Money," "Wounded in the House of Friends," and "A Boston Ballad," all of which directed Gothic rhetoric toward an attack on the social elite and a defense of the masses. In "Resurgemus," Whitman, with a Lippardian flourish, described social rulers as "liars" responsible for "numberless agonies, murders, lusts," and "worming from his simplicity the poor man's wages" (38–40). Also Lippardian was the poem's blackly humorous glee over the 1848 revolutions ("God, 'twas delicious!/That brief, tight, glorious grip/upon the throats of kings") as well as gloom over the suppression of the revolt (figured in the "bloody corpses of young men") and the concluding warning that rebellion is very much alive in the hearts of the people (Whitman 38–40).

But the three writers sought different solutions to the social inequities they perceived. Marx was an atheistic German intellectual who believed that a proletarian revolution was the inevitable result of deterministic forces set in motion by capitalism. After the revolution would come a classless society. Whitman, like Lippard, was a Jacksonian Democrat who opposed both slavery and the exploitation of white labor, but, unlike Lippard, he thought he could heal his fractured nation and embattled foreign nations by offering them a loving, democratic poetic "I" who absorbed every facet of American life and people of different nationalities, creeds, and ethnicities.[17]

Lippard shared the transnational vision of Marx and Whitman but adopted a plan of action different from theirs. Long intrigued by secret revolutionary societies, Lippard in 1849 formed one of his own, the Brotherhood of the Union. He saw his group as the outgrowth of a long line of working-class orders that, he believed, had since ancient times resorted to secrecy for protection. "Secret Societies," he wrote, "have for countless ages been the lever by which the poor

---

[17] See David S. Reynolds, *Walt Whitman's America: A Cultural Biography* (New York: Alfred A. Knopf, 1996).

and oppressed have moved the world" ((Reynolds, *George Lippard, Prophet of Protest*, 203). These brotherhoods spread, feeding into international secret societies like the Rosicrucians and the Illuminati as well as more recent European ones like the Society of Seasons, the League of the Just, and the Society of the Rights of Man.

That Lippard absorbed the radical spirit of such transatlantic groups distinguished him from most other devotees of fraternalism in nineteenth-century America. Membership in secret societies soared during that era. At the beginning of the nineteenth century, there were only a few thousand members of secret brotherhoods. Over the course of the century, more than six hundred orders were established, so that by the late 1920s, according to one estimate, nearly half of all Americans belonged to secret societies, whose membership numbered around thirty million (Merz 329).[18] Lippard's Brotherhood of the Union was distinctive for two reasons: its radicalism and its transatlantic emphasis. The great majority of American fraternal orders, typified by the Masons and Odd Fellows, were politically conservative. The largest secret society of Lippard's day was the Know Nothings, a nativist, anti-Catholic organization so large that it influenced state and national politics in the 1850s. Lippard detested nativists, whom he viewed as narrow-minded sectarians, and satirized them at length in his novels, including *The Quaker City*. When he designed his Brotherhood of the Union, he drew from the radicalism that he saw in a number of European working-class orders. He also integrated into the Brotherhood the kind of sensational imagery that had controlled his fiction. He wrote a long ritual for the order by which initiates into the Brotherhood were led into an inner sanctum in which they watched a skit of three capitalists—the Lord of Law, the Lord of Land, and the Lord of Labor— conspiring against the poor. The three villains toast each other by drinking from a cup "filled with the blood and tears of landless laborers," and they join hands on the skull of a poor man who had resorted to crime because society had deprived him of an education and a well-paying job (Reynolds, *George Lippard, Prophet of Protest*, 81). The three evildoers acknowledge that they would lose their power if laborers formed a mighty "COMBINATION" against them (Reynolds, *George Lippard, Prophet of Protest*, 82).

It was this spirit of working-class unity that Lippard was trying to enforce through his Brotherhood. Previous efforts at labor combination in America had been impermanent, such as the National Trades' Union (1834–37), or fragmentary, such as George Henry Evans's land reform congresses in the 1840s. Lippard hoped to replace such "partial" reforms with a universal Brotherhood, so that the "hundred thousand arms" of American workers would form "one Great Arm,

---

[18]   Illuminating information about Lippard and the Brotherhood of the Union can be found in Roger Butterfield, "George Lippard and His Secret Brotherhood," *Pennsylvania Magazine of History and Biography* 74 (July 1955): 291–309.

their hundred thousand separate Dollars, one Great Purse" (*QCW* June 2, 1849).[19] No race, creed, sex, or trade, Lippard emphasized, would be excluded from the Brotherhood. An intricate network of groups called circles would link all states, cities, and towns, where hundreds of producers' and consumers' cooperatives would work to correct the inequities of capitalism peacefully, while also providing the cohesiveness necessary to bring about such reforms as homestead exemption, prison reform, the shorter work day, and education reform. In its appeal to a broad spectrum of Americans, Lippard's society proved a success: within four years of its founding, almost 150 circles had been formed in twenty-four states. It directly anticipated the powerful post-Civil War secret society the Knights of Labor, whose founder, Robert C. Macauley, had joined the Brotherhood in the 1860s. It also appealed to foreign radicals. Since Lippard was outspokenly determined to complete the work begun by European societies in the revolutions of 1848, it is not surprising that the Brotherhood counted among its associates some English Chartist and German followers of Wilhelm Weitling, as well as radicals who in the late 1860s and early 1870s would play important roles in the International Workingmen's Association. The Brotherhood outlasted most other secret orders founded in nineteenth-century America, reaching a peak membership of 30,000 in 1914 and surviving as a mutual aid society until 1995.

It failed, however, to achieve Lippard's goal of holding the nation together peacefully. Like Whitman, Lincoln, and Harriet Beecher Stowe, Lippard, while deeply sympathetic to enslaved blacks, opposed William Lloyd Garrison's extreme form of abolitionism because it called for the dissolving of the American Union. To prevent the division threatened by both Garrison and his arch-opponents, Southern fire eaters, Whitman affirmed national togetherness poetically in *Leaves of Grass*, Lincoln pursued antislavery politics, and Stowe wrote *Uncle Tom's Cabin*. Lippard's gesture toward national unity was the creation of the Brotherhood of the Union. "Aiming at the destruction of no part of our glorious national fabric," he wrote, "but pledging itself to the support of this Union, in its integrity, and to the defense of the *rights of Labor*, it is fast spreading from one end of this continent to the other," offering an "olive branch" to all Americans and binding the North and South in an "unfailing and impenetrable" union (*Spirit World* 143).

The words proved overly optimistic. A more realistic assessment came in an 1850 letter Lippard wrote to a North Carolina friend, the newspaper editor Lawrence Badger. If tensions over slavery continued, Lippard predicted, America would soon be involved in the most terrible war imaginable. "We shall have a Civil War," Lippard wrote; "one of your old-fashioned infernal affairs; with Disunion

---

[19]   For further information on Lippard in the context of other American labor reformers, see Lorman A. Ratner, Paula T. Kaufman, and Dwight L. Teeter Jr., *Paradoxes of Prosperity: Wealth-Seeking versus Christian Values in Pre-Civil War America* (Urbana: University of Illinois Press, 2009), 101–118; Laura Hapke, *Labor's Text: The Worker in American Fiction* (New Brunswick: Rutgers University Press, 2001), 26–29; and James L. Bronstein, *Land Reform and Working-Class Experience in Britain and the United States, 1800–62* (Stanford: Stanford University Press, 1999), 238–241.

for its text and hell-fire for its fruits. We will have armies in the North and you will have armies in the South…There will be such a burning of houses, such a cutting of throats, … as will make the heart of a Devil leap for joy."[20]

And so, the author who had written stirring sensational narratives about the past and the present had, with uncanny prescience, sketched his most terrifying narrative yet: a blood-drenched prophecy of his nation's immediate future.

Works Cited

Aléman, Jesse, and Shelley Streeby, eds. *Empire and the Literature of Sensation: An Anthology of Nineteenth-Century Popular Fiction*. New Brunswick: Rutgers University Press, 2007.

American Phrenological Journal. March 27, 1858.

Anthony, David. "Banking on Emotion: Financial Panic and the Logic of Male Submission in the Jacksonian Gothic." *American Literature* 76 (December 2004): 719–747.

Bronstein, James L. *Land Reform and Working-Class Experience in Britain and the United States, 1800–1862*. Stanford, Calif.: Stanford University Press, 1999.

Butterfield, Roger. "George Lippard and His Secret Brotherhood." *Pennsylvania Magazine of History and Biography* 74 (July 1955): 291–309.

Callaghan, Gavin. "George Lippard: Revolutionary Horror Writer." *Studies in Weird Fiction* 23 (1998): 1–15.

Carver, Stephen James. *The Life and Works of the Lancashier Novelist William Harrison Ainsworth, 1805–1882*. Lewiston: Edwin Mellen Press, 2003.

Castronovo, Russ. *Fathering the Nation: American Genealogies of Slavery and Freedom*. Berkeley: University of California Press, 1995.

Daily Chronicle. August 17, 1844.

de Crèvecouer, Hector St. John. *Letters from an American Farmer*. New York: Fox, Duffield, and Co., 1904.

DeGrazia, Emilio. "The Life and Works of George Lippard." Diss., Ohio State University, 1969.

Denning, Michael C. *Mechanic Accents, Dime Novels, and Working-Class Culture in America*. London: Verso, 1987.

Ehrlich, Heyward. "The 'Mysteries' of Philadelphia: Lippard's *Quaker City* and 'Urban' Gothic." *ESQ: A Journal of the American Renaissance* 18 (1972): 50–65.

Erickson, Paul Joseph. "Welcome to Sodom: The Cultural Work of City-Mysteries Fiction in Antebellum America." Diss., University of Texas–Austin, 2005.

Fiedler, Leslie. "The Male Novel." *Partisan Review* 37 (1970): 74–89.

Godey's Lady's Book. January 1849.

Hall, Cynthia. "'Colossal Vices' and 'Terrible Deformities' in George Lippard's Gothic Nightmare." *Demons of the Body and Mind: Essays on Disability in*

---

[20]   Letter from Lippard to Lawrence Badger, reprinted in *QCW*, March 2, 1850; in Reynolds, ed., *George Lippard, Prophet of Protest*, 164.

Gothic Literature. Ed. Ruth Bienstock Anolik. Jefferson, N.C.: McFarland and Co., 2010. 35–46.

Hapke, Laura. *Labor's Text: The Worker in American Fiction*. New Brunswick: Rutgers University Press, 2001.

Helwig, Timothy. "Denying the Wages of Whiteness: The Racial Politics of George Lippard's Working-Class Protest." *American Studies* 47 (Fall-Winter 2006): 87–111.

Keetley, Dawn. "Victim and Victimizer: Female Fiends and Unease over Marriage in Antebellum Sensation Fiction." *American Quarterly* 5 (June 1999): 344–384.

Leader. April 13, 1850.

Lippard, George. *Adonai: The Pilgrim of Eternity. The White Banner* (July 1851).

———. *The Ladye Annabel; or, the Doom of the Poisoner*, rpt. as *The Mysteries of Florence*. Philadelphia, Penn.: T.B. Peterson and Bros., 1864.

———. *Paul Ardenheim, The Monk of Wissahickon*. Philadelphia, Penn.: T.B. Peterson, 1848).

———. *The Quaker City; or, The Monks of Monk Hall. A Romance of Philadelphia Life, Mystery, and Crime*. Ed. David S. Reynolds. Amherst: University of Massachusetts Press, 1995).

———, ed. *The Quaker City Weekly*.

Living Age. 240. March 26, 1904: 793.

Manners, Motley [A.J.H. Duganne]. "The Author of *The Quaker City*." *Holden's Dollar Magazine* 1 (July 1848).

Marx, Karl. *Capital: A Critique of Political Economy*. New York: Modern Library, 1906.

Merz, Charles. "Sweet Land of Secrecy: The Strange Spectacle of American Fraternalism." *Harper's Magazine* 154 (February 1927).

Nash, Gary B. *First City: Philadelphia and the Forging of Historical Memory*. Philadelphia: University of Pennsylvania Press, 2006.

New Mirror. A Saturday Paper of Literature and the Fine Artsr 2 November 18, 1843: 102.

New York Observer and Chronicle. October 1, 1857.

Nineteenth Century: A Quarterly Miscellany. Philadelphia 3 (January–June 1849).

Northern Star, and National Trades' Journal. February 1, 1845.

Ostrowski, Carl. "Inside the Temple of Ravoni: George Lippard's Anti-Exposé." *ESQ: A Journal of the American Renaissance* 55 (2009): 1–26.

———. "Slavery, Labor Reform, and Intertextuality in Antebellum Print Culture: The Slave Narrative and the City-Mysteries Novel." *African-American Review* 40 (Fall 2006): 493–506.

Otter, Samuel. *Philadelphia Stories: America's Literature of Race and Freedom*. New York: Oxford University Press, 2010.

Public Ledger. Philadelphia. October 5, 1844.

Ratner, Lorman A., Paula T. Kaufman, and Dwight L. Teeter, Jr. *Paradoxes of Prosperity: Wealth-Seeking versus Christian Values in Pre-Civil War America*. Urbana: University of Illinois Press, 2009.

Reynolds, David S. *Beneath the American Renaissance: The Subversive Imagination in the Age of Emerson and Melville*. New York: Oxford University Press, 2011.

———. *George Lippard*. Boston: G.K. Hall and Co., 1982.

———, ed. *George Lippard, Prophet of Protest, Writings of an American Radical, 1822–1854*. New York: Peter Lang, 1986.

———. *Waking Giant: America in the Age of Jackson*. New York: Harper Collins, 2008.

———. *Walt Whitman's America: A Cultural Biography*. New York: Alfred A. Knopf, 1996.

Ridgely, J.V. "George Lippard's *The Quaker City*: The World of the American Porno-Gothic." *Studies in the Literary Imagination* 7 (Spring 1974): 77–94.

Rose, Anne C. *Voices of the Marketplace: American Thought and Culture, 1830–1860*. Lanham, Md.: Rowman and Littlefield, 2004.

School Friend and Ohio School Journal 5 (June 1851).

Sloan, William David, and Lisa Mullikin Parcell, eds. *American Journalism: History, Principles, Practices*. Jefferson, N.C.: McFarland and Co., 2002.

Spirit World 2 (May 3, 1851).

Stewart, David M. "Cultural Work, City Crime, Reading, Pleasure." *American Literary History* 9 (Winter 1997): 676–701.

Streeby, Shelley. *American Sensations: Class, Empire, and the Production of Popular Culture*. Berkeley: University of California Press, 2002.

———. "American Sensations: Empire, Amnesia, and the US-Mexican War." *American Literary History* 13 (Spring 2001): 1–40.

———. "Haunted Houses: George Lippard, Nathaniel Hawthorne, and Middle-Class America." *Criticism: A Quarterly for Literature and the Arts* 38 (1996): 443–472.

———. "Sensational Fiction." *A Companion to American Fiction, 1780–1865*. Ed. Shirley Samuels. Oxford: Blackwell, 2004. 179–190.

Sue, Eugène. *The Mysteries of Paris*. New York: Harper & Brothers, 1843.

Vaughan, Stephen L. *Encyclopedia of American Journalism*. New York: Routledge, 2008.

Wainwright, Nicholas B., ed. *A Philadelphia Perspective: The Diary of George Fisher*. Philadelphia: Historical Society of Pennsylvania, 1967.

Ward, Geoff. *The Writing of America: Literature and Cultural Identity from the Puritans to the Present*. Cambridge: Blackwell, 2002.

Whitman, Walt. *The Early Poems and Fiction*. Ed. Thomas L. Brasher. New York: New York University Press.

Zboray, Ronald J., and Mary Saracino Zboray. "The Mysteries of New England: Eugene Sue's 'Imitators,' 1844." *Nineteenth-Century Contexts* 22 (September 2000): 457–492.

Zecker, Robert. *Metropolis: The American City in Popular Culture*. Westport, Conn.: Greenwood, Press, 2008.

Chapter 5
The Scourge of "Foreign Vagabonds": George Thompson and the Influence of European Sensationalism in Popular Antebellum Literature

Alexander Moudrov

The works of George Thompson (1823–ca. 1873), who in his day was better known under such mischievous pennames as "Greenhorn," "Eugene de Orsay," and "Appollonius of Gotham," cover almost the entire spectrum of nineteenth-century sensationalism: seduction tales, criminal adventures, erotica, racy journalism, urban horror, and related genres. An amazingly prolific writer, Thompson in just two decades published somewhere between sixty and one hundred pulp novels (some estimates go even higher) as well as enough "tales, sketches, poetry, essays and other literary stock of every description," he boasted, "to constitute half a dozen cart loads" (Thompson, *Venus* 315). The great majority of these literary productions exploit provocative themes which certainly could not help but infuriate some readers: sadism, meaningless violence, pornography, cross-dressing, voyeurism, and pedophilia. But what is perhaps most bewildering about Thompson's subject matter was his line of defense. He claimed that he indulged in the scandalous for no other reason than to promote traditional American values and to warn his compatriots about the dangers that their culture faced, particularly what he considered the pernicious influence of European art and literature.

Thompson's defense of his literary proclivities was actually well founded in the argument that was widely accepted by many Americans at the time. Like other popular antebellum writers, such as George Lippard, Ned Buntline, and George Foster, Thompson easily justified the lurid character of his fiction by claiming that it was his patriotic duty to expose and condemn the most unsavory aspects of American life, including political corruption, urban crime, and prostitution. In this respect, Thompson could even be considered a literary patriot. After all, his approach was deeply rooted in the enduring American tradition of *didactic sensationalism*. It relied on the principle that various shocking situations, particularly sex scandals and appalling crimes, could be exploited in print for ostensibly legitimate purposes. Its proponents saw this form of sensationalism as a viable didactic tool to promote important religious and political ideas in ways that were both effective and memorable. As Karen Halttunen and Daniel A. Cohen demonstrate in their cultural histories of crime in the U.S. before the Civil War, this tradition emerged early in the colonial period and made a substantial impact on nineteenth-century American literature.[1] To extend this point further, didactic sensationalism grew to dominate American popular literature and ultimately became regarded as a distinctly American rhetorical form.

We should not assume, of course, that Thompson, Lippard, and Foster merely followed the literary conventions of their predecessors. They were innovative writers whose works transcended the confines of didacticism—the trend that reflected the growing diversity of American popular literature and, as we will see, the influence of European sensationalism. One of the most notable literary developments in the antebellum period was the proliferation of new forms of sensationalist literature, particularly works in which various provocative subjects were exploited not for moralistic but rather for titillating purposes. Such works relied on the strategy which can be termed *voyeuristic sensationalism*; instead of emphasizing their social value, those works appealed to readers' voyeuristic inclinations and gratuitous obsession with the scandalous and titillating. The trend was thought to originate in Europe, which in the United States was commonly perceived as a major source of moral corruption. Americans were apprehensive of European influence, but they eagerly consumed European literary imports, including crime novels, erotica, and even frankly pornographic materials. The popularity of such works was so tremendous that American popular writers like Thompson could not avoid the temptation of adopting some elements of European sensationalism in their novels. The way it was done, as we will see, reveals a great deal about the intricacies of the antebellum sensationalism.

The central argument in this essay is that Thompson was engaged in the precarious task of balancing his readers' fondness for European literary imports with Americans' ambivalent attitude toward European cultural influence in the United States. To this effect, he consistently exploited in his fiction the themes which his compatriots commonly—even if mistakenly—associated with European culture: aristocratic opulence, decadence, and eroticism. What is noteworthy, however, is that Thompson allowed his readers to hide their voyeuristic appreciation of such titillating subjects under the guise of pseudo-patriotic moralizing about the corrupting influence of European culture. He established himself as an ardent American patriot who derided European influence and saw it as his duty to expose the crimes committed by various "foreign vagabonds" (*Venus* 246). As a result, his fiction is characterized by an odd juxtaposition of cultural patriotism, and his indulgence in the sensationalist techniques borrowed from the works of his European counterparts.

---

[1]   In *Pillars of Salt, Monuments of Grace: New England Crime Literature and the Origins of American Popular Culture, 1674–1860* (New York: Oxford University Press, 1993), Cohen demonstrates that colonial authorities in New England popularized the strategy of turning executions of notorious criminals into educational spectacles. This strategy ultimately contributed to the rise of didactic publications that exploited various provocative subjects. Halttunen, in *Murder Most Foul: The Killer and the American Gothic Imagination* (Cambridge, Mass.: Harvard University Press, 1998), explores the impact of this tradition on nineteenth-century popular crime literature.

An excerpt from his novel *The Magic Night Cap: A Story for Husbands and Wives* exemplifies the tension between voyeuristic sensationalism and didacticism that runs through much of his work.[2] The basic premise of the novel immediately betrays Thompson's indebtedness to the voyeuristic streak of European sensationalism. It tells a story of a young man who is granted the power to be invisible at will. He uses it to visit, unnoticed, the most inappropriate and forbidden places: people's bedrooms, bohemian orgies, girl-school dormitories, and other alluring locations. One of the most provocative scenes takes place in the so-called "Palace of Voluptuous Delights," a secret denizen "dedicated to pleasure" in which some depraved New York worthies indulge their vices. In one particularly provocative episode, which has many voyeuristic overtones, Thompson describes a group of men watching naked children perform a lascivious dance:

> [T]he fat parson, who seemed to be the grand master of ceremonies, rang a silver bell, whereupon there issued from a door ... a troop of rosy children, both boys and girls, of ages ranging from ten and fourteen. These children had been carefully selected with special reference to their youthful beauty, and they had been trained to the base employment for which they were designed. They were all innocent of drapery of any kind, and carried silver goblets filled with spiced wines, which they handed around to the guests, singing, meanwhile, in melodious voices, a Bacchanalian song ... Having distributed the wines until the guests were all satisfied, these children, each one of whom represented a Cupid and a Psyche, began to dance in the most graceful and winning manner, charming the eye with their rapid and exact evolutions, and heating the passions of the beholders by their personal symmetry and loveliness ... When the children had concluded their dancing, they were kissed and caressed by the company as a reward for their cleverness; and then, having withdrawn to their own apartment, these young disciples of inequity amused themselves by an unrestricted indulgence in every species of lasciviousness with which they had become acquainted during their apprenticeship to that abominable trade. (January 29)

As we read this passage, there is little doubt that Thompson was drawn to salacious details. His description of the dance is long and fairly detailed. He dwells on sensual details, particularly the children's loveliness and grace, which were meant to have an arousing effect on the audience. One can easily assume that Thompson wanted his readers to share his own voyeuristic and lascivious fascination with the scene. But then, to deflect an accusation of licentiousness, he suddenly interrupts this description with the following denunciation of aristocratic decadence:

> What punishment could be too severe for the man or the woman who would wantonly instil [*sic*] into the mind of a child a knowledge of the ways of vice! And yet such sacrilege is daily perpetrated. We shrink from the task of describing the lewd enormities committed by the children who were employed as cup-bearers to the visiters [*sic*] who frequented the *Palace of Voluptuous Delights*. (January 29)

---

[2]   Only parts of the novel survive in a few extant issues of *The Broadway Belle*, the weekly which Thompson edited at the time (January 8, 22, 29, and March 12 1855).

Such an awkward contrast between voyeuristic and moralistic elements is characteristic of Thompson's fiction. He was, at once, a stern patriotic moralist who denounced the corrupt sensuality of European culture and a purveyor of sensual pleasures. He drew vivid and sometimes arousing images of sensual delights—only to denounce them moments later.

This strategy was apparent not only in his fiction but also in his work as a publisher, particularly in the way he promoted *The Broadway Belle*, the weekly which he occasionally edited and where he published excerpts from many of his novels. When it was launched in 1855, Thompson advertised it as a paper devoted to "fun, frolic and fashion" (Thompson, "A Fashionable Introduction" 4). A few years later, when he resurrected the paper after a brief hiatus, he felt compelled to defend his publication by calling it "a model of purity and morality," whose goals were "religious instruction and moral improvement of the human race" (November 6: 2).[3] It is doubtful that he expected his readers to take him seriously.

Thompson's assurances of his works' didactic character reflected the approach shared by many antebellum sensationalist writers. Their books about such unsavory subjects as seductions and murders were typically introduced as legitimate studies of social problems and even religious issues. The explanation offered by the editor of *The Lives of the Felons, or American Criminal Calendar* (1846) is a standard line of defense used in books of this sort: "This work is ... offered to public, not only as an object of curiosity and entertainment, but as a publication of real and substantial use, to guard the inexperienced from the allurement of vice, and to protect the weak from the flattering temptations that eventuate only in destruction" (*Lives* iv). George Lippard adopted the same strategy in *The Quaker City* (1844), probably the most infamous sensationalist novel of the period; he claimed that the book should be appreciated not as a work of literature but as a project to expose "all the phases of corrupt social systems" (2). Harrison Gray Buchanan, likewise, commented that his scandalous exposé of city crimes entitled *Asmodeus: Mysteries, Vices and Doings as Exhibited by the Fashionable Circles of New York* (1848) was written "not merely for idle talk, but ... from a desire to do good—to promote the ends of Truth, Justice, Equity, Humanity and Right" (25). This approach allowed American popular writers to distance themselves from the voyeuristic principles of European sensationalism and to prove their cultural patriotism by upholding the didactic conventions of their predecessors.

Rituals of exposure of various transgressions, which made an enduring impact on American sensationalist literature, became popular in New England right at the onset of colonization. In contrast to a popular misconception about Puritan prudishness, civil and religious authorities in Massachusetts and Connecticut did not shun scandals but eagerly embraced them as opportunities to promote important religious and political ideas. William Bradford, the governor of the Plymouth colony, explained this approach in fairly simple terms. Since the settlers

---

[3]   This issue is dated 1858 on the first page and 1856 on the second. It was likely published in 1858.

were in constant danger of being corrupted by the heathenism of the New World, the authorities felt compelled to expose every transgression, regardless of how scandalous it was, as a way to discourage criminal behavior. The churches were expected to "look narrowly to their members" and drag each crime "into the light" so that it could be made "conspicuous to the view of all" (386). What it meant was that New Englanders made substantial efforts to prosecute crime in public and to exploit scandalous transgressions for political and religious purposes.

What is striking about colonial records is not so much the frequency of various of crimes but the custom of turning them into public spectacles. Executions for such serious crimes as murder and piracy in New England drew thousands of spectators. The ceremonies were long and elaborate, and they were usually well attended at every stage. Sex crimes in particular were prosecuted with amazing diligence. As Bradford pointed out, cases of adultery, sodomy, buggery, and other "things fearful to name" were, as a rule, made public and even "marveled at" as horrifying examples of human depravity (385). Punishments ranged from hangings to branding, mock-executions, and public whippings. Adulterers, for example, were often branded with a hot iron or required to wear marks of shame similar to the one described in Hawthorne's *The Scarlet Letter*. Punishments for sodomy and bestiality were even more elaborate and severe; the transgressors' executions were usually accompanied by ritualistic animal slaying and dramatic sermons claiming that such crimes could surely lead to the downfall of the entire Puritan experiment in America. It was clear that the authorities did not want such scandalous affairs to be ignored. Each crime had to be turned into a moving story. Every stage in punishment rituals was meant to teach the public important religious and social lessons. We can ultimately relate this approach to the structure of popular nineteenth-century American novels, particularly Thompson's, which paraded the worst imaginable crimes under the pretext of educating the public about the realities of American life.

The rise of didactic crime literature in the colonies reflected the strategy of tireless exposure of crime. Cheap broadsides with "dying speeches," in which criminals confessed their transgressions and warned readers about the dangers of crime, formed a distinct genre that remained popular well into the nineteenth century. Sermons, particularly those that dwelled on exceptionally shocking crimes, created yet another enduring crime genre. It was inaugurated with Samuel Danforth's *Cry of Sodom Enquired Into* (1674), which was published on the occasion of a young man's execution for bestiality. Cases of piracy and murder inspired scores of other pamphlets with such titles as *Speedy Repentance Urged: A Sermon Preached at Boston ... at the Request of One Hugh Stone, a Miserable Man under a Just Sentence of Death, for a Tragical and Horrible Murder* (1690) and *It is a Fearful Thing to Fall into the Hands of a Living God: Sermon Preached to Some Miserable Pirates* (1726). Some innovative writers went beyond the simplicity of broadsides and composed elaborate works that included interviews with criminals, dramatic confessions, and didactic essays, thus paving the way for literary experimentation that reached its peak in the nineteenth century. An indisputable classic of the genre is Cotton Mather's *Pillars of Salt: An History of Some Criminals Executed in this Land for Capital Crimes* (1699), a collection of cases involving New England's most infamous criminals. Mather made notable efforts to make the book appealing to common readers who were not particularly interested in religious issues (in fact it was published as a cheap, pocket-sized paperback), but he was faithful to the principles of didacticism and emphasized that the book could be used to "correct and reform" the public's sinful propensities and "to suppress growing vice" (59). In this respect, *Pillars of Salt* was a forerunner of an immensely popular literary trend represented by such works as *The American Bloody Register* (1784), *The United States Criminal Calendar: or An Awful Warning to the Youth of America; Being an Account of the Most Horrid Murders, Pirac[i]es, Highway Robberies, & c. & c.* (1832), *Confessions, Trials, and Biographical Sketches of the most Cold Blooded Murderers* (1837), and *The Lives of the Felons, or American Criminal Calendar* (1847). Antebellum sensationalist novels, including those of Thompson, were to a large extent shaped by the conventions of didactic sensationalism which were established in early American literature of this kind.

The influence of didacticism in the nineteenth century was in fact so strong that Thompson and many other popular writers of the day went so far as to deny the literary character of their works. It was assumed that to read a book simply for pleasure was a self-indulgent and useless habit. As Thompson claimed, literariness distracted readers from social issues. On one occasion he simply called fiction "a mess of trashy nonsense" composed by people with "a vitiated literary taste" and too much time on their hands (*Countess* 3). He clarified this point in his opening remarks in *Venus in Boston*: "most of the tales of fiction that are written and published at the present day ... are not sufficiently *natural*—their style is too much exaggerated—and in aiming to produce startling effects, they depart too widely from the range of probability to engage the undivided interest of the enlightened and judicious reader" (*Venus* 3). He followed such observations with repetitive assurances that his novels were so realistic that they could not be called novels at all. Other popular American writers followed the same strategy. As Ned Buntline wrote in the introduction to *Mysteries and Miseries of New York* (1848), his goal was not to appeal to his readers' literary sensibility but to expose "heart-sickening, *too-real* life." Even though "this book bears the title of a *novel*, it is written with the ink of truth and deserves the name of a *history* more than that of a romance" (Part II 5). Harrison Gray Buchanan was even more direct by drawing a clear line between fiction and reality; he called his *Asmodeus* a "'plain unvarnished tale,' of the sins and iniquities of the city of New York," a book of "facts without fiction" (5).

These writers' anti-literary sentiment is not surprising if we consider it in its cultural context. The notion that literature was utterly useless and dangerous was fairly common among American moralists of that period. When John Robert McDowall launched his infamous campaign against prostitution in the early 1830s, he was convinced that young women grew to appreciate licentiousness precisely by reading European novels. He meant sensationalist novels in particular—stories about "seducers, and debauchees, and rakes, and assignations, and seductions, and illicit amours" (27). Lydia Maria Child assumed a similar position by denouncing fiction and what she called "strongly exciting works" for their "unhealthy influence upon the soul" and such negative effects as "bodily intoxication," "weakness," and even "delirium" (93). The American Tract Society, an organization famous for its evangelical efforts, further emphasized the dangers of reading fiction by comparing it to "poison" that causes "a dissolution of the mind" and leads to crime (Gutjahr 59). It was concluded that if novelists were allowed to flourish, they would "undermine half the churches of the land" and "render half the statutes of our courts nugatory" ("Books" 521). Young readers were assumed to be particularly at risk of being harmed by reading novels. To save them from the dangers of reading fiction, some educators even proposed purging school libraries of "novels and other fictitious creations of the imaginations" as well as what they described as "revolting publications which cultivate the taste for the marvelous, the tragic, the horrible, and the supernatural" ("New School" 40).

European literature was a convenient target because Americans often regarded it as decadent and corrupt. As if echoing the infamously boring moralists of ancient Rome, some American writers insisted that literary sensibility bred sensuality, homosexuality, pedophilia, and other sexual proclivities. They lashed out against "the infidel writers of the present day," particularly that "deity Don Juan," whom one minister described as "the most corrupt hero of the most corrupt work of the impure mind of Byron." Greek antiquity, from which Byron and other English writers drew their inspiration, was summed up in one phrase: "sodomy, rape, incest, and bestiality." In short, literature was a pagan rite of sensuality that threatened the young republic. If its influence was unchecked, the United States could become enslaved to the ideals of Greek antiquity and turn into a Sodom of the literary world where "priestesses were avowed courtesans, and the worst deeds of the gods were celebrated with all the fascinations of music, poetry, painting, and the drama" (Beecher 4).

It is quite understandable that European sensationalist literature and erotica were perceived as a particularly dangerous source of corruption. What shocked many American commentators, whose dismay Thompson felt compelled to echo in his works, was not the subject of sex itself but that European writers introduced it without any legitimate sense of purpose. Voyeuristic in their nature, such European works dwelled on titillating subjects simply for the sake of excitement they could impart. Consider, for example, *The Cuckold's Chronicle; Being Select Trials for Adultery, Imbecility, Incest, Ravishment, & c.* (1793), a popular British collection of stories about sexual proclivities, crimes, and misdemeanors. Unlike typically didactic books, which expected readers to react to accounts of various crimes with indignation, *The Cuckold's Chronicle* gave its readers absolute freedom to read it in any way they wanted, even for pleasure. The book was marketed as "an inexhaustible fund of amusement" to be appreciated by "the youthful, the gay, and the fashionable" (*Cuckold's* v). Its stories were meant to be cherished for their "farcical absurdities" and "ridiculous propensity," not to mention the rather explicit illustrations that accompanied them (*Cuckold's* iii). Similar observations can be made about some other works of this sort which were published in Britain in the eighteenth century, many of which were loosely adopted from French originals: Charlotte Smith's *The Romance of Real Life* (1787), based on François Gayot de Pitaval's extensive crime collection *Causes célèbres et intéressantes* (1734–41), *The Triumphs of Love, Containing the Surprizing Adventures, Accidents and Misfortunes ... For the Recreation of Gentlemen, Ladies and Others, Who are Pleased with Such Innocent Diversions and Amusements* (1784), and Louis-Pierre Manuel's *Anecdotes Recorded by the Police of Paris Of All the Affairs of Gallantry ... With Biographical Sketches of the Parisian Women of Pleasure* (1794).

The works of the provocative English artist Thomas Rowlandson (1756–1827) offer some revealing examples of the voyeuristic trend in European sensationalism. Many of his sexually explicit drawings depict people caught *in flagrante delicto*: priests with their female parishioners, young men debauching maids, and pupils seducing their teachers. The settings of such works might seem to replicate scenes common to didactic sensationalist pamphlets in that they all exposed the duplicity and hypocrisy of some people's sexual behavior. What was noteworthy about Rowlandson, however, was that he clearly departed from the didactic conventions and championed new ways of exploiting scandalous materials.

His drawing "Sanctified Sinner" is a case in point (Figure 5.1). It is provocative in its frank depiction of a woman masturbating a minister. Another detail in the image is equally important. The couple is being secretly observed by an indignant man who hides behind the window. What betrays Rowlandson's disrespect for didacticism is the way he portrays the intruder. He looks like a fool. His reaction appears to be nothing more than a rehearsed farce, an expression of quaint Puritanism. The voyeuristic aspect of this image can be related to Rowlandson's drawing "A Finishing Stroke." It depicts two people having sex underneath the portrait of a haughty man who seems to seethe with indignation. Meanwhile two bewildered gentlemen break into the room, indignantly pointing fingers at the love scene. What Rowlandson suggests is that the public should not look at his works in the same way such intruders look at provocative sex acts. The reaction which his images solicit is not some form of moral indignation but a simple delight in a chance to witness something unusual—a purely voyeuristic pleasure of watching images that capture the spontaneity of unique moments. We can decide for ourselves how to look at such scenes.

Such an openly voyeuristic approach was something antebellum sensationalists like Thompson could not freely replicate in their works. As we saw earlier in the excerpt from *The Night Cap*, Thompson's enticing descriptions of lascivious scenes, which readers could appreciate with voyeuristic pleasure, are usually interrupted under various pretexts. Indeed Thompson was often quite indirect in his descriptions of such scenes. More often than not, he left a lot to readers' imagination. It can be assumed that he did it because of his concern for decency or fear of persecution for indecency. What is also likely is that he did it because he wanted to emphasize the difference between his ostensibly didactic fiction and the sensationalist imports from across the Atlantic.

THE SANCTIFIED SINNER.

Fig. 5.1   Thomas Rowlandson, "The Sanctified Sinner." Courtesy of the
Thomas Rowlandson Collection. Graphic Arts. Department of Rare
Books and Special Collections. Princeton University Library.

The volume and variety of European sensationalist materials imported into
the United States could not help but put American writers on the defensive. In
Philadelphia, by far the most liberal place in the colonies, imported erotica and
pornography were available as early as the 1750s (Lyons 115–184). Booksellers in
other American cities lagged behind, but not for long. By the end of the century they
offered a wide selection of literary imports with which popular American writers
had to compete. Lascivious tales from mythology—works of Ovid, Petronius,
Propertius, and Apuleius—could be published without any legal hurdles. Their

reprints, based on European editions, went through numerous printings, sometimes sporting "splendid engravings" of an erotic nature. Pseudo-medical publications on human anatomy and reproduction formed yet another subgenre of European literature about sex. Ostensibly serious in their intent, such well-known works as *Aristotle's Masterpiece* (1684) and *A Treatise of the Use of Flogging in Venereal Affairs* (1718) were often marketed in ways that betrayed consumers' prurient interests. It is noteworthy that works of this kind were often advertized alongside popular sensationalist novels, including Thompson's. One typical announcement advertised several novels by Charles Paul de Kock, Harriett Wilson, and George Thompson along with such pseudo-scientific titles as *Origin of Love* ("a popular treatise on the Philosophy and Physiology of reproduction"), *Conjugal Felicities and Infelicities* ("a physical view of man and woman, in marriage, illustrating the whole origin of love"), and *The Married Woman's Private Medical Companion* ("New and Valuable" 3).

Erotic and pornographic novels from Europe (dubbed "fancy goods" in America) and their American imitations were available in major American cities and, with some effort, could be obtained by mail in others parts of the country.[4] As one contemporary commentator claimed, New York was flooded with "the most disgustingly obscene works that have ever been issued from the Paris and London presses, accompanied with plates too filthy for description" (*London* 44). The first known American edition of Thomas Sterne's *A Sentimental Journey* (1768), which follows the amorous adventures of an English pastor in Italy, appeared in New York in 1795. Its frontispiece featured a fairly explicit image of a young woman in a man's arms. John Cleland's unapologetically pornographic *Memoirs of a Woman of Pleasure* (1748–49), a masterpiece of voyeuristic sensationalism, went through numerous editions in spite of attempts to ban the novel; some editions were ornamented with frankly pornographic woodcuts. Book advertisements in the so-called flash press listed many other enticing titles from Europe such as *The History of a Rake* ("the Adventures, Amours, and Intrigues of a General Lover, or Ladies' Gentleman, with many colored amatory illustrations"), *Adventures of a Bedstead* ("containing many singular and interesting and amorous tales and narratives, particularly Lord K———'s Rapes and Seductions, Peep into a Seraglio, Intrigues in a Boarding School, London Licentiousness Displayed, and forming one of the most moving histories ever displayed to the public of amours in high life"), and *Memoirs* of Harriet Wilson (the famous British courtesan).[5] The racy novels of Charles Paul de Kock, whose sexually suggestive penname was meant to give a

---

[4]   See the "Venus in the Mail" chapter of Donna Dennis's *Licentious Gotham: Erotic Publishing and Its Prosecution in Nineteenth-Century New York* (Cambridge, Mass.: Harvard University Press, 2009), which offers an extensive survey of the pornographic trade in antebellum America.

[5]   Announcement, "Works of Wit, Fancy, and Humor," in George Thompson, *Mysteries of Bond Street* (New York, 1857), n.p., and "Books that are Books," in *The Broadway Belle*, September 10, 1855, 4.

good idea about his interests, were so popular that their importation created an industry of its own and even inspired a number of American imitators.

The market of obscene artifacts and pornographic images imported from Europe—what Thompson prudishly described as "immodest productions of the French school"—thrived in spite or perhaps because of its illegality (*Venus* 13). Such items could be obtained in many places—in shops, from newsboys, or by mail. Well-to-do customers enjoyed a wide selection of expensive prints and objects, including "obscene snuff-boxes, with false tops or covers, musical boxes of similar construction, and ... pictures and albums of a similar character, some of them executed in a superior style, and valued at from $25 to 60" ("Destruction"). There were also plenty of fairly cheap prints, which were sold by young peddlers "at all hours round hotels, steam-boat docks, rail-road depots, and other public places."[6] When in 1842 Congress banned importation of images which were deemed indecent and obscene, American printers quickly met the demand for pornography with robust domestic production. What is remarkable is that even domestically produced materials, similar to the one pictured here (Figure 5.2), were meant to give an impression that they were imported from Europe. It appears that Americans preferred to regard pornography as an entirely European concept.

The notoriety of the *tableau vivant* shows, which in American cities were better known as the "Model Artistes" exhibitions, even further exposed the tensions between Americans' fascination with European sensationalism and their disdain for its influence. The shows were introduced in New York and other American cities in the late 1840s. In their most recognizable form, *tableaux vivants* were still displays of live models replicating familiar episodes from literature, sculpture, and painting. The scenes were elaborately arranged, artfully illuminated, and sometimes accompanied with music, which gave an impression that the *tableau vivant* was a respectable art form. The exhibitions were in fact often promoted as a sophisticated European import that appealed to "connoisseurs and gentlemen of taste" ("Temple").

What Thompson and other American commentators were quick to observe was that such exhibitions were merely cover-ups for licentiousness. The most popular *tableaux vivants* staged in New York were advertised under such suggestive titles as "Adam's First Sight of Eve," "Three Graces" (Figure 5.3), and "Venus Rising from the Sea." Their lascivious appeal was undeniable. The models in such scenes were nude, or nearly nude. Their appearance and poses were often meant to be sexually enticing. One report in *National Police Gazette* aptly described them as "the little naked nymphs who nightly exhibit themselves to the lovers of the classic and the antique" (*National* 98). George Foster, in another contemporary account, observed that such exhibitions had absolutely no aesthetic value whatsoever.

---

6   William W. Sanger, *The History of Prostitution Its Extent, Causes, and Effects Throughout the World* (New York, 1858), 521. See also John Robert McDowall's *Memoir and Select Remains of the Late Rev. John R. M'Dowall, the Martyr of the Seventh Commandment in the Nineteenth Century* (New York, 1838), 222–223, 253, 294, 338.

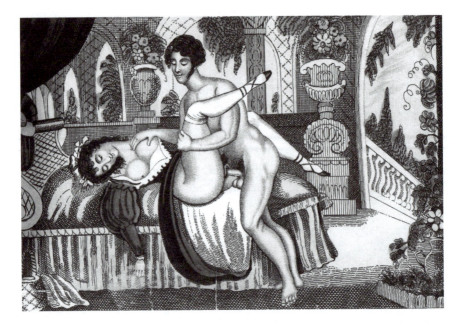

Fig. 5.2   Confiscated Pornography, 1850. Courtesy, American Antiquarian
                  Society.

The models were tramps. The people in the audience were voyeurs who hid their
proclivities under the cloak of sophistication. He described them as

> the worn-out rakes and sensualists, the ambitious young libertines and
> hypocritical old lechers, who sneak into these exhibitions, spy-glass in hand, to
> gloat over the salacious developments of the poor models who are thus forced
> by necessity or a beastly shamelessness, to expose themselves to public gaze for
> a few dollars a week. (Foster 16)

At least on one occasion, the authorities felt compelled to shut down an exhibition
because it was deemed obscene (McCullough 3–8). The coverage of the scandal in
press reminded New Yorkers that there was a wide gap between their fascination
with European novelties and American sense of propriety.

Thompson, who was always well informed about various cultural trends, was
clearly fascinated with *tableaux vivants* but always approached them under the
guise of a stern American moralist. He claimed to have visited several of such
"obscene exhibitions of Model Artists," but as a staunch cultural patriot and
scourge of foreign vagabonds, he derided the exhibitions as a manifestation of bad
European influence. He called them "the orgies of the rich and the fashionable" and
insisted that Americans' fascination with this phenomenon betrayed the downfall
of republican values. He also emphasized the erotic character of such exhibitions,
which is apparent in the following account of one of the several *tableaux* he visited:

Fig. 5.3   "The Three Graces as Exhibited by the Model Artists of New York."
Courtesy, American Antiquarian Society.

> Never was seen so beautiful and voluptuous a scene. It seemed as if every fold
> of drapery, of which there was not an inch too much, had been arranged with
> diabolical art, to excite poor human nature. Every limb, every outline, every
> beauty, was revealed in its most exciting aspects; still there was nothing that
> could be called indecent. Yet I saw eyes that shot forth lurid fires, and heard here
> and there deep respirations, such as mark the prevalence of certain emotions.
> (*New-York* 51)

In his novels Thompson was far more imaginative in his descriptions of such
displays and their corrupting influence. His works feature many episodes about
arousing spectacles, erotic art, and even pornographic plays. *The Magic Night
Cap* includes a telling scene that describes a pornographic play staged in a private
house:

> An oriental garden was represented; in the midst was a fountain whose waters
> sparkled like diamonds. Reclining on a mossy bank, by the side of the fountain,
> were the forms of two persons—a youth and a maiden, or, rather, a female
> who was supposed to *represent* a maiden, although her claim to the title was
> somewhat questionable. The maiden was playing on a guitar, and singing a soft
> and plaintive love-strain; the youth seemed to be entranced, and encircled the
> slender waist of his fair companion with his arm. He whispered in her ear—
> she blushed—he gazed into her eyes with ardor—her bosom heaved with the
> delicious intensity of her emotions—their lips were glued together in one long
> and burning kiss—and then—a round of applause from the audience attested the
> excellence and naturalness of the acting. The curtain fell on a grand tableau that
> was far more effective than those which are usually seen within the walls of a
> theater. (January 29, 1855)

This description accurately represents Thompson's strategy of conflating
aestheticism, sensuality, and eroticism. He was convinced that for many of his
compatriots European art mattered only if it satisfied their cravings for erotica.
This is why he starts this scene by emphasizing the play's aesthetic pretensions
and ends it with details that suggest the play's lascivious effect on the audience. In
other words, European art was meant to be associated with erotica. To make this
idea even clearer, he repeatedly points out in his novels that seducers are addicted
to sensual art works and commonly use them to corrupt their victims.

To some extent, American antipathy toward European aesthetics reflected the
strangely popular notion that even visual appreciation of beauty, one of the most
essential components of aesthetic experience, was marred by lasciviousness and
voyeurism. The fate of many beautiful women in American sensationalist fiction,
particularly in Thompson's novels, offers some sad examples. Their enchanting
descriptions often serve merely as preludes to miserable tales of their seduction,
rape, and even death—perhaps no one more than Thompson's Hannah Sherwood,
the beautiful, carefree prostitute-heroine of *The Gay Girls of New York, or, Life
on Broadway* who, in the novel's conclusion, is grotesquely disfigured, raped, and
turned into a circus freak before she dies of starvation in the Five Points. Many

episodes in Thompson's novels reinforce the notion that women's beauty was dangerous, because it could easily excite lecherous rakes who were believed to lurk on every city street. Women's mere presence in public seemed to be perilous. A scene in the opening chapter of *Venus in Boston* offers a telling example of how some men, according to Thompson, reacted to young women in public:

> As she passed along the street, her beauty and prepossessing appearance attracted the attention of many gay loiterers, who regard[ed] her with various feelings of admiration, pity and surprise that one so lovely should pursue so humble an occupation; nor were there wanting well-dressed libertines, young and old, who gazed with eyes of lustful desire upon the fair young creature, evidently so unprotected and poor. (8)

To make his point unavoidably clear, Thompson gives the story a bad turn. The woman is subsequently kidnapped and, before she gets miraculously rescued, is nearly raped by an old rake.

Real life was even worse—at least according to the press. Crimes against women, routinely sensationalized in cheap newspapers, were reported with alarming frequency. In 1832 the press went into a frenzy over the murder of a young Rhode Island woman named Sara Maria Cornell, whose story is told in Catherine Williams's "docudrama," *Fall River: An Authentic Narrative* (1833).[7] The 1836 murder of Helen Jewett, a high-class New York prostitute, was even more sensational because of its brutality and the subsequent acquittal of the man who was implicated in it. These events were followed by a number of other widely publicized cases. In 1838 New York was shocked by the death of the teenage actress known as Miss Louisa Missouri. The mysterious murder of Mary Rogers, "the beautiful cigar girl" whose mutilated body was found floating in the Hudson in the summer of 1841, created yet another storm of sensationalist reportage. So did the deaths of young Sophia Smith in New York and Maria Bickford in Boston in 1845.[8] Contemporary reports of lesser crimes, such as rapes and assaults on women, are simply too numerous to tabulate. What we can conclude is that for an avid American reader of sensationalist novels and newspapers, beauty was not so much an object of aesthetic contemplation but a catalyst for crime. As one savvy

---

[7]   Patricia Caldwell, for lack of a better term, has called Williams's *Fall River* a "docudrama," a popular genre of twentieth-century sensationalism. See Catherine Williams, *Fall River: An Authentic Narrative*, ed. Patricia Caldwell (Oxford: Oxford University Press, 1993), xvii.

[8]   Scholarly studies of these events include Patricia Cline Cohen's *The Murder of Helen Jewett: The Life and Death of a Prostitute in Nineteenth-Century New York* (New York, Alfred A. Knopf, 1999), Amy Gilman Srebnick's *The Mysterious Death of Mary Rogers: Sex and Culture in Nineteenth-Century New York* (New York: Oxford University Press, 1995), Daniel Stashower's *The Beautiful Cigar Girl: Mary Rogers, Edgar Allan Poe, and the Invention of Murder* (New York: Dutton, 2006), and John Walsh's *Poe the Detective: The Curious Circumstances behind "The Mystery of Marie Roget"* (New Brunswick, N.Y.: Rutgers University Press, 1968).

Fig. 5.4   "Rape of Ann Murphy in New York." Courtesy, American
              Antiquarian Society.

character in Ned Buntline's *Mysteries and Miseries of New York* put it, "Beauty is
a dangerous possession! ... It has been the ruin of many a poor girl!" (Vol. 4, 61).

   The anti-European sentiment of Thompson's novels reflected the notion that
the threat of moral corruption, which Thompson believed led to proliferation of
sex crime, emanated precisely from Europe. He lambasted the eccentricities of
American aristocrats who in his view replicated European lifestyles and grew
morally corrupt because of it. His novels and articles also feature many characters
who are corrupt Europeans: suave con-artists, gentlemen of "fashion and pleasure,"
pedophiles, and other foreign vagabonds who infested the U.S. *The Magic Night
Cap* mentions a seductive and well spoken French dentist who takes liberties with

his chloroformed patients. *City Crimes; Life in New York and Boston* includes a scene in which one "Spanish ambassador," a "miserable sodomite," tries to seduce a boy. Even worse are the foreign villains in *The Gay Girls of New-York*, Monsieur Michaud and his English business partner Dick Flipper; they team up to abduct an American woman whom they exploit in a gruesome freak show. To emphasize his disdain for foreigners, Thompson even dedicated one of his novels, *The Locket*, to George Law, the presidential candidate of the Know-Nothing Party in 1856, to whom he turned "for salvation from the accursed effects of foreign influence."

Whether Thompson was genuine in his denunciation of foreign influence is, however, hard to say. What we have to acknowledge is that his novels actually reflect many conventions of European sensationalist literature, including elements of voyeurism and exoticism. If we look at book advertisements in the antebellum flesh press, we should notice that Thompson's works were often advertised alongside European imports, particularly his chief rival Charles Paul de Kock. It is remarkable that at least on one occasion Thompson even allowed his book, *New-York Life*, to be marketed as that of de Kock; in the tradition of European erotica, its cover sported an enticing image of a reclining semi-nude woman (Figure 5.5). What is more, Thompson's novels contain many other signs of his fondness for European sensationalism.

On many occasions, for example, Thompson writes about debauchery and sexual depravity without a hint of disapproval. In some novels he seems eager to forgo moralizing digressions and instead indulges his readers with enticing images of forbidden pleasures. Thus in *The Countess; or, Memoirs of Women of Leisure,* Thompson is far more enthusiastic about describing the eccentricities of the "Daughters of Venus," a libertine cult that originated in France and spread to America, than condemning its members' immoral behavior or the luxury in which they wallow. He outdid himself in *The Loves of Cleopatra; or, Mark Anthony and his Concubines*, one of his most extravagant antebellum novels, which stuns readers with fanciful descriptions of Egyptian opulence: the lavish interior of imperial palaces, the lascivious art that adorns their walls, and the orgies that take place in their halls. Perhaps the most telling example of Thompson's fascination with decadence is his recollection of a visit to a brothel at the age of twelve. What he fondly remembers about it is its enticing luxury and hints of licentiousness:

> The costly and elegant furniture—the brilliant chandeliers—the magnificent but rather *loose* French prints and paintings—the universal luxury that prevailed—the voluptuous ladies, with their bare shoulders, painted cheeks, and free-and-easy manners—the buxom, bustling landlady, who was dressed up with almost regal splendor and wore a profusion of jewelry ... all these things astonished and bewildered me. (Thompson, *New-York Life* 323)

In the same work he recalls with pleasure an episode when, at the age of fifteen, he spied on his master's unfaithful wife having intercourse with an acquaintance. His novels are full of similar scenes of mischievous voyeurism that readers were meant to share. "The Courtezan's Story" chapter of *City Crimes* is rather typical

Fig. 5.5   Cover. George Thompson. *New York Life*. Courtesy, American Antiquarian Society.

Fig. 5.6   Frontispiece. George Thompson. *Venus in Boston*.

in this respect. In that lengthy vignette, a young prostitute recalls spying on her parents, each of whom brought their respective paramours to the house, from the vantage point of a keyhole. Many who bought Thompson's novels likely dismissed his perfunctory moralizing and took pleasure in their titillating erotica. This is why Thompson occasionally promoted his works by downplaying their didactic character and appealing to readers with promises of voyeuristic pleasure. As one advertisement of *The Bridal Chamber* stated, the book's "sundry *spicy adventures*" were so vividly described that the reader could become "a personal spectator of the scenes" (Thompson, "New and Beautiful Tale" 4).

If we turn to illustrations in Thompson's novels, we can get an even better picture of the voyeuristic streak in his writing. As a rule, they position the reader as a witness of titillating episodes, essentially serving as invitations to enjoy Thompson's tales vicariously. Thus the illustrations in *The Adventures of Lola Montez*, which was serialized in *Venus' Miscellany*, show its protagonist in various amorous situations. The frontispiece to *The Ladies' Garter* is clearly meant to be enticing in that it depicts three nude women in a sensuous pose. The cover of *G'Hals of Boston*, a collection of short biographies of famous prostitutes, features a bare breasted dancer as well as some enticing details of city life. Particularly symbolic is the frontispiece to *Venus in Boston* in that it perfectly captures Thompson's strategy of exploiting his readers' penchant for voyeurism (Figure 5.6). It shows two lovers whose dalliances are being observed by a maid and a lapdog, as well as the novel's readers who are invariably implicated in the act of voyeurism. What is immediately noticeable about the image is that it is completely devoid of didactic elements. The same can be said about the novel as a whole, which reads like a sequence of titillating scenes and stunning crimes. Almost from the start, the novel invites us to overlook its occasional moralizing and simply enjoy characters' "devious wanderings" and amorous adventures (*Venus* 104). What these examples suggest is that Thompson often intentionally undermined his image of a moralist and instead experimented with different forms of sensationalism.

In the final analysis, it is difficult to classify Thompson's literary approach as either didactic or voyeuristic, even as his work draws from both traditions. His political and cultural views are equally uncertain. It is, for instance, hard to say if he sincerely believed in his mission to uphold American values, if he was indifferent to them, or if he wanted to subvert them. Scholars' disagreement over these questions reminds us about the ambiguity of Thompson's fiction, with respect to his cultural views and particularly in terms of his attitude toward the influence of European culture in the United States. Some scholars, most notably Christopher Looby, believe that Thompson invariably reinforced dominant American values instead of undermining them.[9] David S. Reynolds and Kimberly R. Gladman, in contrast, emphasize the subversive spirit of Thompson's novels and argue that he questioned many American values, including "domesticity and Christian nurture, the cult of true womanhood, institutional power structures such as the church and big business; white supremacy, the commonsensical view of the human mind as rational and guided by ethics, and the notion that literature must teach a clear moral lesson" (*Venus* xxx). The differences between these interpretations reveal the complexity of Thompson's fiction, which does not lend itself to straightforward reading. But what can be concluded with some certainty is that Thompson's strategy registered the collision of American and European literary conventions in the antebellum period as well as how American sensationalist literature departed from the didactic conventions that emerged in the colonial period.

Works Cited

Beecher, Edward. "New York Bible Society—Sermon by Rev. Dr. Edward Beecher." *The New York Herald.* May 7, 1849: 4.
"Books which are Books," *The American Review: A Whig Journal of Politics, Literature, Art and Science.* May 1, 1845. New York: Wiley and Putnam: 521–525.

---

9   Christopher Looby, "George Thompson's "Romance of the Real": Transgression and Taboo in American Sensation Fiction," in *American Literature* 65.4 (1993): 651–672. One of the central points in Looby's analysis of the novel *House Breaker* is that Thompson "wants to affirm sentimental domestic norms even as he violates them" (653). Robin Gray Nicks, in "Fairy Tales and Necrophilia: A New Cultural Context for Antebellum American Sensationalism" (Diss., University of Florida, 2006), takes this point even further: "Thompson's ... works do not actually subvert dominant ideologies of antebellum America; they only pretend to do so" (133).

Bradford, William. *History of Plymouth Plantation*. Ed. Charles Deane. Boston, 1856.

Buchanan, Harrison Gray. *Asmodeus; Or, Legends of New York. Being a Complete Exposé of the Mysteries, Vices and Doings, As Exhibited by the Fashionable Circles of New York*. New York: Munson & Co., 1848.

Buntline, Ned. *Mysteries and Miseries of New York*. New York: Berford, 1848.

Child, Lydia Maria. *The Mother's Book*. Boston, 1831.

Cohen, Daniel A. *Pillars of Salt, Monuments of Grace: New England Crime Literature and the Origins of American Popular Culture, 1674-1860*. New York: Oxford University Press, 1993.

Cohen, Patricia Cline. *The Murder of Helen Jewett: The Life and Death of a Prostitute in Nineteenth-Century New York*. New York, Alfred A. Knopf, 1999.

The Cuckold's Chronicle; Being Select Trials for Adultery, Imbecility, Incest, Ravishment, & c. 2 vols. London, 1793.

Dennis, Donna. *Licentious Gotham: Erotic Publishing and Its Prosecution in Nineteenth-Century New York*. Cambridge, M.A.: Harvard University Press, 2009.

"Destruction of Indecent Prints ..." [Boston, 1835].

Foster, George. *New York by Gas-Light: With Here and There a Streak of Sunshine*. New York: Dewitt & Davenport, 1850.

Gutjahr, Paul C., ed. "Beware of Bad Books," *Popular American Literature of the 19th Century*. New York: Oxford University Press, 2001: 59–61.

Halttunen, Karen. *Murder Most Foul: The Killer and the American Gothic Imagination*. Cambridge, M.A.: Harvard University Press, 1998.

Lippard, George. *The Quaker City*. Ed. David S. Reynolds. Amherst: University of Massachusetts Press, 1995.

The Lives of the Felons, or American Criminal Calendar, Compiled in Part from the New-York "National Police Gazette," and Corrected, Enlarged and Revised on Careful Comparison with the Criminal Records of the Various States. New York: George F. Nesbitt, 1846.

London v. New York. London: Bosworth, 1859.

Looby, Christopher. "George Thompson's "Romance of the Real": Transgression and Taboo in American Sensation Fiction." *American Literature* 65.4 (1993): 651–672.

Lyons, Clare A., *Sex among the Rabble: An Intimate History of Gender & Power in the Age of Revolution, Philadelphia: 1730–1830*. Chapel Hill, N.C.: University of North Carolina Press, 2006.

Mather, Cotton. *Pillars of Salt: An History of Some Criminals Executed in This Land, for Capital Crimes ...* Boston: B. Green and J. Allen, 1699.

McCullough, Jack W. "Model Artists vs. the Law: The First American Encounter." *The Journal of American Culture* 6.2 (1984): 3-8.

McDowall, John Robert. *Magdalen Facts*. New York, 1832.

———. *Memoir and Select Remains of the Late Rev. John R. M'Dowall, the Martyr of the Seventh Commandment, in the Nineteenth Century*. New York, 1838.

National Police Gazette, February 26, 1848: 98.

"New and Valuable Works." *Life in Boston & New England Police Gazette*. June 23, 1851: 3.

"The New School Act. With Explanations." *District School Journal*. May 1843: 33–48.

Nicks, Robin Gray, "Fairy Tales and Necrophilia: A New Cultural Context for Antebellum American Sensationalism." Diss., University of Florida, 2006.

Sanger, William W. *The History of Prostitution Its Extent, Causes, and Effects Throughout the World*. New York: Harper & Brothers, 1858.

Srebnick, Amy Gilman. *The Mysterious Death of Mary Rogers: Sex and Culture in Nineteenth-Century New York*. New York: Oxford University Press, 1995.

Stashower, Daniel. *The Beautiful Cigar Girl: Mary Rogers, Edgar Allan Poe, and the Invention of Murder*. New York: Dutton, 2006.

"Temple of the Muses!!" New York, [1848].

Thompson, George. *The Countess, or, Memoirs of Women of Leisure Being a Series of Intrigues with the Bloods, and a Faithful Delineation of the Private Frailties of Our First Men*. Boston: Berry & Wright, 1849.

———. "A Fashionable Introduction." *The Broadway Belle*. January 8 1855: 4.

———. *The Magic Night Cap: A Story for Husbands and Wives. The Broadway Belle*. January 8, 22, 29, and March 12, 1855.

———. *Mysteries of Bond Street*. New York, 1857.

———. *New-York Life: or, The Mysteries of Upper-Tendom Revealed*. New York: Charles S. Atwood, n.d.

———."New and Beautiful Tale, by a Great Author." *The Broadway Belle*, January 8, 1855: 4.

———. *Venus in Boston and Other Tales of Nineteenth-Century City Life*. Ed. David S. Reynolds and Kimberly R. Gladman. Amherst: University of Massachusetts Press, 2002.

Walsh, John. *Poe the Detective: The Curious Circumstances behind "The Mystery of Marie Roget."* New Brunswick, N.Y.: Rutgers University Press, 1968.

Williams, Catherine. *Fall River: An Authentic Narrative*. Ed. Patricia Caldwell. Oxford: Oxford University Press, 1993.

Chapter 6

Charles Reade:
The British Harriet Beecher Stowe
and the Affect of Sensation

Dorice Williams Elliott

Very soon after British sensation writer Charles Reade's *It Is Never Too Late to Mend* (1856) was published, stage adaptations by other writers began to appear. Consequently, Reade, who considered himself a dramatist more than a novelist, wrote his own dramatic version of the novel, partly in an attempt to stamp out these unauthorized versions. Nine years after the publication of his novel, Reade's play opened in London at the Princess Theater—"the home of sensation drama in the West End"—on October 4, 1865 (Barrett 4).

Reade had collaborated before with well-known British sensation dramatists such as Tom Taylor and Dion Boucicault. Produced by George Vining and designed by Frederick Lloyds, who had also worked with Taylor and Boucicault, the play was staged in their heavily sensational style. In the theater, however, sensation had a somewhat different meaning than it did for literary critics of the novel. Sensation dramas were those that created thrilling theatrical effects by introducing scenery, props, and stunts that simulated real-life situations—real horse races or waterfalls on stage, for instance. The first scene of *It Is Never Too Late to Mend*, set on a farm, included a rustic cottage, real horses and stables, pigeons in the dove-cote, and real water drawn from the pump, all of which the audience greatly admired (Barrett 4). When the second act opened, however, the audience was stunned by an authentic depiction of a modern prison, including a working treadmill, a "crank," prisoners picking oakum, and an "ominous silence, relieved only by mournful music" (Barrett 5–6). This was realism of a different sort—shocking, rather than merely entertaining.

In the next scene, in the middle of what was viewed as an amazing reproduction of a prison interior based on the model prison at Pentonville, the actress playing the young prisoner Josephs "was revealed strapped to the corridor wall with a punishment jacket" (Barrett 6). Clement Scott, a member of the audience, recorded that:

> All went well until the second act of the prison scene, when poor little Josephs was tied up to be thrashed for some minor offense at the command of the Governor, and to the righteous indignation of the tender-hearted Chaplain. Well, the discipline was so rigorously and so vigorously administered, and the

> shrieks of the wretched little Laura Moore as the boy Josephs were so piercing, so heartrending, and so natural, that an absolute thrill of horror went through the house. (qtd. in MacMahon 133–134)

After being released from the jacket, the prisoner Josephs is sent to his cell, where his gas, food, and bed are taken away from him. Alone in the cell, the actress playing Josephs prepared, in full view of the audience, to hang himself / herself. As Daniel Barrett describes it, "At this point the playhouse erupted into shouts of 'Revolting!' 'Shame!' and 'Stop the piece!' and indeed the play did stop. A confrontation ensued between Vining, dressed as the convict protagonist Tom Robinson, and the drama critics represented by their unofficial spokesman, [F. G.] Tomlins" (Barrett 6). After exchanging insults with the critics, Vining turned to the audience and asked for a vote on whether to continue the performance. The audience responded positively and the critics were silenced for the moment, but their pens were certainly not silent the following day when the reviews appeared. The play was altered after the first night, losing the treadmill and Josephs' suicide, and, a day or two later, the crank was gone as well. Not surprisingly, the play enjoyed even greater success because of notoriety generated by the controversy— even though the most controversial parts had been removed (Barrett 8). Like the many stage versions of Harriet Beecher Stowe's *Uncle Tom's Cabin*, *It Is Never Too Late to Mend* became a standard part of the stage repertoire in the provinces and in America for at least the next thirty years, but, significantly, reviewers of these later productions do not mention the prison scenes (they are more likely to comment on the portrayal of the stage Aboriginal, Jacky, from the Australian section of the play).

Of course, what was so sensational about the prison scenes in Reade's play was that they were so grimly realistic. Nineteenth-century stagecraft had advanced beyond the simpler eighteenth-century auditorium and seating arrangements, now favoring the "picture-frame stage," where the actor was "part of a stage picture, integrated with scenic effect and lighting in a manner previously impossible" (Booth 71). "Spectacle and the large-scale reproduction of the environment," enabled by new methods of suspending and moving scenery as well as developments in lighting, became the norm and were written into more and more plays (Booth 75). Certainly these developments apply to the 1865 staging of *It Is Never Too Late to Mend*.

In addition, the acting, particularly that of young Louisa Moore as Josephs, contributed to the sensational effect. According to Reade's biographer Malcolm Elwin, when flung to the ground by the jailer, Moore "entered too thoroughly into the spirit of the part and just 'let myself go to the ground,' with 'a smack similar to a cod's tail slapped on the marble slab of a fishmonger's shop—the effect was horrible'" (183). The reviewer for *The Era* reported that Moore's performance of the suicide scene "caused distress for 'several ladies in the stalls'" (apparently he means that some fainted) and "there was 'an indescribable thrill of horror running through the whole body of spectators'" (qtd. in Henderson 100).

Although the term "thrill of horror" was already a cliché in the mid-nineteenth century, it is actually an apt description of the affect of sensation created by Reade's prison scenes in both the play and the earlier novel. The descriptions in the novel and the depictions onstage in the play created feelings of horror, but also a simultaneous thrill, which suggests pleasure. The pleasure, of course, is two-sided. On the one hand, it is the pleasure of masochism, or pleasure from vicariously feeling the pain. On the other hand, , there is pleasure in knowing that one is in a theater, seeing a framed picture on the stage, and not really feeling any pain at all. Thus the play's realism is predicated precisely on its not being real. Ironically, at least for literary critics, such literal realism with its sensational effects was exactly the opposite of what they were trying to define as literary realism, the characteristic of writers such as George Eliot and William Dean Howells. Richard Nemesvari, in fact, argues that literary realism was constructed by its difference from sensation fiction and drama (17). While literary realism, as it has come to be defined, may depend more on psychological effects and a focus on everyday life rather than carefully staged material imitations of reality and scenes of high emotion (or sensation), both forms could be said to rely on the double consciousness of feeling vicariously along with the characters while simultaneously being detached from the action portrayed. The resulting affect of sensation that depends on this double consciousness is common to sensation literature on both sides of the Atlantic. Reade's fiction and plays, however, especially *It Is Never Too Late to Mend*, use this technique of creating physical sensations through realistic details to excruciating effect. In large part, Reade learned to do this from his famous American contemporary, Harriet Beecher Stowe, as well as his compatriot Charles Dickens.

Using facts to create the affect of sensation

Although little known today except among a few Victorian scholars, Charles Reade was considered by many of his contemporaries to be one of the major writers of nineteenth-century Britain and America.[1] Walter Frewen Lord, for instance, included Reade among the twelve "great artists" in his *Mirror of the Century* (1906). Whether readers acknowledged Reade as one of the greatest writers of the century or not, he was certainly recognized as one of the major authors of the genre popularly called "sensation fiction." Walter C. Phillips's 1919 retrospective account of sensation novelists places Reade alongside Charles Dickens and Wilkie Collins as one of the foremost practitioners of that form. Reade's brand of sensation fiction, however, was somewhat different from British contemporaries such as Collins, M.E. Braddon, Ellen Wood, and Ouida, Australian writers such as Marcus Clarke, or Americans such as George Lippard, Louisa May Alcott, or E.D.E.N. Southworth. The method Reade consciously developed for writing his novels and

---

[1]   For a discussion of how and why Reade's reputation plummeted in the twentieth century, see Poovey.

plays depended on heavily researched factual realism to create vivid sensations and emotions in his audience in order to motivate them to social action. Reade's very specific formula for his sensation fiction complicates any simple definition of sensation fiction as a genre and differentiates him from most of the other novelists lumped together as sensation novelists, while at the same time involving him in the transatlantic conversation about what constituted a first-rate novel.

Charles Reade's first sensational novel was published before the term "sensation fiction" had even been coined by the hostile English reviewers of the early 1860s, although "sensation" had been used by Margaret Oliphant to describe novels as early as 1855 and American critics had used the word much earlier. Reade's literary reputation commenced with the simultaneous publication of his third novel, *It Is Never Too Late to Mend*, in England and America in 1856. Despite the fact that this novel was published before the term "sensation fiction" came into common circulation in England, reviewers have usually lumped this novel—especially the prison section—with those published by British authors publishing in the 1860s, especially Braddon, Collins, and Wood. With *It Is Never Too Late to Mend*, Reade developed the artistic method that was to characterize the rest of his works, both fictional and dramatic. With his subtitle, *A Matter of Fact Romance*, Reade signaled the hybridity of his new novel's genre and introduced his fact-based "system," which he described in his *Diary*:

> June 20, 1853—The plan I propose to myself in writing stories will, I see, cost me undeniable labor. I propose never to guess where I can know. For instance, Tom Robinson is in gaol. I have therefore been to Oxford Gaol and visited every inch, and shall do the same at Reading. Having also collected material in Durham Gaol, whatever I write about Tom Robinson's gaol will therefore carry (I hope) a physical exterior of truth ... Such is the mechanism of a novel by Charles Reade ... If I can work the above great system, there is enough of me to make one of the writers of the day; without it, No, No. (qtd. in Burns 130, 132).

Reade's biographer, Malcolm Elwin, goes so far as to say that "With Reade, the passion for truth became veritably a vice":

> Whenever he published a novel or produced a play and an unfortunate critic ventured to suggest the exaggeration or to doubt the probability of an incident or character, Reade dived into his cherished notebooks and concocted a bombastic epistle, triumphantly demonstrating that his fiction was founded on actual facts. (116)

The "unfortunate" critics of the day, with whom Reade had a generally combative relationship, frequently decried his and other sensation novelists' works because, among other things, they created unhealthy emotions in their readers. Deborah Wynne observes that "the sensation novel, as its name suggests, was ... designed to stimulate the senses; whether in the form of entertaining thrills or heavy doses of addictive arousal depended on one's point of view" (6). Alfred Austin, writing in the *Temple Bar* in 1870, maintained that "No doubt the reading of sensational novels must have a deteriorating effect on the mind ... They stimulate only to depress" (424). Because sensation fiction was usually set in the present in a geographically close locale, it was thought to create suspicion and fear about one's own or one's neighbors' domestic surroundings, or even doubt about the basic institutions of society.[2] I contend, however, that even though readers and audiences of sensational fiction and drama might indeed feel the thrill of horror, there was always a simultaneous awareness that they were voluntarily subjecting themselves to the power of an author. In Reade's case, his factual system of writing sensation fiction promised his readers an even more striking affective state of excitement because his stories were "real"—based on facts gleaned from careful research. The thrill he promised readers, however, was granted in exchange for their social involvement and action. This bargain or implied contract is noticeable in the novel version of *It Is Never Too Late to Mend*, but is even more evident in the dramatic incident that occurred on the opening night of his stage version of the story. The aftermath of that evening's events, however, indicates a breakdown in this social contract and a reversion to the more simplistic thrills characteristic of stage melodrama.

Reade was indebted to earlier novelists in both England and America who also focused on prison narratives or secret dungeons as a way to create thrills for readers seeking stimulation of their senses. The popular *Newgate Calendar* had been publishing narratives about sensational crimes and the hangings of notorious criminals since the mid-eighteenth century. Building on the popularity of the *Calendar*, novelists in the 1820s began writing novels based on well-known criminals' lives; these novels, which were written throughout the 1820s, 1830s, and 1840s, came to be called "Newgate novels." Accused of idealizing crime and criminals, the Newgate novels, written by authors such as Edward Bulwer-Lytton, Harrison Ainsworth, Charles Whitehead, and the early Charles Dickens, were controversial but popular and are often seen as the forerunners of British sensation fiction (Pykett 19). Most of them focused, however, on the melodramatic life of crime leading to execution, while Reade's novel centers on the new technologies of the prison system and the reform of the criminal. Similarly, "sensational" novels published earlier in America, such as George Lippard's *Quaker City; or, The Monks of Monk Hall* (1844), may have influenced Reade, though such lurid and melodramatic tales were more akin to the "penny dreadfuls" in Britain than to the later "sensation fiction" of the 1860s. Lippard's novel itself, however, did have a social purpose like Reade's, even if its message leaned toward working-class politics rather than Reade's more conservative reform agenda (Streeby 40–41).

The most obvious influences on Reade's writing, however, were Harriet Beecher Stowe and Charles Dickens. Though Reade had embarked on his method of using extensive research in writing his 1853 play *Gold* (on which the non-prison sections of *It Is Never Too Late to Mend* are based), when he came to write this

---

[2] In an influential article in the *Edinburgh Review*, James Fitzjames Stephen accused Reade (and Dickens) of undermining trust in the government, its leaders, and its institutions.

novel, he had found a model for his system—Stowe's *Uncle Tom's Cabin* and her *Key to Uncle Tom's Cabin*. It was the success of Stowe's novel, especially in conjunction with its *Key*, that cemented Reade's commitment to his system. Several of Reade's critics have briefly noticed his indebtedness to Stowe, but none have noted the way both authors strove to effect social and political change through creating visceral emotions by means of embodying researched facts. The best evidence of Stowe's influence on Reade is that within the pages of *It Is Never Too Late to Mend* itself.[3] The most explicit of these references occurs in the account of a conversation between the heroic prison chaplain Mr. Eden and one of the prison warders, Mr. Fry:

> Great by theme, and great by skill, and greater by a writer's soul honestly flung into its pages, Uncle Tom, to the surprise of many that twaddle traditional phrases in reviews and magazines about the art of fiction, and to the surprise of no man who knows anything about the art of fiction, was all the rage. Not to have read it was like not to have read *The Times* for a week.
>
> Once or twice during the crucifixion of a prisoner Mr. Eden had said bitterly to Fry "Have you read 'Uncle Tom'"?
>
> "No!" would Fry grunt.
>
> But one day that the question was put to him, he asked with some appearance of interest, "Who is Uncle Tom?"
>
> Then Mr. Eden began to reflect. "Why not?" said he to himself. "Who knows?" The cases are in a great measure parallel. Prisoners are a tabooed class in England, as are blacks in some few of the United States. This Lady writes better than I can talk. If she once seizes his sympathies by the wonderful power of fiction, she will touch his conscience through his heart. The disciple of Legree is fortified against me; Mrs. Stowe may take him off his guard. (261)

Reade here not only gives Stowe's novel high praise, but explicitly compares its subject matter to his own: "The cases are in a great measure parallel. Prisoners are a tabooed class in England, as are blacks in some few of the United States." Reade notes that *Uncle Tom's Cabin* was "all the rage" in London, making it evident that he hoped to capitalize on Stowe's artistic method to create a successful novel of his own. In fact, Reade even wrote *A Key to It Is Never Too Late to Mend*, obviously patterned after Stowe's description of her "true" historical sources (Burns 132).

It was not only Stowe's factual method that Reade intended to imitate, however. According to the same passage from *It Is Never Too Late to Mend*, *Uncle Tom's Cabin* has the power to "seize [the reader's] sympathies by the wonderful power

---

3   See especially Burns and Sutcliffe, "*Uncle Tom* and Charles Reade." Even one of Stowe's American obituaries cites her influence on Reade. See "Death of Harriet Beecher Stowe," the Unsigned Editorial in *The Chicago Tribune*.

of fiction" and to "touch his conscience through his heart." Mr. Fry, the character in question here, is the chief henchman of Reade's own Simon Legree figure, the sadistic prison governor, Mr. Hawes. The copy of *Uncle Tom's Cabin* is eventually passed on to Hawes himself, who, as Reade shows with pointed irony, fails to see the parallel between his own treatment of the prisoners in —Gaol and the slaves in Stowe's compelling novel, though he is sentimentally affected by the breaking-up of slave families (327–331).[4] Fry, however, who takes Hawes's cruel orders, ironically dictated while the governor is in the process of reading *Uncle Tom*, perhaps does glimpse the similarities between the case Reade is representing and Stowe's novel, leading him to later rebel against his master. While these characters are not quick to see the parallels, however, Reade assumes that his readers will, and thus he borrows some of the pathos generated by Stowe's novel to enhance the emotional appeal of his own.

Generically, Stowe's *Uncle Tom's Cabin* is usually classified as domestic or sentimental melodrama or as a social problem novel rather than as sensation fiction. Nonetheless, as Reade's imitation shows, Stowe's novel was clearly also a precursor to 1860s sensation fiction partly because of the strong emotional responses it provoked in readers—typical of sentimental fiction—but also the explicit scenes of violence or physical suffering that it portrayed—one of the chief characteristics of sensationalism.[5] Also, like sensation fiction, Stowe's novel portrayed this violence and suffering occurring within familiar, contemporary spaces, thus generating fear in the reader that was both exciting and intimate, not distanced as it usually was in novels classified as Gothic. Writing in 1981, Ann Douglas claimed that "*Uncle Tom* is one of the first two American novels to accept and thus exemplify our native fiction's essential preoccupation with excitation"; I would suggest that the "preoccupation with excitation" was not exclusively a quality of America's "native fiction" and that the relationship between fiction and reality was not as fixed in England as Douglas presumes it to have been (31–32). Stowe's novel, in fact, was a significant intervention in England's literary scene quite as much as any novel published there.[6] The main difference between Stowe's novel and many of the British sensation novels is that her novel's powerful emotional impact is meant to reinforce the sanctity of home and family, the purity of women, and the clear distinction between good and evil.[7] While most sensation

---

[4]   Although the prison on which Reade based this section of the novel was Birmingham Gaol, he refrained from giving his jail a name. He calls it "—Gaol" in order both to claim its fictional status and to broaden the potential criticisms to other jails and penitentiaries.

[5]   Monika Fludernik also comments on the way Reade used both sentimental and sensational conventions, as Stowe did.

[6]   Denise Kohn, Sarah Meer, and Emily B. Todd note in the introduction to *Transatlantic Stowe* that for many Europeans *Uncle Tom's Cabin* became a book that reflected issues of oppression and reform in their own nations, while Stowe herself was shaped by European, especially British, models (xviii, xv).

[7]   Sarah Meer qualifies this assumption when she asserts that Stowe's use of blackface routines "enable[s] fantasies of revolt against the ordered domestic realm the novel (mostly) endorses" (12).

writers' thrills are built on challenges to these very values, many of them turn back to reinforce them in their endings. In Reade's case, he borrowed Stowe's method more than her content, although he clearly saw parallels between the stories as well. Obviously, however, what he most wanted to produce was the same kind of impact she achieved, though his "virile," "manly," and "forcible" style differed from hers significantly.[8]

Reade's novel and the sensational technology of punishment

It Is Never Too Late to Mend is not only about prisons and prisoners. The first section of the novel features a conventional melodramatic plot set in the English countryside, whereas later sections portray the Australian gold rush and the resolution of the plot with the last-minute rescue of the heroine, Susanna Merton, by the hero, George Fielding, just as she is about to wed the villain, Mr. Meadows. While Reade used his system of gathering facts to write all of *It Is Never Too Late to Mend*, the sensation comes in large part from his detailed focus on the misapplied technologies of inflicting pain used by evil overseers in —Gaol. The jail is portrayed at length in the section when Tom Robinson, one of the two protagonists of the novel, is incarcerated there before being transported to Australia.

Like Stowe and the equally famous Dickens, who both created strong emotions in their readers in order to move them to action, Reade obviously intended his novel not only to amuse his readers, but also to achieve a social purpose, in his case the reform of abuses in the British "separate and silent" prisons. Like Stowe, who conducted detailed inquiries of the treatment of slaves in the American South, as well as Dickens, who also carefully investigated the conditions exposed in his social problem novels and wrote about prisons, Reade did extensive research into new technologies of prison management for the prison section of his novel. Since the translation and publication of Michel Foucault's *Discipline and Punish: The Birth of the Prison*, most American literary critics have assumed that Jeremy Bentham's "Panopticon" was the model for British and other modern nations' prisons. However, Bentham's design for a model prison was rejected by the British government before any were built, and the rival "separate and silent" system became the new norm in both prison architecture and the management of prisoners (see Grass 4–5). In this system, as in the Panopticon, prisoners were separated from each other and housed in individual cells but, unlike Bentham's proposed model, the prisons were not circular with an unseen guard in the center nor were the prisoners open to view at all times. Instead, they were isolated in their scrupulously clean bare cells behind heavy doors with openings only for a guard to look through or for food to be passed in. When the prisoners went to chapel, they wore hoods over their heads and worshiped in pews with individual

---

⁸   Nicola Thompson notes that critics considered *It Is Never Too Late to Mend* "a quintessentially masculine novel" (196).

walls designed so they could see the chaplain but not other prisoners. Even when they exercised, they used lanes or small yards with high walls that allowed them to experience fresh air but not communicate with their peers. In addition to being isolated from the sight of other prisoners, they were prohibited from speaking to anyone except the chaplain (besides an occasional minimal exchange with a guard or warder). Punishment for prison infractions was even more separation and silence. Prisoners who violated the rules were put in solitary confinement in specially designed cells that blocked out all light and most sounds; a cell of this type became known among prisoners as the "black hole" or the "dark cell."

The abuses in Reade's nameless jail, as he acknowledged, were based on a scandal at the Birmingham Gaol that was reported in *The Times* in 1853. Birmingham was a county jail, not a penitentiary, but it, along with several other county jails, had adopted the separate and silent system. The idea of the penitentiary originated in England, but the most famous example of such a prison was the Eastern Penitentiary in Philadelphia (Teeters and Shearer viii).[9] The Pennsylvania Prison Society, which designed and promoted the legislation that fostered the building of the Eastern Penitentiary, or Cherry Hill, as it was called informally, exchanged ideas with most of the major English penological reformers, including the famous John Howard, as well as French and Russian penologists (Johnston 26). Birmingham Gaol, the source for Reade's novel, and —Gaol, his fictional version, were both based on the system as it was practiced at the American Eastern Penitentiary, which also served as a model for Pentonville and Millbank, the most famous British model prisons.

Reade's portrayal of separate and silent prisons was preceded by more than a decade by Dickens's *American Notes* (1842), in which he includes a description of his visit to Cherry Hill. Dickens was very critical of the separate and silent system: "The system here, is rigid, strict, and hopeless solitary confinement. I believe it, in its effects, to be cruel and wrong" (146).[10] Dickens's account caused resentment among his American readers and Eastern Penitentiary officials who had hosted his visit felt betrayed. According to historians Negley K. Teeters and John D. Shearer, "the members of The Philadelphia Prison Society were compelled to repair the damage [Dickens] had wrought throughout the world" (114). Teeters and Shearer themselves feel compelled to contrast Dickens's account carefully with historical evidence and demonstrate that the penitentiary "was not as bad as the novelist painted it." This reaction to Dickens's observations, from both American contemporaries and later historians, is similar to attacks made on Reade for exaggeration of his evidence. For example, in 1857, shortly after *It Is Never Too Late to Mend* was published, James Fitzjames Stephen took him to task in the

---

9   See Bender for a discussion of how the idea of the penitentiary and the narrative technique of the novel developed in eighteenth-century England.

10   Dickens also attacks the separate and silent system satirically in *David Copperfield* (1850) when he has the hypocritical villains Uriah Heep and Mr. Littimer incarcerated there. Not surprisingly, they manipulate the system to their advantage.

Edinburgh Review for twisting the facts. A century later, in 1960, literary critic Sheila M. Smith similarly censured Reade for the "lurid quality of the imagination which worked upon the hard facts of [his] research" (141). However, applying imagination to "hard fact" is precisely what Reade, Dickens, and Stowe saw as their strength. Even Dickens's "documentary" travelogue intentionally used imagination and personal impressions (Reynolds 15). In Stowe's case, as is well known, the method of using the artistic imagination to vivify factual information generated not only criticism, but elaborate defenses from proponents of slavery in response to *Uncle Tom's Cabin*. As Reade has Mr. Eden express it in *It Is Never Too Late to Mend*, even writers who base their works on careful research use the "art" and "wonderful power" of fiction. Like Stowe and Dickens before him, then, Reade used this power to involve himself and his readers in an international debate about a crucial social policy, but even more than they did, he used the emotional techniques that would come to be known as "sensational" in order to engage in that debate.

While Reade used the facts he found from his research to write the prison section of his novel, the sensation comes in large part from his imaginative focus on the suffering bodies in —Gaol. Reade portrays prisoners as young as eleven collapsing after having been forced to do hours of backbreaking but useless work on "the crank," a machine with a handle hooked to a wheel which counted the number of revolutions and could be adjusted for pressure. He recreates the sensations of the infamous "wheel," a large treadmill with steps that a prisoner had to keep climbing to avoid falling off or getting caught in the machinery. He also describes in careful detail the hunger they feel when deprived of meals for not meeting their quotas on the crank, and the additional torment of having their beds removed after they have been flogged or put in the "punishment jacket." The latter, which is what Reade means when he refers to "crucifixion," was a straitjacket into which the prisoner would be strapped tightly for several hours. The pain it caused is described in harrowing detail aimed directly at the reader's own sensations:

> Were you ever seized at night with a violent cramp? Then you have instantly with a sort of wide and alarmed rapidity changed the posture which had cramped you; aye, though the night was never so cold, you have sprung out of bed sooner than lie cramped. If the cramp would not go in less than half a minute, that half-minute was long and bitter. As for existing cramped half an hour that you never thought possible [*sic*]. Imagine now the severest cramp you ever felt artificially prolonged for hours and hours. Imagine yourself cramped in a vice, no part of you moveable a hair's breadth, except your hair and your eye-lids. Imagine the fierce cramp growing and growing, and rising like a tide of agony higher and higher above nature's endurance, and you will cease to wonder that a man always sunk under Hawes's man-press. Now then add to the cramp a high circular saw raking the throat, jacket straps cutting and burning the flesh of the back-add to this the freezing of the blood in the body deprived so long of all motion whatever (for motion of some sort or degree is a condition of vitality), and a new and far more rational wonder arises, that any man could be half an hour cut sawed crushed cramped Mazeppa'd thus without shamming [what Hawes calls fainting]—still less be four, six, eight hours in it and come out a living man. ([*sic*], 294)

Although based on interviews, personal observation, and government blue books, this kind of description clearly goes beyond fact-gathering by using the imagination to intensify the evidence, creating the vicarious sensation of pain in the reader, while simultaneously reminding the reader that s/he is in fact not in pain. Reade's descriptions, of course, do linger on the pain in a way that his sources did not. In fact, Sheila Smith accuses Reade of attempting "to inculcate an emotion in the reader, hatred against Hawes and his system, rather than soberly ... explor[ing] a problem affecting society." For her, as for many earlier critics, this is a flaw in the novel (141). For Reade, however, emotion was exactly what he hoped to create in his reader—a powerful sensation that would move him or her to action.

In addition to the physical suffering that the characters and, vicariously, the readers experience in *It Is Never Too Late to Mend*, Reade inflicts another sensational horror. The most serious punishment for infractions in —Gaol is putting the prisoners into solitary confinement in the "dark cell." This particular torture works not on the suffering body, but instead on the mind of the fractious (or unfortunate, in the novel's view) prisoner. In his *American Notes*, Dickens had commented on the debilitating psychological effects of what he called "solitary confinement" in the Eastern Penitentiary: "[the prisoner] is a man buried alive; to be dug out in the slow round of years; and in the mean time dead to everything but torturing anxieties and horrible despair" (148). Though what Dickens was actually referring to was only the regular form of separate and silent treatment, his description is even more apt for those confined for hours or days in the even more severe solitary confinement of the "dark cell." When condemned to the cell for twenty-four hours, Robinson exclaims to the chaplain Mr. Eden that "here is one of your brothers being taken to hell before your eyes. I go there a man, but I shall come out a beast" (195). Reade goes on to describe Robinson's mental agonies as graphically as he describes the physical punishments, taking them hour by hour. By the third hour, Robinson's past haunts him, figures he has wronged seem to come alive, and devils whirl around him, driving him to "[fling] himself madly against the door" until he is "bruised and bleeding." By the sixth hour, the narrator explains that Robinson is genuinely going mad. He prays to be put in the punishment jacket or anywhere rather than in the cell he occupies. Finally rescued from insanity by Mr. Eden coming in the night to talk to him through the door, Robinson manages to keep his senses and go to sleep. Eden calms and amazes him by explaining that he himself has voluntarily experienced confinement in the dark cell (as he has also done with the punishment jacket) in order to be able to sympathize with his charges, the tormented prisoners. It is this human contact that relieves Robinson's intense suffering and effects his conversion. Like Reade's descriptions of physical pain, his hour-by-hour portrayal of mental anguish is also sensational. It inflicts voluntary pain on readers, who are, however, unlike Mr. Eden, simultaneously aware that they themselves are not in the dark cell, but in a lighted room that allows them to read. Creating these sensations in his readers, Reade hoped, would provoke them to speak out, as Mr. Eden models, against solitary confinement for prisoners and other abuses of the separate and silent system.

The stated purpose of the new separate and silent system was, unlike most earlier penal practices, reformative. Rather than simply punishing criminals and serving as a deterrent to future crimes, the new prisons aimed to reform the prisoner so that he could be reintegrated into society as a law-abiding citizen.[11] As the Reverend Whitworth Russell, a prison inspector and former chaplain at Millbank, put it, "in his separate cell, all the moral machinery of the system is brought to bear" on the prisoner, in effect turning him into a new man (qtd. in Grass 30). This "machinery" of the new penal system was a way to enforce "morality" by instilling it deep within the prisoner's psyche, which sounds very Foucauldian. A key difference between the secular Panopticon, however, and the new penitentiaries was that the Christian chaplain was central to the reformation expected of the prisoners. Confined separately and prohibited from communication with their peers, criminals were supposed to spend their time in meditation on the folly of their past lives and rehabilitate themselves. In order for their meditations to take the correct form, however, frequent conversations with the chaplain were advised.

Reform through affective submission in *It Is Never Too Late to Mend*

In Reade's novel, the hero of the prison section of the book is Mr. Eden, the chaplain of —Gaol. It is he who, despite physical frailty and the machinations of Hawes, manages not only to expose the sensational abuses in the jail, but also to convert most of its inmates, including Tom Robinson. By the end of the prison section, in fact, all of the mismanagement and cruel practices have been reformed and the prison truly is a model (in Reade's view). All of Hawes's instruments of torture are eliminated and only some of the prisoners who are deemed to need it are subjected to the separate—and silent—system. This development in plot suggests that Reade was not so much opposed to the system itself as to abuses of it that ignored the humanity of the prisoners. This insistence on the humanity of the prisoners is one of the key sentiments that links *It Is Never Too Late to Mend* to *Uncle Tom's Cabin*, which insists that the reader see the suffering slave as a fully redeemable person, not a piece of property, as well as the efficacy of Christian conversion.

While Reade's insistence on Christian conversion in *It Is Never Too Late to Mend*, which is implied in the title, could be seen as just another way to exercise Foucauldian disciplinary power, Anna Maria Jones's *Problem Novels* offers a way of looking at conversion as a method of exercising "critical agency" and "the possibility of culturally embedded subjects engaging with and critiquing forms of power in self-conscious ways" (14). She offers masochism, or voluntary submission to suffering, as a "position from which submission and self-consciousness are possible simultaneously" (17). Jones's own readings focus on female characters

---

[11]   I use "he" advisedly; women were not systematically subjected to this kind of imprisonment, though some experienced it.

who submit to their gender roles and gain a sort of agency in return. In Reade's novel, by contrast, Mr. Eden voluntarily submits himself to the same punishments that cause torment for the prisoners. In addition, Tom Robinson, the convict, submits himself to the discipline of Mr. Eden, at first reluctantly but later willingly. By extension, of course, this means a submission to God, or a conversion. Though at first Robinson's attraction to Mr. Eden leads to more punishment from Hawes, even in the early stages Robinson gains an access of agency by viewing his punishment as voluntary rather than forced. His masochism also expresses his criticism of Hawes's system at least as effectively as did his earlier defiance; in fact, it infuriates Hawes. Thus, Robinson's conversion requires him to give up his rebellious and pugnacious identity and take on a new one that is more masochistic, but also more free. After the expulsion of Hawes, Robinson's new demeanor leads to more physical freedom, as well as meaningful work. Both his new sense of agency and the trade he learns in the jail allow him to succeed, despite setbacks, in the Australian portion of the novel that follows. The novel ends, in fact, with Robinson in a position of power; his former master becomes his servant and he becomes a member of the colony's legislature. Becoming part of the disciplinary mechanisms of culture, of course, does not overturn those structures, but it does give the character more agency to effect change within them.

In her reading of Wilkie Collins's *No Name*, Jones also claims that the reader experiences "suspenseful pleasure" not from following a detective's revelation of a secret, as in many sensation novels, but from voluntarily sharing sensations of suffering with a wayward but still sympathetic character. The novel "paradoxically demands a reader who is well disciplined and deviant—one who understands and accepts literary and social conventions, even as he or she is driven by the affective power of the novel to *feel* at odds with those conventions ... the novel forces the reader to examine individual agency in relations to the mechanisms of disciplinary power" (36). In Reade's sensation novel the reader feels along with a convicted criminal as he learns to submit to prison surveillance and to God's will, both authoritative apparatuses of power. Even more than in *No Name*, the reader's masochism in *It Is Never Too Late to Mend* is so evident as to be almost literal, since s/he is voluntarily submitting to intense vicarious pain, whether physical or mental. Simultaneously, though, that reader is also experiencing pleasure from this pain, pleasure that derives in large part from the mental contrast between imaginative suffering and actual physical and emotional comfort.

While the separate—and silent—system that Reade is critiquing isolates prisoners from each other in their regular cells and, more extremely, in the dark cell, in mid-Victorian England and America the prisons themselves became increasingly more cut off from the public. Whereas the old prisons had allowed visitors, including both relatives and friends of the prisoners and curious onlookers, who sometimes paid admission to gaze on the spectacle of the criminal, the new penitentiaries allowed virtually no visitors to individual prisoners and made public access increasingly difficult. Grass notes that even newspaper reporters were barred from the prisons, so that what went on behind the heavy doors of the penitentiary was a virtual secret from the ordinary citizen (26). John Pratt connects this isolation of the prison from public view to the Victorian notion of its own advanced civilization:

> punishment in the civilized world ... became largely anonymous, remote, encircled by the growing power of the bureaucratic forces presiding over it which then shaped, defined and made it understandable; and where *precisely because of this framework*, which differentiated it from the uncivilized world, brutalities and privations could go largely unchecked or unheeded by a public that preferred not to be involved in such matters. (3, emphasis original)

As Pratt points out, while isolating the prison from public view made it seem more civilized, it also enabled abuses of disciplinary power that were most uncivilized. The social purpose of Reade's novel was, as we have seen, to expose such abuses through his fiction. Thus, while sensation writers like M.E. Braddon lift a veil to expose a theatrical secret underneath the smooth surface of the Victorian home (see Mattacks), Reade lifts a veil to reveal the torture being inflicted inside a building anyone might walk by any day and exposes horrors more "real" (because factual) than those in the novels of contemporaries like Braddon and Collins.

The abuses at Birmingham Gaol came to light because of the suicide of fifteen-year-old Edward Andrews, who hung himself from the window bars of his cell. In Reade's novel, Andrews becomes "Josephs, No. 15, Corridor A" (136). Josephs, like his historical counterpart Andrews, commits suicide after being subjected to outrageous work assignments on the "crank," torture in the "punishment jacket," withholding of food and light in his own cell, and time spent in the "dark cell." Though Robinson endures even more cruel treatment than Joseph—including time on the infamous "wheel"—he manages to survive long enough for Mr. Eden to reform his soul and expose the abuses of Hawes (Mr. Austin, in the Birmingham Gaol incident).

Significantly, Mr. Eden reforms the private prison by making its abuses public by appealing in turn to the various officials who oversee the gaol's management. Before he finally gets the Home Office to take his accusations seriously and actually send someone to investigate, though, Mr. Eden vows that he will

> Lay the whole case before her Majesty the Queen and the British nation, by publishing it in all the journals. Then I shall tell her Majesty that, having thrice appealed in vain to her representatives, I am driven to appeal to herself; with this I shall print the evidence I have thrice offered you of this gaoler's felonies and their sanguinary results. That Lady has a character; one of its strong, unmistakeable features is a real, tender, active humanity ... Nor will the public hear unmoved the awful tale. Shame will be showered on all connected with these black deeds. (320)

Reade's heroic chaplain thus threatens to use the press to appeal to the civilized public, symbolized by the womanly Queen with her "real, tender, active humanity," just as Reade himself did through his sensational novel, modeled on the book by the "Lady" whose "soul [was] honestly flung into its pages," Harriet Beecher Stowe. Thus Reade offers his readers his own tender, feminine icon with whom to identify. The Queen, of course, was the best model of someone who could experience sympathetic emotions and effectively act on them to prevent abuses of hidden power.

It Is Never Too Late to Mend brought Reade the success he had been seeking for many years. The system that he developed by imitating Stowe's, along with Dickens's, fact-finding and emotional appeal to audiences brought him fame and wealth, and, shortly after the publication of the novel, the prisons he had exposed were reformed so that abuses like the ones he portrays in the novel became rare. As successful as it was in England, Reade's novel sold even more copies in the U.S., and his relations with publishers and critics there were considerably more amicable than with those in his own country (Elwin 108–109, 115). His American success sustained him through nine years of wrangling with English publishers over commissions and payment, as well as a drawn-out trial over the copyright of the stage version of his novel—which he eventually won. Reade's novel was thus successful in several ways. It brought him financial security and international notoriety, especially in America, but it also succeeded in its avowed mission of using the "wonderful power of fiction" to motivate the reform of social abuses, as Stowe's *Uncle Tom's Cabin* had done so well before him.

It Is Never Too Late to Mend—The play's return to melodrama

Although one might presume that Reade's motives in staging the play were similar to his intentions in the earlier novel—to make facts come alive in a sensational way in order to motivate the audience to act on social reforms—that view is open to some question. For one thing, as Michael Booth explains, "the picture-frame stage ... well suited the growing passivity and detachment of the Victorian middle-class audience" (71). Rather than being provoked to action by the realism, in the dramatic sense, of the play's staging, the critics and audience were scandalized and disturbed by the graphic nature of the prison scenes and demanded that they be toned down and, so to speak, censored.[12]

Another difference in the effect created by the stage version was that, in the nine years intervening between the novel and the play, most of the reforms Reade was agitating for had already been achieved. As we have seen, Reade, unlike many of the other writers who have been called sensation novelists, intended his sensationalized facts to contribute to social reform, as did Stowe. The novel version of *It Is Never Too Late to Mend* could be said to have had this effect, with the readers' agreement to Reade's proffered bargain in which sensational pleasure was provided as a condition of social action. Ironically, however, in his onstage argument with the critics the actor/manager Vining, who stepped

---

[12]   Barrett discusses Reade's skillful manipulation of the play's actual censor (from the Lord Chamberlain's office) before it was allowed to open (4).

out of his character as Tom Robinson to address the hostile critics, justified the sensationalism of the play precisely because social action was no longer needed:

> Ladies and Gentlemen,—With all due submission to public opinion, permit me to call your attention to one fact, which appears to have been overlooked. It has been acknowledged that the work from which this piece is taken has done a great deal of good. We are not here representing a system *as it is*, but the abuses of a system, and I may refer to the Blue Book—here a voice from the pit shouted out 'We want no Blue Books on the stage'—for the truthfulness of these things. (qtd. in Barrett from *The Era* 6; my emphasis).

Vining suggests that the reform Reade was working toward in the novel has already been accomplished and thus the play no longer represents the system "as it is." But the "voice from the pit" expresses the more disengaged sentiments of the stage audience—"We want no Blue Books on the stage." Even if the facts are accurate, the audience wants them to remain hidden behind a pretty "stage picture" like the picturesque set of Act I, reinforcing Booth's conclusion about their "growing passivity and detachment." In 1865, apparently, Victorian stage audiences wanted the sensation that the "realistic" technologies of stagecraft could provide without a social message attached. By making the prison scenes too graphic, Reade aroused the sensibilities of the audience in a painful, not a pleasurable way, and in a way that seemed to demand action on their part rather than passivity.

Pratt's analysis in *Punishment and Civilization* astutely suggests that one of the characteristics of modern civilization, as its members conceive it, is "the increased sensibility to the suffering of others and the privatization of disturbing events" (4). As "internalized controls on an individual's behavior became more automatic and pervasive, more and more a taken for granted aspect of cultural life," they "thereby again raised the threshold of sensitivity and embarrassment" (5). This is, of course, what both Bentham's Panopticon, as Foucault interprets it, and the separate and silent prisons aimed to create in their reformed criminal—"internalized controls on an individual's behavior." But if the "internalized controls" on the behavior of the middle-class theater-going public were also becoming more "automatic and pervasive," we might expect that their sensitivity to disturbing scenes was also growing, thus causing them to reject suicidal tortured prisoners and Blue Books on stage. Significantly, however, Pratt points out that this very "civilizing process itself can bring about most uncivilized consequences" (8). In other words, if the public refuses to see what goes on in private, then those behind the closed doors of the prison can enact the very abuses Reade was trying to expose with his use of the affect of sensation.

Works Cited

Austin, Alfred. "Our Novels: The Sensational School." *Temple Bar* 29 (June 1870): 410–424.

Barrett, Daniel. "*It is Never Too Late to Mend*." *Theater Research International* 18.1 (1993): 4–12. Gale Database, 1–10.

Bender, John. *Imagining the Penitentiary: Fiction and the Architecture of Mind in Eighteenth-Century England.* Chicago: University of Chicago Press, 1987.

Booth, Michael R. *Theater in the Victorian Age.* Cambridge and New York: Cambridge University Press, 1991.

Burns, Wayne. *Charles Reade: A Study in Victorian Authorship.* New York: Bookman, 1961.

Burns, Wayne, and Emerson Grant Sutcliffe. "*Uncle Tom* and Charles Reade." *American Literature* 4 (January 1946): 334–347.

"Death of Harriet Beecher Stowe." *The Chicago Tribune.* Unsigned Editorial. 1 July 1896. Institute for Advanced Studies in the Humanities, University of Virginia Press.

Dickens, Charles. *American Notes for General Circulation.* 1842. Ed. John S. Whitley and Arnold Goldman. London: Penguin, 1985.

———. *David Copperfield.* 1850. Ed. Jerome H. Buckley. New York: Norton, 1990.

Douglas, Ann. "Introduction: The Art of Controversy." In Harriet Beecher Stowe, *Uncle Tom's Cabin or, Life Among the Lowly.* 1852. Ed. Ann Douglas. New York: Penguin, 1981.

Elwin, Malcolm. *Charles Reade: A Biography.* London: Jonathan Cape, 1931.

Fludernik, Monika. "'Stone Walls Do (Not) a Prison Make': Rhetorical Strategies and Sentimentalism in the Representation of the Victorian Prison Experience." In *Captivating Subjects: Writing Confinement, Citizenship, and Nationhood in the Nineteenth Century.* Ed. Jason Haslam and Julia M. Wright. Toronto: University of Toronto Press, 2005. 144–174.

Foucault, Michel. *Discipline and Punish: The Birth of the Prison.* Trans. Alan Sheridan. 2nd ed. New York: Vintage, 1995.

Grass, Sean. *The Self in the Cell: Narrating the Victorian Prisoner.* New York: Routledge, 2003.

Henderson, Ian. "Jacky-Kalingaloonga: Aboriginality, Audience Reception, and Charles Reade's *It is Never Too Late To Mend* (1865)." *Theater Research International* 29.2 (2004): 95–110.

Johnston, Norman, Kenneth Finkel, and Jeffrey A. Cohen. *Eastern State Penitentiary: Crucible of Good Intentions.* Philadelphia, Penn.: Philadelphia Museum of Art, 1994.

Jones, Anna Maria. *Problem Novels: Victorian Fiction Theorizes the Sensational Self.* Columbus: Ohio State University Press, 2007.

Kohn, Denise, Sarah Meer, and Emily B. Todd, eds. *Transatlantic Stowe: Harriet Beecher Stowe and European Culture.* Iowa City: University of Iowa Press, 2006.

Lord, Walter Frewen. *The Mirror of the Century.* London: John Lane, 1906.

MacMahon, Donald Hutchins. *Charles Reade as a Dramatist.* Diss., Cornell University, 1935.

Mattacks, Kate. "Beyond these Voices: M.E. Braddon and the Ghost of Sensationalism." *Women's Writing* 15.3 (December 2008): 320–32.

Nemesvari, Richard. "'Judged by a Purely Literary Standard': Sensation Fiction, Horizons of Expectation, and the Generic Construction of Victorian Realism." *Victorian Sensations: Essays on a Scandalous Genre*. Ed. Kimberly Harrison and Richard Fantina. Columbus: Ohio State University Press, 2006. 15–28.

Meer, Sarah. *Uncle Tom Mania: Slavery, Minstrelsy and Transatlantic Culture in the 1850s*. Athens: University of Georgia Press, 2005.

Phillips, Walter C. *Dickens, Reade, and Collins: Sensation Novelists*. New York: Columbia University Press, 1919.

Poovey, Mary. "Forgotten Writers, Neglected Histories: Charles Reade and the Nineteenth-Century Transformation of the British Literary Field." *ELH* 7 (2004): 433–453.

Pratt, John. *Punishment and Civilization: Penal Tolerance and Intolerance in Modern Society*. London: SAGE, 2002.

Pykett, Lyn. "The Newgate Novel and Sensation Fiction." In *The Cambridge Companion to Crime Fiction*. Ed. Martin Priestman. Cambridge: Cambridge University Press, 2003. 19–39.

Reade, Charles. *It Is Never Too Late to Mend*. 2 vols. Boston: Ticknor and Fields, 1856.

Reynolds, Ernest. *Early Victorian Drama*. Cambridge: W. Heffer, 1936.

Smith, Sheila M. "Propaganda and Hard Facts in Charles Reade's Didactic Novels: A Study of *It is Never Too Late to Mend* and *Hard Cash*." *Renaissance and Modern Studies* 4 (1960): 135–149.

Stephen, James Fitzjames. "The License of Modern Novelists." *Edinburgh Review* 106 (July 1857): 124–156.

Stowe, Harriet Beecher. *Uncle Tom's Cabin or, Life Among the Lowly*. 1852. Ed. Ann Douglas. New York: Penguin, 1981.

Streeby, Shelley. *American Sensations: Class, Empire, and the Production of Popular Culture*. Berkeley: University of California Press, 2002.

Teeters, Negley K., and John D. Shearer. *The Prison at Philadelphia Cherry Hill: The Separate System of Penal Discipline 1829–1913*. New York: Temple University Press, 1956.

Thompson, Nicola. "Virile Creators Versus 'Twaddlers Tame and Soft': Gender and the Reception of Charles Reade's *It Is Never Too Late to Mend*." *Victorians Institute Journal* 23 (1995): 193–218.

Wynne, Deborah. *The Sensation Novel and the Victorian Family Magazine*. Houndmills, Basingstoke, Hampshire and New York: Palgrave, 2001.

Chapter 7

Women in White:
The Tragic Mulatta and the
Rise of British Sensation Fiction

Kimberly Snyder Manganelli

Published the year before *Lady Audley's Secret*, Mary Elizabeth Braddon's *The Octoroon; or, The Lily of Louisiana* (1861) opens in a crowded ballroom during the London season of 1860. Cora Leslie, an American girl born in New Orleans but educated in England, has attracted the interest of Gilbert Margrave, a British engineer celebrated for inventing machinery to replace slave labor. Pointing out Cora's beauty to Mortimer Percy, an American planter, Gilbert asks his acquaintance if he knows who the lovely beauty is. Mortimer responds, "No. But I can do more. I can tell you *what* she is" (4). The southerner then explains to the naïve British gentlemen that Cora is the daughter of a slave:

> Had you been a planter, Gilbert, you would have been able to discover, as I did, when just now I stood close to that lovely girl, the fatal signs of her birth. At the extreme corner of the eye, and at the root of the finger nails, the South[ern] American can always discover the trace of slavery, though but *one drop* of the blood of the despised race tainted the object upon whom he looked. (4)

Gilbert is not the only character unable to read the signs of Cora's racial ancestry. While American Tragic Mulatta narratives traditionally pivot on the mixed-race woman's discovery that she is not free, Braddon's story revolves around a more shocking secret: Cora does not know she is an octoroon. Upon learning that her father has been injured in a slave revolt on his plantation, she returns to New Orleans ignorant of her racial ancestry. "The courted, the caressed, the admired beauty of a London season" (61) soon learns, however, that she is not white. Braddon's novel follows Cora's struggle to escape a narrative that offered only two choices to mixed-race slaves: sexual violation or death.

In American abolitionist texts, such as Lydia Maria Child's "The Quadroons" (1842), Harriet Beecher Stowe's *Uncle Tom's Cabin* (1852), and William Wells Brown's *Clotel* (1853), the Tragic Mulatta is a sentimental figure of true womanhood whose compromised bloodline prohibits her from marrying her white suitor. However, as British sensation authors such as Braddon capitalized on the popularity of *Uncle Tom's Cabin*, the Tragic Mulatta was transformed into a mysterious figure in the 1850s and 1860s. In lesser-known texts, such as Captain

Mayne Reid's *The Quadroon; or, a Lover's Adventures in Louisiana* (1856), Dion Boucicault's play, *The Octoroon* (1859), and Braddon's serial, the mixed-race slave becomes an embodiment of dangerous secrets as British authors coupled abolitionist sentiment with narratives of detection and discovery. Although literary history has maintained a national divide between British and American sensation authors, I argue that American abolitionist fiction gave rise to British sensation fiction. Indeed, although Wilkie Collins's *The Woman in White* (1860) is traditionally given as the starting point for the British sensation novel, this particular genre of sensation fiction begins to emerge in the American Tragic Mulatta narratives of the 1840s and 1850s, racial generation literature that was read alongside the city mystery romances of George Lippard, George Thompson, and others.

"Genres," Michael McKeon explains, "are formal structures that have a historical existence in the sense that they come into being, flourish, and decay, waxing and waning in complex relationship to other historical phenomena" (1). Although the abolitionist works of Child, Brown, and Stowe are traditionally categorized as sentimental texts meant to elicit tears and sympathy from readers, the realities of slavery interrupt these narratives by introducing mysterious identities, sexual transgressions, madness, and violence—elements that would later define British sensation novels—into the genteel drawing rooms of characters and readers alike. In fact, as British periodicals such as *Blackwood's Edinburgh Magazine*, *The Quarterly Review*, and *The Sixpenny Journal* sought to define sensation fiction in their reviews of such novels as *The Woman in White* and *Lady Audley's Secret*, reviewers compared the works of Collins and Braddon to Stowe's *Uncle Tom's Cabin*.[1] "Wilkie Collins's extremely clever romance," writes one reviewer of *The Woman in White*, "we regard as the greatest success in sensation writing, with the single exception of Mrs Stowe's deservedly popular work" (qtd. in Page 109).[2] Indeed, Stowe's Cassy, the brutalized quadroon slave on Simon Legree's plantation, could be read as an early sensation heroine.[3] The violation Cassy

---

[1]   See Margaret Oliphant's articles, "Sensation Novels" and "Novels," published in the May 1862 and September 1867 issues of *Blackwood's*, as well as H.L. Mansel's "Sensation Novels," which was published in the April 1863 issue of *The Quarterly Review*. *The Sixpenny Journal*, which also serialized sensation novels, began publishing installments of *Lady Audley's Secret* in January 1862.

[2]   Other examples of reviewers describing *Uncle Tom's Cabin* as a sensation novel include an 1858 article in *The English Woman's Journal*, which explained, "though 'Uncle Tom's Cabin' may be a sensation novel, the Key to it is a sad and trustworthy statement of facts" (91), as well as a reference to the work as "Mrs. Stowe's great-sensation novel" in an 1864 issue of *The New Monthly Magazine* (Jacox 37).

[3]   For works of literary scholarship that examine Stowe's novel as a work of gothic fiction, see Karen Halttunen's "The Haunted House of Lyman Beecher, Henry Ward Beecher, and Harriet Beecher Stowe," in *New Essays on Uncle Tom's Cabin*, ed. Eric J. Sundquist (New York: Cambridge University Press, 1986): 107–134, and Jeanne Elders Dewaard's "'The Shadow of Law': Sentimental Interiority, *Gothic* Terror, and the Legal Subject," *Arizona Quarterly* 62.4 (2006): 1–30.

endures at her master's hands "hardened womanhood within her" (Stowe 409), transforming her into a manipulative *femme fatale* who uses Legree's superstitions and guilt about his sadistic acts against him. In an unsettling scene of domestic intimacy between the quadroon and her master, the sensation genre serves as a means of Cassy's escape when Legree begins reading one of her books, "one of those collections of stories of bloody murders, ghostly legends, and supernatural visitations, which, coarsely got up and illustrated, have a strange fascination for one who once begins to read them" (Stowe 409). Legree's reading of Cassy's penny dreadful makes him susceptible to her haunting of the garret, a Gothic space in which Stowe asks readers to imagine the sexual violence and torture one of his previous victims suffered when she was confined there: "What passed there, we do not say; the negroes used to whisper darkly to each other; but it was known that the body of the unfortunate creature was one day taken down from there, and buried" (407). After masquerading as the ghost of Legree's dead mother and escaping in the disguise of a Spanish lady, Cassy is reunited with her son and daughter in a Canadian Quaker community. Stowe's ending reveals the previously unknown familial connections between the mother and children obfuscated by slavery.

Stowe's novel created such a sensation in Britain that, as Audrey Fisch explains, "Uncle Tom-mania" inspired illustrated songbooks, wallpaper, curio ornaments, dolls, paintings, a card game, a set of quadrilles, abolitionist stationery, not to mention the many theatrical and literary adaptations of the story (13–14). As a result of its commercial success, *Uncle Tom's Cabin* became a site of cultural conflict in Britain as reviews revealed "anxieties underlying Victorian questions about the definition and role of culture, of the expanding reading public, and about working-class revolt" (Fisch 16). The *Spectator*, for example, described how "'the mob,' Victorian shorthand for the working classes, those without education and cultural taste, having 'read a popular book,' are 'rushing to see the leading personages placed in a visible shape before its eyes'" (qtd. in Fisch 12). In *The Times*, the author of an editorial worries, "I fear that the book will…be immortalized at the Victoria and Bower Saloon, and no doubt 'the Secret Chamber in Legree's house,' and the 'Death of Tom at the Whipping-post,' will be faithfully recorded; or, 'Legree, the Man of Crime and the Murderer of Uncle Tom,' will attract the unwashed inhabitants of the Transpontine districts. The book, which might have done worlds of good in other hands, will sink into the sewer of literature in penny numbers, and be turned to the worst instead of the best purposes" (qtd. in Fisch 23–24). Fisch observes that this battle between high and low culture in British reviews of *Uncle Tom's Cabin* reflects a deeper anxiety that Stowe's novel would "'excite the passions'" of the masses, "leading them to a dangerous state of excitement approaching anarchy" (21). The criticism leveled against *Uncle Tom's Cabin* in British reviews would be echoed in attacks on the sensation novel in the 1860s (although worries in the latter arose over its power to rouse women rather than working class readers).

More than a decade before *Uncle Tom's Cabin* became an international "media event," to borrow William Warner's term, that inspired several British sensation narratives about imperiled mixed-race slaves, Britain was inundated with a range of American sensations. Shelley Streeby observes that this "culture of sensation" in 1840s America extended far beyond the popular fiction of George Lippard and Ned Buntline to the circulation of daily newspapers and "cheap, sensational story papers such as the *Flag of Our Union* and the *Star Spangled Banner*" (11) via the railway (itself a symbol of sensation), along with various forms of popular entertainment such as blackface minstrelsy. Although writers and critics in the United States almost never used the term to refer to their literature and culture, the British perceived "sensation" as a thoroughly American phenomenon. As a poem in an 1861 issue of *Punch* surmises,

> Some would have it an age of Sensation,
> If the age one of Sense may not be—
> The word's not *Old* England's creation,
> But New England's over the sea. ("Some Would Have It," lines 1–4)

Described in the poem as a "land of fast life and fast laws" (line 9), America was regarded as a place where everything from a steamer explosion or a senator "goug[ing] a friend / In the course of a lively debate" (lines 17–18) to the "last new sermon, or wash for the mouth, / New acrobat, planet or drama" was proclaimed a "sensation" (lines 25–26). The "pois'nous exotic 'Sensation'" (line 38) generated in America was quickly transported to Britain where audiences eagerly crowded theaters to see P.T. Barnum's shows, which featured such spectacles as Tom Thumb, Jenny Lind the "Swedish Nightingale," and Mrs. Bloomer, "an American, whose revolutionary championing of a short skirt and long loose trousers fascinated British women, to the bemusement, and often derision, of British men" (Diamond 3). British lecture halls in "small towns such as Ledbury and Ventnor in Hampshire and the Isle of Wight," as well as in "the major industrial centers such as Manchester, Birmingham, and Leeds" (Fisch 70) were also filled with spectators who came to see African-American abolitionists, including Frederick Douglass, Henry "Box" Brown, William Wells Brown, and William and Ellen Craft, describe in vivid detail how they escaped the horrors of American slavery. Indeed, between his arrival in 1845 and his return to America in 1847, Douglass delivered at least 300 lectures (Fisch 70). A blend of empirical inquiry and entertainment, the lectures allowed audiences to see the fugitive slaves display their scars along with instruments of torture while narrating their heroic flights to freedom.

The sensation generated by "Box" Brown and his fellow abolitionists threatened to draw attention away from the abolitionist cause, but also threatened to turn other African-American abolitionists into spectacles, since after Brown, their events were advertised by enthusiastic British abolitionists in a manner akin to the "oddities" who received top-billing in Barnum's shows. During William and Ellen Craft's visit to Bristol, for example, the British abolitionist J.B. Estlin wrote to his American colleague, Samuel May, "The Crafts ... had kind but not judicious, (& some vulgar) advisers in the North of England, neither their interest nor *respectability* (Ellen's espy) being properly consulted. Some of their hand-bills have been headed 'Arrival of 3 Fugitive Slaves from America'!! as if 3 monkeys had been imported, and their public appearance has been too often of the *exhibitive* kind" (qtd. in Fisch 120). Ellen Craft in particular stoked British fascination in the "almost white" slave who, as an article in *The Liberator* described, "may become a mother, but not a wife ... What passes under the name of marriage, is but a sort of concubinage, which exists not at the will of the parties, but at the will, the whim, caprice, or interest of another" (qtd. in McCaskill 521). Craft escaped this fate by running away to Philadelphia disguised as a white southern gentleman, her husband serving as her valet. However, the obsession with her whiteness recorded in the British press seems to reflect public curiosity in the concubinage (or sexual violence) between her master and mother that produced her fair complexion. Referring to her as a "gentle, refined-looking young creature of twenty-four years," the 1853 antislavery tract, "Singular Escapes from Slavery," declared that Craft was "as fair as most of her British sisters, and in mental qualifications their equal too" (qtd. in McCaskill 521). Both embodying and resisting the stereotype of the sexually imperiled mixed-race slave, Craft was a silent figure on the lecture hall's stage. Margaret McCaskill cites the following account of William Wells Brown and William Craft's joint lecture published in the Scotland *Advertiser*: "When the meeting was about to disperse, a general wish was expressed that Mrs. Craft, who was seated on the platform, should present herself to the audience. She seemed rather reluctant to do so, but on the persuasion of the Provost and several other gentlemen, she consented to offer a standing position on the left side of the former ... At first she seemed abashed, but the cheering continued, she courtesied [*sic*] gracefully, and retired." As McCaskill asserts, Craft had escaped the auction block only to be "displayed as a specimen of Victorian femininity" in the lecture hall (523).

Indeed, shortly after the Crafts arrived in England in 1851, the American abolitionist Henry Wright suggested that they be showcased in the Great Exhibition:

> Above all, an American slave-auction block must be there, with William and Ellen Craft on the block, Henry Clay as auctioneer, and the American flag floating over it ... Or, if they cannot be admitted *into* the Fair, with other specimens of American ingenuity and skill, they must be exhibited in some place *outside*, but near it, so that they can be seen and examined with convenience. (qtd. in Zackodnik 48–49)

The Crafts resisted being reduced to mere spectacles by instead promenading through the Crystal Palace on the arms of their British abolitionist friends. William Farmer, who accompanied William Craft through the exhibit, remarked, "This arrangement was purposefully made in order that there might be no appearance of patronizing the fugitives, but that it might be shown that we regarded them as our equals, and honored them for their heroic escape from slavery" (qtd. in Still 375). Upon reaching the American section of the exhibit, the abolitionists encountered Hiram Powers's statue, *The Greek Slave*. Farmer writes that William Wells Brown took a copy of the *Punch* cartoon, "The Virginia Slave. Intended as a Companion to Powers's 'Greek Slave,'" produced by one of their companions and "deposited it within the enclosure by the 'Greek Slave,' saying audibly, 'As an American fugitive slave, I place this 'Virginia Slave' by the side of the 'Greek Slave,' as its most fitting companion" (qtd. in Still 376). Brown's remarks underscore the disparity between the demure Greek slave with eyes cast downward and the weary Virginia slave with sorrowful eyes cast upward. Standing upon a podium decorated with crossed whips, the ebony slave is stripped to her waist and her wrists are bound with thick shackles. Unlike in Powers's work," Kate Flint explains, "the nakedness here cannot be seen as classical homage" (172). Whereas Powers's celebrated statue transmutes slavery into a classical form, *Punch*'s image of slavery is one of grotesque realism.

Why would the United States invite universal scrutiny by including Powers's statue in its section of the exhibition? Perhaps the prominent display of *The Greek Slave* reflects America's failure to realize that slavery, specifically as it was embodied by the figures of "almost white" slaves, had become an inextricable feature of its national identity. To the United States, Powers's statue was the pinnacle of American artistic achievement, but to British critics, she was not a Greek slave, but one of the persecuted mixed-race slaves they had heard about in the lectures of Douglass, William Wells Brown, and the Crafts. While America sought to defend its claim to the title of "model republic" (Fisch 71) under the critical eye of Mother England, in the years following the Great Exhibition and the publication of *Uncle Tom's Cabin*, novels, illustrations, songs, and dramas emblazoned with the word "quadroon" or "octoroon" saturated both American and British culture.[4] Ironically, in Britain, this "octoroon fever" was fueled by the Irish authors Captain Mayne Reid and Dion Boucicault, whose appropriations of the Tragic Mulatta's narrative dramatized the efforts of an innocent British hero to rescue the mixed-race heroine from the sexual perils of American slavery. Perhaps their interest in America's octoroons and quadroons was inspired by similarities between Ireland's struggle for independence and the ambiguous status of the mixed-race slave's unstable colonized body.

"Do you know what I am?": The tragic mulatta as sensation heroine

Born in Ireland, Captain Mayne Reid sailed for New Orleans in 1839 at the age of twenty-one. In the ten years that followed, Reid migrated from New Orleans to New York, working a variety of jobs along the way, including those as a private tutor, storekeeper, actor, and soldier (Dunae). Although he left America in 1849, settling in London after being wounded in the Mexican-American War, he earned his living by publishing novels based on his adventures in North and South America, such

---

4   In Britain, America's mixed-race slaves were the subjects of popular songs, such as Charles Hall's "The Octoroon Quadrilles" (1861), Albert Wagner's "The Octoroon Waltz" (1862), W.H. Montgomery's "The Octoroon Galop" (1862), and Carl Veley's "Quadroon Dance for the Pianoforte" (1867), as well as the heroines of such plays as *Quadroona, or, The blot upon Humanity* (1857) and *Quadroon, The Slave Bride* (1857).

as *The Rifle Rangers; or, Adventures of an Officer in Southern Mexico* (1850), *The Scalp Hunters; or, Romantic Adventures in Northern Mexico* (1851), *The Desert Home; or, The Adventures of a Lost Family in the Wilderness* (1852), and *The Boy Hunters; or, Adventures in Search of a White Buffalo* (1853). Reid's novels were so popular in both Britain and America that Barnum announced in newspapers, "I have succeeded in engaging Captain Mayne Reid to write a series of plays, founded on his own novels, to be produced simultaneously in England and the United States. Captain Reid's picturesque romances are equally popular on both sides of the Atlantic; millions have read them, and few without feeling intense interest in the scenes and characters he has created" (E. Reid 214–215). In 1856, Reid published what is arguably his most influential work, *The Quadroon; or, A Lover's Adventures in Louisiana*, a tale that was a departure from his romances of the American frontier. Although this novel capitalized on the recent public obsession with mixed-race slaves generated by *Uncle Tom's Cabin* and the lectures of African-American abolitionists touring Britain, Reid insists in a note to his preface, "The book is 'founded' upon an actual experience. It was written many years ago, and would have been then published, but for the interference of a well-known work, which treated of similar scenes and subjects. That work appeared just as the 'Quadroon' was about to be put to press; and the author of the latter, not willing to risk the chances of being considered an imitator had determined on keeping the 'Quadroon' from the public" (Reid 444). But unlike Stowe's novel, which focused on reuniting Cassy with the children born from her concubinage with a New Orleans lawyer, Reid's text transformed the Tragic Mulatta's narrative from one of seduction to one of courtship. Indeed, his interracial courtship plot introduces several new elements to the Tragic Mulatta's narrative, from which Boucicault and Braddon later borrowed in their adaptations.[5]

In these retellings the British hero travels to New Orleans, falls in love with the mixed-heroine, and resolves to rescue her from slavery and marry her despite America's anti-miscegenation laws. The English gentleman's unfamiliarity with the American South renders him unable to read the mixed-race heroine's racial identity. As Reid's narrative reveals, the allure of the "almost white" slave was coupled with a fear that her mixed-race body could pass into white society undetected. Although Reid's, Boucicault's, and Braddon's heroines do not conceal the secrets of their bodies, later sensation narratives pivoted on a character's fear

---

[5]   When *The Octoroon* debuted in London, Reid wrote a letter to the *Athenaeum* to address similarities between his novel and Boucicault's drama: "With regard to the 'Quadroon' and the Adelphi drama, the resemblance is just that which must ever exist between a melodrama and a romance from which it is taken; and when the 'Octoroon' was first produced in New York—January, 1860—its scenes and characters were at once identified by the newspaper critics of that city as being transcripts from the pages of the 'Quadroon'... It might be ... in good taste if the clever dramatist were to come out before the public with a frank avowal of the source whence his drama has been drawn" (E. Reid 138–139).

that their body would betray their true identity.[6] For example, Braddon's Lady Audley is anxious that the "dreadful taint" (374) of madness she inherited from her mother will expose her.

In Reid's novel, and the adaptations that followed, the British hero is unable to detect the secrets of the heroine's body on his own. When Reid's narrator, Edward Rutherford, travels to America in search of adventure on a steamer bound for St. Louis, he meets the Louisiana Creole, Eugénie Besançon, whom he helps swim ashore when the ship capsizes. When he later awakens at her plantation, recovering from his wounds, it is with "an impression on [his] mind of having beheld amid this confusion a face of extraordinary beauty—the face of a lovely girl!"—but it was not the face of Eugénie (72). He is informed by one of her slaves that the mysterious face, "of a strange type—its strangely-beautiful expression, not Caucasian, not Indian, not Asiatic," instead belongs to Aurore, a quadroon slave (95). At first repelled by his discovery, Edward's interest returns when he learns that she is an accomplished lady who can read, write, and play the piano. In Boucicault's adaptation, Zoe, the octoroon, is forced to reveal her racial identity to George Peyton, who was born in Louisiana but educated in Europe, when he proposes she become his "wife—the sharer of my hopes, my ambitions, and my sorrows" (153). Referring to herself as though she is a specimen of mixed-race, Zoe asks, "George, do you see that hand you hold? look at these fingers; do you see the nails are of a bluish tinge?" (Boucicault 153). She points out a similar "faint blue mark" in her eyes (153). Zoe's account of her body echoes the writings of eighteenth-century scientists, such as Jean-Baptiste Labat, who believed that fingernails could reveal signs of racial difference. However, the color of the mark varied from author to author. While Boucicault represents the mark as blue, Labat asserts that if a mark at the root of the nails is "white or nearly white, one may say with certainty that the child is a Mulatto" (qtd. in Sollors 155–156).[7] After revealing signs of her racial difference, Zoe asks, "Do you know what I am?" (153). When George declares that he does not know, Zoe, who exhibits more self-loathing than Reid and Braddon's heroines, exclaims, "I'm an unclean thing—forbidden by the laws—I'm an Octoroon!" (154).

The Tragic Mulatta's crime was in her mixed blood, which placed her outside the conventions of ideal womanhood. She did not commit murder, adultery, or bigamy, but like later sensation heroines, such as Lydia Gwilt, Aurora Floyd, Lady

---

[6]　While the sensation narratives of Reid and Boucicault are structured around the crime of the mixed-race heroine's free papers being stolen by the villain, other narratives of this period centered on the secret of race. In Charles Kingsley's *Two Years Ago* (1857) a mixed-race slave, Marie Lavington, escapes slavery by refashioning herself into the Italian diva, La Cordifiamma, yet she lives in constant fear that her body will eventually betray the secret of her ancestry. For further discussion of Kingsley's La Cordifiamma, see Kimberly Snyder Manganelli, "The Tragic Mulatta Plays the Tragic Muse," *Victorian Literature and Culture* 37 (2009): 501–522.

[7]　For an extensive discussion of this motif, see Werner Sollors's chapter, "The Bluish Tinge in the Halfmoon; or, Fingernails as a Racial Sign" in *Neither Black nor White Yet Both*.

Audley, and Lady Isabel Vane, the Tragic Mulatta was an affront to domestic stereotypes. As Lyn Pykett explains, "The sensation 'heroine'… offers a complex and contradictory range of significations, and is not simply the iconic embodiment of transgressive femininity, or a fantasy version of a feared or desired female power, as some critics have argued. If the sensation heroine embodies anything, it is an uncertainty about the definition of the feminine, or of 'woman'" (82). The British adaptations of the Tragic Mulatta's narrative highlight this questioning of Victorian femininity by offering a reversal of Walter Scott's *Ivanhoe* in which Ivanhoe chose the fair Rowena over the Jewess or "dark lady," Rebecca. In Reid's, Boucicault's, and Braddon's texts the British hero chooses the slave over the beautiful white heroine who puts aside her own desires to help the hero rescue the octoroon.

Race is not the only secret that must be detected in these British retellings of the Tragic Mulatta's narrative. The mixed-race heroine, with the help of the hero, must uncover whether she is a slave or free. As in the later works of Braddon, Collins, and Mrs. Henry Wood in which the sensation heroine's true social class must be revealed, the Tragic Mulatta's identity is defined solely by paper. During the height of the British sensation movement, the construction of Victorian identity in such works as *The Woman in White* frequently hinged on ephemeral documents such as Parish registries. In *Lady Audley's Secret*, for example, Lucy Graham's extensive paper trail finally proves that she is a bigamist. However, without documents to prove otherwise, sensation characters could exchange an old identity for a new one. In Reid's novel the question of Aurore's status begins as one of ownership—who owns Aurore? Eugénie Besançon or the villain, Gayarre? By the end of the novel, Reid reveals that neither of these people has a claim to Aurore because Eugénie's father had signed free papers for her, which Gayarre, a New Orleans lawyer, later stole and hid away.

Whereas Aurore believes that she is a slave and then discovers that she is free, Boucicault's stage drama reverses this plot. In *The Octoroon*, Boucicault depicts the mixed-race heroine, Zoe, as a free woman, who is later sold to pay off her deceased father's debts. Again, stolen documents are central to the plot. In Boucicault's play, a letter releasing the Peyton plantation from debt has been stolen by the villain, M'Closky. The villain's theft of Zoe's free papers and a letter releasing the estate from its debt (a letter which he commits murder to obtain) is motivated by more than his desire to possess the octoroon. It is also a skirmish in class conflict: M'Closky declares, "Curse their old families—they cut me—a bilious conceited, this lot of dried-up aristocracy. I hate 'em. Just because my grandfather wasn't some broken-down Virginia transplant, or a stingy old Creole, I ain't fit to sit down to the same meat with them…I'll sweep these Peytons from this section of the country" (Boucicault 145). In proposing to Zoe, he asks her to become his lover and partner in ruining the Peytons: "You shall be mistress of Terrebonne…these Peytons are bust; cut 'em; I am rich, jine me; I'll set you up grand, and we'll give these first families our dust, until you'll see their white skins shrivel up with hate and rage" (146). Realizing that she will not come to him of her own free will, M'Closky steals her free papers so he can then purchase her as a slave. In the American version of the play, Zoe commits suicide before the discovery of M'Closky's crime is revealed, while in British performances, George discovers the villain's treachery in time to rescue her. In both Reid and Boucicault's texts, the mixed-race heroine's fate hinges on whether the villain's theft of her free papers will be discovered.

Unlike Reid's Aurore and Boucicault's Zoe, Braddon's heroine, Cora, must not only detect her free status but also her race and the sexual transgressions that led to her birth. As Franny Nudelman explains in her examination of Harriet Jacobs's *Incidents in the Life of a Slave Girl* (1861): "The tragic mulatta is both the sign and site of sexual abuse: the color of her skin makes visible the fact that her forefathers raped her foremothers, and she is imagined as the object of the white man's continued violence" (947). In British versions of the Tragic Mulatta's narrative, the threat of sexual violence looms over the domestic space, but Reid's, Boucicault's, and Braddon's heroines do not suffer the physical or sexual violence that Child's Xarifa, Stowe's Cassy, or Brown's Clotel endure. Moreover, Reid and Boucicault show no interest in the possible sexual violence that resulted in the birth of their mixed-race heroines. Neither Reid nor Boucicault provide any background about Aurore's and Zoe's mothers and the possible violation they suffered at the hands of their masters. Braddon's text, however, narrates the violence suffered by the heroine's mother, Francilia, who is the quintessence of the Tragic Mulatta stereotype. Upon returning to her father's plantation, Cora is informed by the planter, Augustus Horton, "There is, perhaps, a secret; there is, it may be, a fatality which overshadows your young life. Be mine, and none shall ever taunt you with that fatal secret; be mine, and you shall be the proudest beauty in Louisiana, the queen of New Orleans ... be mine, and the debt owed me by your father shall be canceled" (53). Cora dismisses Augustus, but asks Toby, Francilia's slave-husband, to reveal the secret of her birth: "One day, Francilia left for Saint Louis, with her master and mistress. They were absent some weeks ... When Francilia—returned—she ... had become your father's mistress. She confessed all to me, with tears, and heart-rending grief!" (55). After her daughter is sent to England, Francilia is sold because the "glance of those mournful black eyes became an eternal reproach, which irritated and tormented" her master (56). She later commits suicide to avoid being raped by her new master. Cora, upon learning that she is the daughter of a slave, confronts her father and fiercely taunts him when he threatens to whip Toby for revealing the secret. "Strike me rather than him," she exclaims, "Prove to me, sir, that I am before my master; for if I am indeed your daughter, I demand of you an account of your conduct to my mother." When her father asks what more he could have done beyond trying to educate her abroad to protect her from the knowledge of her birth, Cora vehemently responds, "You could have refrained from giving me life!" (59).

In most sensation fiction, the exposure of secrets and past transgressions is contained by the domestic sphere. In *Lady Audley's Secret*, for example, forced by Robert Audley to confess, Lady Audley falls on her knees before her husband and admits all, including the "hereditary taint" of insanity from which she was desperate to escape. Everything in the novel has led up to this moment, when Robert Audley has gathered enough information to expose his aunt. However,

instead of being tried for the attempted murder of her first husband, Lady Audley is placed in a private asylum. The transgressions that occur in the domestic sphere are resolved in the privacy of the home rather than in the public court of law. However, in British and American abolitionist tales of the Tragic Mulatta, the mixed-race heroine is ripped from the comfort and privacy of the domestic sphere and subjected to public exposure and sale on the auction block. Exposed on the auctioneer's platform, she is stripped of her whiteness (Roach 217). She becomes a spectacle, in which her white body is read as black. In *Scenes of Subjection*, S. Hartman explains that the Tragic Mulatta's "white or near-white body ... makes the captive's suffering visible and discernable" (16). On the auction block, the Tragic Mulatta's body becomes a blank screen upon which are inscribed all the wrongs of slavery.

The auction block scenes in abolitionist fiction are sensational in two senses— not only is the body of the mixed-race slave exposed, but both spectators and readers are invited to witness her physical sensations. Since Cassy is a spectacle of fallen womanhood, Emmeline assumes the role of the virtuous and sexually imperiled Tragic Mulatta. Emmeline's exposure on the auction block is a figurative rape, yet the sensations she feels there make her more beautiful: "The blood flushes painfully in her otherwise colorless cheek, her eye has a feverish fire, and her mother groans to see that she looks more beautiful than she ever saw her before" (Stowe 343). She is "more beautiful" in her public shame because her flushed cheeks emphasize her whiteness. P. Gabrielle Foreman points out in her reading of Louisa Picquet's autobiography, *The Octoroon Slave and Concubine*, that Picquet "recognizes that enslaved women are placed in front of viewers not only to be bought, as she explains to Mattison derisively, but as spectacle, 'to be seen'" (515).

While the slave auction scene is a sensational moment in both American and British abolitionist texts, it becomes a climactic moment of exposure in British versions of the Tragic Mulatta's narrative. In Reid's, Boucicault's, and Braddon's texts public exposure on the auction block immediately follows the heroine's discovery of her true identity. As in the novels of Stowe and Brown, Reid's Tragic Mulatta, Aurore, "beautiful as ever," creates a sensation among the crowd witnessing her auction: "every voice became hushed, and every eye was bent upon her as she moved across the floor. Men hurried forward from distant parts of the hall to get a nearer glance; others made way for her, stepping politely back as if she had been a queen" (346). Reid invokes the image of Powers's *Greek Slave* in his description of Aurore standing "upon the dais like a statue upon its pedestal—the type of sadness and beauty" (350). Beautiful as she is, Aurore upsets this fantasy of exploited white womanhood because she wears the "head-dress worn by all quadroons—the 'toque' of the Madras kerchief, which sat upon her brow like a coronet, its green, crimson, and yellow checks contrasting finely with the raven blackness of her hair" (M. Reid 347).[8] The illustration that accompanies

---

[8]   Although New Orleans law required quadroons to wear the toque to distinguish themselves from white Creole women, there are no references to Aurore wearing this headdress while residing on Eugénie's plantation.

this scene, however, depicts the traditional image of the "white" woman for sale. Aurore does not wear the toque in the sketch, and like Stowe's Emmeline, her hair is undone. While Reid's text uses the toque as a sign of Aurore's racial difference, the accompanying illustration removes it, perhaps because the illustrator did not want to surrender the fantasy.

Braddon, similarly, calls attention to the female slave's status as an object to be seen as well as possessed: "Eyeglasses were raised, spectacles put on, and looks of insolent admiration were fixed upon the unhappy girl" (161). Her body is not only a spectacle, but it also becomes a focal point of social conflict as her British fiancé and his American rival feverishly bid against each other for ownership of her, one desiring her as his wife, the other as his mistress. However, whereas the slave auction is the pinnacle of Reid's and Boucicault's works, Braddon offers a different climax: Cora's confrontation with her new master, Augustus Horton. Though Cora briefly thinks of suicide, Braddon guides her away from the traditional fate of the Tragic Mulatta, explaining that, "to this girl, religiously educated, there was something horrible in the idea of suicide. It seemed a doubt of Providence even to think of this worst and last resource" (173). Instead, Cora decides to flee Horton's villa. Using the rope that bound her wrists at the slave auction, Cora climbs over the balcony and runs, but when Horton captures her, he says, "It is not the right of a master that I would exercise, but that of a lover ... The rigours of slavery are not for you. Reward my devotion with one smile, one word of encouragement, and a life of luxury shall be yours." Rebuffing him, Cora raises the rope that had previously bound her and says, "One step further, and it is I who will inflict upon you the chastisement of a slave, by striking you across the face" (175). Instead of rebelling against Victorian womanhood sexually as Lady Audley and Aurora Floyd do, Cora rebels against a narrative that would inflict on her the fate of her mother. However, although Cora defies her master verbally and threatens physical violence, her agency is short-lived. Before Horton can respond to her raised arm, her father and fiancé rescue her.

"If your fancy deign to act": The tragic mulatta's ending as British sensation fiction's beginning

The later sensation fiction of Braddon, Collins, and Wood culminates in the removal of all threats to the domestic sphere and the assertion of middle-class virtues. (Lady Audley awaits death in a Belgian asylum, Lydia Gwilt commits suicide, and a repentant Lady Isabel Vane dies of grief). Indeed, with few exceptions, these authors return both characters and readers to "a 'pure,' closed, middle-class" space (Gilbert 3). But what of the mixed-race heroines who were rescued from the tragic fates of their American predecessors, such as Child's Xarifa, who fractures her head against a wall, or Brown's Clotel, who dives into the Potomac? Reid's, Boucicault's, and Braddon's heroines survive their narratives, but the authors diverge in the endings they give to these mixed-race slaves and their English lovers. While Braddon's ending explicitly alludes to marriage, Reid's conclusion is more ambiguous:

> Would you have me paint the ceremony—the pomp and splendour—the ribbons
> and rosettes—the after-scenes of perfect bliss? Hymen, forbid! All these must
> be left to your fancy, if your fancy deign to act. But the interest of a 'lover's
> adventures' usually ends with the consummation of his hopes—not even always
> extending to the altar—and you, reader, will scarce be curious to lift the curtain,
> that veils the tranquil after-life of myself and my beautiful QUADROON. (444)

Although he seems to give readers license to imagine Aurore and Edward
united in marriage or in concubinage, the couple remains in Louisiana where
anti-miscegenation laws prohibit marriage. Reid's reluctance to imagine a
definitive ending for the quadroon reflects the conflict between sensation fiction,
which transformed America's mixed-race slaves into romantic figures, and the
abolitionist project seeking to expose the horrific truths of slavery. In Reid's
novel and the adaptations that followed, British literature subsumed America's
sensational abolitionist fiction and thereby changed the terms of the Tragic
Mulatta's consumption. Both Reid and Braddon obscure the realities of slavery to
offer their mixed-race heroines romantic endings.

Boucicault, however, resolved to give his octoroon a realistic conclusion. In
the original version of the play performed for American audiences in 1859, Zoe
commits suicide to escape the sexual violence that awaits her at the home of her
new master, M'Closky. Zoe's death not only restores order on the Peyton plantation
by leaving George free to marry the white heroine he rejected in favor of the
octoroon, but it also erases the "fatal mark" of difference from Zoe's eyes (154).
"Dat's what her soul's gwine to do," remarks a fellow slave, "It's going up dar,
whar dere's no line atween folks" (183). In this ending, Boucicault condemns an
institution and its adherents who would rather see the mixed-race slave kill herself
than marry her white lover. British audiences, however, rejected this ending when
the play premiered in London in 1861. Responding to pressure from the public and
the press, Boucicault revised the play's final act. In what has become known as the
English ending, George walks on stage after the infamous steamboat explosion,
carrying an unconscious Zoe in his arms. Many spectators welcomed this change,
including Reid, who praised Bouciault for having "had the good taste to alter
[the ending], restoring the beautiful quadroon to the happier destiny to which the
romance had consigned her" (E. Reid 139). But as Boucicault explains in a letter
to the London *Times*, this new ending rang false:

> In the death of the Octoroon lies the moral and teaching of the whole work. Had
> this girl been saved, and the drama brought to a happy end, the horrors of her
> position, irremediable from the very nature of the institution of slavery, would
> subside into the condition of temporary annoyance ... Has public sentiment in
> this country veered so diametrically on this subject ... that the feeling of the
> English people is taking another course? (qtd. in Sollors 356–357)

Indeed, a decade earlier, interracial unions between Englishmen and mixed-race
West Indian women had been the source of gothic horror in *Jane Eyre* (1847) and

racist caricature in *Vanity Fair* (1847).[9] Although Zoe survives, her unconscious state in the English ending seems to indicate a refusal on Boucicault's part to allow the sensation genre to diminish the realism of American slavery and anti-miscegenation laws.

Braddon's narrative, however, offers readers the ending that both Reid and Boucicault resist: "Cora is a happy wife in our dear native land—happy in the society of the father she loves, secure in the devotion of her proud English husband" (210). Braddon makes the interracial marriage of Cora and Gilbert explicit, but as Kimberly Harrison argues, "Braddon's narrative is less forceful in its antislavery design … While [Gilbert] Margrave goes to America with the goal of mitigating slavery, the novel ends without reference to a large-scale vision of abolition" (213). Instead, after a brief visit to Francilia's grave, Cora and Gilbert travel to England where American slavery is the subject of sensation dramas and penny dreadfuls rather than a way of life. Cora is reabsorbed into Britain's domestic sphere, but as I observe in a previous article, "Braddon does not explain how Cora's race fits within her new identity as an English wife. Do her British neighbors know she is a former slave? Or is this a secret of omission protected by her husband and father?" (517). Instead, Cora passes into the domestic realm, carrying the secrets of American slavery and miscegenation into her middle-class English home where she becomes what Henry James describes as one of "'those most mysterious of mysteries, the mysteries which are at our own doors'" (122).

Works Cited

"America," *English Woman's Journal* 13, no. 74 (1864): 91.

Boucicault, Dion. *The Octoroon. Selected Plays of Dion Boucicault*. Ed. Andrew Parkin. Washington, D.C.: Catholic University of America Press, 1987.

Braddon, Mary Elizabeth. *Lady Audley's Secret*. Ed. Jenny Bourne Taylor. New York: Penguin Books, 1998.

———. *The Octoroon; or, The Lily of Louisiana*. Ed. Jennifer Carnell. Hastings: Sensation Press, 1999.

Brontë, Charlotte. *Jane Eyre*. Ed. Richard J. Dunn. New York: W.W. Norton, 1987.

Dewaard, Jeanne Elders. "'The Shadow of Law': Sentimental Interiority, *Gothic* Terror, and the Legal Subject," *Arizona Quarterly* 62.4 (2006): 1–30.

Diamond, Michael. *Victorian Sensation: or, The Spectacular, the Shocking and the Scandalous in Nineteenth-Century Britain*. London: Anthem, 2003.

Dunae, Patrick. "(Thomas) Mayne Reid." *Victorian Novelists Before 1885*. Ed. Ira Bruce Nadel and William E. Fredeman. *Dictionary of Literary Biography Vol. 21*. Detroit: Gale Research, 1983. *Literature Resource Center*.

---

[9]   With Bertha Rochester's wild mane and "giant propensities" (Brontë 302) and Miss Rhoda Swartz's "big rolling eyes" and "woolly hair" (Thackeray 4), the mixed-race West Indian woman is constructed as a grotesque and dangerous presence that reflected British anxieties about racial mixing.

Gale. Clemson University. 31 May 2009 <http://go.galegroup.com/ps/start. do?p=LitRC&u=clemson_itweb>.

Fisch, Audrey. *American Slaves in Victorian England: Abolitionist Politics in Popular Literature and Culture*. New York: Cambridge University Press, 2000.

Flint, Kate. "Exhibiting America: The Native American and the Crystal Palace." *Victorian Prism: Refractions of the Crystal Palace*. Ed. James Buzard, Joseph W. Childers, and Eileen Gillooly. Charlottesville: University of Virginia Press, 2007. 171–185.

Foreman, P. Gabrielle. "Who's Your Mama?: "White" Mulatta Genealogies, Early Photography, and Anti-Passing Narratives of Slavery and Freedom." *American Literary History* 14.3 (2002): 505–539.

Gilbert, Pamela. *Disease, Desire, and the Body in Victorian Women's Popular Novels*. New York: Cambridge University Press, 1997.

Halttunen, Karen. "The Haunted House of Lyman Beecher, Henry Ward Beecher, and Harriet Beecher Stowe," *New Essays on Uncle Tom's Cabin*, ed. Eric J. Sundquist. New York: Cambridge University Press, 1986: 107–134.

Hartman, Saidiya V. *Scenes of Subjection: Terror, Slavery, and Self-Making in Nineteenth-Century America*. New York: Oxford University Press, 1997.

Jacox, Francis. "Brutish Affinities of the Human Face Divine." *The New Monthly Magazine* 132 (1864): 35–53.

James, Henry. "Miss Braddon." *Nation* 9 (November 1865): 593–595.

Kingsley, Charles. *Two Years Ago*. 2 vols. Leipzig: Bernhard Tauchnitz, 1857.

Manganelli, Kimberly S. "The Tragic Mulatta Plays the Tragic Muse." *Victorian Literature and Culture* 37 (2009): 501–522.

McCaskill, Margaret. "'Yours Very Truly': Ellen Craft—The Fugitive as Text and Artifact." *African American Review* 28.4 (1994): 509–529.

McKeon, Michael, ed. *Theory of the Novel: A Historical Approach*. Baltimore, Md.: Johns Hopkins University Press, 2000.

Mansel, H. L. "Sensation Novels." *Quarterly Review* 113 (April 1863): 481-514.

Nudelman, Franny. "Harriet Jacobs and the Sentimental Politics of Female Suffering." *ELH* 59.4 (1992): 939–964.

Oliphant, Margaret. "Novels." *Blackwood's Edinburgh Magazine* 102 (September 1867): 257–280.

———. "Sensation Novels." *Blackwood's Edinburgh Magazine* 91 (May 1862): 564-584.

Page, Norman, ed. *Wilkie Collins: The Critical Heritage*. London: Routledge & Kegan Paul, 1974.

Pykett, Lyn. *The 'Improper' Feminine: The Women's Sensation Novel and the New Woman Writing*. London: Routledge, 1992.

"Some Would Have It an Age of Sensation." *Punch* 41 (1861): 31.

Reid, Elizabeth. *Captain Mayne Reid: His Life and Adventures*. London: Greening & Co., Ltd., 1900.

Reid, Mayne. *The Quadroon; or, Adventures in the Far West*. Ridgewood, NJ: Gregg Press, 1967.

Roach, Joseph. *Cities of the Dead: Circum-Atlantic Performance*. New York: Columbia University Press, 1996.

Sollors, Werner. *Neither Black nor White yet Both: Thematic Explorations of Interracial Literature*. New York: Oxford University Press, 1997.

Still, William. *The Underground Railroad*. New York: Arno Press, 1968.

Stowe, Harriet Beecher. *Uncle Tom's Cabin*. Ed. Jean Fagan Yellin. New York: Oxford University Press, 1998.

Streeby, Shelley. *American Sensations: Class, Empire, and the Production of Popular Culture* Berkeley: University of California Press, 2002.

Thackeray, William Makepeace. *Vanity Fair*. Ed. Peter L. Shillingsburg. New York: W.W. Norton, 1995.

Zackodnik, Teresa C. *The Mulatta and the Politics of Race*. Jackson: University Press of Mississippi, 2004.

Chapter 8
Slavery, Sensation, and Transatlantic Publishing Rights in Mary Elizabeth Braddon's *The Octoroon*

Jennifer Phegley

It was not until the passage of the Chace Act of 1891 that foreign writers were offered copyright protection for their publications in the United States. Up until that time, American publishers were free to reprint foreign works at will without seeking permission from or providing compensation for the authors or original publishers. However, the works of American authors could be protected in England if they were published there first. This state of affairs led the *Critic* to proclaim in June 1851 that "the British Author is subjected to a double injury; the American writer shares the patronage of readers in England, and the American Publisher plunders him in America ... So long as the American Authors and Publishers can *command the monopoly, both of our markets and of their own*, they will *not* follow our example" ("The Copyright Question" 251). By February 1852, the *Critic*'s rhetoric had intensified: "We are not craving a boon; we are demanding justice. If American privateers were to seize our merchantmen, they would not ... be committing a greater crime than is the piracy of English books by American publishers. The demand for reparation would be swift in the one case; let it be no longer delayed in the others" ("International Copyright with America" 88). Other writers were even less judicious in their criticism, comparing the state of transatlantic copyright law not only to the piracy of a merchant ship, but also to slavery.[1]

While pirating intellectual property and enslaving people are by no means comparable, the trope of slavery was, nonetheless, commonly used to agitate for an international copyright law. The use of this trope suited the critique of American literary piracy because it doubled as a nationalistic argument against a country that continued to support a slave economy.[2] This tactic is exemplified in an 1847 *Punch* essay entitled "English Authors—American Booksellers." *Punch* complains that:

---

[1] Technically "piracy" is not any more appropriate a word to describe unauthorized reprinting than "slavery," considering that piracy implies the violation of a law. Since there was no international copyright law to be violated, there could be no true piracy. However, that didn't stop anyone from using the word to promote the cause of copyright law.

[2] Audrey Fisch argues that abolitionism "became a compelling touchstone for English nationalism" as it was used to redefine the public's sensationalized and voyeuristic fascination with slavery as "the philanthropic and noble interest of a superior nation called to witness the degradation of American society" (10, 8).

> An English writer is treated by America as America treats its negroes: he is turned into ready money for the benefit of the smart dealer who robs him. His brains are taken to market, and knocked down to the highest bidder ... Indeed, whilst America sells the bodies of blacks, and steals the brains of the whites, she ought to take second thoughts about a design for her flag. The stripes may remain ... lines of bloody red, red as the gore that trickles from a negro's back; but the stars, we think, admit of improvement. We would therefore have them rounded into dollars. (178)

This disturbingly graphic commentary points to the anger that the issue of international copyright inspired, particularly among the English literati.[3] *Punch's* critique, while much bolder, is similar to one made several years earlier by Charles Dickens in *American Notes for General Circulation.*

Dickens was perhaps the first to draw a connection between piracy and slavery with his own unauthorized reprinting of advertisements for the return of runaway slaves from U.S. newspapers. Meredith McGill notes that "Dickens explicitly links a depraved indifference to slavery" depicted in the ads "to the licentiousness of the American press" in its indiscriminate reprinting of his own fiction (110). The publication of *American Notes* followed Dickens's 1842 American lecture tour, during which his promotion of an international copyright agreement was met with a stunning lack of interest. His protests against the unfair treatment of foreign writers in the United States were not well received in a nation whose democratic ideals about publishing were intended to protect the interests of readers rather than writers, keeping printed materials cheap and easily accessible rather than protecting the authors who produced them. McGill points out that in the United States "Opponents of international copyright saw the decentralization of the literary marketplace as an important hedge against the tyranny of centralized power" (75). There is also evidence directly linking the nation's stance on copyright to slavery itself. As McGill argues, "southern legislators worried that granting copyrights to foreign authors would embolden British abolitionists and encourage the circulation of anti-slavery publications" (94). However, Melissa Homestead claims that the equation of slavery with the status of international copyright only increased and intensified as the century wore on and "slavery as a present reality receded" (147). In this largely semantic battle over the metaphorically equivalent practices of piracy and slavery, both camps claimed to be on the side of freedom and liberty. The question was who would be "enslaved" by copyright laws: authors (in the case of the status quo and from the perspective of the British) or readers and publishers (in the case of an international copyright agreement and from the perspective of many Americans).

Despite the over-heated rhetoric from England, American writers were not immune to problems caused by their own laissez-faire national publishing system, nor were they sheltered from British publishing pirates. Harriet Beecher Stowe, whose *Uncle Tom's Cabin* was nothing short of a literary and abolitionist

---

[3]   Melissa Homestead outlines similar arguments made in the American press (49–52).

phenomenon, had to fight to stop America's rampant culture of reprinting from depriving her of any claim to the profits from translations and adaptations of her work. Stowe lost a court battle to prevent foreign translations of her novel from being published in America on the grounds that these publications significantly transformed her original work into something new (Homestead 123). Though Stowe benefited from the sales of her novel in England, she also lost out on transatlantic publishing profits as a result of the proliferation of unauthorized English editions of *Uncle Tom's Cabin* in periodicals and single-volume reprints. Likewise, E.D.E.N. Southworth, who was eager to publish her work in England to avoid laws that funneled her U.S. profits to her estranged husband, serialized several of her novels in the *London Journal* between 1859 and 1869 (Homestead 46; King 136–137). As Homestead explains, "Even though she remained an American citizen, she could claim copyright in England on the basis of her residence in England at the time of publication, as long as her works were published in England *first*. She could *also* still claim U.S. copyright protection on the basis of her U.S. citizenship even though she resided abroad" (46). Despite the measures she took to control her profits by publishing on the other side of the Atlantic, some of her English publications were reprinted without permission or payment and even the *Journal*, which commissioned several original novels from her, was not above stealing her serials from American periodicals (King 161–162). While the British copyright and publishing systems were more refined, individual publishers still benefited from unauthorized foreign reprints. Though accusations of piracy were most often made by British writers, maintaining control over one's literary property once it crossed the ocean was problematic for writers on both sides of the Atlantic. For women writers, this problem was even more acute because, as Graham Law notes, "they were excluded from full membership in the emerging profession of authorship" and often had less control over their publishing rights (180).

Mary Elizabeth Braddon fought for greater control over her professional identity and her profits, with the help of her publisher and future husband John Maxwell. But even before taking direct action to maintain control of her publications, she entered the overwrought transatlantic publishing debate by pairing the subjects of slavery and transatlantic exchange in *The Octoroon; Or the Lily of Louisiana*. In taking on this serious copyright debate through the metaphor of slavery, Braddon worked to bolster her own reputation as a more serious peddler of sensational wares.[4] As Audrey Fisch argues, "Under the politically acceptable mantle of abolitionism ... the slave narrative offered Victorian readers the excitement for which they were eager: graphic scenes of torture, murder, sexual violence, and the thrill of escape (54). Yet, it also projected "the uncultured tastes" of the Victorian reading public—whose desire for sensationalism was seemingly insatiable—

---

[4]   This was a project Braddon took up more forcefully several years later in *Belgravia Magazine*. See *Educating the Proper Woman Reader* for a complete discussion of Braddon's project in *Belgravia*. In this case, I argue that Braddon was just beginning to experiment with ways to claim respectability for herself and her popular forms of writing.

"across the Atlantic onto the site of American slavery" (64). *The Octoroon* follows the fate of Cora Leslie, whose father—the owner of a plantation in Louisiana—sends her to England to be educated at the age of five. Cora, now a beautiful young woman, hears that her father has been injured in a slave revolt and insists on making an unannounced transatlantic visit to see him. This decision defies her father's demand that she stay away from New Orleans, which she assumes is linked to the unhealthy climate and to her mother's untimely death there. Once in the United States, Cora is shocked to discover the real reason she has been sent away: she is both Gerald Leslie's daughter and his slave. Her visit to America comes at the worst possible time; her father's property is being seized due to outstanding debts. Silas Craig, an unscrupulous money-lender, sets his sights on Cora, the most valuable of her father's assets. Silas captures and sells Cora to Augustus Horton—her schoolmate Adelaide's brother—who hopes to make her his mistress. Meanwhile, Gilbert Margrave, an Englishman who has romantically pursued Cora across the Atlantic, sets out to save her. Adelaide secretly sells Cora to Margrave to make up for mistreating her friend upon discovering her true identity. Finally, Margrave is able to marry Cora and take her back to England. While this brief summary does not do justice to the numerous twists and turns of the plot (and the completely separate cast of characters in a major subplot), it highlights how Cora's experience in the United States serves as a metaphorical example of the plight of British texts as they traveled across the Atlantic.

It is not a difficult leap to see how the transformation of the identity of an Englishwoman (according to her education and upbringing if not her birth) followed by her enslavement in the United States serves as an allegory for the repackaging and "enslavement" of British fiction by the speculative and exploitative American publishing system. Examining this novel within the context of Braddon's nascent publishing career provides both a practical and a metaphorical example of what could happen to British literature when it hit the "outlaw" American nation. Furthermore, the complexity of Cora's dual identity as Englishwoman and slave parallels Braddon's own conflicting roles as a known middlebrow author of sensation novels and an anonymous cheap penny press writer. Braddon's dual identity, like that of her character Cora, is under threat of exposure when her cheap sensation fiction crosses the Atlantic and is "outed" as the production of her pen.

Sensational copies: Plagiarism, theatrical adaptations, and penny press publishing

Braddon's life as a professional writer may best be described as one that was necessarily attentive to the complexities of adaptation, plagiarism, and the crossing of literary boundaries. Braddon's earlier career in the theater exposed her to a world that thrived on borrowing, copying, and imitation. Furthermore, as a former actress, Braddon was adept at forging multiple literary identities simultaneously, writing both cheap working class serials for penny magazines—such as *The Black Band*

(1862), *The Octoroon* (1862), and *The White Phantom* (1863)—and middlebrow novels destined for the circulating library—such as *Lady Audley's Secret* (1862), *Aurora Floyd* (1863), and *The Doctor's Wife* (1864). Wearing multiple masks as an author sometimes got Braddon into trouble. She was accused of plagiarism several times during her career for "rewriting" French works. For example, *The Doctor's Wife* was based on Gustave Flaubert's *Madame Bovary*, and *Circe* (1867) was a version of Octave Feuillet's *Dahlia*.[5] Jennifer Carnell speculates that, "[w]riting so much at once in the 1860s—numerous three deckers, penny bloods," as well as editing her own magazine and revising other people's books, may well have pushed her to fall back on old theater practices, such as borrowing plots from French novels, in order to keep up "with the frenetic pace" of her bourgeoning career (*Literary Lives* 220). Braddon's connections to the theater also facilitated alliances that would serve to advance her career in innovative ways.

It seems that Braddon was using theater productions as an inspiration for her cheap fiction and writing cheap fiction specifically to be adapted for the stage. The overlapping serialization of *The Black Band* (July 1, 1861–June 23, 1862) and *The Octoroon* (November 11, 1861–March 17, 1862) in the *Halfpenny Journal* facilitated a double-billed theatrical production performed at the Royal Pavilion Theater, Whitechapel timed to coincide with the debut of the *Octoroon* in print. These performances were advertised in the *Halfpenny Journal* to stimulate interest in the *Octoroon* and bring readers already hooked on *The Black Band* out to the theater. Carnell surmises that "Braddon sold a rough idea of what she was going to do in her serial to the theater ... or, perhaps, in exchange for allowing the dramatization of *The Black Band*, Braddon decided to use [the theater manager's son's] play about Cora, the Octoroon, as a basis for her serial" ("Introduction" xiv). Whatever the impetus for the novel and the subsequent stage production, Braddon's *Octoroon* and its dramatization at the Pavilion were certainly intended to capitalize on the popularity of Dion Boucicault's play of the same name.

Boucicault's *Octoroon*, which had opened to great acclaim in New York in 1859, debuted in London at the Adelphi Theater on Monday November 18th, a week after the debut of Braddon's novel by the same title. The *Halfpenny Journal* denied any relationship between the two works in a footnote placed at the bottom of the first page of the opening serial part of *The Octoroon*: "Octoroon signifies eighth blood, or the child of a Quadroon by a White. The word is asserted to be the invention of Mr. Boucicault, the dramatist, whose drama, 'The Octoroon, or Life in Louisiana' is said to have introduced it into the American vocabulary ... The tale appearing in this publication is not taken from the drama in question" (161). In its earlier advertisement for the serial, the magazine called *The Octoroon* "An entirely original, powerful, and most truthful Romance" ("Advertisement" 160). For the most part, this advertising was true, though the tales certainly had

---

[5]   Most notably, Braddon was embroiled in a battle with Frederick Greenwood of *The Pall Mall Gazette* who accused her of plagiarism in a series of articles in September and October 1867 (Phegley 121–122).

much in common. Braddon's novel includes a nationalistic message as well as a happy ending, both absent from Boucicault's drama. Carnell maintains that Braddon's *Octoroon* has more in common with *Uncle Tom's Cabin* and its stage productions—which Braddon had certainly seen and possibly performed in during the 1850s—and Thomas Morton's play *The Slave* (1818), in which Braddon played the quadroon heroine ("Introduction" xiii).[6] Furthermore, Carnell outlines some significant differences between Cora and Zoe, Boucicault's heroine, key among them the fact that Zoe knows she is a slave and commits suicide to avoid being sold into slavery at the end. This scenario was a famously unpopular ending against which English audiences and reviewers overtly revolted. That Boucicault was forced to revise his concluding scene for English audiences to bring it more in line with Braddon's plot is an interesting twist in this story of sensational copies.[7]

Braddon's extensive experience with adaptation, copying, and even plagiarism in the realms of theater and penny fiction did not translate into her work for the circulating library audience. Braddon had two parallel writing careers that ran side by side like train tracks—one for the cheap fiction audience and the other for middlebrow readers—and she was not eager to involve her middle-class sensation novels in such a promiscuous marketplace. She tried to maintain the separation of these career tracks by keeping her name off the penny press novels and promoting her "better" fiction with a signature.

---

[6]   Interestingly, in an unpublished response to the controversy in England over his play's ending, Boucicault cites as his own inspiration an actual case that even more closely resembles Braddon's plot:

> The author has been informed of the strong objection to the scenes in this drama representing the slave sale at which Zoe is sold and to avoid her fate commits suicide ... In reply to these remarks he begs to quote from a slave history the following episode: A young lady named Miss Winchester, the daughter of a wealthy planter in Kent had been educated in Boston where she was received in the best circles of society and universally admired for her great beauty and accomplishments. The news of her father's sudden death recalled her to Kentucky. Examination into the affairs of the deceased revealed the fact that Miss Winchester was the natural child of the planter by a quadroon slave; she was inventoried in chattels of the estate, and sold; the next day her body was found floating in the Ohio. (unpublished note, qtd. in Devere Brody 103)

[7]   There are other possible models for Braddon's story. The idea of a free "British" subject being enslaved in Louisiana echoes the true story of the sailor John Glasgow told in John Brown's *Slave Life in Georgia* (1855). Glasgow, a free black married to an Englishwoman, is captured and sold into slavery. Fisch argues that "Glasgow's story epitomizes the encroachment of American slavery on English freedom and on English power" (65). Braddon's novel likewise reflects another specter of slavery raised by Sarah Parker Remond while on her 1859 British lecture tour: sexual exploitation. *The Anti-Slavery Advocate* noted that, according to Remond, "If the veriest scoundrel, the meanest coward, the most loathsome ruffian, covets ... a defenceless female, provided she be known to be, ever so remotely, of African decent, she is in his power ... it has only to be known that she is the child of a slave and a slave herself, she is liable to the brutality of the vilest wretches" (qtd. in Fisch 87).

Despite Braddon's initial inspiration from and collaboration with the theater, as her career progressed she became more and more concerned about controlling her "brand" and the profits she earned. For example, she sued T.H. Lacy in the Court of Chancery to prevent unauthorized theatrical adaptations of *Lady Audley's Secret* and *Aurora Floyd* from being published. She won the case, though on the narrow grounds of publication rather than performance (Wolff, *Sensational Victorian* 145–146). Still, the fact that Braddon freely offered her penny press fiction for theatrical productions but sought to restrict the adaptation of her middlebrow novels further indicates her desire to keep what she saw as distinct literary forms in their separate spheres. The proliferation of unauthorized versions of her work was even more pressing in the United States since it was difficult to find out how her name and property were being used and nearly impossible to control it.

"At the mercy of any American publisher": Braddon's battle against piracy

Braddon's effort to prevent the piracy of her works was spearheaded by her partner and publisher, John Maxwell. Maxwell was the maverick publisher who helped Braddon break into the literary business by publishing her work in his periodicals (he also hired her mother to edit his *Halfpenny Journal*). Soon, Braddon was living as well as working with Maxwell and the two of them proved to be a formidable publishing team.[8] Maxwell's array of journals facilitated Braddon's dual authorial identities. Weekly working-class family magazines such as the *Halfpenny Journal* housed her "penny bloods" while the more prestigious monthlies *Temple Bar* and *Belgravia* were home to her triple-deckers aimed at the circulating library reader.[9] While all of Braddon's early fiction was of a sensational nature, the

---

[8]   The fact that Maxwell was married (his mentally ill wife was living in Ireland under the care of relatives) was damaging to her reputation, but it may well have been good for her finances. As Carnell points out, if they had been married before 1874 (when his first wife died), Braddon's "earnings would have been sequestered to pay his debts" when in 1862 Maxwell was forced to mortgage his magazines to secure what he owed (*Literary Lives* 151). Instead, Braddon's novels brought her a great deal of money that allowed her to purchase several homes that she shared with Maxwell and their brood of legitimate and illegitimate children.

[9]   The success of *Lady Audley's Secret*, published in *The Sixpenny Magazine* and issued by Tinsley's Publishing as a three-volume circulating library novel, seems to have inspired Braddon's two-tiered publishing plan. Carnell points out that "*Lady Audley's Secret* went through eight editions in three volumes in three months" (*Literary Lives* 147). After this breakthrough, Braddon was able to simultaneously fill John Maxwell's penny press periodicals with anonymous serials and generate better, signed novels for his middle-class magazines. However, the republication of both *Lady Audley's Secret* and *Aurora Floyd* in the working-class *London Journal* complicate this conception of Braddon's two-tier career. Braddon would also go on to publish two of her last penny dreadfuls as three-volume novels: *The Banker's Secret* (serialized in the *Halfpenny Journal* from November 21, 1864, to June 5, 1864) became *Rupert Godwin* (1867) and *Diavola* (serialized in the *London*

cheaper novels emphasized fast-paced plots, criminality, and heroism and featured stereotyped characters engaged in dialogue more than in self-reflection. Although her middle-class sensation fiction was criticized for being overly plot-driven and too concerned with female criminals, these novels were markedly different in their more complex language and style, more carefully developed plots, and more fully drawn characters. Braddon acknowledged this distinction in a December 1862 letter to Edward Bulwer Lytton:

> I do an immense deal of work which nobody ever hears of, for Half penny & penny journals. This work is most piratical stuff, & would make your hair stand on end, if you were to see it. The amount of crime, treachery, murder, slow poisoning, & general infamy required by the Half penny reader is something terrible. I am just going to do a little paracide [*sic*] for this week's supply. (Wolff, "Devoted Disciple" 11)

The two novels Braddon would have been working on at the time were *Aurora Floyd* for *Temple Bar* and *The White Phantom* for the *Halfpenny Journal*. Carnell points out that "it was not widely known that Braddon was moonlighting amidst the mysterious world of lower class magazines and penny part novels" (*Literary Lives* 200). In the early days of her success, the advertisements on the covers of the *Halfpenny Journal* promote the division of her works into separate categories. M.E. Braddon is touted as the author of *The Lady Lisle* (1862) and *The Captain of the Vulture* (1862)—serials appearing in the *Welcome Guest* and the *Sixpenny Magazine* that aspired to reach some middle-class readers—but there is no mention of her name as the primary contributor to the *Halfpenny Journal* itself. As Carnell argues, "even at this early stage she was keeping her Braddon work separate from the hack work" (*Literary Lives* 210).

This advertising strategy indicates that the novels originally published in Maxwell's the *Welcome Guest* and *Sixpenny Magazine* were considered of a slightly higher level than those that appeared in the *Halfpenny Journal*, though they had overlapping audiences among the working and lower-middle classes. In partnership with Maxwell and his array of magazines that spanned the entire range of target audiences, Braddon was wildly successful in all sensational

---

Journal from October 27, 1866, to July 20, 1867) was published as *Run to Earth* (1868) (Wolff, *Sensational Victorian* 122–125; Carnell, *Literary Lives* 383). Perhaps in these cases the promise of making a quick profit outweighed the desire to deliver separate kinds of sensational fiction to separate audiences. Or, perhaps these reprinting decisions were made by Maxwell who was savvy at garnering as much money as possible from Braddon's works in a variety of publication formats. However, by 1863 Braddon would have been much less motivated by profit as she had earned enough to set her up for life: "Affluence was at hand, literary hackwork abandoned, and the future rendered secure, all within five years after the first appearance of *Lady Audley's Secret* (Wolff, *Sensational Victorian* 142). Regardless of these complications in sorting out Braddon's dual authorial identities, it holds true that she was increasingly moving away from working-class audiences toward middle-class readers as her career progressed.

forms, much like her literary alter ego, Sigismund Smith. Smith, who appears in *The Doctor's Wife* (1864) as a penny dreadful writer and then reemerges as a three-volume novelist in *The Lady's Mile* (1866) with the more sophisticated surname of Smythe, follows a career path similar to Braddon's own. Robert Wolff characterizes Smith/Smythe as a satirical self-portrait that Braddon used to assert that there was "very little difference between a penny-dreadful and a three-decker, except for the number of murders needed: for a three-decker, one was enough; for a penny-dreadful there was no limit" (*Sensational Victorian* 132). Yet, Braddon clearly saw other differences in her various fictional forms, differences that were marked enough that she only wanted her name attached to those she considered to be of higher quality. While the distinction may have been slight, there was, nonetheless, a distinction to be made and Braddon and Maxwell insisted upon making it.

The more famous and popular Braddon became, the more desirable a target she was for American publishers who reprinted each new novel without her permission and without upholding the distinctions Braddon made in the English press. However, Braddon and Maxwell worked together to mitigate her losses. For example, Maxwell cut a deal with Harper and Brothers, selling advance sheets of his star writer's works for authorized publication in *Harper's Weekly* and *Harper's Bazaar* as well as in cheap bound editions.[10] Yet these efforts took time to put into place and did not immediately solve the piracy problems Braddon faced, particularly with her *Halfpenny Journal* serials, which "achieved immediate book publication in pirated, crudely printed paperback form in America" (Wolff, *Sensational Victorian* 119). In 1866 Braddon expressed outrage at her lack of control over her work in the United States in a letter to the editor of the *Round Table*. This American magazine had reviewed a novel called *What is This Mystery?* described by its publisher as "Miss Braddon's latest and best" work. In contrast to this flattering characterization, the *Round Table* review claims that the real mystery is how "any one could write such a supremely silly book" filled with "rampant vulgarity and low-mindedness" that could only be considered "delightful" by milliners and lady's maids ("A Novel by Miss Braddon"). In response, Braddon angrily informs the editor "that I never wrote a novel with the title given, and that I have never had any correspondence with its publishers, who, nevertheless, announce their book as printed from my 'advance sheets.'" She goes on to admonish American publishers by imagining the tables turned:

---

[10]   *Harper's Bazaar* may have first published an unauthorized Christmas story by Braddon in December 1868. During March and April of 1870, they serialized her novella *My Sister Caroline*, originally published in her own *Belgravia Magazine*. It seems likely that this was the first publication in a series of authorized copies as a torrent of her novels soon appears: *The Lovel's of Arden* (April 15, 1871–March 30, 1872); *To the Bitter End* (March 2, 1872–January 25, 1873); *Lost for Love* (April 25, 1874–November 28, 1874); and *Hostages to Fortune* (February 20, 1875–October 30, 1875). Graham Law provides a useful list of Braddon's novels published in *Harper's Weekly* and several other American periodicals through agreements with W.F. Tillotson beginning in 1873 (232–237).

"should such trading ever arise in England, then perhaps, American statesmen will see the urgent necessity for an international copyright, to protect the characters of American writers from the outrageous dishonesty into which unrestrained literary piracy can degenerate. For the present, the reputation of every English writer is at the mercy of any American publisher" ("A Letter from Miss M.E. Braddon"). In her spirited self-defense, Braddon disregards the fact that British publishers also pirated American works and instead casts England as a place where authors are treated fairly by self-controlled publishers and the United States as a place where authors are abused by indiscriminate printing practices. She also conveniently fails to mention that she did, in fact, write the novel in question. *What is This Mystery?*, as she well knew, was a copy of her penny-press novel, *The Black Band*. The important point here is that Braddon took action to protect her anonymity when threatened with the collapse of her two-tiered authorial identity by the unauthorized U.S. publication of her penny press novels with her name prominently displayed.

In the same issue in which Braddon's letter appeared, the *Round Table* printed its reply. In "Miss Braddon and International Copyright," the editors defend their critique of the novel and their exposure of Braddon as its author. They point out that Braddon "studiously avoids" denying that she wrote the novel and cite this omission as proof that she is indeed the author. Perhaps surprisingly, given the vehemence with which the magazine belittles Braddon's writing, the editors come to her defense on the issue of international copyright and the unscrupulous behavior of some American publishers:

> Literary piracy is of course much more shocking to people who are fortunate enough to live in a community where literary property is respected; and our publishers are so much in the habit of filching English books—and our public in that of profiting by it—that even when the offense is aggravated by a direct misrepresentation—rebaptizing a work and professing to have received the author's advance sheets—it is more than doubtful whether the exposure will have any constraining influence in the future ... The fault lies in our own legislature, which cares little for our own authors because they are few and therefore weak, and nothing for foreign ones, because they cannot help themselves.

While authorizing Braddon's complaint about piracy, the *Round Table* stands by its ridicule of her penny-press sensationalism and disregards her efforts to keep her cheap serials anonymous.

Back in England, copies of Braddon's letter to the *Round Table*, which were sent to several London papers, inspired a series of articles in the *Athenaeum* called "The Manufacture of Novels" printed between February and March of 1867.[11] These articles focus on the reprinting of Braddon's penny-press fiction under new titles in America and speculate about her authorship of *What is This Mystery?* and *Nobody's Daughter*, another work serialized with her name on it in the *New*

---

[11] I would like to thank Jennifer Carnell for calling my attention to this series of articles.

Correspondents weighed in on the "squabble" raised by "a Grub Street tempest on the other side of the Atlantic" and sought to discredit Braddon and other penny-press novelists for reprinting works under different titles on the grounds that the practice misled and even defrauded readers (February 16). The correspondents first demanded an explanation from Braddon and then from Maxwell, claiming that the interests of literature at large were at stake. Maxwell took the bait, defending Braddon's right to maintain her anonymity and her ability to authorize the reprinting of her work while denying "the right to demand information" from authors and protesting against the "bad taste of threatening Miss Braddon" (March 9). The following article concludes that Maxwell's reluctance to explain the origins and authors of these novels provides "an instructive peep into" his role as overseer of "a factory of novels for the halfpenny press" that are the result of a "patchwork of many 'hands'" (March 16). Interestingly, this statement equates Braddon's writing with an image of industrialized authorship that is akin to slavery.

Finally, in May of 1867, the focus was shifted away from the protection of Braddon's anonymity and toward the condemnation of immoral publishing practices across the Atlantic in a two-part article called "English Authors in America." Maxwell contends that while the *Sunday Mercury* "honestly paid" for *Nobody's Daughter*, the editors must not have protected the advance sheets from "rival American publishers, who live upon the policy of stealing as much literature as they can." Messrs. Hilton & Co., the New York publishers of *What is This Mystery?*, also entered the fray, claiming that they published Braddon's novel under a new title and with the addition of her name to avoid the novel's association with another novel called *The Black Band*. The Hiltons unwittingly make Maxwell's point for him by asserting that Braddon was, in fact, the author of the work that they "fairly" stole from an English periodical rather than from American advance sheets as Maxwell accused (May 16). Their own letter to the *Athenaeum* claims:

> Almost instantly, we were assailed ... and charged with having imposed upon the reading public, through palming off, as a work of Miss Braddon's the production of some obscure novelist. The lady herself or some person representing her interests, thought proper to encourage presumption of fraud ... whereas our offense appears to have consisted in the fact of reprinting, without her express sanction, from a London publication, a work for which the London publisher had, as we presume, paid its market value. (May 11)

Thus, the American publisher denies any wrongdoing since piracy is, after all, only a crime if a law exists to prevent it. Maxwell provided one final protest against the exposure of Braddon's penny-press fiction in the United States by arguing that "Messrs. Hilton & Co. appear to think that, by adding insult to injury, they can extenuate their conduct and cast aside the opprobrium which their dishonesty should entail. They do not attempt to deny the charges against them ... they had no justification for ascribing the authorship to Miss Braddon ... whose name they most unfairly used for their own dishonest purpose" (May 18). While Maxwell argued that American publishers blew Braddon's cover and thereby sullied her efforts to maintain separate authorial identities, this dubious distinction between sensational forms was met with skepticism by both the English and the American correspondents who continued to thwart her use of anonymity.

The public exposure of Braddon's dual authorial identities had serious consequences. For Braddon, it meant the loss of both status and profit. As a result, she and Maxwell sought new ways to reign in licentious transatlantic publishing practices. The most effective solution was Maxwell's formation of an alliance with W.F. Tillotson's Fiction Bureau, which in 1882 began selling the rights to publish the works of several British authors to a consortium of American newspapers and periodicals. Graham Law explains that in December of that year, Tillotson "prepared a detailed circular advertising for a coterie of state-wide papers to take up advance sheets of Braddon's latest work" for £25 per paper (73). Maxwell worked with the Fiction Bureau and, later, with another literary syndicate, W.C. Leng, to ensure that while Braddon's work would be copied into many local newspapers, she would receive a substantial flat sum payment, ranging from £350 to £1,250 per book. Maxwell played a major role in the growth and development of these syndicates, yet he continued to fear that Tillotson's practice of sending advance sheets to U.S. newspapers too early "risked allowing American newspaper publication to conclude before the first complete appearance in a British journal, thus perhaps imperiling the entire British copyright" (Law 81). This partnership was productive but still perilous. Law argues that Braddon's reputation as someone who had "breached bourgeois social and sexual conventions" in her own life and her fame as a writer of "sensational works which transgressed the social and sexual norms of domestic fiction" fit perfectly with her "engagement in modes of fictional production that challenged the conventions of the dominant mode of 'gentlemanly' publishing of the mid-Victorian period" (170–171). Furthermore, Braddon's personal and professional partnerships with Maxwell allowed her to negotiate more forcefully than most women writers could. With Maxwell's support, Braddon entered into agreements that would eventually transform transatlantic publishing practices.

"The man who makes money is *respectable*": *The Octoroon* crosses the Atlantic

Braddon's and Maxwell's relationships with literary syndicates came too late to combat the unauthorized reproduction of the *Octoroon* in the United States. The novel seems to have been first published in the U.S. by DeWitt publishing of New York in 1869. Other American editions of the novel appear to be based on this presumably pirated copy, including two undated 1800s editions published in Chicago by W.B. Conkey and Homewood Publishing and an 1895 edition published in Philadelphia by Henry Altemus. All of these American editions advertise Braddon as the author. They also all have one very significant chapter missing. This chapter, entitled "The Lawyer's Map of the United States," focuses on Silas Craig, the most villainous character in the novel, whose many despicable acts include selling Cora into slavery. Surely it is no coincidence that this chapter was cut from the pirated American edition of the novel as it implicitly decries the practice of literary piracy by explicitly critiquing the American obsession with making a profit at any cost.

At the opening of this excised chapter of *The Octoroon*, we are shown Craig's office, which is decorated with an enormous map of the United States framed in "polished ebony, handsomely carved in a floriated pattern, and ornamented on each side with the arms of America" (42). This ornate image of the nation becomes a more threatening specter of deception when it is revealed that the map happens to hide the entrance to a secret gambling saloon where "There were no exclamations, no oaths, no laughter, no animation. There was the solemn calm of men whose very lives are staked upon the venture; the awful silence of men whose inmost souls revolve with every turn of the fatal wheel" (43). Those who enter the gambling hall are described as willing but naïve participants who leave as empty and will-less shells of their former selves, people whose "vast riches were melting nightly away" while they were "powerless to resist the fiend" (43). American publishers who reprinted the *Octoroon* may well have eliminated this chapter in protest against its relentless characterization of the United States as a nation that preys on people in the name of profit. As one character observes earlier in the novel, in America "the man who makes money is *respectable*, no matter by what shameful means he makes it. Userer, oppressor of the helpless, trafficker in human flesh—what matters by what hideous trade the gold is got? The yellow guineas will not sparkle less—the hollow world will not be less ready to bow to the *respectable* member of society" (25). Annette Van argues that by mid-century, England felt threatened by America's growing economic importance and therefore often perpetuated "the stereotype of the greedy, amoral American" while also harnessing the financial growth of the U.S. by "promoting America as a market and Americans as consumers for English exports" (80). Yet, Braddon's yoking of the gambling house with the slave auction highlights the depravity of all American markets, including the book market. As Van argues, such a characterization "preserve[s] the integrity of English culture while instantiating a logic of transatlantic relations wherein England can play both innocent victim and power player in a world experiencing the rapid emergence of global capitalism" (95). *The Octoroon* dramatizes Braddon's version of this economic "power play" as she depicts Cora as an innocent victim, travelling across the Atlantic to be exploited in the American marketplace.

As soon as Cora Leslie crosses the Atlantic, she is violated in ways that she could not previously have imagined as an Englishwoman. Indeed, she is "an utter stranger in her native land" (22). Cora is now regarded as a commodity and she falls prey to those around her who hope to exploit her for their own benefit. While Adelaide Horton suddenly refuses to see her old friend out of a sense of propriety, her brother's interest in Cora as a sexual conquest is increased. Cora's changing status weakens her and makes her more vulnerable and attractive prey. When

Cora refuses to accept Augustus Horton's offer to marry her and pay her father's debts, he hatches a plan to buy Cora and make her his slave and, presumably, his mistress. In one crucial scene illustrated for the original serial, Augustus Horton publicly reads a paragraph from the newspaper in front of Cora in order to humiliate her. The paper announces that "The conduct of Mr. Leslie in daring to foist the child of one of his slaves upon the highest circles of society, merits the punishment with which he has met. The citizens of New Orleans have shown their indignation at his offense ... Gerald Leslie walks the streets of his native city a stranger, a ruined man" (94). Despite this denouncement of her father and, implicitly of herself, as outsiders who have violated social rules, Cora resolves not to react to the sensationalized report or to Augustus' ungentlemanly behavior in reading it in public.

Though the news of Cora's status spreads quickly in the local press, she is the last to know that she is her father's property and will be sold to cover his debts. When Gerald Leslie's slave Toby tells Cora that her mother died as the result of her father's neglect, she finally confronts her father about his conduct. He defends himself by declaring: "My crime is the crime of all. Is the punishment to fall on me alone? ... Do you know that every citizen in New Orleans would blame and ridicule me for my devotion to you? Do you know that I am even amenable to the laws of Louisiana for having dared to educate your mind and enlighten your understanding?" (60). Leslie absolves himself of responsibility for his immoral acts because of the irresistible cultural economy of slavery, just as the American publishers Braddon and Maxwell tussled with blamed their actions on a publishing system that was beyond their control.

Luckily for Cora, Margrave—"the artist, the poet, the enthusiast!" and inventor of a machine "which might, as he fondly hoped, supersede slave labour" (44–45)—endeavors to rescue her from slavery (much as Maxwell tried to defend his wife's work from American pirates). Margrave does not forget Cora's innate value as a woman even when she becomes a slave. Indeed, he not only hopes to save Cora from her cruel fate, but also to bring about an end to slavery through scientific innovation. As an Englishman, he is able to resist the negative press coverage and new packaging she has received in America and commits himself to marrying her and taking her back to England regardless of the repercussions. As he tells Adelaide when she refuses to see Cora, "Whatever danger I may incur of being either ridiculed or persecuted, I shall never conceal my detestation of prejudice and tyranny, and my sympathy with the weak ... Pardon me, if I speak warmly on the subject, Miss Horton; it is not to be supposed that you and I should think alike. We represent the opposite sides of the Atlantic" (47). Margrave helps Cora escape and Augustus then signs the missing girl over to his sister in disgust instead of pursuing her in the press as he had threatened to do. With the power of the press and of her brother neutralized, Adelaide returns to her English roots and decides to relinquish her ownership of Cora to Margrave, who is then free to make her his wife rather than his slave.[12]

---

[12]　There is no mention of whether or not Margrave frees Cora before marrying her.

The novel concludes with Cora and Gilbert visiting her mother's tombstone, on which "the star of hope shone" as "a prophetic whisper in the hearts of both" foretelling "of a day when the terrible institution which enables man to traffic in the body and soul of his fellow men, should be only a dark memory of the past" (209). Braddon describes the couple's voyage back to England as a return to the true land of freedom and liberty, reversing the myth of America by projecting it back across the Atlantic. Braddon's plot echoes what Homestead argues was a commonly drawn parallel "between the slave trade, in which traders 'stole' people from Africa and transported them to Europe and the Americas, where they were forced to work without compensation, and international literary piracy, in which authors' properties produced by their labors, rather than the authors' bodies, are transported across the Atlantic and 'put to work' for the financial benefit of piratical publishers" (51). In the *Octoroon*, America is not a land of freedom and liberty, but of enslavement, for both people and texts. Furthermore, it is not only the publishers who violate standards of common decency, but the press, which takes every opportunity to sensationally exploit people's misfortunes for profit.

The plot and transatlantic publishing adventures of the *Octoroon* serve as an apt analog to Braddon's own attempts to establish herself as what may seem to be an oxymoronic figure: the respectable sensation novelist. By keeping her penny press fiction a secret and promoting her circulating library sensation novels with her name, Braddon endeavored to raise the level of critical discourse surrounding sensationalism while continuing to please a vast reading public with her exciting plots and characters.

Works Cited

Advertisement for *The Octoroon* in the *Halfpenny Journal* (November 11, 1861): 160.

Braddon, Mary Elizabeth. "A Letter from Miss M.E. Braddon." *Round Table* 4:51 (August 25, 1866): 57.

———. *The Octoroon, or the Lily of Louisiana.* Ed. Jennifer Carnell. Hastings: The Sensation Press, 1999.

[———]. *The Octoroon, or The Lily of Louisiana. Halfpenny Journal* (November 18, 1861): 161.

Brody, Jennifer DeVere. "The Yankee Hugging the Creole: Reading Dion Boucicault's *The Octoroon.*" *Creole: The History and Legacy of Louisiana's Free People of Color.* Ed. Sybil Kein. Baton Rouge: Louisiana State University Press, 2000. 101–116.

Carnell, Jennifer. "Introduction." *The Octoroon, or the Lily of Louisiana.* Hastings: The Sensation Press, 1999. vii–xviii.

———. *The Literary Lives of Mary Elizabeth Braddon: A Study of Her Life and Work.* Hastings: The Sensation Press, 2000.

"The Copyright Question." *Critic: London Literary Journal* (June 1851): 251–252.

"English Authors—American Booksellers." *Punch* (April 24, 1847): 178.

"English Authors in America." *Athenaeum* (May 11, 1867): 623–624.

"English Authors in America." *Athenaeum* (May 18, 1867): 663.

Fisch, Audrey. *American Slaves in Victorian England: Abolitionist Politics in Popular Literature and Culture*. Cambridge: Cambridge University Press, 2000.

Homestead, Melissa. *American Women Authors and Literary Property, 1822–1869*. New York: Cambridge University Press, 2005.

"International Copyright with America." *The Critic: London Literary Journal* (February 1852): 88.

King, Andrew. *The London Journal, 1845–83: Periodicals, Production, and Gender*. Aldershot, Hampshire, England: Ashgate Press, 2004.

Law, Graham. *Serializing Fiction in the Victorian Press*. Houndmills, Basingstoke, Hampshire: Palgrave, 2000.

"Manufacture of Novels." *Athenaeum* (March 9, 1867): 323.

"The Manufacture of Novels." *Athenaeum* (February 16, 1867): 221–222.

"The Manufacture of Novels." *Athenaeum* (March 16, 1867): 354.

McGill, Meredith. *American Literature and the Culture of Reprinting, 1834–1853*. Philadelphia: University of Pennsylvania Press, 2003.

"Miss Braddon and International Copyright." *Round Table* (August 25, 1866): 53.

"A Novel by Miss Braddon." *Round Table* (July 14, 1866): 437.

Phegley, Jennifer. *Educating the Proper Woman Reader: Victorian Family Literary Magazines and the Cultural Health of the Nation*. Columbus: Ohio State University Press, 2004.

Van, Annette. "Ambivalent Speculations: America as England's Future in *The Way We Live Now*." *Novel: A Forum on Fiction* (Fall 2005): 75–96.

Wolff, Robert Lee. "Devoted Disciple: The Letters of Mary Elizabeth Braddon to Sir Edward Bulwer-Lytton, 1862–1873." *Harvard Library Bulletin* 22 (1974): 5–35, 129–161.

———. *Sensational Victorian: The Life & Fiction of Mary Elizabeth Braddon*. New York: Garland Publishing, 1979.

Chapter 9
Business Sense and Sensation: The Transatlantic Trade in Domestic Drama

Kate Mattacks

I offer a sincere expression of regret that I have at length allowed myself to follow the disreputable example of some New York and Boston publishers and appropriate property to which I have no moral right. I have for years wholly repudiated the practice of pilfering from Americans, and should never, at any time, have assumed what I consider to be a degrading, if not dishonest position, had I not been the victim of hundreds of instances of similar delinquency from the other side of the Atlantic. The most annoying and injurious instance of this is the case of "The Amateur's Guide," which in design and treatment, was altogether original ... I did not expect that the gentleman who terms himself my agent in New York should hurriedly thrust a mutilated version of it on the American public with a *studious withholding of my name from the book altogether*, and that my own Preface should be copied, and signed by Tony Denier as *the author of the book*. Sympathising with the honest movement now agitating the public attention in America for a reciprocal protection of literary property—I have taken this step to aid it, and deliberately assert that had Mr Daly possessed the right to introduce this drama into England and her Colonies—its merit is such that he might have hoped to derive an important pecuniary result therefrom for years—all which is sacrificed by the disinclination of the American Government to believe in the genius and inventive power of its own citizens. (Augustin Daly, Preface to *Under the Gaslight: or, Life and Love in These Times*)

Thomas Hailes Lacy's edition of Augustin Daly's drama *Under the Gaslight* (1867) offers a key insight into the relationship between sensationalism and the transatlantic marketplace created by the specific conditions in copyright law. Given Lacy's reputation as the leading British theatrical publisher of accessible, practical performance texts, his reprint of Daly's pivotal drama was partly a response to a market demand for the first sensation drama to stage what Michael Booth describes as one of the definitive sensation scenes in which the hero is rescued from the path of an oncoming train (Booth 170). However, Lacy's preface also reveals a complex set of political and personal impulses behind this reprint, indicating the creative and legal tensions that underpinned the transatlantic trade in texts. Entering into the contemporary debate on how copyright protection could defend what Claudia Stokes terms "literary nationalism," Lacy's defense of the American right to gain income from dramatic adaptations and original works is an interesting counterpoint to Charles Dickens's public declaration of American piracy in his reading tour of 1867.[1] Lacy's opening apology for effectively stealing the royalties from Daly and the performance rights from his publisher Wemyss is a calculated attempt to reconstruct himself as an agitator in the copyright debate of the 1860s. Problematically positioning America outside the protection afforded by English colonization, Lacy's emotive rhetoric shifts from a paternalistic tone to personal outrage unwittingly revealing publishing practices that manipulated or even circumvented existing copyright law altogether. Lacy's self-styled role as a champion for copyright legislation was partly upheld by his inclusion of *Under the Gaslight* in later editions of *The Amateur's Guide* as a play not subject to performance fees. Having waived the rights to potential performance revenue, his public refusal to appropriate the play into his vast portfolio of over a thousand plays by the late 1860s suggests another motive for publication. What really appears to be at stake in this preface's attack on transatlantic trade in dramatic piracy is the breach of trust by Lacy's New York agent, Samuel French in targeting a developing market for amateur and private theater products.

Lacy's tirade against piracy stressed the temporal, editorial and imaginative investment in *The Amateur's Guide* (1866), declaring it an original work specifically designed for an identifiable gap in the marketplace. The preface to the actual guide lodged in the British Library a year later argued that it was created with "no fear of trenching on vested interests or occupied ground," making a significant departure from the often piratical practices of theatrical publishing that I will focus on later (Lacy, *The Amateur's Guide* 2).[2] What is crucial here is the move towards a textual record of theater practice that was directed at a reading public rather than practitioners. The rise of the domestic consumer of theatrical products that paralleled the public demand for melodramatic narratives of the sensation novel was crucial to Lacy's continued business strategy in a changing world of performance revenues. In pirating the manual, French breached their reciprocal arrangement whereby Lacy and French reprinted texts in New York and London in order to afford them protection under both American and British copyright law respectively. Denied the possibility of legal injunction preventing further publication or distribution, Lacy sought recourse in publishing a play that would be in direct competition with French's publication of Dion Boucicault's *After Dark* (1868), a sensation play which famously appropriated Daly's spectacular

---

[1]   See Claudia Stokes, "Copywriting American History: International Copyright and the Periodization of the Nineteenth Century" in Susan Manning and Andrew Taylor (eds), *Transatlantic Literary Studies: A Reader* (Edinburgh: Edinburgh, 2007), 23–30.

[2]   A second title page gives the lengthier title of *The Amateur's Hand-Book and Guide to home or Drawing Room Theatricals to Which is Added How to "Get Up" Theatricals in a Country House*. The first section was written by W.J. Sorrell, the second by Captain Sock Ruskin and a supplement was added by Lacy in 1869 to provide a comprehensive list of plays after a description of the legalities of performance and setting up an amateur company.

train scene.[3] The issue of lost revenue is clearly at the heart of Lacy's thinly veiled attacks on French's status as both a gentleman and business agent.

What is problematic here is that Lacy felt the desire to publicly berate French over *The Amateur's Guide* for the very publishing practices that their businesses were effectively based upon. The legal battles between authors, theater practitioners and publishers over ownership of texts and subsequent performance rights during the early 1860s raise a complex set of questions concerning the commercial and cultural value of drama, particularly that of sensationalism in its variant literary and dramatic forms. Is it possible to discern the editorial practices behind their canonical catalogue of Victorian drama? How far did Lacy and French's reciprocal arrangements shape the production and reception of the sensational into a transatlantic form? What can Lacy and French's back catalogue tell us about the development of sensation drama and its symbiotic relationship with its literary double, the sensation novel?

To begin this re-negotiation of the sensational as a complex cultural form shaped by the tensions between economic and artistic concerns, this chapter will focus on the mobile dramatic form as the lynchpin of the transatlantic market in sensationalism. Using evidence from the financial records of Samuel French and Thomas Hailes Lacy, I begin by outlining their business and editorial methods that circumvented or exploited copyright laws. Lacy's much publicized legal dealings with the sensation novelists M.E. Braddon and Charles Reade shaped the way in which sensation dramas, particularly those with literary origins, were published, disseminated and reinvented both in the British domestic market and overseas. The final strand of my argument is that Lacy not only published professional acting editions of sensation dramas which articulated their own fragile status as legitimate texts, but that he more significantly commissioned two sets of sensation dramas for private performances. Aimed at a reading public familiar with the frisson created by sensation fiction's location of theatricalized events and personae in the home, Lacy's *Sensation Series* (1864–67) and H.J. Byron's *Sensation Dramas for the Back Drawing Room* (1864) indicate a sustained attempt to debate the intercultural, hybrid nature of the sensational from within the domestic sphere.

The business practices of T.H. Lacy and Samuel French were as sensational as any of the narratives they commissioned for the stage. Often cast as a pirate and profiteer, the figure of the theatrical publisher had a not altogether undeserved reputation for exploiting legal loopholes for financial gain. By the time French bought Lacy's business for £5,000 in 1873,[4] Lacy had published more than 1,500

---

[3]   See D. Boucicault, *After Dark* (New York: Samuel French, Standard Drama no. 360, 1868).

[4]   The actual transaction began in 1872 with a set of promissory notes from French to Lacy for £500, each post-dated for July of each year from 1873 to 1876. Part payment of £2,750 was made in 1872. See Samuel French Business Archive 81/2366, Box 10. It is often cited that Lacy sold the business to French in 1873 just months before his death as he had no family to inherit the business. Indeed his will gives all his estate to various dramatic

plays while French claimed to have more than 100,000 plays available by 1856.[5] Both capitalized on developments in publishing to generate an income from the text. Contextually, the acting edition was analogous with the serial form in terms of its speed of production in response to public demand and the palatable size of each volume attracting what Altick termed the emergent, semi-literate "common reader" keen to access more than advertising material (303). In a rapidly shifting marketplace, Lacy and French's transatlantic business practices relied on the exploitation of copyright laws and a theatrical culture grounded in adaptation and appropriation. Their catalogues reveal the vibrant, hybrid quality of Victorian drama as satirical burlesques and pantomimes appeared alongside comedies, farces, sketches, melodramas and domestic dramas. The range of material was marked by its metacultural nature, aligning the theater's creative use of novels, successful predecessors, paintings, journalism and topical events with the sensational. What is less clear is the selection policy and editorial practice of Lacy which influenced the subsequent transatlantic trade in drama.

Lacy's business began with his appropriation of *Cumberland's British Theatre, Duncombe's British Theatre*, and *Webster's Acting Editions* in the 1840s. The corresponding copyright assigns from surviving papers and ledgers passed to Samuel French exist only as signed receipts from playwrights, with W.T. Moncrieff typically earning just £2 for the play *The Cook and the Secretary* in 1833.[6] When Lacy began to procure texts for his own *Acting Editions* he typically paid £15 for a three-act drama in the 1850s, increasing the amount to £20 in the 1860s. This sum effectively doubled the playwright's income from each play, but transferred the performance rights to Lacy, perpetuating his reputation as a pirate despite his work for The Royal Theatrical Fund, a major beneficiary of Lacy's estate.[7] How Lacy selected plays for publication is difficult to discern despite

---

funds so his son must have either predeceased him (Lacy's wife Frances, a former actress, died in 1871) or been completely disinherited. Thus far I have been unable to trace his son Thomas Lacy, Jr., who appears in the 1861 census aged 11 and at the age of 15 had signed the receipt for F.C. Burnand's *Pirithoüs, The Son of Axion*, first performed at the New Royalty Theatre 13 April 1865 and printed in volume 65 of Lacy's List. See Samuel French Business Archive 81/2366, Box 1, Assignments Book 3 for Lacy, (renumbered by French as 1), f. 152.

[5]   This claim seems exaggerated. French was notoriously unreliable about dates or figures according to the writer of *Truly Yours: One Hundred and Fifty Years of Play Publishing & Service to the Theatre* (London: Samuel French, 1980), 1.

[6]   See Samuel French Business Archive 81/2366, Box 1, Assignments Book 1, dating from 1860, receipt from W. Moncrieff for £2 for *The Cook and the Secretary*, dated 26 October 1833.

[7]   An interview with Samuel French for the New York Times 19 September 1878 declared that Lacy bequeathed $70,000 to the Dramatic Fund thereby returning the money he had made from them. This interview is given in full in Anon, *Truly Yours: One Hundred and Fifty Years of Play Publishing & Service to the Theatre* (London: Samuel French, 1980), 7. Lacy's will bequeathed much of his London property to the Royal Theatrical Fund.

John Russell Stephens's suggestion that Lacy was the most "catholic" of the theatrical publishers, presumably a reference to a traditional, less experimental approach (130). His connections with the Dramatic Author's Society and *Punch*'s circle of writers are evident in the number of plays authored by Mark Lemon, Tom Taylor and the Morton brothers. Indeed, it was a requirement of the Society that plays be made available in printed form for the provincial market in order to collect fees. Frequently upheld as the authoritative list of performance texts in answers to correspondents in advice columns of the major theatrical paper *The Era*, Lacy's list appears to be a comprehensive selection of Acting Editions. He even included a flagrant act of self-promotion in Wilmot Harrison's *Special Performances* (1868) where the characters use Lacy's List to find an ideal farce for an amateur performance (Harrison 11). However, a brief comparison between the Lord Chamberlain's complete list of plays sent for licensing in 1860 and the plays Lacy printed reveals how selective he was. Lacy's process shows a preference of the comic over the drama, with 45% of the farces and 50% of the burlesques appearing in print as opposed to only 12% of the drama (what we might subdivide into melodrama, nautical drama, domestic drama). His publication of only 5% of the pantomimes would seem to support Tracy Davis's questioning of the residual value of a pantomime script once the specific scenery and costumes were sold off to avoid storage costs (Davis 345).

The timing of his publications also problematizes the immediate cultural relevance of certain genres. Whilst the majority of his comedies and farces are published within weeks of the London première, the dramas are more difficult to place in terms of popularity. Lacy's publication of Douglas Jerrold's *The Mutiny at the Nore* (1830) and Edward Fitzball's *The Inchcape Bell* (1828) in 1867 could suggest a revived interest in the nautical drama or that he was only given the rights to certain plays once they were not profitable in performance terms.[8] What is at stake here is the question of Lacy's creation of a textual resource that resembles a dramatic canon filtered by personal connections and economic concerns rather than immediate cultural value. Indeed, Thomas Postlewait critiques Jeffrey Mason's use of the limited playtexts left available by publishers like French such as *The Drunkard* (1844) and *Uncle Tom's Cabin* (1859) which create false impressions of cultural representation in nineteenth-century American drama (Postlewait 46–47). Given the publishing history of W.H. Smith's *The Drunkard*, it is particularly problematic to reclaim it as a formative point in American history, as Lacy and French simultaneously printed the play on both sides of the Atlantic.[9] This suggests that not only were they trading plays before their first meeting in 1859, but that the play was interchangeable in terms of cultural resonance, an idea borne

---

[8]   See Douglas Jerrold, *The Mutiny at the Nore* (London: T.H. Lacy's Acting Edition, Vol. 78, no. 1167) and Edward Fitzball, *The Inchcape Bell* (London: T.H. Lacy's Acting Edition, Vol. 79, No. 1173).

[9]   Lacy printed *The Drunkard* in Vol. 7, No. 102 c.1852 whereas French's Standard Drama List shows *The Drunkard* in Vol. 11, No. 89.

out by Lacy's direction that the costumes and therefore context were "precisely similar to those that would be worn if the Scene was laid in England instead of America" (2). Lacy also commissioned adaptations of *Uncle Tom's Cabin* (1853) and *Clarissa Harlowe* (1846),[10] supporting the notion of his List as a secondary canon as "canonicity, it has been posited, is almost a required feature of the raw material for adaptation and appropriation" (Sanders 120). The complex political, legal and personal concerns in which Lacy's List were grounded are at their most evident in the transatlantic exchange of plays between Lacy and French.

Initially, it would appear that the specific socio-legal conditions of copyright law before the Berne Convention of 1884 created a dramatic culture grounded in the interdependence of transatlantic exchange. However, here it would be useful to relate the variant forms of "transatlanticism" to Lacy and French's trade in order to show how the theater created a culture which resisted categorisation. Joseph Roach defines three primary types of the transatlantic: "Cis-Atlantic," the national or regional history within an Atlantic context; "Trans-Atlantic," the international history of the Atlantic world; and "Circum-Atlantic," the transnational history of the Atlantic world which centers on the diasporic histories of Africa and the Americas (Roach 236–248). Whilst Lacy and French's exchange of English and American playtexts and reciprocal collection of fees is an example of transatlantic trade, the way in which ethnic identities of African Americans were alternately defined for their respective audiences shows the slippage in definitions of the circumatlantic and the cisatlantic. The demand for African-American entertainments following the transatlantic phenomenon of *Uncle Tom's Cabin* (1859) in both narrative and dramatic form resulted in French's creation of a series of Ethiopian Dramas, with familiar titles such as *Box and Cox* (based on John Madison Morton's 1847 play of the same title), *Corsican Twins* (based on Boucicault's *The Corsican Brothers* 1852), and even *Old Dad's Cabin*. The reception and performance possibilities of these versions of popular plays that Lacy and French had canonized were controlled through the publishing medium. Whereas French published the series in single 6d acting editions ready for performance, Lacy anthologized the plays in shilling volumes containing nine dramatic texts. Here I deliberately use the word "text" to signal the literary value of such anthologies designed for reading and storing in a library as opposed to the single duodecimo acting edition that once backed with card covers became a portable, serviceable script for amateur and professional practitioners. Lacy's repackaging of the Ethiopian series into what were then called "Darkey Dramas" priced the common reader and performer out of the market, problematically disenfranchising their relationship with the spectator as other and de-ethnicizing the subject. This act of homogenizing emergent African-American identities made possible by the theatrical phenomenon of *Uncle Tom's Cabin* indicates the dual interplay of cultural and political impulses

---

[10] See Anon., [Henry Addison] *Uncle Tom's Cabin*, (London: T.H. Lacy's Acting Edition, Vol. 12, No. 178, 1853) and T.H. Lacy and John Courtney, *Clarissa Harlowe*, (London: T.H. Lacy's Acting Editions, Vol.77, No. 1043, 1867)

of globalization (Rebellato 5–6). It was politic to reprint French's plays to obtain British copyright, but their cultural value was literary rather than performative, a notion borne out by Lacy's encounters with the sensation novelists M.E. Braddon and Charles Reade and the sensation dramatist Dion Bouciault.

As an Irish playwright/actor-manager working in New York and London, Boucicault epitomized the culture of sensational transatlanticism. Boucicault's self-fashioned "sensation dramas" attracted and sensitized audiences through unlikely plot structures punctuated by realistic representations of spectacular events such as horse races, train crashes, and courtroom scenes. Making practical use of advances in engineering and science, sensation drama staged modernity but often arguably at the expense of narrative depth. Dramatizing innovation rather than character development allowed an immediate cultural impact based upon economic gain that defines the sensational. John Barton and Jennifer Phegley's introduction to this volume argues for a re-visioning of the sensation novel as a genre with a clear cultural trajectory across the long nineteenth century, one that complicates its initial critical reception as a response to the specific concerns of the 1860s. Yet the publishing practices surrounding sensation drama openly acknowledge a generic style that was grounded in perpetual re-invention, evolution, and cross-cultural influence to attract wider, shifting audience demographics. Initially, Lacy acted merely as the agent for French's text of Boucicault's *Life of An Actress* (1855) and *The Poor of New York* (1857),[11] but openly manipulated loopholes in copyright protection to appropriate the performance rights to Boucicault's *The Corsican Brothers* (1852) and *The Colleen Bawn* (1860). Although Boucicault had secured the British rights to his *Corsican Brothers* by publishing it through J.R. Chapman in 1852, Lacy created his own Acting Edition of *The Corsican Brothers* (1852) by bypassing Boucicault to reassert the play's complex origins. Entitled "*Les Frères Corses; or, The Corsican Brothers. A Dramatic Romance in Three Acts and Five Tableaux.* Adapted from the Romance of M. Dumas by MM. E Grange and X. De Montepin,"[12] the title page effectively displays the complex nature of Victorian theater as an intercultural space where modern definitions of legal, authorial identity were deeply problematized. Lacy continued to capitalize on Boucicault's brand of transcultural sensationalism, acknowledging the genre's adaptative qualities that ensured its continued survival in variant forms. He commissioned Thomas Egerton Wilks to write *Eily O'Connor* (1860), a near-perfect copy of Boucicault's *The Colleen Bawn* (1860).[13] French held the performance rights to Boucicault's *The Colleen Bawn* and exchanged publishing rights with Lacy

---

[11]   See Dion Boucicault, *The Life of An Actress* (New York: Samuel French's Standard Drama, Vol .20, No. 159)[1855], and Dion Boucicault, *The Poor of New York* (New York: Samuel French's Standard Drama, Vol. 24, no. 189)[1857].

[12]   Published as Lacy's Acting Edition, Vol. 6, No. 79.

[13]   Published as Lacy's Acting Edition, Vol. 47, No. 693. No place of performance is given.

in 1864 after initial profits had been maximized.[14] As Lacy's statement reveals, however, the impetus to publish had changed:

> in consequence of the production of this Drama, and others by the same Author, in the United States of America, with which there is no existing International Treaty of Copyright. Vice-Chancellor Wood decreed that no property *could exist* in their representation in this Country; therefore the Assignees of the Author, in whom his property was vested at his bankruptcy, have not title whatsoever in or to them, and *The Colleen Bawn*, with the Dramas named on the title page of this Play are Performance Free. (Boucicault 3)

In waiving performance rights, the financial value of the play rested in the act of reading and owning a copy. The new market force of the reader transformed the acting edition into a literary text whose fixity remains distinctly problematic for theater critics such as Jacky Bratton who argue that performative meaning is located *outside* the text.[15] Whether or not a distinction between literary and performative value is valid, what is clear is that the Victorian reading public increasingly read plays, countering Daniel Barrett's contention that the cheap paper and transient cultural value of mid-Victorian drama facilitated the rise of the novel to the extent that no one read plays (173–187). Lacy sold his editions in half-calf bound volumes of 12 plays and as early as the 1860s was advertising for complete runs available at 15s and his *Amateur Theater*, an anthology of 225 dramas, bound in half-morocco for £6. These aspiring middle-class bindings in uniform runs ensured the survival of Lacy's Acting Editions in county and national libraries as many single issues and disposable popular literary forms were pulped in the war effort.[16] Whilst the validity of Lacy's editions as a cultural reference point is still open to question given that his relationship to canonicity was irrevocably tied to publishing practice, what emerges is how the printed script became an increasingly valuable commodity in literary terms.

The legal disputes among publishers, playwrights and theater managers constructed a public space for debating how a script formerly ascribed with commercial and visual value could be re-sold in a new literary marketplace. Surviving evidence from Lacy and French's business archives show transactions which ranged from swift private resolutions of outstanding performance fees to

---

[14]   Published as Lacy's Acting Edition, Vol. 63, No. 932 (London: T.H. Lacy, 1864) and in Samuel French's Standard Drama, No. 366 (New York: French's Standard Drama, 1860).

[15]   Jacky Bratton, *New Readings in Theater History* (Cambridge: Cambridge University Press, 2003).

[16]   I am grateful to Eileen Mann, former county librarian, for discussing how the enormous influx of books given to be recycled into bandages for the war effort meant that only books that were printed in or before the seventeenth century were saved for sorting by archivists. This would explain the rarity of first editions of novels by popular sensation writers such as Ellen Wood and M.E. Braddon.

sensational public appearances in the Chancery Court. The papers transferred from Duncombe to Lacy show a receipt dated 9 June 1831 from W.T. Moncrieff for meager £5 "in damages and costs and in full settlement of an action commenced by me against him in the Chancery Court for infringement of copyright of *Gates of Italy*."[17] This sum was derisory, given that Lacy's accounts show an average revenue of £20 per play from each provincial performance. When French attempted to appropriate the performance rights for William Suter's *Little Faults* (1864), he was faced by a double assault on his integrity by both Leo Conquest, the commissioning theater manager and Suter himself.[18] French had attempted to assuage Conquest by declaring that his mistake was genuine, given that Lacy had originally brokered the deal, punning on the play's title in that "we all have our little faults."[19] However, Conquest's response was severe, claiming the piece was his "*sole and exclusive* property. I hastily allowed Mr Lacy to print it and I gave him no other right of any sort."[20] Interestingly, this response was pasted in top of a letter from Suter himself, authenticating the piece through a piratical source; "Mr Conquest *has* rights—I cannot now remember to what extent—in *Little Faults* and several other pieces, and if I have rights Mr Lacy was of course perfectly aware when he dealt with me. *Little Faults* was done to order for Mr Conquest, who furnished me with the French original."[21] The collaborative if piratical creative practices that shaped mid-Victorian theater were brought into focus when Lacy was forced to defend a theatrical culture grounded in adaptation.

Lacy's publication of unauthorized adaptations of M.E. Braddon's novel *Lady Audley's Secret* represented a challenge to the iconographic status of the sensation novel as the dominant literary form. Once published, Suter's version of *Lady Audley's Secret* (1863) constituted a breach of literary copyright, and Braddon's publisher Tinsley instigated proceedings against Lacy. Despite the potential for secondary sales of the novel from audience members wanting to "fill up from memory [the] many dramatic gaps in the story," Braddon applied for an injunction against the play's proposed performance on 23 April 1863. This application was delayed until July as Lacy failed to respond, indicating either his clerical ineptitude or a more likely cynical attempt to delay the process in order to maximize initial revenues in the wake of the impending trial. By the second hearing on 4 July,

---

[17]   Samuel French Business Archive 81/2366, Box 1, Assignments Book 3 for Lacy, (renumbered by French as Book 1), n.f.

[18]   William E. Suter, *Little Faults* (London: T.H. Lacy Acting Edition, Vol. 78, No. 1156, 1864).

[19]   Letter from French, see Samuel French Business Archive 81/2366, Box 1, Assignments Book 3 for Lacy, (renumbered by French as Book 1), f. 146.

[20]   Letter from Conquest dated 3 July (1877?), see Samuel French Business Archive 81/2366, Box 1, Assignments Book 3 for Lacy, (renumbered by French as Book 1), pasted on f. 146.

[21]   Suter's letter to French, dated 8 March, 1877 pasted under Conquest's letter, see Samuel French Business Archive 81/2366, Box 1, Assignments Book 3 for Lacy (renumbered by French as Book 1), pasted on f. 146.

Tinsley presented a second Lacy's Acting Edition as evidence, that of Suter's *Aurora Floyd* (1863).[22] The court found against Lacy, as his acting editions were in infringement of literary copyright law. The permanent injunction against Lacy prevented not just the reprinting of the text, but any subsequent performances. Tinsley claimed a moral victory and waived the costs, but his action failed to control the dissemination of the play as a literary work which was still available when complete runs or single volumes of Lacy's List were purchased. Rather, the injunction transformed the performance text into a dramatic text, paradoxically replacing the practitioner with the reader as the primary target market to effectively compete with the sensation novel.

When Lacy published Colin Hazlewood's adaptation of *Lady Audley's Secret* (1863) he included the by-line "based on Miss Braddon's novel," avoiding further litigation. The case of Tinsley v. Lacy had created a precedent which protected an identifiable literary product from unauthorized dramatic versions, creating a link between the theater, literary commodity, and sensationalism. This image of a performance text which acknowledges a narrative source mirrors the theatrical devices located within sensation fiction and argues for a symbiotic link between the novel and the drama. However, the cultural form of sensationalism was clearly shaped by the specific legalities of copyright. Having been allowed to print Hazlewood's version of *Lady Audley's Secret*, an adaptation that has ironically been more consistently available than the novel,[23] Lacy and French held a transatlantic monopoly over the dissemination of dramatic products carrying the Braddon name. In response to the legal identity of the playscript as text, Lacy's business records become more organized. Evidence of copyright and transfer of performance rights was fragmentary prior to 1860, raising doubts over Lacy's claim of ownership. Press accounts of the case of *Lacy v. Rhys* in 1863 record its initial adjournment due to Lacy's failure to submit the correct paperwork, indicating Lacy's papers were in disarray even before they were archived (*Daily News*, 11 February 1863). However, by the mid-1860s Lacy had introduced clear printed contracts witnessed by two additional signatories, although in some cases these were the marks of his clerks and therefore open to question in terms of legitimacy. The contracts between the prolific domestic dramatist Colin Hazlewood and Lacy show both the specific distinction made between provincial and London rights to plays and the rights of

---

[22]   Details of the case were reported in *The Times* and in *The Glasgow Daily Herald*, Saturday, 4 July 1863, p. 3. William E. Suter's adaptation of *Aurora Floyd* (1863) was performed at the Queen's Theatre on 4 April and appeared in Volume 58 of Lacy's List of Acting Editions. It is also available at http://victorian.worc.ac.uk.

[23]   *Lady Audley's Secret* was made into a film, directed by Jack Denton in 1910, the play was still being performed until WWI, and Colin Hazlewood's version came back into print in George Rowell (ed.), *Nineteenth Century Plays* (Oxford: Oxford University Press, 1953). Brian Burton's *Lady Audley's Secret or Death in Lime Tree Walk* (New York and London: Samuel French, 1966) ran into three editions. Constance Cox's one act melodrama *Lady Audley's Secret* (London: Samuel French, 1976) is still readily available. All of these predate the novel's reappearance and subsequent inclusion on the undergraduate syllabus.

the commissioning theater manager. Hazlewood typically opted out of signing over total rights to Lacy in the contract for *Early Guilt and Late Repentance* dated 18 September 1862, giving Lacy the "out of London rights" alone.[24] The deed of copyright for Hazlewood's adaptations of M.E. Braddon's novels *Aurora Floyd* and *Lady Audley's Secret* gave the commissioning theaters of the Britannia and Victoria respectively the right to perform the plays free for the period of a year from October 15, 1863 while selling the remaining rights to Lacy for £6.[25]

Despite Lacy's apparent agreement with Tinsley to sustain the marketable image of Braddon, Lacy published plays which depict how sensationalism was grounded in a creative, organic culture of inferences that undermines the validity of any claim to single authorship. Watts Philips's *Maud's Peril* (1867) resonates with themes from *Aurora Floyd*, including the re-appearance of a presumed dead lover. Interestingly this play was the victim of transatlantic piracy, as Philips dedicated the Lacy Acting Edition to "the thief or thieves, who by means of shorthand, or other petty larceny devices, caused a mutilated copy of the work to be circulated in America, to the detriment of its author" (Philips 2). As arguably the official publisher for authorized versions of Braddon's narratives, Lacy went on to publish Tom Taylor's adaptation of *Henry Dunbar; or, The Daughter's Trial* (1865) before sustaining his publishing momentum through standardized dramatic texts of nautical dramas from the 1830s and contemporary comedies. By the mid-1860s, the dwindling number of domestic dramas available through Lacy's List suggests that the market for sensationalism was in decline. However, the sensation drama was relocated in the domestic sphere with Lacy's publication of Henry J. Byron's *Sensation Dramas for the Back Drawing Room* (1864).

Whereas Lacy's *Sensation Series* (1864–67) was a run of eight plays by favored authors such as F.C. Burnand which were designed for fêtes and amateur events,[26] Byron's *Sensation Dramas* was at first glance commissioned to supply the increasing demand for amateur theatrical material. Following the work of Jenny Bourne-Taylor, modern critics are familiar with the connection between sensationalism and a theatricalized sense of self within the narrative form, yet little has been written on the actual practices of home performances.[27] Private theatricals repeatedly appeared in the early sensation novels of M.E. Braddon; *Only A Clod*

---

[24] Samuel French Business Archive 81/2366, Box 1, Assignments Book 3 for Lacy (renumbered by French as Book 1), f. 86. Interestingly, this play does not appear in Lacy's List.

[25] Samuel French Business Archive 81/2366, Box 1, Assignments Book 3 for Lacy (renumbered by French as Book 1), f.114.

[26] Titles were priced at 6d each and were short pieces which were amalgamations of popular dramas derived from Boucicault, Sir Walter Scott, Sir Edward Bulwer-Lytton, and M.E. Braddon. The titles were 1: The Blazing Burgee, 2: *The Port-Admiral*, 3: *Briganzio the Brigand*, 4: *The Tyrant, the Slave, the Victim and the Tar*, 5: *The Domestic Hearthstone*, 6: *Pretty Jane*, 7: *Alice the Mystery*, 8: *The Rosebud of Stinging Nettle Farm*.

[27] Jenny Bourne-Taylor, *In The Secret Theater of Home: Wilkie Collins, Sensation Narrative, and Nineteenth Century Psychology* (London: Routledge, 1988).

(1865) featured a performance of Bulwer-Lytton's *The Lady of Lyons* (1838) and *Strangers and Pilgrims* (1873), published in Lacy's final year of trading, uses Charles Reade's *Masks and Faces* (1852). What is interesting here is how the sensation drama was relocated in the home through being partially subsumed into the amateur market. The demand for dramatic products and practitioner guides from the aspiring middle-classes corresponded to the theater's rising status as an art form that received royal patronage. Lacy and French's catalogues give a key insight into the level of scenography that bordered on professional to which amateurs could aspire through purchasing tableaux lights, make-up, back scenes, borders and sides. As argued by Lacy in the preface to *The Amateur's Guide*, the possibilities presented by private theatricals for "a meeting of the sexes upon a neutral platform" were of transatlantic appeal (Lacy, *The Amateur's Guide* 2). Materials designed for American and British markets appeared, including Lacy's series *Comic Dramas for College, Camp and Cabin* (1862–72). However, Byron's volume of sensation plays engages with the idea of theater as an alternative cultural space where boundaries between nationhood, culture and gender are contested to argue that no space is ever neutral.

Sensation Dramas for the Back Drawing Room is a collection of the most popular mid-Victorian domestic dramas in miniature, including recognizable versions of *The Heart of MidLothian* (1819), *The Colleen Bawn* (1860), and *Black Ey'd Susan* (1829). What is interesting about these heavily condensed plays is Byron's technique of relocating the action to an alternative metatheatrical space in which cultural and national boundaries are contested. Byron's version of *Black Ey'd Susan*, entitled *The Mendacious Mariner; or, Pretty Poll of Portsea and the Captain with his Whiskers*, recasts the eponymous and virtuous Susan as Mary the cross-dressing sailor. Her rousing cry to gain the audience's approval is overshadowed by a finale which undermines the possibility of the play being performed in a domestic setting: "The crew cheer—land appears on the lee-bow—a rainbow spans the back of the scene—the enemy's vessel blows up, and Lieutenant Lee Scupper expires from the effects of a slow poison, as the curtain descends rapidly" (Byron 50). Whereas the ship functions as an alternative space where normative definitions of gender and corresponding actions are questioned, in other plays Byron conflates class and geographical boundaries to produce a satirical commentary on the very audience who engaged in private theatricals. *Green Grow the Rushes, oh; or, The Squireen, the Informer, and the Illicit Distiller. A Hibernian Sensation Drama*, a condensed version of *The Colleen Bawn*, sets the action in Scotland rather than Ireland and allows the heroine Eily to claim a universal sentiment. Her final speech argues that "virtue gilds the cottage of the peasant with gold as refined as the manners of the aristocracy ... there *are* homes without a sewing machine ... where you DO double up your perambulators in spite of a censorious world and all are happier for the deed" (Byron 32). This speech undercuts any suggestion of middle-class superiority involved in performing lower class characters as "other" whilst connecting social mobility to domestic theatricality. Byron's sensation plays resonate with the tension created by locating the middle-class reader's values within alternative cultural frameworks. This destabilizing quality is most evident in the play *The Ever-so-Little Bear; or, The Pale Faces and The Putemindecauldron Indians*. Here Byron juxtaposes two Indian chiefs, one a Native American and the other a former British sailor masquerading as a tribal leader. The dissemblance continues in the figure of Paramatta, a woman who allegedly disguises herself as a sailor, tracker and then infant child in order to unmask the impostor. The definitions of civilized/uncivilized, British and American collide in the finale, where Paramatta addresses the audience in order to reinstate the common human values of "the heart that can feel for another" (Byron 69). Here a humanistic claim seeks to unite the ethnic diversity of the "copper-coloured children of the Prairies" and the "pale-faces" whilst revealing the theatrical medium as a place where cultural differences can be debated.

Byron's brand of sensationalism capitalized upon the frisson created by domesticated theatrical form which addressed the needs of a transatlantic audience. As a hybrid genre, sensationalism was marked by its ability to resist containment in cultural, literary or dramatic terms, yet its protean nature was also paradoxically shaped by the specific social and legal conditions of the mid-Victorian transatlantic literary marketplace. Sensation drama evolved from its inception in the spectacular yet momentary events typified by Boucicault and Daly through to a form of self-parody that involved a sustained interaction with the reader as intended performer. Their publishers Lacy and French shifted the emphasis from the professional to a domestic market for sensationalism, strategically capitalizing on the lack of transatlantic copyright protection to attract an expanding international readership. The resulting publishing practices were as complex as their material, with both resisting legal, social or geographical containment. What emerges is an image of sensationalism that was analogous with theatricality and theatrical practice. Much more needs to be done in terms of the symbiotic relationship between literature and theater. However, what is clear is that the development and dissemination of the sensational form was in response to the transatlantic trade in drama.

Works Cited

Altick, Richard D. "Publishing." In Herbert F. Tucker (ed) *A Companion to Victorian Literature and Culture*. London: Blackwell, 1999. 289–304.

Anon. *Truly Yours: One Hundred and Fifty Years of Play Publishing & Service to the Theatre*. London: Samuel French, 1980.

Barrett, Daniel. "Play Publication, Readers, and the 'Decline' of Victorian Drama." *Book History* 2 (1999): 173–187.

Booth, Michael. *English Melodrama*. London: Herbert Jenkins, 1965.

Boucicault, Dion. *After Dark*. New York: Samuel French, 1868.

Bratton, Jacky, ed. *Acts of Supremacy: British Empire and the Stage, 1790–1930*. Manchester: Manchester University Press, 1991.

———. *New Readings in Theatre History*. Cambridge: Cambridge University Press, 2003.

Byron, H.J. *Sensation Dramas for the Back Drawing Room*. London: T.H. Lacy, 1864.

Daily News. February 11, 1863.

———. March 2, 1863.

Daly, Augustin. Preface to *Under the Gaslight: or, Life and Love in These Times*. London: Lacy's Acting Edition, 1868.

Davis, Tracy C. *The Economics of the British Stage 1800–1914*. Cambridge: Cambridge University Press, 2000.

Harrison, Wilmot. *Special Performances*. London: T.H. Lacy Acting Edition.

Lacy, T.H. *Lacy's Acting Editions in 100 Volumes*. London: T.H. Lacy, 1848–1873. Texts are available at http://victorian.worc.ac.uk.

———. *The Amateur's Guide*. London: T.H. Lacy, 1866.

Philips, Watts. *Maud's Peril*. London: T.H. Lacey, 1867.

Postlewait, Thomas. "From Melodrama to Realism: The Suspect History of American Drama." In Michael Hays & Anastasia Nikolopoulou (eds.) *Melodrama: The Cultural Emergence of a Genre*. London: Macmillan, 1999. 39–60.

Rebellato, Dan. *Theatre & Globalization*. Basingstoke: Palgrave Macmillan, 2009.

Roach, Joseph. "Introduction: History, Memory and Performance." In Susan Manning & Andrew Taylor (eds.) *Transatlantic Literary Studies: A Reader*. Edinburgh: Edinburgh, 2007.

Sanders, Julie. *Adaptation and Appropriation*. London: Routledge, 2006.

Smith, W.H. [adapted for the British stage by Thomas Hailes Lacy. *The Drunkard*. T.H. Lacy's Acting Edition 7.102 (1852): 2.

Stephens, John Russell. *The Profession of the Playwright: British Theatre 1800–1900*. Cambridge: Cambridge University Press, 1992.

Stokes, Claudia. "Copywriting American History: International Copyright and the Periodization of the Nineteenth Century." In Susan Manning & Andrew Taylor (eds.) *Transatlantic Literary Studies: A Reader*. Edinburgh: Edinburgh, 2007. 23–30.

Chapter 10

Transatlantic Magnetism: Eliot's "The Lifted Veil" and Alcott's Sensation Stories

Susan David Bernstein

Under the name A.M. Barnard, Louisa May Alcott published *Behind a Mask: or, A Woman's Power* in *The Flag of Our Union* in four installments during October and November 1866. While many of these stories did not make their way into print in British publications, there are several angles to reading Alcott transatlantically. Scholars such as Elaine Showalter have linked Alcott's American brand of sensation fiction to recycled portrayals of powerful, ambitious heroines from Charlotte Brontë's *Jane Eyre* to Mary Elizabeth Braddon's *Lady Audley's Secret* and Wilkie Collins's *Armadale*. After her prizewinning thriller "Pauline's Passion and Punishment" appeared in *Frank Leslie's Illustrated Newspaper*, Alcott continued to publish anonymously several sensational stories in this weekly periodical modeled after the *Illustrated London News*. "A Pair of Eyes" appeared anonymously in *Frank Leslie's* in two installments in late October 1863. Although Alcott's celebrated *Little Women* (1868–69) and its sequels were circulated in Britain, her earlier sensation stories remained anonymous and were only in print in the United States.

If Brontë's fiction offers an obvious source text for Alcott's sensation fiction, Alcott's "A Pair of Eyes" has surprising ties to "The Lifted Veil," the only sensation story written by George Eliot. "The Lifted Veil" was published anonymously in *Blackwood's Edinburgh Magazine* in July 1859, and then reprinted for American readers in *The Living Age* in August 1859. Whereas Eliot's name has become identified with canonical Victorian realism for novels like *Middlemarch* and Alcott's with family fiction like *Little Women*, both writers published sensational short stories early in their careers. Alcott's transatlantic rewriting of Eliot's tale about parapsychological phenomena might suggest distinctions between British and American sensation fiction.[1] Proper names alone indicate that both writers rework elements of *Jane Eyre*, with Eliot's Bertha Grant as a counterpart to the demonized Bertha Mason, and Alcott's Agatha Eure in "A Pair of Eyes" as a

---

[1] The use of mesmerism and other paranormal phenomena in these stories suggest again how sensational fiction is a hybrid form, with links to the gothic and the supernatural, but with a more contemporary bent.

medley of Bertha and Jane Eyre.[2] By exploring these transatlantic depictions of mesmerism, clairvoyance, and other forms of mental agency, I propose that both writers use this subject as an extended and exaggerated trope for the power and liabilities of female authorship. While both writers use sensationalism to explore the problems and possibilities of gendered knowledge while hiding behind veils of anonymity, Eliot demonizes her female mesmerist; in contrast, Alcott's Agatha Eure is a morally hybrid character who uses this capacity to redress her powerlessness as a wife and as an artist. Along with drawing out similarities between these sensation stories, and especially their heroines endowed with psychic powers, I explore differences within the narratives and between print culture contexts as a way to gain purchase on how sensationalism played out differently across the Atlantic. One clear distinction is the unevenness of the Anglo-American publishing history, as Amanda Claybaugh has noted, where more British authors and their writing circulated in American periodicals than the reverse of American popular fiction in Britain (Claybaugh 19). Eliot's anonymously printed sensational story appeared nearly immediately in American print, while Alcott's short fiction was almost entirely absent in British pages. The only exception was Alcott's Civil War stories, which carried a kind of sensational accent that appealed to British reading diets drawn to the subject of American slavery and her family fiction.

In "The Lifted Veil," Latimer's first-person narrative accentuates the ability to think others' thoughts, to see future events, also the attributes of an omniscient narrator, qualities that Eliot's later narrators complicate or limit. This masking of character thoughts and narrative outcome, both subjects of form explored through psychical powers in the story, works differently in Alcott's sensational stories. In the later story, "Behind a Mask," the omniscient gaze of the narrator allows readers to view beyond the masquerade of Jean's public performances as governess. But the suggestion of a mesmeric force manipulated by Jean Muir, a femme fatale, also functions as a conduit for the sensational powers of fiction. With this 1866 story, as with Alcott's other contributions to *The Flag of Our Union* where *Behind a Mask* appeared, she adopted her own mask through the pseudonym "A.M. Barnard," like the anonymous earlier 1863 "A Pair of Eyes," along with her other sensational stories published in *Frank Leslie's*. So too did Eliot publish anonymously "The Lifted Veil," while she used "George Eliot" for her novels published before and after that.

---

[2]   Jean Muir, the sensational governess in Alcott's "Behind a Mask," also alludes to Brontë's Jane Eyre. In other of her sensational thrillers, Alcott seems to wink at other British heroines in her choice of names. The earliest of these, "Marion Earle: or, Only an Actress!" (*American Union*, July–September 1858), echoes Elizabeth Barrett Browning's poor, sexually abused, Marian Erle in *Aurora Leigh*, first published in 1856 in London and in New York (by C.S. Francis & Co.). There are many reviews of and excerpts from *Aurora Leigh* in American periodicals from December 1856, including a review in early 1857 in *The Living Age*, and excerpts in *The Saturday Evening Post* in January 1857. Marian Erle, of course, could be considered a precursor to the 1860s British sensation heroine.

Alcott's interest in animal magnetism or mesmerism is explicit in "A Pair of Eyes," a story with evident resemblance to and crucial differences from "The Lifted Veil." These two tales have first-person male narrators, both artists drawn to mysterious women who are magnetic operators. Female mental agency behaves differently within these stories, variations that open up space for speculating about cultural differences between British and American sensationalism. In addition to analyzing the role of mesmerism within these sensational tales, I link these depictions of gendered mental powers to the question of female authorship transnationally in two other ways. First, I consider how paratextual elements of titles and attribution in *Blackwood's, Littell's Living Age, Frank Leslie's Illustrated Newspaper*, and *The Flag of Our Union* function as veils or masks for Eliot and Alcott early in their careers. Second, I explore the framing of the stories by periodicals in which these texts first appeared. These investigations yield some interesting comparisons between American and British printing of sensation fiction. Consistent with American tolerance of class mixing in popular fiction, in contrast to British reviews of sensation fiction's blurring tendencies, Alcott's suggests a more fluid and heterogeneous readership, with her "thriller" stories as popular entertainment, their only claim to literariness through allusions to British fiction. Because Eliot's story was published transatlantically, we can see that its *Blackwood's* appearance in Britain and the paratextually marked Britishness of its American publication granted the text a kind of prestige despite its sensational elements. Where "The Lifted Veil" in its initial British print publication is merely part of a cast of items bearing sensational elements, its American reprinting elevates its literary status as the story carried cultural authority due to the *Blackwood's* origin.

The transatlantic appearances of "The Lifted Veil"

"The Lifted Veil" was first published in *Blackwood's* in July 1859. Although the advent of sensation fiction in England is usually credited to the serialized debut of Collins's *The Woman in White*, from November 1859 in *All the Year Round*, and Braddon's *Lady Audley's Secret* two years later, scholars have noted some sensational features of Eliot's fiction (Pykett 69–70). Eliot[3] wrote what she described to John Blackwood as "a brief magazine story" on the heels of the successful reception of her first novel *Adam Bede* a few months earlier in February 1859 (Haight iii 112 n.6). When she sent it to Blackwood in late April, she included a note, "Herewith the dismal story" (Small x).

Why was this a "dismal" story? First, the narrator is off-putting, as alienating as he is alienated. Latimer, a failed poet full of gloom, is tormented by his clairvoyant

---

[3]   I use "Eliot" as the conventional moniker for this writer, whose renaming has an extensive history. Around the time of writing this story, she used both "Marian Evans Lewes" and "Marian Evans" in her personal correspondence. See Rosemarie Bodenheimer, "A Woman of Many Names," *The Cambridge Companion to George Eliot*, ed. George Levine (Cambridge: Cambridge University Press, 2001), 10–37.

powers to read the future and to read the thoughts of others. He becomes attracted to his brother's fiancée Bertha because the contents of her mind, unlike those of others in his world, are not available to him. Once married to her, however, Latimer gains access to the contents of her mind and discovers her thoughts to be appallingly cruel and self-serving, in no way consistent with Bertha's angelic external beauty. He also learns that Bertha possesses a power that opposes his own: while he can read the thoughts of others, she can write them through her animal magnetism or thought control. Deviating in troubling ways from ideal middle-class femininity, Bertha, with her nasty sentiments and disturbing powers, is a precursor to aggressive British sensation heroines like Lady Audley or Lydia Gwilt in *Armadale*. And Latimer, with his feminine physical frailties and nervous sensitivity, also resembles the gender-bending qualities of many sensation fiction characters including Marian Halcombe and Philip Fairlie in *The Woman in White*.

Its plotting and performance of suspense are also consistent with the formal, narrative dimensions of sensational stories. Through the attention to prevision and reading the minds of others, Eliot suggests that desire is shaped by limited knowledge that stimulates a craving for more. "The Lifted Veil" functions as an allegory for the powers of insight aligned with the reading and writing of fiction. Latimer's manipulation of readerly desires by pointed and periodical glimpses of the future also bespeaks the formal operations of narrative suspense, something sensation fiction's serial form exploits.[4] However, "The Lifted Veil" was not published serially, either in its British *Blackwood's* appearance in July 1859 or in its American arrival a month later. Without this enforced suspension of narrative through weekly or monthly installments, so characteristic of sensation novels of the 1860s, Eliot foregrounds its absence in "The Lifted Veil." For Latimer's narration makes manifest a convergence of suspenseful conclusion at the start. "The time of my end approaches," begins Latimer in the opening paragraph of the story, while the last sentence of this initial paragraph forecasts, and thus problematizes, the suspense of closure: "For I foresee when I shall die, and everything that will happen in my last moments" (3). The reader knows the ending by the bottom of the first paragraph. Still, its attention to the tension between concealment and disclosure, whether of the thoughts of others or of future events in Latimer's life, offers a useful parallel to the forms of suspense in Victorian fiction. As we shall see, Alcott's stories conformed in this way to the serial nature of sensational suspense since her "thrillers" were issued in periodical parts.

In terms of plot elements, "The Lifted Veil" is replete with sensational features of extraordinary, paranormal occurrences, from Latimer's prevision and mind-reading and Bertha's mesmeric capacities to a penultimate scene of revivification, perhaps the most "dismal" moment of all. The transfusion scene, with the animated

---

[4]   Although "The Lifted Veil" was published on both sides of the Atlantic in one installment only, the story itself is divided into two chapters. For an intriguing discussion of suspense in this story, see Caroline Levine, *The Serious Pleasures of Suspense: Victorian Realism and Narrative Doubt* (Charlottesville: University of Virginia Press, 2003), 127–137.

corpse of the servant Mrs. Archer revealing Bertha's murder plot against her husband, anticipates the shocking incidents of sensation heroines whose penchant for the unladylike feelings of hatred and revenge along with the agency to commit crimes undercuts the conventional domestic angel.[5]

In response to Eliot's remark that the story was "dismal," Blackwood replied in admiration of the writing itself, but advised her to cut the transfusion scene, as he found it in objectionable taste. Quality of writing, although an unstable value across cultures and time, also distinguishes British sensation fiction from its transatlantic counterpart. As I have argued elsewhere, the very term "sensation fiction" in British reviews signifies an attempt to categorize the popular stories in the periodical press that seemed to blur class lines between elitely educated and newly literate readers (Bernstein, "Ape Anxiety" 253–254). Yet most American fiction was viewed as popular, lacking refinement, or downright vulgar by British readers. Put differently, American readers understood the class distinctions of literature through the lens of nationality, with British writers as refined or cultured in contrast to the popular writing of American authors. Blackwood's advice here reveals how principles of decorum mediated British fiction. Eliot refused to accommodate this suggestion to remove the transfusion scene, an incident, Blackwood's comment implies, that was dubiously fit for the pages of *Blackwood's*.

Eliot wrote "The Lifted Veil" during a public controversy over the authorship of her first published fiction, *Scenes of Clerical Life* and *Adam Bede*. George Henry Lewes recommended "George Eliot" as the authorial signature for "The Lifted Veil." Instead, Blackwood insisted on the magazine's editorial policy of anonymity and asserted that it was preferable to withhold this proper name as it was "better not to fritter away the prestige which should be kept fresh for the new novel" (Haight 112 n.6). Lewes had lobbied to include Eliot's name at the end of the story as a way to quash a lively rumor, that a Nuneaton clergyman Joseph Liggins was the author of *Adam Bede* and *Scenes from Clerical Life*. Given that this controversy about the identity of "George Eliot" spiraled around the time she wrote "The Lifted Veil" and was resolved in late June 1859, just before its publication, when Marian Evans admitted her identity to Blackwood, the story is frequently read as an allusion to the veiling and unveiling of female authorship with its references to scandal, duplicity, and secret identity, features of later sensation stories and its heroines of many names.[6] Reacting to this public disclosure of her name, William Hepworth Dixon, editor of the *Athenaeum,* on 2 July 1859 in the pages of his periodical described Eliot as "a clever woman with an observant eye and an unschooled moral nature...a rather strong-minded lady, blessed with abundance of showy sentiment and a profusion of pious words, but

---

[5]   The transfusion scene actually inspired a painting by a French artist: H.É. Blanchon, "La Transfusion du sang" (1879), reprinted in Small, frontispiece.

[6]   The title character of *Lady Audley's Secret* is perhaps the most well known example; the novel circulates some five different proper names for her. See Small (x–xi) for an account of Eliot's correspondence with Blackwood and the controversy over revealing her identity.

kept for *sale* rather than for use" (emphasis original; qtd. in Ashton 223). The personal identity behind the name "George Eliot" unleashes such accounts that seem to characterize the author as a sensation heroine herself.[7]

The story's initial reception in Britain also anticipated the kind of language critics would use a few years later to decry sensation novels. Blackwood wrote to Eliot about early reactions to the story: "All admire the excellence and power of the writing, lovers of the painful are thrilled and delighted, others like me are thrilled but wish the author in a happier frame of mind and not thinking of unsympathising untrustworthy keepers of secrets" (Haight 112). These words bespeak the strong passions that became a hallmark of sensation fiction, while the "secrets" here allude not to elements of the story itself but rather to the hidden identity behind "George Eliot," and the publisher's anxiety that neither name be disclosed as the author of "The Lifted Veil." Because Lewes, her spouse, was legally married to someone else, Marian Evans Lewes, as she called herself, lived a sexual scandal, a topic frequently found in the pages of sensation fiction, something Hepworth Dixon's acerbic words imply.[8]

Across the ocean, Henry James reviewed the story for *The Nation*, although not until *Blackwood's* published it under Eliot's name in 1878.[9] James's brief description of "The Lifted Veil" showcases the climactic finale that reveals Bertha's plot to murder Latimer: "a wicked lady…whose guilt is brought to light by the experiment of infusing blood into the heart of a person just dead" (James 994). James is ambivalent about a story he finds both "very wonderful" and "rather violent" (994), again traits usually applied by the British press to British sensation fiction of the 1860s.

Despite Blackwood's professed interest in eschewing "dismal" themes of crime and revivification in his magazine, sensational elements do punctuate the content. Besides "The Lifted Veil" other items in the July 1859 pages of *Blackwood's* forecast the 1860s cultural obsession with shocking subjects (Figure

---

[7]   Eliot's other short story, "Brother Jacob," published in *The Cornhill* in July 1864, also reads as an allegory about the ethics of false identity where Jacob's brother, the aptly named "David Faux" disguises himself after returning from some years in the Jamaican sugar industry as "Edward Freely." That Liggins was the son of a baker prompts an affiliation with Faux/Freely, a confectioner whose shop sells delectable sweets and pastries, a favorite trope for sensation novels as addictive sugarplums or corrupt "mental food" (Oliphant 259) that stimulate the "cravings of a diseased appetite" (Mansel 483). The eponymous Jacob of the story might be aligned with the readers of popular fiction too. Jacob is mentally disabled, an "idiot" according to the language of the story and the day. David, who absconds to Jamaica with family money, repeatedly tries to trick his brother, but Jacob proves himself a more adept reader, and even sees through David's disguise as Edward Freely. Jacob's partiality for all sweets further prompts a reading of this story as an allegory about sensation fiction readers and writers

[8]   As Lyn Pykett has observed, "The sensation novel's preoccupation with marriage questions was frequently articulated in the form of the bigamy plot" (45).

[9]   Blackwood's 1878 Cabinet Edition of Eliot's work included in one volume "The Lifted Veil," "Brother Jacob," and *Silas Marner*.

BLACKWOOD'S

EDINBURGH MAGAZINE.

No. DXXV.   JULY 1859.   Vol. LXXXVI.

CONTENTS.

EDINBURGH:

WILLIAM BLACKWOOD & SONS, 45 GEORGE STREET,

AND 37 PATERNOSTER ROW, LONDON;

To whom all Communications (post paid) must be addressed.

SOLD BY ALL THE BOOKSELLERS IN THE UNITED KINGDOM.

Fig. 10.1   *Blackwood's Magazine.*

10.1). The lead article, a review of Thomas Babington Macaulay's treatment of the massacre of Glencoe in his writing on British history, advertises this retelling of political crime so that "after the lapse of a century and a half, the blood curdles at it as if it were a deed of yesterday" (1). Following Eliot's story is an article about H.L. Mansel's Bampton Lectures at Oxford University on theology and rationalism. Although this topic might bear no relation to sensationalism, its author does. Four years later Mansel published "Sensation Novels," an unsigned review of twenty-four novels issued in 1862 from *Lady Audley's Secret* and *No Name* to the anonymously authored *The Woman of Spirit*. For Mansel, sensation fiction "aims at convulsing the soul of the reader" and "electrifying the nerves of the reader" (483, 488–489), qualities that resemble the magnetic field influencing a mesmeric subject. Using scientific language to imagine the effects of reading, Mansel classifies some sensation fiction as "the galvanic-battery type" and compares the embodied sensations produced in the reader to those stimulated by "heat, electricity, galvanism" (487). Finally, the review dismisses the whole lot as "an impure or a silly crop of novels" (512), words that recall Eliot's 1856 *Westminster Review* essay "Silly Novels by Lady Novelists."

In contrast to Mansel's disparaging view of current fiction, a further essay in the magazine, "The Novels of Jane Austen," regrets that her books are not read more extensively since Austen is "an artist of the highest rank, in the most rigorous sense of the word" (99). Here the writer deplores the current state of British literary culture in which Austen's "name is still unfamiliar in men's mouths," and remarks, "So far from the name of Miss Austen being constantly cited among the glories of our literature, there are many well-informed persons who will be surprised to hear it mentioned among the best writers" (99). Instead, the essayist observes that when readers do remember *Pride and Prejudice*, they often forget the author's name, and when prompted with "Miss Austen," they confuse her with a "Mrs. Austin" who translates from German. This opening parley about the merit of a woman novelist whose name seems barely alive functions as an ironic corollary to the current controversy around "George Eliot" and its veiling as author of "The Lifted Veil" in the same issue of the magazine. The question of the durability of a female author's name here suggests too the problem of female agency thematized through Bertha's mesmeric powers in the story. As I will show later, women writers' names seem to have more longevity in American culture, especially British authors like Eliot, Braddon, or Brontë.

Also part of the magazine issue in which "The Lifted Veil" appeared in Britain is the fifth installment of "The Luck of Ladysmede," a historical romance set in medieval England; this episode begins with a chapter "The Confession" that sensationalizes the secrecy of Catholic religious rituals.[10] Again switching between fiction and essay, the pattern of the items in the July 1859 contents of *Blackwood's*, the next article, "Sentimental Physiology," invites the reader "to shape for himself the forms of events in the darkness of the future" of Paris, a practice that "The

---

[10]   William Lucas Collins is the author of *The Luck of Ladysmede*, published in volume form by Blackwood in 1860.

Lifted Veil" details through Latimer's clairvoyant prevision of Prague (87). By examining these items that accompanied Eliot's story in *Blackwood's*, we can see how elements of sensationalism accent other features in the periodical and across discourses from fiction and history to religion and science.[11] More than the American papers that carried Alcott's thrillers, this British periodical context balances or subdues the sensational elements of Eliot's story with its array of writing about loftier topics including the scholarship of an Oxford don.

A month after the initial British publication of the tale in *Blackwood's*, "The Lifted Veil" appeared in *The Living Age*, an American miscellany weekly entirely comprised of unauthorized reprints (McGill 23). Similar to Elisa Tamarkin's argument about Anglophilia,[12] Meredith McGill comments on the prestige of British reprints in American periodicals such as Littell's *Living Age*: "Reprinted foreign texts carry with them the authority of an older, established, and centralized media" (24). Substituting nationality for authorship in this American reprint magazine, titles of British journals supplanted the authors' proper names in the table of contents. "The Lifted Veil" in the August 6, 1859, issue of *The Living Age* accordingly lists "*Blackwood's Magazine*" in the right column opposite the story's title in the left column of the contents page (Figure 10.2). Rather than Foucault's "author function," we might read this paratextual feature as a "nation function" since the periodical title has signifying weight, something that would trump the taint of sensation. The table of contents for the volume version groups together documents according to periodical titles including *Quarterly Review*, *North British Review*, *Fraser's Magazine*, *Spectator*, and S*aturday Review* (Figure 10.3). Whereas British readers would have pre-selected themselves according to the political, religious, and class profiles of the journals, American readers instead gravitated toward such magazines as *The Living Age* which grouped together documents from heterogeneous British sources. While McGill transposes a convention of "gentlemanly anonymity" in British periodicals to "democratic anonymity" in American reprints, this framing through the British magazine title also suggests a kind of transatlantic cultural hegemony (26). Although Eliot's proper name does not promote this instance of the American recycling of her fiction, the title of the British periodical as its source does indicate cultural capital. In this case, the British journal title masks the author's name of "The Lifted Veil" too, even as the veil had literally lifted on the identity behind "George Eliot" in Britain.

---

[11] While Braddon edited *Belgravia*, a series of articles titled "Sensationalism in Science" appeared in the magazine in 1868 and 1869. See my essay, "Sensation and Science," *The Blackwell Companion to Sensation*, ed. Pamela Gilbert (Oxford: Blackwell, 2011).

[12] Tamarkin identifies "the compulsive patternings and devotional respects of what I can only call American Anglophilia" (445) in American abolitionist discourse; her argument here extends to a wider tendency to measure literary merit in nineteenth-century United States through British standards, or through "an idealized, civilized world in which the highest cultural accomplishment is its likeness to Britain" (473).

THE LIVING AGE.

No. 793.—6 August, 1859.—Third Series, No. 71.

CONTENTS.

PLATE.—PORTRAIT OF KLOPSTOCK.

☞ "Holmby House" comes out *once a month* in Frazer's Magazine,—so that we could only have given several parts in weekly succession, by the accumulation of our material for several months past. And now, having printed all we have, we must wait awhile for more. This is the more inconvenient as some of our subscribers demand its regular continuance. Next week we shall print up the arrears of "Town and Forest."

PUBLISHED EVERY SATURDAY BY

LITTELL, SON, & CO., BOSTON.

For Six Dollars a year, in advance, *remitted directly to the Publishers*, the Living Age will be punctually forwarded *free of postage*.

Complete sets of the First Series, in thirty-six volumes, and of the Second Series, in twenty volumes, handsomely bound, packed in neat boxes, and delivered in all the principal cities, free of expense of freight, are for sale at two dollars a volume.

Fig. 10.2 *The Living Age.*

TABLE OF THE PRINCIPAL CONTENTS

OF

THE LIVING AGE, VOLUME LXII.

THE SIXTH QUARTERLY VOLUME OF THE THIRD SERIES.

JULY, AUGUST, SEPTEMBER, 1859.

QUARTERLY REVIEW.

The Italian Question, ... 9
Editions of Shakspeare, ... 265
Invasion of England, ... 515
Life of Erasmus, ... 643

EDINBURGH REVIEW.

Queen Marie Antoinette, ... 579

WESTMINSTER REVIEW.

Effect of Local Causes on National Character, ... 782

NORTH BRITISH REVIEW.

Memoirs of Port Royal, ... 202

BENTLEY'S QUARTERLY REVIEW.

France, ... 473

NATIONAL REVIEW.

The People of the Arabian Nights, . 327
The Settlement of New England, . 392
Sir E. B. Lytton, ... 707

CAMBRIDGE ESSAYS.

The Ancient Bashan and the Cities of Og, 70

BRITISH QUARTERLY REVIEW.

Physical and Moral Heritage, . . 140

FRASER'S MAGAZINE.

Holmby House, . . 172, 232, 281, 344

BLACKWOOD'S MAGAZINE.

The Lifted Veil, ... 360
Novels of Jane Austen, ... 424
The Luck of Ladysmede, 451, 539, 599, 676, 727, 796
Macaulay and the Highlands of Scotland, 771

TITAN.

A Strange Life, ... 31

SPECTATOR.

The Crusade of To-day, ... 123
The Diplomatic Crisis of Europe, . 306
Actual Position of Austria, . . . 508
The Peace: its Purposes and Prospects. 570

EXAMINER.

The Peace of Villafranca, . . . 567
The Seven Weeks' War, ... 569
Western Indies and Mexico in 1599–1602, 574
The Liberal Party in France, . . 745
New African Discoveries, . . . 750
Life of Garibaldi, ... 763
England and the Congress, . . . 767

ECONOMIST.

Confining the War to Italy, . . . 113
Is the Anti-Gallican Panic Justified? . 115
The Anti-Gallican Press, ... 191
The European Crisis—England's Duty, 249
The Relations of England with France, 251
France, Russia, and Germany, . . 252
True Duties of Neutrals, ... 307
Austria—a Supposed Political Necessity, 440
The Armistice—What it Means, . . 509
Cavour's Resignation, ... 572
The Peace Analyzed, ... 633
Deficiency of Labor in the West Indies, 752
Hopes of Italy and Intentions of France, 754

PRESS.

American Preachers, ... 104
Russia and the East, ... 126
France and Sardinia, ... 127
The Revolutionary Element, . . . 308
Prospects, ... 442
Battle of Solferino, ... 443
The Armistice, ... 510
The Peace, ... 634
Blighted Prospects, ... 636
Closing Scene of the Italian Drama, . 637
First Fruits of the War, ... 638
Attitude of Italy, ... 695
The *Moniteur* and its Announcements, . 695
A Photograph from St. Cloud, . . 703
Can Italy be Worse? 755
Waiting Italy, ... 767

SATURDAY REVIEW.

Policy of Germany, ... 112
Chinaman's Journey in Japan, . . 186
Foreign Policy of the New Government, 254
Prince Metternich, ... 304
The French Alliance, ... 310

Fig. 10.3 "Table of Contents." *The Living Age.*

Where the assortment of different intellectual discourses mitigated the appearance of sensationalism in the contents of *Blackwood's* surrounding Eliot's story, in this initial American printing of "The Lifted Veil" the frequent British labeling through magazine titles lends a highbrow veneer to any sensationalizing themes. In a *National Review* essay on Edward Lane's 1859 translation of "The Thousand and One Arabian Nights," the reviewer suggests that the stories, much like dreams, induce readers to become Aladdin in a kind of promiscuous reading identification.[13] This blurring of reader and character constitutes a profile that would increasingly identify sensation fiction, its characters and plots, and its effects on readers. As the reviewer of "The People of the Arabian Nights" here explains, "To read of these things was a sort of intellectual 'hasheesh,' an intoxicating stimulant to that early imagination which does not consciously subdue other things into its own forms, but delights to lose itself in suggestions from without" ("People" 328). In this way Eliot's story is framed through the tenets of reviewers' assessment of sensational literature. Middle chapters from a historical romance set in seventeenth-century Britain, "Holmby House," reprinted from *Fraser's Magazine*, next appear in the pages immediately prior to "The Lifted Veil."[14] A note at the bottom of the list of contents explains the logistical problems of reprinting a serial from a British monthly magazine in an American weekly: "And now, having printed all we have, we must wait awhile for more. This is the more inconvenient as some of our subscribers demand its regular continuance." Transatlantic serialization necessitates additional suspended suspense. With Cromwell and King Charles as characters in the novel, this installment begins, "Deeper and deeper still, Mary Cave found herself engulphed [*sic*] in the whirlpool of political intrigue" (344). Also similar to sensation fiction, the story accentuates female agency.

In "The Lifted Veil," the treatment of gender and power is also ambivalent. The narration of "The Lifted Veil" is unusual for Eliot inasmuch as it is the only first-person narrative among her fiction, until her final collection, *The Impressions of Theophrastus Such*. However, the reflexive narrators who punctuate the pages of all her novels echo some of the speculations on authorial and narratorial agency "The Lifted Veil" probes. The story's evident interest in paranormal psychic powers might suggest a stronger adhesion to the Gothic rather than sensationalism, yet as many scholars have noted, the Gothic novel is a crucial supporting branch in the literary genealogy of sensation fiction (Wynne 7). For Kate Flint, the sensational scene of Mrs. Archer's revivification through the experimental blood transfusion reads as an allegory about female authorship: "this text functions as an experiment … in George Eliot's awareness of the complications involved in a woman author writing with masculine authority—whether one takes 'masculine' in the sense of personal identity or dominant discourse" (470). For Helen Small, Mrs. Archer's

---

[13] For a discussion of reading through "promiscuous identification," see Bernstein, "Promiscuous Reading."

[14] George John Whyte-Melville (1821–78) wrote *Holmby House: A Tale of Old Northamptonshire*.

shocking revelation about Bertha's murderous designs is contingent on the scientific experiments and literal life blood of the male doctor; thus, female agency necessarily draws on male authority just as the author does by using "George Eliot" as her pen name (Flint xxiv). Latimer, as first-person narrator, functions as a device for experimenting with the power and problems of authorial omniscience, especially the dubious effects of knowing the thoughts of others and future events. Like many sensation characters, Latimer seems a gender hybrid, a man with many feminine attributes including his acute and frustrated sensitivity as a voiceless poet: "the poet's sensibility that finds no vent but in silent tears" (7).[15]

It is in relation to Bertha Grant that the story's most complex stance on gendered power emerges. While many readers focus on the paranormal abilities of Latimer including his previsions, Bertha's mesmeric powers work as both catalyst and limit for Latimer's clairvoyant agency. This arrangement reverses the argument that female authority, whether authorial or sensational, is contingent on masculine power. Malcolm Bull maintains that both the plot and title of the story only make sense if we assume that Bertha is the mesmeric or magnetic operator, Latimer her subject, again an arrangement that inverts the more typical roles of male mesmerist and female subject (246). Even the word "sensation" makes its most salient appearances in the text around these moments in which Bertha's gaze stuns Latimer into "double consciousness." The initial description of Bertha Grant anticipates the portraits of Braddon's sensation heroines like Lady Audley: "…a tall, slim, willowy figure, with luxuriant blond hair, arranged in cunning braids and fold that looked almost too massive for the slight figure and the small-featured, thick-lipped face they crowned. But the face had not a girlish expression: the features were sharp, the pale grey eyes at once acute, restless, and sarcastic. They were fixed on me in half-smiling curiosity, and I felt a painful sensation as if a sharp wind were cutting me" (11). This "painful sensation" matches what William Gregory, who published about animal magnetism in 1851, described as the effect of the magnetizer on the patient (Bull 245–246). Eliot knew about Gregory's mesmeric experiments through George Combe, the British phrenologist (Flint xvi–xix). Combe read a cast of Eliot's head in 1844 as belonging to a man and read her head in person in 1851 when he declared that she was "the ablest woman whom I have seen …with a very large brain" (Flint xvii).

Eliot's treatment of mesmerism and clairvoyance in the story stems from her knowledge of these new sciences that captured a wide interest in British print in the 1840s and 1850s.[16] Latimer's loss of consciousness immediately following this experience of Bertha's mesmeric gaze implies the phenomenon of animal magnetism—the transference of power from one body to another—Gregory details in his account. Latimer dates his prevision or direct clairvoyance from this scene in which he feels Bertha's gaze as "a painful sensation." The only other time

---

[15]   All quotations from "The Lifted Veil" are taken from the Oxford edition edited by Helen Small.

[16]   For another recent treatment of this subject, see Willis.

the word "sensation" appears in the story occurs when Latimer visits a gallery in Vienna and reacts to "Giorgione's picture of the cruel-eyed woman, said to be a likeness of Lucrezia Borgia. I had stood long before it, fascinated by the terrible reality of the cunning, relentless face, till I felt a strange poisoned sensation" (18–19). If the confluence of gazes were not sufficient to fasten the identification between Bertha and Borgia here, immediately after this "sensation" Latimer feels Bertha's touch, "a light hand gently pressing my wrist" (19), at which point "a strange intoxicating numbness passed over me, like the continuance or climax of the sensation I was still feeling from the gaze of Lucrezia Borgia" (19). A few years later, Braddon also compares Lady Audley to this early modern woman famed for bewitching beauty and ruthless power including murder (310).[17]

Not only does this reading anticipate popular profiles of 1860s sensation heroines, but also it implies that the act of reading (or viewing a representation of a dazzlingly beautiful and powerful woman) inflicts readers with mesmeric effects, much as critics compared sensation novels to addictive stimulants, "striving to act as the dram or the dose, rather than as the solid food" (Mansel 485). Although I would not categorize "The Lifted Veil" as sensation fiction in the way the term is circulated a few years later to describe popular serialized novels, it does have evident marks of resemblance within the story through shocking scenes and especially through the attention to gender construction and female power. Even so, the crafting of sensationalism is as much the work of its periodical context and the internal substance of the story. In these two transatlantic publications of "The Lifted Veil," that sensationalism is both bolstered by echoes within surrounding material and yet muted by the intellectual topics included in *Blackwood's*, on the one hand, and the Anglophilic effect of the titles of British periodicals listed in *The Living Age*, on the other. Neither inscribes author names, but the style of anonymity clearly differs. Given the prestige of British culture in the mid-century American popular press, Alcott's sensationalism carries the transatlantic mystique when she clearly mimics British fiction, evident in *Behind a Mask* with its ample allusions to novels by Charlotte Brontë, Braddon, and Collins. But the earlier "A Pair of Eyes," the story connected to "The Lifted Veil" through the entwined subjects of mesmerism and female power, offers a different form of sensationalism— internally and in its periodical context—from its British and British-modeled counterparts.

Alcott's American "Modern Magic"

Unlike Eliot, Louisa May Alcott had not been recognized widely as a prominent novelist, and she had not apprenticed, as Eliot did with the *Westminster Review*, as an editor of a respected periodical. But she did win a newspaper story contest for "Pauline's Passion and Punishment," a prize which proved her incentive and

---

[17] In "A Pair of Eyes," the narrator imagines Agatha Eure as Lady Macbeth (68, 78).

promise. Both appearing in serial form, "A Pair of Eyes" and "Behind a Mask" likewise investigate double consciousness and mesmerism, but in Alcott's stories this mental agency is explicitly aligned only with a female character. Like Latimer and Bertha, Alcott's mesmeric heroines offer a "mask" for the power and problems of female authorship and artistic creativity. Alcott also deploys animal magnetism to wield a critique of marriage, gender relations, and romantic love as magnetic attraction. While I hesitate from using this comparison of psychic powers in "The Lifted Veil" and "A Pair of Eyes" to assert broadly transatlantic distinctions of sensationalism in fiction, I do find Alcott's American variety far bolder, less convoluted and ambivalent, about using sensational devices to launch a social critique.

In this tale, published in two installments in October 1863 in *Frank Leslie's Illustrated Newspaper*, Agatha Eure possesses the power of a magnetic operator. *Frank Leslie's Illustrated Newspaper*, as I elaborate in what follows, promoted itself as a brand of sensational press in contrast to middle-class periodicals like *Harper's* with its resemblance to British fare like *Blackwood's Edinburgh Magazine*. Publishing venue and content combine to render Alcott's "A Pair of Eyes" more audacious in its strains of sensationalism than Eliot's single foray in that direction. Both stories attribute mesmeric powers to these two characters, powers that suggest ways of working out the force of female fictive authorship. For Eliot, in order to assert that authorial power, a woman needs to assume a male identity: Marian Evans as "George Eliot" follows her narrator as Latimer. Bertha Grant's narrative agency, the ability to speak her own version of that marriage, remains unvoiced, much like Brontë's mute Bertha, speechlessly mad in the attic. For Alcott too, female creative agency works "behind a mask" of conventional femininity, but in "A Pair of Eyes" the male artist's creativity is dependent on and ultimately subjected to a woman's will through her magnetic powers. Unlike the British Berthas, Agatha Eure, the magnetic operator and wife in "A Pair of Eyes," does voice her version of the marriage, male art, and female subjection. And she also pursues a vocation as a visual artist, unlike her counterpart Bertha in Eliot's story.

Besides the name "Eure," so close to "Eyre," Alcott's debts to both Charlotte and Emily Brontë are numerous, with assorted links to *Jane Eyre, Villette,* and *Wuthering Heights*. A review from the *Boston Post*, circulated through *The Living Age* in 1848, immediately depicts the heroine of *Jane Eyre* as "an impassioned temperament, a quick and sound intellect, extraordinary strength of nerve," and "moulded from a heap of opposites."[18] The reviewer also mentions Brontë's paranormal plot device, where Jane apprehends Rochester's appeal to her as "the intellectual hearing of voices a hundred miles off is extravagant if not absurd." Even the mixed assessment of *Jane Eyre*'s masked author links sensationalism with female authorship: "The author *ought* to write a first-rate novel, for he or

---

[18] The short review indicates that *Jane Eyre* was reprinted by Harper & Brothers in New York and by Redding & Company in Boston in 1848.

she (perhaps) is gifted with passion, power, will, and fluency of language ... from the present specimen it would seem as if her forte lay in throwing one strong and intense light from one side of her lantern, leaving all surrounding objects in comparative darkness." This instance of uneven praise for a novelist presumed to be a woman substantiates the Brontës' use of the gender-neutral names of "Currer Bell" (for Charlotte) and "Ellis Bell" (for Emily), similar to Alcott's "A.M. Barnard."

With all its excessive and nearly farcical allusions to *Jane Eyre*, *Wuthering Heights*, and *Lady Audley's Secret*, Alcott plays with British prestige in *Behind the Mask*, as nearly a parody of Anglophilia, although it appeared in *The Flag of Our Union*, a periodical with a title and content tooled to the American Civil War.[19] The story of Jean Muir employed as governess to a young girl manages to marry the patriarch of the family despite the "furtively watching" eyes of Mrs. Dean, a maidservant described as "a grave, middle-aged woman with keen eyes" (159, 161).[20] The narrator comments, "The metamorphosis was wonderful, but the disguise was more in the expression she assumed than in any art of costume or false adornment" (106). Notwithstanding the demure damsel Jean often portrays, the narrator credits Jean's eyes with power. During a scene in which she and other members of the household perform a tableau of Judith and Holofernes, her impersonation of the biblical murderess accentuates her eyes which "darkened and dilated till they were as fierce as any southern eyes that ever flashed" (147). If Alcott suggests that Jean's eyes reveal a cunning agency "behind the mask" of her various domestic performances, "A Pair of Eyes" three years earlier owe the heroine's power to mesmerism.

Like Bertha Grant, Agatha Eure moves from an object of fascination as the wife of the narrator in "A Pair of Eyes," but her mesmeric gaze arrests the

---

[19]   Advertised a week before its first installment, *The Flag of Our Union* promises "one of the most intensely exciting and interesting novels ever published" (October 6, 1866). A marked contrast from *Blackwood's Edinburgh Magazine* as well as *The Living Age*, *The Flag of Our Union* promised original material "to please all tastes, and which makes it a welcome visitor to the Home Circle, The Camp, The Counting-Room, The Workshop, and The Farmer's Fireside" (October 6, 1866). Its 1854–1870 run spanning the Civil War, this paper likewise offered a print vehicle for Alcott's Americanized sensation tales, published under the name "A.M. Barnard." Alcott's serialized novel "A Marble Woman:—or, The Mysterious Model" appeared in *The Flag of Our Union* a year earlier on May 20, 27, June 3, 10, 1865. "Behind a Mask" also was issued in four installments: October 13, 20, 27, November 3, 1866.

[20]   Despite these evident allusions, "Behind a Mask" has its most salient sources in Braddon's *Lady Audley's Secret* and in Collins's *Armadale*, as Elaine Showalter points to Alcott's depictions of "ambitious and passionate governesses, who use their ambiguous position within the family to initiate romantic plots" (xxix). Like Lady Audley, Jean Muir becomes Lady Coventry despite an ongoing rivalry with a Coventry cousin, Lucia Beaufort. Like Lydia Gwilt, Jean Muir skillfully applies cosmetics and artificial teeth like an actress to perform her femininity in a way designed to seduce the Coventry men.

attention of a neglectful husband who is "married" more to his art. The story, divided into two parts, like "The Lifted Veil," focuses initially on Max Erdmann, the narrating artist who is in "want of a pair of eyes" for the finishing touches of his painting (59). During the opening scene, which takes place at a theatrical performance, Erdmann senses "a disturbing influence whose power invade my momentary isolation ... the conviction that someone was looking at me" (60). The eyes belong not to the actress on stage, but to Agatha Eure, and so Erdmann asks Eure to pose as his model for his painting. Alcott remakes some of the elements from the theater scene in *Villette* where the actress performing Vashti, the wronged wife, wears a "demoniac mask" where "in each of her eyes sat a devil" (257). To seal the allusion to Brontë's Lucy Snowe, *Villette*'s narrator, the surname of the people accompanying Agnes Eure to the theater is "Snow." When Erdmann goes to Agatha's "West End square" (66) home—a likely reference to London—to paint her eyes, he succumbs to an inexplicable trance when his model appears. The painter seems to enter an alternative consciousness as a result, and the description of his sensations indicate a mesmeric trance. When he emerges from this altered state and completes his painting, Agatha then tells him that the studio she has provided for him actually was once her working space, for, she claims, "I, too, was an artist then, and dreamed aspiring dreams here, but was arrested on the threshold of my career by loss of sight." She concludes, "I have learned to desire for others what I can never hope for myself" (69). Alcott clarifies Agatha's psychic gaze not only as compensatory power for an earlier somatic blindness, but also as a female artist compelled to exert her own creative visions through a male artist. Love for art and artist, like the blurring of artist and model, become confused, and the first part of the story ends with their marriage. The second half of "A Pair of Eyes," like "The Lifted Veil," reveals the disaster of that marriage, as the balance of the story also shows the battle of wills between this couple. Through mesmerism, Agatha forces Erdmann to be "possessed" by her rather than by his art. Erdmann attempts to retaliate but ends a widowed father with a mute and blind son, while "with a power made more omnipotent by death Agatha still calls me" (80), suggesting Rochester's supernatural call to Jane, or Cathy from the grave summoning Heathcliff in *Wuthering Heights*. Before detailing Alcott's use of mesmerism to show a woman's subjugation as an artist and as a wife, I want to provide a parallel background on the print context for this American sensation story.

Alcott first wrote her thrillers for income she needed for her family during the Civil War and found a ready customer through Frank Leslie. After her prize story "Pauline's Passion and Punishment" appeared in *Frank Leslie's Illustrated Newspaper* in January 1863, she supplied similar stories about designing women including "A Pair of Eyes." Leslie was English by birth and worked as an engraver at the *Illustrated London News* for six years until he arrived in New York City in 1848 (Brown 8). Originally named "Henry Carter," Leslie changed his name as he crafted an American identity, and launched his weekly pictorial newspaper as an alternative to the successful and more elite *Harper's Monthly Magazine*, the dominant middle-class periodical since its inception in 1850. By the early 1860s,

Leslie aggressively pursued an editorial policy of "sensation and revelation" so that this paper "teetered on the cusp of respectability" as it "delved into the realm of sensation" with visual and verbal representations of lurid crimes and sexualized entertainment (Brown 24–25).

The January 3, 1863 issue of *Frank Leslie's Illustrated Newspaper* front-loads large engravings from Civil War battles, yet inserts an announcement that the winner of "Our American Prize Story"—depicted in the advertisement as one "of high merit as well as absorbing interest, purely American and excellent in morals"—appears in this issue. The first chapters of "Pauline's Passion and Punishment" commences a few pages later, surrounded by additional full-page engravings of eye-witness scenes from the war front. Within the same issue are installments from British sensation novels—Ellen Price Wood's *Verner's Pride* (with the byline "by the author of *East Lynne*") and Braddon's *Aurora Floyd*.[21]

A few years later in *Little Women*, Alcott transposes her experiences as a contributor of sensational stories with Jo March writing for a "pictorial sheet" called the "Weekly Volcano" filled with "that class of light literature in which the passions have a holiday" (291, 292). After Jo wins the prize for her story, she continues producing "rubbish" in order to support their household during wartime: "'The Duke's Daughter' paid the butcher's bill, 'A Phantom Hand' put down a new carpet, and 'The Curse of the Coventrys' proved the blessing of the Marches in the way of groceries and gowns" (294). While the last title clearly alludes to *Behind a Mask*, Alcott also mentions the "metaphysical streak" of Jo's sensation stories like the mesmeric plot of "A Pair of Eyes" (296). Because of this breadwinner benefit, Jo "began to feel herself a power in the house" from writing such prize-winning "rubbish" (294). Her authorial name and her personal name converging on the cover of *Little Women* in 1868, Alcott distances herself from her earlier "rubbish" within this autobiographically laced novel which became both a commercial and critical success, yet she continued publishing these thrillers through 1870 in Leslie's various papers.[22] The mask of anonymity or a pen name used with her thrillers sanitized "Louisa M. Alcott" as a respectable author of fiction for American girls.

And it was this breed of writing, not her newspaper shockers, that circulated across the Atlantic. *Little Women* "by Louisa M. Alcott" appeared first in London in late 1868 issued by Sampson Low. A review in *The Athenaeum* comments on the American scenes to which English women readers would be "unaccustomed,"

---

[21] Clearly Leslie was able to obtain installments of Braddon's novel rapidly from London since this segment in the early January 1863 issue of the American weekly had appeared in the November 1862 issue of the monthly periodical *Temple Bar*.

[22] *Little Women* was first published in two parts in Boston by Roberts Brothers in October 1868 and in April 1869, and another girls' novel, *An Old-Fashioned Girl*, followed in 1870. However, in 1868, 1869, and 1870, Alcott continued to publish her periodical sensation stories in *Frank Leslie's Illustrated Newspaper*, *Frank Leslie's Lady's Magazine*, and *Frank Leslie's Chimney Corner*. For a bibliography of Alcott's stories, see Stern (75). For details on her full publishing history, see Alton edition of *Little Women*.

and depicts Jo March as "one of the strong-minded race of young women." The reviewer also mentions that "Miss Jo in her early days aspires to literary success." That she relinquishes this ambition, the critic implies, mitigates her "strong-minded" propensities. Perhaps one reason why Alcott's anonymous thrillers did not travel the transatlantic print network is because they imitated British fiction, using English settings and thinly disguising character names.

If on the surface Alcott's stories seem indebted to the robust passions of the Brontës and even current sensation novelists, the interest in thought control and clairvoyance ties these stories to Eliot's 1859 "dismal" tale. In Alcott's "A Pair of Eyes; or, Modern Magic," written a few years after "The Lifted Veil" appeared transatlantically, feminine mastery emerges explicitly through animal magnetism. Alcott's abiding interest in mental control, whether through writing sensation stories themselves or by developing plots about insanity or drug experimentation, takes a particularly compelling turn in "A Pair of Eyes." Where Eliot uses mesmerism and clairvoyance to investigate creative and authorial powers, Alcott deploys paranormal agency to bolster a "strong-minded" or feminist critique of marriage as well as women's curtailed access to artistic careers. Several full-fledged 1860s British sensation novels by Braddon, Wood, Collins, and Rhoda Broughton feature female characters who chafe against restrictions of their gender. Although Eliot's heroine clearly has nefarious powers, it is difficult to assess her agency because "The Lifted Veil" limits Bertha's perspective. Latimer's initial attraction to her springs from his inability to read her thoughts. Like Eliot's story, "A Pair of Eyes" is also a first-person narration by Max Erdmann, "the rising artist" who paints "ghosts and goblins" that generate sensational effects in viewers by making "their hair stand on end" (60). Ultimately the sensationalism of the story derives not from Erdmann's art but from the mesmerizing eyes of Agnes whom he first meets, as we have seen, at a theatrical performance when he experiences a "vague consciousness that some stronger nature was covertly exerting its power upon my own" (60). It turns out, however, that she has already seen him at an early occasion and expressed interest in meeting him to their mutual friend; here is another gender reversal where a woman's desires, rather than the man's social and sexual agency, drives the initial introduction of the couple.

Agatha Eure's animal magnetism closely approximates the description of mesmeric operations detailed by William Gregory in 1851. Like Eliot, whose interest in mesmerism followed a wider cultural fascination, Alcott's Boston literary world joined the American wave of clairvoyants and mesmerists. Ralph Waldo Emerson, Alcott's Concord neighbor, noted that mesmerism "broke into the inmost shrines, attempted the explanation of miracle and prophecy…it affirmed unity and connection between remote points" (Stern xxii). In the story, Agatha's mesmeric eyes explain the artist's initial attraction: "They exercised a curious fascination over me and kept my own obedient to their will, although scarce conscious of it at the time and believing mine to be the controlling power" (62). An earlier version of Jean Muir's "woman's power" and a more explicit rendering of Bertha Grant in Eliot's story, here the female mesmerist subtly works the magnetic force in an eroticized way that captivates Erdmann.

If Latimer only intuits Bertha's animal magnetism as the source of her appeal and his clairvoyance, Erdmann is increasingly explicit about Agatha's mental powers. As a dedicated bachelor-artist, who claims, "Art is my wife, I shall have no other"(66), Erdmann asks Agatha to model for him. During the session, he experiences a role reversal where he feels her eyes on him and then he succumbs to a mesmeric trance: "my eyelids began to be weighed down by a delicious drowsiness…Everything grew misty, and the beating of my heart sounded like a rapid, irregular roll of a muffled drum; then a strange weight seemed to oppress and cause me to sigh long and deeply" (67). There is no question that Agatha Eure is the cause of this subliminal state, and presumably Erdmann's proposal three months later results from the force of her desires. Erdmann observes, "Agatha Eure was a strong-willed, imperious woman, used to command all about her and see her last wish gratified" (70). Unlike Eliot's use of mesmerism, here Alcott aligns this mental agency with Agatha's "strong-willed" determination to have her husband's affections, especially when he begins wandering away from home to his work as an artist. But it is also possible to read her paranormal gaze as an assertion of a visual artist despite a handicap that forced her to relinquish that career.

The second part of the story, published a week after the first in *Frank Leslie's* on October 31, 1863, opens after their wedding when Erdmann quickly recognizes that Agatha resents that his art is "the mistress dearer than the wife" (71). Soon he finds himself drawn away from his painting and toward Agatha as she subjects him to a magnetic force field that expresses an "iron determination" which Erdmann describes as "some new power had taken possession of me, swaying my whole nature to its will, a power alien yet sovereign" (74). This mesmeric power, aligned with the neglected wife, might also be read as a corollary for the power of sensational reading. Where "The Lifted Veil" accentuates the process and powers of Latimer as reader of future events and others's minds, "A Pair of Eyes" focuses on Erdmann's enthrallment to Agatha's mesmeric abilities. After months of experiencing this power, Erdmann consults a medical friend, much like Latimer's Charles Meunier who experiments with revivification through blood transfusion in the climactic sensation scene toward the finale of "The Lifted Veil." In Alcott's story, this doctor diagnoses "Magnetism" as the name for Erdmann's condition, and the narrator relays some background on the "occult magic" of "Mesmer's mystical discoveries" (75–76). The British press lamented the tendency of sensation fiction to "preach to the nerves" instead of the loftier qualities of readers, like morals or reason, such as Mansel mentions in his review about such stories "electrifying the nerves," an effect which might be compared with the magnetic force of a mesmerist. So does this American sensation story explore compulsive and obsessive ways of reading or being read, yet Alcott exploits this interest in magnetic reading practices to offer a broader social critique of gender and power, an accent that is latent at best in Eliot's tale.

The most striking departure from "The Lifted Veil" is in the last pages of "A Pair of Eyes" where Alcott quotes Agatha's account of her "mysterious gift" which she directs on her husband out of anger as the forsaken wife: "You have brought this fate upon yourself, accept it, submit to it, for I have bought you with my wealth, I told you with my mystic art, and body and soul, Max Erdmann, you are mine!" (77). Yet Erdmann determines to resist Agatha's magnetic powers, "that mental telegraph which stretched and thrilled between us," by acquiring counterbalancing mesmeric abilities of his own which lead to Agatha's death and the birth of a son, "dumb, blind and imbecile" as "punishment for my sin" (79–80). The story concludes with Erdmann, like Latimer, awaiting his death as Agatha continues to summon him "with a power made more omnipotent by death" (80).

By comparing these stories, I am interested in how Eliot and Alcott use mesmerism differently to reshape the marriage plot by demonizing, in "The Lifted Veil," feminine erotic power, or justifying a neglected wife's use of this occult "Modern Magic," in "A Pair of Eyes." Both women were at pivotal—yet different—places in their careers as fiction authors. For Alcott, her early sensational stories earned her necessary income as she published either anonymously in *Frank Leslie's Illustrated Newspaper* or under the name "A.M. Barnard" in *The Flag of Our Union*. Asserting herself as a fiction writer for money, Alcott's determination to succeed might be affiliated with her "strong-willed" sensation heroines. Yet once she achieves more respectable critical success through her *Little Women* series of family reading, Alcott no longer produces these stories of thrilling passion and intrigue. At this point Alcott has secured for herself a career as a literary artist, something her heroine Agnes Eure does not accomplish; Alcott has proven herself more durable than her willful sensation character. She no longer needed to bewitch readers through sensational fare because she had cultivated through her tamer, domestic novels a large readership of devoted girls. Unlike the newspaper thrillers, her *Little Women* novels were rousingly American in setting and in the subject matter of the March sisters' struggling self-reliance during the Civil War. Yet it is primarily British women writers who provide the models for Alcott's apprenticeship in fiction work. While I would be hesitant to take this transatlantic comparison of the uses of mesmerism in sensation stories as the basis for distinguishing American from British varieties, it does seem clear that Alcott imports from British sources, but she does so not to extol an Anglophilic fascination, but to hone her skills as a fiction artist by using some of the designs of the Brontës, Braddon, and Eliot.[23]

In contrast, "The Lifted Veil" seems less interested in recuperating transgressive women or frustrated women artists than in the politics of reading itself, whether future events or characters' minds, both powers that fiction writers and omniscient narrators possess. For Eliot, "The Lifted Veil" provided an opportunity at a juncture in her career as a novelist, already in full gear with her critically acclaimed novel

---

[23]   Although I have no secure evidence that Alcott had read "The Lifted Veil" as one of her sources inspiring "A Pair of Eyes," I want to reiterate that Eliot's publication in *The Living Age* makes manifest its English authorship, if not the specific proper name of the author. For aspiring American writers intent on British models, *The Living Age* was a valuable and well circulated resource.

Adam Bede published earlier that year, to speculate on the hazards of powerful realism, through this foray into sensationalism.[24] Yet if Alcott recreates herself in her fictional Jo as a writer of "rubbish," Eliot, or Marian Evans Lewes, had to contend with her immediate society that portrayed her as a sensation heroine, a fallen woman living with a married man without benefit of a legally or religiously sanctioned union. I am suggesting that Bertha Grant's mesmeric powers, like Latimer's clairvoyance, are vehicles for Eliot to apprehend the ambivalent significance of revealing others' thoughts, either through narrating a character or through writing or reading a novel or even the exposure of ignominious gossip around herself. When she began writing "The Lifted Veil," John Blackwood did not know the identity behind the alias "George Eliot" affixed to *Adam Bede*, which he had published; but by the time the story was ready to go, he did. Whether he found the transfusion scene at the end more "objectionable" than the risk of Eliot's reputation as an author compromised by the revelation of her intimate connection with Lewes, these diverse circulatory systems were a matter of concern.

Here too around this matter of authorial naming and masking we can discover some suggestive transatlantic differences. George Eliot's publishing name never reverted to "Marian Evans" or other forms in Britain, but it did in American publications of her fiction, perhaps an indication that gender and sexual politics were more liberal in this new, and less traditionally fixed, culture. *Harper's New Monthly* wrote in its June 1863 "Editor's Drawer" about how to access the popularity of *East Lynne* and *Aurora Floyd* from the current publications. "What eye is sharp enough to foresee the future, and distinguish in any contemporary novelist, for instance, the page moistened with a drop of the immortal elixir?" (135). As if searching for some prevision capacity, the editor speculates on literary value, and then offers this list of writers which mixes British and American, sensation and realism, women and men: "Is it Dickens, or Thackeray, or Bulwer, or James, or Wilkie Collins, or Reade, or Charlotte Brontë, or Miss Evans, or Mrs. Gaskell, or Hawthorne, or Mrs. Southworth, or Miss Braddon, or Mrs. Stowe, or Charles Lever, or Sylvanus Cobb, Jun.—or who is he or she who is really first in the immortal race?" (135). That *Harper's* uses "Miss Evans" here is particularly interesting in light of a comment in the magazine nine months earlier which reviews the early installments of *Romola* as it is serialized in *Harper's:* "This work must satisfy us all that English literature has a really substantial addition in Miss Evans, or by whatever name the author should be known" ("Editor's Easy Chair" 567).[25] This equivocation hints that Eliot's personal circumstances are now public knowledge, but perhaps not with the sensationalizing and unmentionable

---

[24]   Eliot's realist novels of course contain sensational elements or characters. In *Middlemarch,* Madame Laure, the object of Lydgate's brief infatuation while a medical student in Paris, is a French actress who murders her husband during a performance, but then claims it was an accident she meant to do, is one obvious example.

[25]   Under the name "Marian C. Evans," *Romola* was serialized in *Harper's New Monthly Magazine* from August 1862 to October 1863, a month behind the British run in *The Cornhill* from July 1862 to August 1863.

effect they had in Britain. Unlike the uniform author's name of "George Eliot" in British publications, "Miss Evans" continues to alternate with "George Eliot" and "Marian C. Evans" in American reprints of her fiction.

If we return briefly to these two stories once again, one distinction proves more significant in the context of these transatlantic treatments of female authorship. In "The Lifted Veil," Latimer is the failed artist whose clairvoyance or keen vision proves pointless, while Bertha is not an artist at all, her mesmeric abilities never aligned with visual creativity. In "A Pair of Eyes," both Max Erdmann and Agatha Eure are artists, although he has enjoyed public acclaim and she must settle, but only temporarily, for a subordinate role as his inspiration or ultimate model. The British story perpetuates the male mask of Latimer much like Eliot's male pseudonym as author; the American sensation story is able to remove the masculine masking of female creative endeavors, and in this way seems bolder about registering both the challenges and accomplishments of women writers.

Works Cited

Alcott, Louisa May. "A Pair of Eyes." *Louisa May Alcott Unmasked*. Ed. Madeleine Stern. Boston: Northeastern University Press, 1995. 59–81.

———. "Behind a Mask; or, a Woman's Power." *Alternative Alcott*. Ed. Elaine Showalter. New Brunswick, N.J.: Rutgers University Press, 1988. 95–202.

———. *Little Women*. Ed. Anne Hiebert Alton. Peterborough, ONT: Broadview Press, 2001.

Ashton, Rosemary. *George Eliot: A Life*. New York: Penguin Press, 1996.

Bernstein, Susan D. "Ape Anxiety: Sensation Fiction, Evolution, and the Genre Question." *Journal of Victorian Culture* 6.2 (Autumn 2001): 250–271.

———. "Promiscuous Reading: The Problem of Identification and Anne Frank's Diary." *Witnessing the Disaster: Essays on Representation and the Holocaust*. Ed. Michael Bernard-Donals and Richard Glejzer. Madison: University of Wisconsin Press, 2003. 141–161.

Braddon, Mary Elizabeth. *Lady Audley's Secret*. Ed. Natalie M. Houston. Peterborough, ONT: Broadview Press, 2003.

Brontë, Charlotte. *Villette*. New York and Oxford: Oxford University Press, 1990.

Brown, Joshua. *Beyond the Lines: Pictorial Reporting, Everyday Life, and the Crisis of Gilded-Age America*. Berkeley: University of California Press, 2002.

Bull, Malcolm. "Mastery and Slavery in *The Lifted Veil*." *Essays in Criticism* 48.3 (1998): 244–261.

Claybaugh, Amanda. *The Novel of Purpose: Literature and Social Reform in the Anglo- American World*. Ithaca, N.Y.: Cornell University Press, 2007.

"Editor's Drawer." *Harper's New Monthly Magazine* (June 1863): 131–135.

"Editor's Easy Chair." *Harper's New Monthly Magazine* (September 1862): 563–567.

Eliot, George. *The Lifted Veil and Brother Jacob*. Ed. Helen Small. New York: Oxford University Press, 1999. 1–43.

[Eliot, George]. "The Lifted Veil." *Blackwood's Edinburgh Magazine* 86.525 (July 1859): 24–48.

[Eliot, George]. "The Lifted Veil." *The Living Age* (August 6, 1859): 360–380.

Flint, Kate. "Blood, Bodies, and *The Lifted Veil*." *Nineteenth-Century Literature* 51.4 (1997): 455–473.

Haight, Gordon S. Ed. *The George Eliot Letters*. New Haven, Conn.: Yale University Press, 1954–1978.

"Holmby House." *The Living Age* (August 6, 1859): 344–359.

James, Henry. Review of "The Lifted Veil" and Brother Jacob." *The Nation*. April 25, 1878. Reprinted in *Henry James: Essays, American and English Writers*. New York: The Library of America, 1984. 992–994.

"Lord Macaulay and the Massacre of Glencoe." *Blackwood's Edinburgh Magazine* (July 1859): 1–23.

[Mansel, H.L.]. "Sensation Novels." *Quarterly Review* (April 1863): 481–514.

McGill, Meredith L. *American Literature and the Culture of Reprinting, 1834–1853*. Philadelphia: University of Pennsylvania Press, 2003.

[Oliphant, Margaret]. "Novels." *Blackwood's Edinburgh Review* (September 1867): 257–280.

"The People of the Arabian Nights." *The Living Age* (August 6, 1869): 327-342.

Pykett, Lyn. *The Sensation Novel*. Plymouth, UK: Northcote House, 1994.

Review of *Jane Eyre—an Autobiography*. *The Living Age* (February 12, 1848): 324.

Review of *Little Women*. *The Athenaeum* (September 25, 1869): 399.

Showalter, Elaine. "Introduction." *Alternative Alcott*. Ed. Elaine Showalter. New Brunswick, N.J.: Rutgers University Press, 1988. ix–xliii.

Small, Helen. "Introduction." *The Lifted Veil and Brother Jacob*. New York: Oxford University Press, 1999. ix–xxxviii.

Stern, Madeleine. "Introduction." *Louisa May Alcott Unmasked*. Ed. Madeleine Stern. Boston, Mass.: Northeastern University Press, 1995. xi–xxix.

Tamarkin, Elisa. "Black Anglophilia; or, The Sociability of Antislavery." *American Literary History* 14.3 (2002): 444–478.

Willis, Martin. "George Eliot's *The Lifted Veil* and the Cultural Politics of Clairvoyance." *Victorian Literary Mesmerism*. Ed. Martin Willis and Catherine Wynne. Amsterdam and New York: Rodopi, 2006. 145–160.

Wynne, Deborah. *The Sensation Novel and the Victorian Family Magazine*. New York: Palgrave, 2001.

Chapter 11

Botanical Brews:
Tea, Consumption, and the Exotic in
Braddon's *Lady Audley's Secret* and
Alcott's *Behind A Mask*

Narin Hassan

A domestic scene in Mary Elizabeth Braddon's 1862 novel, *Lady Audley's Secret* presents Lady Audley, "amongst the fragile china teacups" preparing tea. In a novel cluttered with exotic commodities and objects, Braddon reveals how the art of making tea situates Lady Audley as a masterful performer of female domesticity and beauty—"surely a pretty woman never looks prettier than when she makes tea" (222). What characterizes Lady Audley as a particularly dangerous sensational heroine is her innocent exterior and her ability to perform aristocratic femininity, rising from a position as a governess to the lady of Audley Court. Like many of the heroines of sensation fictions, she is a woman of secrets, and clues to her past are hidden in her boudoir—a fantastic and gothic space of exotic objects and goods. The novel offers extensive references to Lady Audley's interior spaces that are cluttered with transported objects and souvenirs such as china teacups, Indian cabinets, and valuable jewels and shawls. Critics of this exemplary sensation novel have shown how it portrays the relationship of Victorian women and female domesticity to the rise of consumer culture and the growing "world of goods" to use Mary Douglas's term.[1] Further, like the consumer goods represented within *Lady Audley's Secret*, sensation novels themselves were critiqued as dangerous material objects of consumption that could entice readers and produce addictive behaviors. As has been noted in the wide range of scholarship on the genre, sensation fiction gained popularity alongside industrial and technological expansion and, further, such progress allowed for the rapid production and dissemination of popular

---

[1]   A number of scholars consider the role of consumer objects in *Lady Audley's Secret*. See for example, Katherine Montwieler, "Marketing Sensation: *Lady Audley's Secret* and Consumer Culture," in Marlene Tromp, Pamela Gilbert and Aeron Haynie, eds., *Beyond Sensation, Mary Elizabeth Braddon in Context* (Albany: State University of New York Press, 1999) and more recently, Eva Badowski, "On the Track of Things: Sensation and Modernity in Mary Elizabeth Braddon's *Lady Audley's Secret*," *Victorian Literature and Culture* 37.1 (2009) 157–175. The "world of goods" has inspired much critical work in the past two decades, most notably in collections such as *Consumption and the World of Goods*, ed. John Brewer and Roy Porter(New York: Routledge, 1994).

fictions designed to thrill and stimulate readers' sensations. As such, the genre was aligned with the development of a broader mass culture and associated with the expansion of markets and with a widening urban and industrial world in which consumers and the journeys of consumer goods were increasingly detached from sources of production.

While Braddon's novel is a key text contributing to the "sensation mania" of the 1860s in Britain, this essay situates Braddon's pivotal work within the context of gender, empire, and global exchange and traces its links to the sustained presence of the sensational genre on the other side of the Atlantic. By reading *Lady Audley's Secret* in relation to its references to foreign objects of consumption such as tea, and through its transatlantic relationship with Louisa May Alcott's novella, *Behind a Mask* (1866)—a Gothic thriller which borrows and extends many of the rhetorical strategies and plots of Braddon's work—I consider how the gendered representation of exotic, consumable goods in both of these fictions emphasizes the "sensational" elements of both texts and reveals a shared investment in representing the figure of the dangerous, domestic woman as dependent upon and engaging with the global circulation of exotic and potentially addictive plants, substances, and colonial goods. Reading these narratives in tandem reveals how the sensation genre itself traveled and flourished on both sides of the Atlantic and how, within both contexts, the genre suggested a link between the domestic home and a broader global culture and economy.

Sensation fictions often featured domestic locales, and placed their central tensions and plots around homes; yet they also revealed how these homes and women within them were inextricably tied to the activities of empire. In the case of Braddon and Alcott, their narratives produce female characters whose masterful performances of polite femininity and domesticity depend upon their consumption of foreign and exotic accessories and goods. While both these works represent aristocratic, English households, their sensational heroines reflect a transatlantic interest in creating "sensation" through the intertwining of foreign commodities with domestic homes. Foreign consumables are embedded within the domestic spaces of these narratives and their ambitious heroines frame and define them, exposing how women fashioned imperial progress and were implicated in the global circulation of objects and goods. Thus, the transatlantic continuities between these works reflect not only the Anglo-American conditions of sensationalism, but also the genre's global ties. Further, like the sensation novel, foreign commodities such as tea, sugar, and opium, began to flood middle-class households in the mid-nineteenth century and in turn inspired widespread cultural anxieties. Questions surrounding tea drinking and production in the nineteenth century resembled those in debates regarding the sensation genre and popular fiction. The properties of tea and its effects on bodies were debated by medical and scientific communities, and tea inspired worries about racial and imperial contamination. In fact, it was often imagined as a foreign object that entered British and American bodies and produced weakness or addiction. Like the sensation genre itself, tea elicited cultural anxiety and exposed the concerns of an increasingly global material culture of exchange.

Lady Audley's Secret and *Behind a Mask* have representational commonalities and share narrative strategies; as such, reading these texts together provides a way to examine concurrent trends and movements in popular British and American fiction. Reading the resonances of Braddon's novel on Alcott's thriller also exposes the ways that American texts were influenced by and revised the modes of British sensation fiction, extending British mid-century sensationalism to nineteenth-century American gothic. While Braddon's text was written at the height of the British sensation trend and defined Braddon as a "sensational author"—a label that stuck even as she wrote an impressive array of novels and short stories over the span of her long literary career—Alcott's work is a rare and radical contrast to much of her other writing. Alcott's production of her sensational thriller, written secretly and pseudonymously, contrasts with her respectable image and was produced a few decades after the height of American sensationalism. However, together these narratives offer a perfect transatlantic pairing as they trace similar plots and fit within the sensational oeuvre, revealing how the genre itself spread and took various forms throughout the nineteenth century.

Braddon's and Alcott's texts also reveal the resonances and traditions of women's writing on both sides of the Atlantic, and have received significant critical attention in recent years. Following Madeleine Stern's assertion, in her 1975 edition of *Behind A Mask* that the narrative was "the most extraordinary" (Stern xvii) of Alcott's "blood and thunder tales," and Elaine Showalter's description of it as "the most skillful of the tales Alcott published under the pseudonym of A.M. Barnard" (Showalter xxix), the story has received attention from a range of other critics including Judith Fetterly, Mary Elliott, and Theresa Strouth Gall. *Lady Audley's Secret* is also well represented in discussions of Victorian women's writing as well as considerations of the British sensation genre. Both works critique the nineteenth-century cult of femininity. Critics have argued that *Behind a Mask* is a challenge to the "separate spheres" and to the confining representations of the "angel in the house" and feminist critics have rigorously examined *Lady Audley's Secret* in light of Victorian notions of femininity, domesticity and sexuality.[2]

Both texts have inspired critics to examine the figure of the dangerous and transgressive heroine as a challenge to and result of the limited opportunities and confining roles for women in the nineteenth century. With a transatlantic lens, *Behind a Mask* has been analyzed in relation to Victorian women's fiction; Christina Doyle compares it to Bronte's *Jane Eyre*, whereas Elaine Showalter writes that Alcott "drew heavily on her childhood reading of *Jane Eyre*, and on best-selling

---

[2]   The sheer volume of critical work on Braddon's *Lady Audley's Secret* is now quite extensive. See for example, the collection, *Beyond Sensation: Mary Elizabeth Braddon in Context* (ed. Pamela Gilbert et al.) as well as work by Ann Cvetkovich, Lynda Hart, Lillian Nayder, as well as biographies by Robert Wolff and, more recently, Jennifer Carnell. Elaine Showalter was one of the first critics to discuss both *Lady Audley's Secret* and *Behind a Mask* in her feminist criticism, arguing that sensation novelists, "made a powerful appeal to the female audience by subverting the traditions of feminine fiction" (*A Literature of Their Own* 158).

English novels of the 1860s such as Mary Elizabeth Braddon's *Lady Audley's Secret* (1861) and Wilkie Collins *Armadale* (1866)" (Showalter xxix). The figure of the governess and issues of class converge in *Jane Eyre*, *Lady Audley's Secret* and *Behind a Mask*, and the narratives share sensational elements such as the use of letters, portraits, theatrical elements, and crimes within the home.

Braddon's novel established her as a "queen" of the circulating library and, as many critics have argued, heralded the beginning of the rise of sensation fiction as a distinctive genre. Braddon was a prolific writer, and although many of her novels, such as *John Marchmont's Legacy*, *Joshua Haggard's Daughter*, and *The Doctor's Wife* have strong elements of realism and sentimental fiction, it is the term "sensation" that was, and continues to be, applied to her work. Her two bestsellers, *Lady Audley's Secret* and *Aurora Floyd*, provided readers with fast paced plots and themes such as bigamy and adultery that became associated with the genre. In turn, critics of the sensation genre associated her work with the "literature of the kitchen"—emphasizing the ways that her novels could pollute readers and heighten their sensations. Alcott, on the other hand, established herself as an author of realistic fiction recognized for its sentimental and genteel mode. However, "behind a mask" of the pseudonym A.M. Barnard, she wrote gothic and sensational tales; and she was thus, as Elaine Showalter has noted, writing with a "double" hand simultaneously producing respectable and more scandalous popular fiction.

As an example of her sensational mode, *Behind a Mask* has much to share with *Lady Audley's Secret*, and at times Alcott seems to be directly invoking narrative conventions of the sensation genre (such as letters and theatrical performances) as well as specific aspects of Braddon's bestselling novel. Both plots outline the invasion of aristocratic domestic settings by dangerous women and trace the strategies of ambitious, lower class women who succeed in gaining social standing through their deception and ability to perform aristocratic femininity— Jean Muir and Helen Maldon (who eventually becomes Lady Audley) are masters of performance, and readers are exposed to who they are on the surface as well as behind the scenes. Both women work as governesses and manage to manipulate, and eventually marry, wealthy patriarchs. Alcott sets her novel in the English countryside and, like Braddon, she provides lengthy descriptions of the wealthy English household and the domestic commodities that lie within it. As such, her narrative performs and reenacts itself as an English sensational story. Alcott distances and tempers her narrative for her American readers at the same time as she associates it more closely with popular British sensational tales that had gripped readers on both sides of the Atlantic. Her Jean Muir is cast as an extreme and diabolical version of the sensational heroine—she is an aging actress able to mask herself as an innocent nineteen-year-old governess and charm those around her, although readers witness the erasure of her mask when she is done with her performance and exposes her true aged features, false teeth, and ugly interior. As in *Lady Audley's Secret*, where, through crucial scenes in the boudoir, Braddon suggests the tie between exotic commodities and Lady Audley's bewitching beauty, Alcott too exposes how makeup, hair dye, and the right goods—such as rich clothing and jewelry—make the aristocratic angel in the house a figure of performance by the skilled actress. Braddon's and Alcott's powerful heroines exemplify how domestic homes and the women within them were linked to empire and to a wider global exchange—not only of goods, but also of cultural anxiety. Thus, together they provide a rich example of how women's transatlantic sensation fiction engaged with the intricate ties between gender, empire and metropole.

Sensation fiction was itself a genre associated with consumption and a widening, interwoven, increasingly technological, industrial, and global culture. As Thomas Boyle's early reading of the genre acknowledges, the Victorian city (and its crime and industry) was linked to the emergence of the genre. The term "sensation" alluded to both the affinity of the genre with consumption itself—books were imagined to be quickly "consumed" by readers and could heighten physical sensations through their exciting plots and character—and with a culture that was becoming increasingly fast paced and interconnected—these books were produced at an alarmingly quick rate, and distributed to a larger reading audience of many classes and backgrounds, challenging ideological boundaries and producing what Susan David Bernstein has termed the "anxiety of assimilation" (217). Like consumer goods, books could be alluring and addictive, and, in the often quoted words of Henry Mansel, "the cravings of a diseased appetite" (482). The emergence of the sensation genre in Britain in the 1860s thus prompted criticism which alluded to the fictions themselves as unhealthy and intoxicating and which associated them with the features of an increasingly fast paced, urban society—they were cheap, quickly produced, and quick to read "railway fictions" which appealed to the appetites of a broad reading audience. Sensation fiction was associated with a rising mass culture, and its emergence collides with the increased production and circulation of exotic commodities that had become staples in the English household. Braddon herself alluded to the relationship of sensation novels to the consumption of exotic commodities when, in her 1864 novel *The Doctor's Wife*, she introduces sensation writer Sigismund Smith as "the author of about half a dozen highly spiced fictions, which enjoyed an immense popularity amongst the classes who like their literature as they like their tobacco—very strong" (11). Viewing the sensation novel itself as stimulating, potentially addictive, and easily consumed, Braddon emphasizes in *Lady Audley's Secret* that the sensational heroine, like the sensational author, is simultaneously the masterful consumer and distributor of such enticing goods.

The inclusion of exotic consumer goods within households of varying classes had, by the nineteenth century, become common and commodities such as sugar, coffee, tea, and chocolate that had been viewed as luxuries in the past, were increasingly considered substances that were a part of everyday life. As Sidney Mintz has shown, in the nineteenth century sugar became a staple part of the English diet and had been transformed from what was originally a medicinal good or a luxury item to a sweetener used by the masses in jams, tea, coffee, and a range of recipes. During the same period, tea became an increasingly popular household good, and became associated with notions of "Englishness." John Sumner prefaced his 1863 *Popular Treatise on Tea* with the claim that "the Anglo-Saxon people are essentially a tea drinking race" (iii). As Julie Fromer has argued, it was during the nineteenth century that tea was transformed from a luxury item to a necessity. While the substance itself became widely available within Britain, the rituals of the tea drinking were linked to notions of gentility and class—the items and goods that made up the tea table, such as cups and saucers and teapots, characterized the nature of a household, and the rituals of tea making defined the genteel Victorian woman. As Fromer notes:

> tea crossed class lines, appearing at the humblest of suppers and gracing the table of Queen Victoria creating a universal English habit…but at the same time, details of tea preparation and consumption marked class status and concomitant moral position within the culture. The rituals of the tea table, however, insist on gender distinctions and they highlight a woman's privileged role in nourishing her family and her nation. (12)

Piya Chatterjee makes a similar claim when she notes that "through rituals of consumption, tea signified a new domain of desire: of femininity and its leisure" (22). Nineteenth-century writers such as Leitch Ritchie assigned tea with transformative social powers calling it a "new agent in civilization" and describing its influence as "a bond of family love; It is the ally of woman in her work of refinement;—it throws down the conventional barrier between the two sexes, taming the rude strength of one and ennobling the graceful weakness of the other" (qtd. in Sumner 43). Thus tea was imagined to temper and regulate the sexes while creating harmonious and ideal partnerships and refined values. Tea was related to both everyday domestic ritual and to consumer habit and while tea drinking produced linkages among peoples and classes, the rituals of the tea table defined gendered and class difference.

Within sensation fictions, conventions of tea drinking and tea making represent the peaceful domain of the home at the same time as they signify the possible dangers of women within them. In the case of Braddon and Alcott, their sensational heroines are able to produce the rituals of consumption and perform the leisurely and calm façade of the tea table, but like tea itself, they crossed class and social boundaries and exposed the dangers of an increasingly uncertain, and sometimes artificial and dangerous world. Ceremonies of tea making and tea drinking evoked American and British notions of domesticity that connected women beyond domestic parlors and boudoirs to the reaches of empire. By nourishing families and nations through tea table rituals, women ensured the production and demand of colonial products such as tea and sugar and by establishing rituals around the tea table, women produced notions of national habit and comfort. Sensation fictions could expose and subvert the dominant image of tea as a symbol of comfort and refinement by revealing how dangerous heroines made use of such goods to perform an idealized femininity and bewitch others through the powers of both the product itself and the rituals that accompanied it.

The trope of the dangerous woman making tea figures in a number of sensational fictions, and tea emerges as the paradox that simultaneously exposes the cocooning comforts of the tea parlor or tea table and the dangers of the expert brewer. Lydia Gwilt, the dangerous heroine of Wilkie Collins' *Armadale* (1864), is described as a powerful brewer: "her hands moved about among the tea things with a smooth, noiseless activity. Her magnificent hair flashed crimson in the candle light as she turned her head hither and thither, searching with an easy grace for the things she wanted in the tray ... perfectly modest in her manner, possessed to perfection of the graceful restraints and refinements of a lady, she had all the allurements that feast the eye, all the siren invitations that seduce the sense—a subtle suggestiveness in her silence, and a sexual sorcery in her smile (377). Here, the tea table is a stage for the performance of female ritual and seduction—it becomes a site where Collins can reveal the subtlety and skill of the masterful femme fatale, who simultaneously embodies the siren and the graceful lady. References to tea are scattered throughout *Lady Audley's Secret*—Robert nurses George Talboys with strong tea at the beginning of the novel and craves a cup of green tea for his headache; he also reads women as they make tea, claiming to himself that "this is a woman who can keep a secret" when he notices how neatly Phoebe, Lady Audley's maid, tends to serving tea (163). These incidents serve as critical moments in the text, as Robert Audley is collecting evidence against Lady Audley. While the representation of Phoebe making tea exposes how, even within the shabby Castle Inn, the tea table is a site of observation and negotiation—Robert, for instance, observes Phoebe's character while she carefully crafts both tea and self.

Braddon's most extended description of Lady Audley's tea making reveals the relationship of the substance to strategies of seduction and witchery. She represents the tea table as the site to witness woman's power and her link to empire. Occurring in the middle of the novel, as Robert Audley is searching for clues to Lady Audley's madness as well as her history, Braddon writes:

> She looked very pretty and innocent, seated behind the graceful group of delicate opal China and glittering silver. Surely a pretty woman never looks prettier than when making tea. The most feminine and most domestic of all occupations imparts a magic harmony to her every movement, a witchery to her every glance. The floating mists from the boiling liquid in which she infuses the soothing herbs, whose secrets are known to her alone, envelop her in a cloud of scented vapour through which she seems a social fairy, weaving potent spells with Gunpowder and Bohea. At the tea table, she reigns omnipotent, unapproachable. What do men know of the mysterious beverage? Read how poor Hazlitt made his tea and shudder at the dreadful barbarism. How clumsily the wretched creatures attempt to assist the witch president of the tea-tray; how hopelessly they hold the kettle, how continually they imperil the frail cups and saucers, or the taper hands of the priestess. To do away with the tea table is to rob woman of her legitimate empire. (243)

In this lengthy description, tea is the substance that ties Lady Audley to the precious commodities of empire. She is linked not only to her gunpowder and bohea teas, but also to the "glittering silver" and "delicate opal china" in her boudoir. Braddon's description is sensual and ethereal, highlighting how Lady

Audley's tea making appeals to the senses and creates an enclosure of "floating mists" and "a cloud of scented vapor." This tea scene stimulates the senses just as the sensation novel itself was imagined to, and conveys the space of the tea table as a space of ritual as well as a space of secrets "known to her alone." Braddon highlights the paradox of tea and of Lady Audley's tea table, representing the scene as simultaneously soothing and bewitching, pretty and dangerous. Her allusions to empire and to the feminine domain implicate the English sensational heroine within a larger colonial nexus and link her to the seductive nature of the product itself as well as its potential contamination.

Exploring the contrasting meanings of the tea table, Elizabeth Kowaleski-Wallace has argued that this scene both "conveys a sense of the precariousness of the tea table" and reveals how "Braddon's tea pourer reserves secrets to herself, intimations of an illicit, transgressive life" (20, 21). Braddon's description also underscores the tea table as a site of performance, where Lady Audley can project the delicacy, comfort, and magic of an idealized and civilized female domesticity. Here Braddon makes a direct link between the English woman's consumption of exotic beverages and her translation of those beverages from raw material to civilized ritual. Delicate cups are protected from the "peril" of gruff English men and the tea tray is safely domesticated through the rituals of the pretty Englishwoman, masking the colonial web underneath the magic and witchery of the exoticized scene. Lady Audley's performance of English femininity then relies upon the exotic objects distributed through the networks of empire, and she makes them magical, sensational and larger than life: "the starry diamond upon her white fingers flashed hither and thither amongst the tea things and she bent her pretty head over the marvellous Indian tea caddy of sandal-wood and silver, with as much earnestness as if life held no higher purpose than the infusion of Bohea" (243). Thus, like the many objects that clutter her boudoir, "handsome dresses … jewelry, ivory-backed hairbrushes, and exquisite china" and the odors of rich perfumes that surround this womanly space, the tea table is an accessory to Lady Audley's performance of aristocratic femininity—and one that provides the illusion of calmness and domesticity just as it evokes mysterious, womanly witchery.

While Alcott's *Behind a Mask* has a less sustained consideration of the tea table, it is crucial in early pages of the narrative when readers are introduced to Jean Muir through her performance of making tea. In the story's opening chapter, the Coventry family awaits the arrival of the new governess, whom they imagine will be a dull nuisance. While she appears to be meek and subservient, she quickly charms Lady Coventry and challenges the family's assumption of governesses when she makes tea. Despite her initial plainness and her "air of resignation" (100)—here Alcott's depiction echoes Bronte's *Jane Eyre*—it is in the process of making tea that we see one of the first examples of her ability to charm and woo others, while fashioning herself as a domestic angel: "she performed her little task with a skill and grace that made it pleasant to watch her" (102). Alcott describes Jean Muir's work at the tea caddy as an artistic and powerful performance:

Miss Muir performed her little task with a skill and grace that made it pleasant to watch her. Coventry lingered a moment after she had given him a steaming cup, to observe her more nearly, while he asked a question or two of his brother. She took no more notice of him if he had been a statue, and in the middle of one remark he addressed to her, she rose to take the sugar basin to Mrs Coventry, who was quite won by the modest, domestic graces of the new governess.

'Really my dear, you are a treasure. I haven't tasted such tea since my poor maid Ellis died. Bella never makes it so good, and Miss Lucia always forgets the cream. Whatever you do, you seem to do well, and it is such a comfort. (102)

Alcott stages this scene as a space of performance that inspires observation. Drawing her readers to watch and observe the governess as the Coventry family does, Alcott reveals Jean Muir's ability to win over Mrs. Coventry by her polite graces and her exceptional tea making abilities. The tea table is a space where Jean Muir can perform domestic femininity under the sharp scrutiny of the family, and particularly of the male characters, Coventry and Edward, who initially are suspicious of her charms but fall in love with her as the narrative progresses.

The elaborate descriptions of Lady Audley's relationship to tea—as a maker and a drinker—expose not only the ways that she performs domesticity, but also provide subtle references to the "sensational" qualities of her heroine and of the text itself. Similarly, the powerful presence of tea in the opening pages of Alcott's work frame our introduction to Jean Muir and reveal how she "bewitches" and convinces the elderly Mrs. Coventry of her domestic qualities and social graces. Just as Braddon's description highlights the tea table as a "feminine" space, where men are unknowing and clumsy intrusions, Alcott juxtaposes Jean Muir's rituals of tea making with the awkward and uncoordinated efforts of Mrs. Coventry's sons who attempt to make tea: "Edward, eager to feed the pale governess, was awkwardly trying to make the tea … as he upset the caddy and uttered a despairing exclamation, Miss Muir took her place quietly behind the urn" (102). Through the tea making scene, Braddon first exposes Jean Muir's powers of performance as well as the glimmers of her controlling and dangerous presence within the household—she nudges the men of the house out of the space, and, fully aware that she is under their watchful gaze, she challenges them directly to witness the power of her performance.

Making tea is the first of a series of Jean Muir's dramatic presentations, and the outwardly simple governess performs multiple roles that expose her powerful charms. If the raging and looming portrait of Lady Audley, viewed secretly by George Talboys and Robert Audley in the dramatic and often quoted boudoir scene of the novel, "had something of the aspect of a beautiful fiend," then Alcott's representations of Jean Muir in tableaux and performance scenes reveal a similar emphasis on the uncanny quality of artificial exteriors and portraits:

Bending over the sleeper was a woman robed with barbaric splendor. One hand turned back the embroidered sleeve from the arm which held a scimitar: one slender foot in a scarlet sandal was visible under the white tunic; her purple

mantle swept down from snowy shoulders; fillets of gold bound her hair, and
jewels shown on her neck and arms ... she had darkened her skin, painted her
eyebrows, disposed some wild black locks over her fair hair, and thrown such
intensity of expression into her eyes that they darkened and dilated till they were
as fierce as any southern eyes that had ever flashed. Hatred, the deepest and
bitterest, was written in her sternly beautiful face, courage glowed in her glance,
power spoke in the nervous grip of the slender hand that held the weapon, and
the indomitable will of the woman was expressed—even the firm pressure of the
little foot half hidden in the tiger skin. (146–147)

In this striking and dramatic scene, Alcott reveals Jean Muir's talent as an actress
and provides exotic orientalized motifs to contrast with the early images we receive
of Jean Muir as a plain, simple governess. Both *Lady Audley's Secret* and *Behind a
Mask* employ such exotic references to reveal the slippery boundaries between the
artificial and the real. Jean Muir's performance highlights her ability to "mask" her
true identity and to perform multiple identities. Muir's performances and outward
appearances, including the "tiger skin," represent the savage rebellion that lurks
beneath the surface illusion of simplicity and innocence. Supporting the tea table
scenes within these texts, such orientalized representations suggest that the foreign
has been consumed within the domestic, and that the figure of the sensational
heroine triangulates the relationship between the two.

If sensation narratives associated the tea table with feminine deception, they
emerged alongside broader cultural anxieties about foreign commodities as
dangerous and potentially contaminating. The benefits or dangers of tea had been
a subject for debate for several decades in the writing of doctors and travelers
and the emergence of the tea trade produced a range of works that described the
"nature" of tea drinkers and the effects of tea on the body. Of particular interest
was the effect of tea on women and upon the household. Unlike coffee that had
traditionally been a substance associated with masculinity (as in the eighteenth-
century coffee-house) and with work and industry, tea had long been considered a
drink of comfort and of feminine ritual. Nineteenth-century writers such as George
Sigmond and Arthur Reade spoke of the domestic comforts of the "tea table" and
traced how tea was a fashionable drink. However, mid-nineteenth century notions
of tea and of tea drinking also alluded to anxieties about the source of tea leaves and
of the potential adulteration of tea itself. The cultural notions of tea as a potentially
adulterating substance emerge during the same period as the rise of the sensation
genre in Britain and together, both tea and sensation fiction inspired anxieties of
pollution and contamination and raised questions surrounding authenticity. As
Erika Rappaport notes, tea illuminated "concerns about the real and the fake and
inspired worries about foreign objects entering British bodies" (129).

Writing specifically of tea history during mid-nineteenth century, Rappaport
suggests that anxieties about the dangers of tea increased in this period: "the
Victorian discussion of adulterated foods and drinks peaked between the 1850s
and 1870s and was the product of wider concerns about public health, the growing
authority of chemistry and food science, the mechanization of food production and

the expansion of international free trade in foodstuffs." Rappaport examines tea in particular, "to reveal how this movement was also animated by and stimulated anxieties about foreign substances entering British markets and bodies and how such concerns defined commodities and altered states" (Rappaport 126). Braddon's and Alcott's use of tea as a metaphor is particularly striking in light of these concerns, particular as their texts are assumed to build sensational thrills for readers.

In a novel that captured and inspired many of the anxieties of sensation fiction itself, Braddon represents tea, and other exotic commodities such as jewels, china cabinets, and silks, as crucial to the aristocratic interiors of her novel as well as the shaping of her female character in her transformation into "Lady Audley." While one reading of the tea table in this novel could suggest Braddon's association of tea with polite domesticity, considering her representations of tea in light of public fears of contamination and adulteration allows us to read tea as a crucial key to Lady Audley's own artificial and contaminating role within Audley Court. Thus, tea not only signifies the ability of sensational heroines such as Lady Audley to adopt and perform polite, domestic rituals and exude respectable femininity, but also assigns them to the categories of the sensational and subversive. Indeed, in other texts, Braddon continues to associate tea with her sensational heroines. For example, in *Aurora Floyd*, the titular character is repeatedly described as "intoxicating" and her tea table includes the gunpowder and bohea that Lady Audley offers. In early chapters of *Aurora Floyd*, we are told, "Mr Mellish did not cherish any great affection for the decoctions of bohea and gunpowder with which his wife dosed him ... he strung his nerves to extreme tension at the post-meridian dishes of tea which his wife poured out for him in the sacred seclusion of her dressing room" (246). Alcott's representation of tea depicts Jean Muir's domain as part of "the first scene" of her many performances, and it is the beginning of her inclusion into the Coventry household and a sign of what is yet to come, as she carefully maneuvers and manipulates the household, and ultimately contaminates the aristocratic line.

Tea ceremonies in these sensation fictions produce gendered notions of space and outline feminine rituals as they also expose the ambivalent boundaries between the global and the local, domestic and foreign. While other sensation texts such as Sheridan LeFanu's *Green Tea*, associated men with tea drinking, Braddon and Alcott emphasize the inclusion of tea within respectable homes and its associations with femininity and domestic ritual. If, as Anne McClintock and other scholars have noted, women bore the burden of "domesticating" and in turn civilizing empire, then, in sensation fictions, empire is configured within the home itself through the inclusion of colonial commodities and the interaction of women with them. Women displayed, upheld, and made ordinary and necessary objects of empire, and as such they were a crucial link to it. In the case of transatlantic sensation fiction, references to exotic goods, particularly tea, suggest that the global circulation of commodities has impacted domestic tranquility and transformed cultural values and rituals. The invasion of the most remote and noble homes—the "stately old place ... befitting the ancestral home of a rich and honorable race" in *Behind a Mask*

(107) and the "glorious old" "noble place" of Audley Court (44)—by sensational heroines produces much of the unease of these popular texts, but empire itself was also a source of anxiety. The products and substances that circulated globally and entered homes referenced the economic and cultural exchanges that constituted empire; as Catherine Hall and Sonya Rose note, "empire linked the lives of people in the metropole to global circuits of production, distribution and exchange, to the exploitation and oppression of millions of other imperial subjects" (20). If mass consumption and production of goods created distance between consumers and producers, imperial products were also a reminder of the connectivity of peoples and of things. The circulation, consumption, and representation of tea culturally reflected the gendered exchanges between empire and homes, while the inclusion of tea as simultaneously a marker of gentility and of subversion and contamination within sensation fictions reflected similar dichotomies and contradictions. Lady Audley and Jean Muir reflect the paradox of tea as well as the link of sensational heroines to the rebellion and anxiety that a widening, transatlantic and global culture produced. Transatlantic sensation fictions, with their common resonances, revisions, and re-articulations of intoxication and consumption, remind us that sources of contamination and of the exotic are already at the heart of the home: within its tea-table.

Works Cited

Alcott, Louisa. *Behind a Mask.* 1866. *Alternative Alcott.* Ed. Elaine Showalter. New Brunswick, N.J.: Rutgers University Press, 1988.

Bernstein, Susan David. "Dirty Reading: Sensation Fiction, Women and Primitivism." *Criticism.* 36.2 (Spring 1994): 213–241.

Braddon, Mary Elizabeth. *Aurora Floyd.* London: Tinsley Brothers, 1863.

———. *Lady Audley's Secret.* Ed. Natalie Houston. Peterborough, ONT: Broadview Press, 2003.

———. *The Doctor's Wife.* Ed. Lyn Pykett. Oxford: Oxford World's Classics, 1998.

Boyle, Thomas. *Black Swine in the Sewers of Hampstead.* New York: Viking, 1989.

Chatterjee, Piya. *A Time for Tea. Women, Labor, and Post/Colonial Politics on an Indian Plantation.* Durham, N.C.: Duke University Press, 2001.

Collins, Wilkie. *Armadale.* New York and London: Harper Brothers, 1902.

Douglas, Mary. *The World of Goods.* New York: Routledge, 1996.

Elliott, Mary. "Outperforming Femininity: Public Conduct and Private Enterprise in Louisa May Alcott's *Behind a Mask.*" *American Transcendental Quarterly.* 8:4, 1994.

Fromer, Julie E. *A Necessary Luxury: Tea in Victorian England.* Athens: Ohio University Press, 2008.

Hall, Catherine, and Sonya Rose. *At Home with the Empire. Metropolitan Culture and the Imperial World.* Cambridge: Cambridge University Press, 2006.

Kowaleski-Wallace, Elizabeth. *Consuming Subjects. Women, Shopping, and business in the Eighteenth Century.* New York: Columbia University Press, 1997.

Mansel, Henry L. "Sensation Novels." *Quarterly Review* 113 (April 1863): 482–514.

McClintock, Anne. *Imperial Leather. Race, Gender, and Sexuality in the Imperial Contest.* New York: Routledge, 1995.

Mintz, Sidney, *Sweetness and Power. The Place of Sugar in Modern History.* New York: Penguin Books, 1995.

Rappaport, Erika. "Packaging China. Foreign Articles and Dangerous Tastes in the Mid-Victorian Tea Party." *The Making of the Modern Consumer. Knowledge, Power and Identity In the Modern World*, ed. Frank Trentman. New York: Berg Publishers, 2006.

Reade, Arthur. *Tea and Tea Drinking.* London: Sampson Low, 1884.

Showalter, Elaine, ed. "Introduction." *Alternative Alcott.* New Brunswick, N.J.: Rutgers University Press, 1988.

Sigmond, George. *Tea; Its Effects Medicinal and Moral.* London: Longman, Orme, Brown, Green and Longman, 1839.

Stern, Madeleine, ed. *Behind a Mask: The Unknown Thrillers of Louisa May Alcott.* New York: Harper Collins, 1975.

Sumner, John. *A Popular Treatise on Tea: its qualities and effects.* Birmingham: William Hodgetts, 1863.

Tromp, Marlene, Pamela K. Gilbert, and Aeron Haynie. *Beyond Sensation: Mary Elizabeth Braddon in Context.* Albany: State University of New York (SUNY) Press.

Chapter 12
Transatlantic Sensationalism in Victorian Domestic Fiction: Failed Settler Narratives in Charlotte Yonge's *The Trial*

Tamara S. Wagner

Charlotte Yonge's domestic fiction sensationalizes a two-way flow of transatlantic and transpacific emigration and repatriation. Throughout her writing, she promotes a missionary agenda through offstage depictions of Africa, Asia, and Australasia, yet the novel that engages most extensively with migration across and beyond the British Empire, *The Trial* (1864), questions the transportability of domesticity that is vital to successful settlement abroad. It is also Yonge's most extensive venture into literary sensationalism, a phenomenon she continued to regard with suspicion. It is no coincidence that the same novel contains her most intricate and far-reaching exploration of foreign spaces. Failed emigration expresses a sense of being unsettled, an extreme version of similar uncertainties back at home in England. What may at first seem an easily typecast projection of current anxieties onto the "other" place registers a tension in the representation of home as an exportable ideal. Not surprisingly, this tension becomes particularly pressing when it is played out in settler colonies that are meant to operate as an extension of English domesticity. But if Yonge simultaneously draws on the narrative potential of failed emigration that, in Victorian culture generally, had come to be associated specifically with fraudulent American land speculation, in *The Trial* she further complicates this transatlantic sensationalism by contrasting the Ward family's failure to settle down in the New World with the May family's missionary ties in New Zealand. At the mid-nineteenth century, New Zealand was in many ways thought of as a relatively new, potential model settler colony, whereas the United States had become typified as the lost or renegade colony that had broken away from the empire. For Yonge, moreover, New Zealand was of particular significance due to her own family's missionary interests. It therefore lent itself as a pointed contrast to more established narratives of both settlement and return, creating a central juxtaposition between opposing movements of emigration. While this contrast addresses the difficulties of transporting English domesticity, it also literalizes genre crossings within the novel. New Zealand qualifies as a domesticated part of the British Empire, eschewing any exoticizing fantasies; America figures as a sensational space.

A dedicated religious, domestic novelist who considered her fiction as "a sort of instrument for popularising Church views that might not otherwise have been taken in" (Romanes 190), Yonge resorted to various fashionable formulae, including sensationalism. But due to her commitment to orthodox Christianity and avowed preference for the domestic, Yonge has seemed emblematic of conservative, antifeminist fiction by Victorian women, and her appropriation of sensational devices has chiefly singled her out as a prime example of a novelist "forced" by market pressures to adopt whatever happened to be fashionable. Ongoing archival work, however, amply shows that there clearly were "various kinds of sensation novel" (Maunder x). It was not merely that throughout the century's second half, domestic writers reacted critically to the sensation phenomenon. Religious novelists especially employed literary sensationalism for their own agenda.[1] Yonge's genre crossings, I wish to suggest, are deliberate and have got a specific narrative function. The geographical projections that create a triangulation of differently unsettled spaces in *The Trial* bring this out most clearly. At the same time, this triangulation showcases how the Victorians saw the transatlantic in conjunction with the transpacific as they increasingly considered emigration to and changing cultural exchanges from these destinations.

Subtitled *More Links of the Daisy Chain*, *The Trial* illustrates the process of rewriting, or redirection, that occurs in Yonge's experimentation with the sensation genre, and how her shifting representation of "other" spaces helps convey this redirection. A sequel to Yonge's most successful domestic chronicle, *The Daisy Chain* (1856), it moves a narrative of mundane family life into the realm of public spectacle. To achieve this end, it prominently features such popular sensational devices as a murder trial and wrongful incarceration.[2] Nevertheless, the detailing of the proceedings in court focuses first and foremost on the innocently accused young man's capability for resignation and the mastery of his various "trials" with the help of God-given grace. As a result, the potentially most sensational effects are redirected into a narrative of spiritual growth that is summed up at the end of the novel, after his release from prison: "all the anguish you describe could and would have been insanity if grace had not been given you to conquer it" (371). Contained in a religious framework, this plotline makes space for a delineation of the aftermath, of emotional reactions and their significance for moral development. This aftermath, however, also includes a twofold emigration: his siblings' move to America and his own settlement in the Antipodes. Both locations are introduced as potentially exotic scenes that promise new beginnings. Their parallel treatment operates through a double sensational projection.

---

[1]   As Deborah Wynne has put it, the "craving for the genre" was "so overwhelming that even the staunch practitioners and defenders of the domestic novel, Margaret Oliphant and Charlotte M. Yonge, were forced at the height of the craze to offer their readers sensational novels featuring murders and mysteries" (3).

[2]   June Sturrock speaks of "quasi-sensation novels" that move "beyond the private realm of the family chronicle to take on many of the horrific, extreme, and mysterious trappings of the sensation novel" (74, 76).

In pairing a murder trial in provincial England with both an America in the midst of civil war and a New Zealand experiencing some of the worst outrages of the Māori Wars, *The Trial* reworks established literary clichés about "other" places while it also finds new ways of dealing with concepts of transportable domesticity. Briefly, Leonard Ward is wrongfully convicted of murder. When his elder brother Henry decides that the rest of the family should emigrate to America for the precise purpose of breaking off any contact with the accused brother, this move is scripted as a form of abandonment that stands in sharp contrast to the promotion of missionary activities in the Antipodes. In exploring parallel new homes across the Atlantic and the Pacific, however, Yonge also taps into cultural anxieties that find revealing expression in sensational transoceanic projections. Both Henry's preference for the unsettled life of an army doctor and Leonard's call to become a missionary after his release from prison add significant layers to a strikingly intricate engagement with emigrants' different agendas as well as destinations.

Indeed, if "the nineteenth-century literary world took for granted" that there was an increasing spread of "literature in English" throughout these destinations (Claybaugh 441), it makes sense that we read not only the re-presentation of the Old and the New World on both sides of the Atlantic in tandem, but that we extend this comparative approach to encompass the parallel exportation of literary formations across the Pacific as well. Amanda Claybaugh has argued for a "New Transatlanticism," reminding us that "[n]ineteenth-century novelists and critics took for granted what present-day scholars have only recently begun to acknowledge: that the literatures of Great Britain and the United States should not be read in isolation from one another" (440). Building on his seminal work on cultural cross-fertilizations between nineteenth-century English language-fiction as an essential part of that "play of opposites, a series of reciprocal attractions and repulsions between opposing national situations" that prompt us "[t]o read national literatures in a transnational way" (Giles, *Transatlantic* 1), Paul Giles has similarly stressed the neglected "significance of antipodean inversions to the formation of US national narratives in the nineteenth century, the ways in which American culture was symbiotically bound to both its British antecedents and its Australian colonial counterparts" ("Antipodean" 24). Clearly, if "the entire shape of English literary history appears different when it is viewed from a transnational critical perspective," "allow[ing] for a remapping of the genealogies for 'English Literature'" (Giles, *Atlantic* 5, 2), this demands what Susan Manning and Andrew Taylor have similarly termed the "widened geographical and discursive parameters" of transatlantic literary studies (6).[3] This extension is all the more crucial since nineteenth-century writers (including such an emphatically domestic novelist as Yonge) were keenly aware of and capitalized on the potential of this parallelism. Since a broader transoceanic (both transpacific and transatlantic) context makes clearer her complex contribution to sensation fiction, I shall therefore first firmly situate the novel within the Victorians' imagining of the United States as a lost

---

[3]   Kate Flint similarly stresses "that 'the transatlantic' is a greatly weakened term if it is taken to apply to British-American traffic alone" (7).

colony and a rising commercial power. Yonge's sensationalization of transatlantic emigration can best be understood as a counterpoise to her anti-sensational, domesticating treatment of missionary activities in likewise potentially exotic spaces "down under," at the Antipodes, that are nonetheless culturally closer to home.

This "terrible severing of all home ties": Transporting domesticity

Although Yonge indisputably participated in the creation of some of the most clichéd representations of the foreign, she reacted critically to typecast narratives of successful and failed emigration. Like most Victorian domestic novelists, she at first indiscriminately featured Britain's main settler colonies—including the lost or renegade colony, the United States—as potential extensions of a peculiarly "English" domesticity. In *The Two Guardians; Or, Home in this World* (1852), for example, a young boy's plans to settle "in one of the colonies" center on the construction of "a regular model of an old English farm-house [...] stout, and strong, and handsome, just to put the people in mind that they do belong to an old country, after all" (210, 208). He may dream of being "an Australian stockman, riding after those famous jockeys of wild bulls" to escape the confines of home, to lead a life "in a great place bigger than all Europe, instead of being stifled up in this little bit of a poky England, [with] every profession choke full of people." Yet when cautioned that such a move might entail "a terrible severing of all home ties," he declares his triumphant return as part of the project: "O, but I should come back again. I should be an Englishman still, and come back when I had made my fortune" (209). A fortune made in the colonies is to restore the family at home. That this restoration goes beyond financial reward encapsulates the driving force of some of Yonge's most hopeful emigrants. The neglected boy's exotic fantasy is informed by the wish to "see if mamma would not think [him] worth something, after all" (209–210). What interests me here is that the projected return sidesteps the fact that the emigrant's "terrible severing of all home ties" is inevitable. In distinguishing settlers from fortune hunters, the severing of ties to England is crucial to the cultural enterprise of settlement abroad. Yet even as the returnee becomes a popular figure in sensation fiction, the distinction between old and new homes is never an easy dichotomy. On the contrary, especially when it comes to the renegade colony in America, the willingness or ease with which characters become absorbed in foreign settlements indicates a desertion of original homes and often of the values that are meant to be exported.

In *The Trial*, precisely this severing of home ties symptomatically decides Henry Ward's choice of his destination. Unable to face his "sense of disgrace" after his brother's conviction for murder, he resorts to emigration because it promises a break with the past. What drives him is the desire to "hurry from old scenes, and sever former connections." In his "burning impatience to be quit of everything, and to try to drown the sense of his own identity," he insists that they take an assumed name, Warden, so "that his sisters might never feel that they were the relative of a convict." Attempting to "break the tie of brotherhood," he forbids his younger sisters from mentioning Leonard in the hope that they may entirely forget him (234–236). The death of one sister in America seems to be caused as much by "the full misery" of "the treatment of his [Leonard's] name as that of one dead" as by a lingering fever (317). Such a radical break from home and family is diametrically opposed to the idea of colonization as a transposition of domesticity: "A colony was not change enough for Henry's wishes; even there he had sure of being recognised as the convict's brother, and [he] was resolved to seek his new home in the wide field of America" (235). Loyal colonies form a network of communication and extended family ties where new settlers are easily traced. The rejection of such loyalty is the key to the novel's pairing of transatlantic and transpacific migration.

Leonard Ward's undeserved imprisonment in England may invite familiar associations of parts of the Antipodes and the Americas with (former) convict settlements, yet the distinction brought out by Henry's flight from shame indicates an important shift to different links between transgression and "transportation." Escape from a perceived criminality literalizes Henry's abandonment of familial responsibilities whereas his wrongfully accused brother ultimately translates his experience of undeserved suffering into missionary activities. The markedly different motivation of their exportation already signals the resulting juxtaposition of opposing narratives of emigration. In New Zealand, Leonard ultimately joins branches of the May family. This makes his move an extension of home that is, of course, meant to include those brothers and sisters brought into the fold of the Anglican Church through conversion. His absorption of the values he first learns among the Mays in England is vital to Yonge's project of promoting a missionary agenda that relies on the transportability of a functioning domesticity.

Transpacific migration successfully exports domestic ideals influenced by a religious doctrine that is in many ways concentrated on everyday living. That this is by no means a straightforward transposition, however, is similarly articulated through an important link between *The Daisy Chain* and *The Trial*, a link that has often been sidestepped in discussions that stress the difference between the original domestic chronicle and its sensational sequel: missionary interests as a motivation for settlement are revisited to demystify some of the prevalent, distorting fantasies of emigration. The end of the earlier novel sees Norman May, one of the seven motherless May siblings, go out to the Antipodes as a missionary.[4] His zeal has been fostered from an early age not only by the family's interest in the local poor and a general atmosphere of religiosity at home, but also by reports of travels. A younger brother becomes a sailor, bringing back accounts both in *The Daisy Chain* and its sequel of adventures that include being shot at in China

---

[4]   Yonge's dedication of her earnings to missions abroad as well as her biography of John Coleridge Patteson indicates the close connections between her writing and her involvement in the Anglican Church. Norman May was partly modeled on Patteson, who left for the Antipodes in 1855 and was to become Bishop of Melanesia. The rewriting of Norman's disappointment there is completed in yet another of Yonge's family chronicles: at the end of *The Pillars of the House*, Leonard is met "circulating among the unhappy deported Melanesians in Queensland" and described as "a noble work" of the Mays (2:681).

(with the bullet safely embedded in a prayer book), as well as of loyal islanders nursing and converting a shipwrecked Englishmen in the South Sea Islands. At the other end of the spectrum, a maternal aunt writes letters home about local conflicts that seem to culminate only in "Aunt Flora [seeing] a Maori walking about in her best Sunday bonnet" (*Daisy Chain* 1:346) in the aftermath of a massacre and general looting. This downplaying of the Māori Wars may strike readers now as one of the incongruities of Victorian domestic fiction's representation of imperial expansion, but here it specifically prepares for Yonge's subsequent demystification of the reputed ease of settling in abroad. Disappointment may be the result of very different causes so that if American land speculation is expectedly swamped in a rehearsal of the plot of Dickens's 1844 *Martin Chuzzlewit*, New Zealand turns out to be too dull almost in its more easily realizable domesticity. The triangulation of exotic spaces becomes particularly complex precisely because all sensationalism is ultimately concentrated on America. This projection frees both England and New Zealand from disruptions of the domestic.

Predominantly due to her identification with domestic fiction, however, Yonge's representation of foreign spaces has rarely received mention in critical work. Symptomatically, Coral Lansbury's seminal study of nineteenth-century representations of Australia references Yonge repeatedly as a typical domestic writer without mentioning at all her invocation of the Antipodes (48, 79). More recently, Diana Archibald acknowledges her as one of the few authors who feature New Zealand to distinguish its narrative function from Australia's (105), and Catherine Vaughan-Pow has suggested that Yonge "finds the Indian experience and context a less fruitful source of information [than] colonies other than India, particularly the Antipodes" (252). Still, even if her India mainly consists of "well-established cities and the presence of an administrative and martial organisation," while Australia features as a "rude colony" (Vaughan-Pow 251–252), foundations for domestication in any British colony are in pointed contrast to a much more emphatically sensationalized America. Native rebellions in New Zealand may be chiefly glossed over, but America is war-ridden as well as undeveloped, and if South Sea Islanders only seem to need a haircut to turn them into civilized members of the British Empire in *The Daisy Chain* (Schaffer 207–208), native Americans are briefly evoked in *The Pillars of the House* (1873) as having nearly scalped an emigrant Englishman and his son. In *The Trial*, the sensationalization of America is really two-pronged: it consists of undeveloped settlements in which fevers make the country a good case study, and it is a land of rampant financial speculation that suggests an accelerated version of the capitalist economy developing on both sides of the Atlantic.

"Vague designs": Demystifying emigration narratives

The Trial contains Yonge's most extensive description of settler life in different parts of the globe. It explores both the potential and the limitations of a globally extended domesticity. Henry's belief in an easily facilitated new start in the American West and Leonard's boyish hope for adventures in "the Feejee Isles" display the same misleading reliance on a profitable move elsewhere. Both undergo enormous changes in their outlook, but in different places, under a different guidance (or lack thereof), and hence they develop into diametrically opposed directions that then become externalized by different geographical spaces and also by the genre elements that likewise become associated with them. At first, however, it is the same reliance on "other spaces" that gets them into trouble. Driven to take up a dull clerkship in his great-uncle's mill, Leonard fantasizes about possible escape "to some diggings or other," or of "turn[ing] up at the Grange— New Zealand" (152). This replication of an English home at the Antipodes is where Norman May—who, we remember, goes out to the Antipodes to become a missionary at the end of *The Daisy Chain*—has just become archdeacon. In pointed contradistinction to Leonard's initial fantasies, missionary work there is restricted to "an under-bred English congregation" for which Norman "need not have gone so far." These "very colonial colonists" may be "as much in need of [missionaries] as unreclaimed savages," but there is indisputably "less apparent glory" in converting them. It is because "Norman's powers were not thought of the description calculated for regular mission work" that "some of the chief aspirations of the young couple had had to be relinquished." His "unmurmuring acceptance" is presented at the opening of *The Trial* (8–9). This act curiously subdues the enthusiasm displayed at the end of *The Daisy Chain* and, in a pointed rewriting of the earlier novel, already explodes Leonard's adventurous boyhood dreams. When Leonard expounds his plans to Norman's brother Aubrey, he tellingly declares New Zealand as "too tame and too settled":

> And the two boys proceeded to arrange the details of the evasion in such vivid colouring, that they had nearly forgotten all present troubles, above all when Leonard proceeded to declare that New Zealand was too tame and too settled for him, he should certainly find something to do in the Feejee Isles, where the high spirit of the natives, their painted visages, and marvellous head-dresses, as depicted in Captain Erskine's voyage, had greatly fired his fancy, and they even settled how the gold fields should rebuild the Market Cross. (152)

The fantasy of this restored icon of both national prosperity, and Christianity plays an important role in one of the novel's most sensational plotlines. Significantly, it counts against Leonard in court: it seems just a typical scheme to abscond, to escape from responsibilities and possibly from justice for committed crimes at home.

It is here necessary to recount some of the details of the England plot. Shortly after the two boys' conversation, Leonard's great-uncle sends him to London with a bag of money to deliver at a bank there because the old man wishes to guard his savings from abuse by another great-nephew in his employ. This scheming young man, it later transpires, kills their employer, deliberately framing Leonard. Only the receipt for the money could clear him, but it is stolen by the real culprit and not discovered until his death in a drunken brawl in Paris more than three years later. Aubrey's admission, during the trial, that "[Leonard] talked of getting gold enough to build up the market-cross, or else of going to see the Feejee Islands" threatens to align Leonard with the figure of the sensational fortune hunter and his updated, more vilified version, the absconder. His boyish fantasies, however, also set him apart from typecast adventurers out to cash in on the opportunities of foreign spaces. Far from expressing "a deliberate purpose," he indulges in "a vague design," in "romantic visions of adventure" that, his counsel maintains, should be "to all who remembered their own boyhood, an illustration of the freshness and ingenuousness of the character that thus unfolded itself," for "[w]here there were day-dreams, there was no room for plots of crime" (197–199). This argument may only help commute a death sentence to penal servitude for life, but it establishes a distinction the novel bears out.

Once divorced from associations with the adventurous, the romantic visions serve as a crucial point of contrast to other emigration plans. In a reversal of the initial demystification of any easy realization of missionary zeal, Leonard's welcome addition to missions in New Zealand and, ultimately, Melanesia is paired with Henry's hopes of a new start in America and Norman's failure to proceed to Melanesia. Lending an additional edge to this juxtaposition of foreign spaces, the two brothers' adoption of different countries and duties is moreover paralleled by their brother-in-law's research project on the impact of different climates on the human body: *The Diseases of Climate*, a study begun in India by a family friend of the Mays, provides Tom May with an excellent reason to pursue the Wards to Indiana. But if Tom's main reason for going to America is to rescue the eldest sister, Averil, from their swamped speculations, his research abroad has previously already provided a vital clue to the murder case involving her brother Leonard. While working in a hospital in Paris, Tom is handed a dying man's pocketbook that turns out to belong to the murderer, the other great-nephew. It still contains the missing receipt that can prove Leonard's innocence. This pointedly anticlimactic end to the murder mystery tellingly takes place abroad, if not offstage. Given the novel's central interest in different motivations for work abroad, it is equally important that Tom's travels never imply a wish to emigrate. What he nevertheless shares with both Norman and Leonard is that he has his work well mapped out. Henry, by contrast, proceeds to America with hardly any more concrete plans than his younger brother's original "vague design" for the "Feejee Isles." Changing his name, moreover, bars him from using his professional certificates; without them, he fails to obtain any employment until the exigencies of the American Civil War make any doctor welcome. Just such impostors, emigrating or returning under a false name, form popular figures in Victorian sensation fiction. As Yonge adapts sensational formulae as well as familiar settlement narratives, she imbues their reworking with a curious ambiguity. The novel's America plot presents the story of an assumed identity from the point-of-view of the emigrant escaping from perceived criminality or shame at home.

Projected sensationalism: Literary maps of American speculations

The Wards's speculations in American swamps capitalize on a growing fascination with foreign speculative ventures. The literalized instability of land speculation abroad had been fictionalized the most memorably in Dickens's *Martin Chuzzlewit*,

published twenty years earlier. The eponymous hero is cheated, returns penniless, and having witnessed the worst exponents of selfishness abroad, is redeemed as his grandfather's heir. The novel pairs swindles on both sides of the Atlantic: in America, plots are sold for an entire city that only exists on paper, while in Britain, a company is set up to issue fake life insurance policies, and Martin's prize-winning architectural drawings are being plagiarized. Despite these parallel forms of fraud, however, the lasting image remains that of the promised city of Eden in America that turns out to be an undeveloped swamp. The failure of Martin's expectation of sudden riches in the land of presumably unlimited opportunities—where one has "the certainty of doing great things ... if he could only get there" (195)—was to become such a pervasive point of reference that Anthony Trollope's only novel set to a significant extent in America, *Dr Wortle's School* (1881), was criticized for displaying "an antique flavour which carries one back to the days of *Martin Chuzzlewit*."[5] Sensational spaces abroad clearly include the Americas and the Antipodes as often as traditionally more "exotic" destinations like India and Africa.[6] Again and again, however, America specifically doubles as a refuge for absconding bankrupts as well as for misguided, all too hopeful, emigrants and as a source of returnees who bring back the worst of both worlds. By the 1860s, Yonge could draw on ready-made stereotypes to situate her emigrants in a recognizable literary landscape.

Throughout nineteenth-century British literature, the United States promised not only a new start and perhaps a greater sense of obscurity that may shelter absconders. It also presented an expanding economy that could be seen to rival Britain in an increasingly speculative global marketplace. From its beginnings, the renegade colony troubled the British imagination, and it has now become widely accepted that far from being "altogether indifferent to the loss of America, as has sometimes been suggested, [Britain] was, rather, wary of the emergence of the United States as a significant presence on the world stage" (Giles, *Atlantic* 15). Giles has suggested that "[t]he first British responses to the prospect of the new

---

[5]   Failed emigration narratives that drew on advice literature of the time to create largely cautionary tales had of course been popular before Dickens's transatlantic reading tour, as Frances Trollope's "American" novels as much as her *Domestic Manners of the Americans* (1832) clearly indicate. Compare Cotugno (251) on Trollope's rewriting of her earlier novels in *The Old World and the New* (1849). Nancy Metz refers to accounts of "the 'How Not To Do It' of trans-Atlantic emigration" (51–52).

[6]   Similarly, the convict's money that turns Pip into a gentleman in Dickens's *Great Expectations* (1861) and the drunken gold-diggers, both male and female, in Trollope's *John Caldigate* (1879) propel sensational plotlines through their intrusion into the often only seemingly solid domesticity back home. At the same time, Australia was developing its own sensational writers. Most prominently among them was Marcus Clarke, whose focus on a penal colony in *For the Term of his Natural Life* (1874) reinforced the association of the Antipodes with convict narratives. Unlike Yonge, most British novelists did not distinguish between different settler colonies. In Ellen Wood's *The Red Court Farm* (1868), a squire's son engages in large-scale smuggling activities and, thinking he has just murdered his brother, escapes to New Zealand.

United States, then, were worked out not so much on the level of philosophical abstraction or theoretical debates about how environment might shape character, but in terms of brute political power" (*Atlantic* 15–16). In the course of the nineteenth century, this brute political power was replaced by commercial power struggles, by rivalry on a world stage dominated by imperial commerce. Finance capitalism ruled by stock-market speculations is shown to be turning the former colony into a formidable competitor. As Annette Van has similarly pointed out, this shift "posits America as an economic frontier space in which speculators can thrive" (75). Van maintains that this suggests a ceding of the future to "financially savvy Americans [who] move forward energetically, speculatively," which "leaves the reader on the brink of a new world" (94). In the majority of British novels, however, this is a brave new world to be dreaded, not welcomed. As a result, land speculation in America serves as an apt metaphor for instability. In Dickens's novel, the elusiveness of domestic foundations or constructions creates important ironies, yet ultimately the nightmare vision of a future based on speculation can be left behind abroad and suitably expelled at home. In popular fiction of the 1860s and 1870s, transatlantic flows of exchange eschew any such containment.

The absconder and the threatening returnee express anxieties about the dreaded reflux of the exported disruptive elements. Transatlantic migration prepares a final resort for impostors. As a professional detective puts it in Mary Elizabeth Braddon's *Aurora Floyd* (1863), "these fellows always go one way. It seems as if the minute a man has taken another man's life, or forged his name, or embezzled his money, his ideas get fixed in one groove, and never can go beyond Liverpool and the American packet" (442). In Elizabeth Gaskell's *A Dark Night's Work*, published in the same year, a murdered clerk is wrongly believed to have defrauded his employer "and then have made off to America!" (67). As a clearly already familiar structure, this intrinsically sensational narrative of the absconding fraudster operates as a suitable false clue.[7] Similarly, in Yonge's novel, it is a young, ambitious physician's cowardly attempt to avoid the disgrace of his brother's prison sentence that drives his endeavor to melt into a mass of anonymous humanity in the United States. His emigration plans are a desertion of his country and his imprisoned brother. Considering America "the only field for him," Henry is "resolved against remaining under British rule" (237). The implications are clear: whereas characters continue to go out to the Antipodes or Melanesia to spread a doctrine that revolves around the expansion of English domesticity, those who feel an affiliation with renegade colonies simply abscond from home responsibilities. The contrast may be somewhat embarrassingly overt, yet an ironic invocation of adoption engenders a poignant extended metaphor that forces it home even more: Henry is shown to be "fretting and wincing over" his brother's convict uniform and "trying to arrange that the farewell interview should precede its adoption" (234). As opposing driving forces, abandonment and adoption link together the novel's negotiation of emigration and repatriation and its central investment in transportable domestic values.

---

[7]   I discuss the figure of the foreign speculator, including the returnee figure, in *Financial Speculation in Victorian Fiction* (chh. 2 and 3).

So if Yonge's New Zealand stands in for adoption that includes the British Empire's appropriation of new lands, the failed domesticity of a new town erected on speculation in the United States is only the more conducive to further abandonment. Averil experiences this literally when Henry finds an opening as a surgeon to the Federal forces. His experience in the war is not only entirely offstage, but is registered as a form of desertion that brings out the "true heroism" of those left behind:

> There was true heroism in the spirit in which this young girl braced herself to uncomplaining acceptance of desertion in this unwholesome swamp, with her two little ailing sisters, beside the sluggish stream, amid the skeleton trees—heroism the greater because there was no enthusiastic patriotism to uphold her—it was only the land of her captivity, whence she looked towards home like Judah to Jerusalem. (309)

At this point in the novel the settler narrative's failure is inevitable. Averil's heroism is not located in her struggles to maintain domesticity in the West, but in her endurance of exile.

Involvement in the American Civil War becomes the final catalyst in a test of familial attachments, of affiliations that question issues of personal loyalties beyond patriotism. Averil may be recurrently exposed to intense discussions on "topics of the day, intensely interesting, and of terrible moment" to a country that remains alien to her: "but that country Averil had not yet learnt to feel her own, and to her all was one dreary whirl of words" (270). A war that is not hers only further alienates the recent emigrant: "Averil was, in Cora's words, 'too English' […] and when Mordaunt Muller had been enrolled in the Federal army, she had almost offended the exultant sister by condolence instead of congratulation." The English girl is not alone in her experience of such ambiguity: after her husband's death in the war, an Irish servant is shown to be "wailing at his dying away from his country." The "intensity of enthusiasm that has shed so much blood in the break-up of the Great Republic" is felt from a doubly domestic point-of-view: that of the sisters left behind and that of British domestic politics (305–306). The continued recourse to the metaphorical potential of adoption then poignantly culminates in the renunciation of the old country, his old life, and old name when America becomes "Henry's truly adopted country." The letter announcing his decision to stay in the West marks out his successful absorption into American culture. It is spelled out through his adoption of the language of advertising. It is the country's "most inflated style" (400), the same style in which the Wards are first introduced to the risky land speculations that are so reminiscent of the swampy Eden of *Martin Chuzzlewit*:

> [Mr. Muller] began to talk of the rising city of Mississauga—admirably situated—excellent water privilege, communicating with Lake Michigan—glorious primeval forest—healthy situation—fertile land—where a colossal fortune might be realised in maize, eighties, sections, speculations. (270)

By the time *The Trial* was published, the quick recourse to a land speculation plot with which we are already familiar from *Martin Chuzzlewit* had become such a recurrent cliché that it could serve almost as a shorthand for doomed settlement projects.

And yet, there is no scheming villainy in Mr. Muller's promotion of the land in which he speculates as well. The Wards' struggles in the swamp are simply the predictable outcome of emigration that is based on an absconding from responsibilities at home. Henry persuades Averil to sink the money she has inherited from an aunt into American speculations just when civil war is looming, laughing Averil's fears "to scorn" (275). As Archibald has pointed out, while "the majority of Victorian English emigrants chose not to go to imperial destinations," preferring the United States, "with Canada a close second, and Australia and New Zealand trailing far behind," the years 1852–1862 were a notable exception because of both the Australian gold rush and the outbreak of the American Civil War (2). But if Australia as a new colony had been conceived as "an alternative version of America, a society modelled around conventional hierarchies where insurrection against the monarch had never taken place" (Giles, "Antipodean" 39), the first full-scale settlements were consciously created with the goal to create a "Better Britain." Australia replaced America as a destination for transported convicts; the "New Zealand colonial settler was able to gather his respectability around him secure in the knowledge that he could never be described as a flogger of convicts" (Lansbury 114). In New Zealand, the logic ran, the empire would not make the same mistakes—either tactical or moral. It was to be a model colony" (Archibald 106). It was from the beginning invested in domestic portability and in the promotion of religion: founded in 1848 the Canterbury Association played a decisive role in the colony's self-imaging as the destination of "pilgrims." Yonge's novels actively helped promote such permanent pilgrimages, whereas migrating to America was literally going into the wrong direction.

When in *The Trial* "all the five quarters of the world [are being] talked of in a wild sort of a way" (236)—a wild way that eerily prefigures the propaganda slogans of American speculators—Tom May's initial reactions to the Wards' emigration plans are admittedly based on preconceptions. Emigration is cast as a rebellion against "British rule": "how could he [Tom] suppose that any man could be crazed enough to prefer to be an American citizen, when he might remain a British subject?" And yet this evocation of subject and citizen is partly ironic. It is, moreover, made clear that Tom is influenced by a school-friend who enhances the "[r]epugnance to America" that is "naturally strong in Tom" by delineating impressions made during "excursions into the States" while quartered in Canada: "such impressions as highbred young officers were apt to bring home from a superficial view of them." Biased as they are, his projections are proven all too true nonetheless: "[Henry] will get no practice in any civilised place, and will have to betake himself to some pestilential swamp, will slave his sisters to death, spend their money, and destroy them with ague" (236–237).

This is exactly what happens. Frustrated by his inability to obtain employment, Henry grasps at the inflated promises of a random American acquaintance (Muller) who has "been founding a new city." Like numerous sensationalized speculators in the fiction of the time, Muller epitomizes instability and risky overconfidence. He has been "in more various professions than Averil could ever conceive of or remember" and discourses in the language of commercial prospectuses and empty commonplaces: "'I hope you feel at home in our great country.' It was so exactly the ordinary second-rate American style" (269, 268). It is this style that Henry adopts at the end of the novel when his letter about "the future well-doing of the Mississauga Company" and "the ultimate triumph over rebellion, &c. &c. &c." is only "decisive" in articulating that he does "not wish to return to a neighbourhood so full of painful recollections" (400). Although no sensational villain, Henry is no great loss to his siblings or to England. Overbearing and self-important, he has consistently rejected the Mays' "patronage" (34), and his creation of domestic conflict has driven Leonard into his great-uncle's employment, even though their father "would as soon have sent Leonard to the hulks as to the Vintry Mill" (129). It is therefore at once unexpected and sadly ironic that the younger brother's position there directly leads to penal servitude.

Henry, by contrast, is suitably exported to a place where his resentment of patronage can be translated into a move "rapidly upwards" in a new field that turns out to be a battlefield (400). But if Yonge capitalizes on the sensational resonance of the American Civil War, she does not enlarge on it. Instead, she plays with the popular transatlantic trope of the (criminal) absconder or escapee. Henry is an easily, symptomatically Americanized emigrant who realizes his typified escape, and with whom more ambiguously presented Americans contrast positively. Mr. Muller may be a barely mentioned, typecast promoter, and his son just one of the many young men proud and eager to join a civil war, but Yonge makes an important contribution to the generally much more notoriously stereotyped representation of American women in nineteenth-century British literature.

The figure of what Archibald has diagnosed as the "'monstrous' fictional Neo-European woman" (10) necessarily lent itself well to sensational representations of colonial spaces, and in general, Victorian novelists did not really distinguish between geographically and culturally very dissimilar areas. Still, American women are simultaneously associated with—and sensationalized for this association—with protofeminist rhetoric. The characterization of Muller's daughter Cora consequently shows Yonge's reworking of clichéd plotlines at its most pointed. Cora is a good friend, good sister, good daughter, and as domestic as the circumstances of a boarding-house or a new settlement in still undeveloped parts of the Midwest—conceptualized as a "wild" west in the novel—allow her to be. Her creation is the result of a self-conscious dismantling of the unfeminine American, or Americanized, women that, in Victorian fiction, embody a lack of domesticity as "the effect of an uncontrollable market, money-grubbing values, cutthroat social relations, and the Wild West on the so-called 'weaker' sex" (Archibald 146). In Yonge's novel, this two-pronged typecasting of the former renegade colony as characterized by cutthroat social and financial relations may remain a submerged issue so that America remains in many ways an unfavorable choice for domestic settlements. Still, the attendant rewriting of the stereotype of the American woman by a domestic woman writer gives an importantly different spin to the fictional stereotyping of an intrinsically "undomestic" America.

Given Yonge's avowed antifeminism, her novels indeed register an intriguing ambiguity. *The Three Brides* (1876), for example, features a virulent women's rights activist. The wife of an American professor of political economy lectures more freely and vociferously than her husband. She is a largely comical, if comically obnoxious figure, but she also displays an amount of good-nature that is singularly lacking among those who have invited her. It is certainly an exaggeration to suggest that "Charlotte [Yonge], like Dickens, regarded the United States as a land of fever-ridden swamps inhabited by a race of uncivilised hoboes" (Battiscombe 149). In *The Trial*, Averil's fortune is, after all, partly retrieved because Cora has "made her father buy all Ave's Mississauga shares—at a dead loss to us of course" (414). There is an important connection between the two young ladies keeping their homes together, a connection that can counterpoise the worst domestic effects of land speculation or war.

The impact of their unsettled lives on the youngest Ward sister, Ella, however, is deplored as the symptom of a particularly American idea of emancipation. Her "precocious Western manner" (414) is the result of advice by American girls her age (she is eight when they emigrate) that "no young lady of [her] age would ask her sister's permission, and not even her mother's, unless her mamma was very intellectual and highly educated" (290). In a revealing contrast of different settlements and the returnees they produce, Norman's eight-year-old son Dickie is not only "perfectly at ease and thoroughly at home" when sent to England from New Zealand, but also proud of being used to cleaning the dishes at home: "I never break anything" (362–363). The pairing of the two young returnees encapsulates a central comparison: "[Ella's] tinge of Americanism formed an amusing contrast with Dickie's colonial ease—especially when she began to detail the discomforts of Mississauga, and he made practical suggestions for the remedies of each—describing how mamma and he himself managed" (414). Throughout the novel, a prevailing domestic point-of-view readdresses the predominant preoccupation with (male) narratives of exploration and adventure. Instead, Yonge depicts daily struggles with accumulating domestic inconveniences as much as with illness.

At the same time, the double standards with which the Māori Wars are downplayed and the bloodiness of the American Civil War accentuated highlight the significance of sensationalist devices in the narrative construction of literary landscapes. Surely there would have been enough material for Yonge to render New Zealand as sensational as the American West. Partly, however, Yonge's interest in missionary work in the Antipodes ensured that she stressed resolution of conflicts, not the conflicts themselves. Her biography of her cousin John Coleridge Patteson, first Bishop to Melanesia, even "purposely omitted" material on "the unhappy Maori war" (vi). In the biography, this omission is paired with a similar elision of "such criticisms on living personages as it seemed fair towards the writer to omit" (vi); in her novels, it signals the need to make New Zealand domestic and even emphatically unexotic.[8]

For Yonge, missionary as well as military outposts around the world function as parts of home, while America remains first and foremost a sensational space. It is a country outside the secure folds of the Empire—engendering an alignment that affects also her representation of Canada in her later fiction.[9] At once undeveloped and endorsing overdevelopment, however, the United States unites the worst of an expanding capitalist economy. Hence in *The Trial*, the mundane domesticity described in letters from New Zealand contrasts with "plenty of bush" in Indiana (268). No more a thriving city than Martin Chuzzlewit's Eden, the Wards' lot in Mississauga combines rough bush-life with the results of speculative ventures in the course of which "all the trees near it have been killed, and stand up all dead and white, because nobody has time to cut them down" (290). As opposed to American swamps that usefully swallow up even the most calculating characters, New Zealand becomes a possible extension of home precisely because it is domestic to the point of being "too tame and too settled."

The end of the novel turns on a twofold return that underscores the thematic significance of failed emigration: Leonard Ward is released from prison once his innocence is established after more than three years of hard labor; his sisters return from America. Their paralleled escape from hardships marks the culmination of a consistent equation of these two places of forceful exile. Leonard is repeatedly said to fare better in a scrupulously clean English model prison than his sisters in swamps abroad. If this may seem a reductively neat, even unduly exaggerated dichotomy of home and elsewhere, the parallelism of transatlantic and transpacific emigration importantly breaks through any neat dichotomies. After his undeserved confinement, Leonard is even better befitted to become a missionary. His exportation as the spokesman of a message that is vital to Yonge's writing is in sharp contrast to his brother Henry's assertion that in preferring to stay in the United States after the surviving sisters' return home, he has himself successfully "broken off his whole connection with England"—an assertion he makes in "the most inflated style of Henry's truly adopted country" (400). Meanwhile, Averil's return home to careful nursing by the extended May family promises a slow recuperation from a variety of ailments brought on in the swampy settlement. Symptomatically, what eventually happens to the Mississauga shares (in which Henry continues to believe) is completely irrelevant. Sensational American speculations, like the swamps

---

[8]   The New Zealand, or Māori, Wars refer to a series of conflicts between 1845 and 1872. After a period of relative peace between 1848 and the early 1860s, the Invasion of Waikato in 1863 started the biggest of the New Zealand Wars. The American Civil War lasted from 1861 to 1865. Both wars were therefore raging when Yonge was engaged in writing *The Trial*.

[9]   *Lady Hester* (1874), for example, is a short novella revolving on a Canadian woman of various mixed blood and upbringing who embodies an infiltration of traditional social and domestic structures at home.

they promote, have fulfilled an important narrative function and are then safely contained as of no consequence to the retrieved English characters. In adapting sensational clichés, *The Trial* presents an intriguingly intricate engagement with the cultural fictions of settlement circulating in Victorian Britain. It asks us to reconsider the complex functions of domestic fiction's evocation of transatlantic or transpacific imaginaries, while prompting us to read the shifting re-presentation of these imaginaries, at home and abroad, in tandem.

Works Cited

Archibald, Diana. *Domesticity, Imperialism, and Emigration in the Victorian Novel*. Columbia: University of Missouri Press, 2002.

Battiscombe, Georgina. *Charlotte Mary Yonge: The Story of an Uneventful Life*. London: Constable, 1943.

Braddon, Mary Elizabeth. *Aurora Floyd*. Oxford: Oxford University Press, 1999.

Claybaugh, Amanda. "Towards a New Transatlanticism: Dickens in the United States." *Victorian Studies* 48.3 (2006): 439–460.

Cotugno, Clare, "'Stay Away from Paris!' Frances Trollope Rewrites America." *Victorian Periodicals Review* 38.2 (2005): 240–257.

Dickens, Charles. *Martin Chuzzlewit*. Oxford: Oxford University Press, 1998.

Flint, Kate. *The Transatlantic Indian, 1776–1930*. Princeton, N.J.: Princeton University Press, 2009.

Gaskell, Elizabeth. *A Dark Night's Work And Other Stories*. Oxford: Oxford University Press, 1992.

Giles, Paul. *Transatlantic Insurrections: British Culture and the Formation of American Literature, 1730–1860*. Philadelphia: University of Pennsylvania Press, 2001.

———. *Atlantic Republic: The American Tradition in English Literature*. New York: Oxford University Press, 2006.

———. "Antipodean American Literature: Franklin, Twain, and the Sphere of Subalternity." *American Literary History* 20.1–2 (2008): 22–50.

Lansbury, Coral. *Arcady in Australia: The Evocation of Australia in Nineteenth-Century English Literature*. Melbourne: Melbourne University Press, 1970.

Manning, Susan, and Andrew Taylor. "Introduction: What Is Transatlantic Studies?" *Transatlantic Literary Studies: A Reader*. Ed. Susan Manning and Andrew Taylor. Edinburgh: Edinburgh University Press, 2007. 1–13.

Maunder, Andrew. "General Introduction." Varieties of Women's Sensation Fiction: 1855–1890. Ed., Andrew Maunder. London: Pickering & Chatto, 2004. x–xi.

Metz, Nancy Aycock. "'Fevered with Anxiety for Home': Nostalgia and the 'New' Emigrant in *Martin Chuzzlewit*." *Dickens Quarterly* 18.2 (2001): 49–61.

Romanes, Ethel. *Charlotte Mary Yonge: An Appreciation*. London: Mowbray, 1908.

Schaffer, Talia. "Taming the Tropics: Charlotte Yonge Takes on Melanesia." *Victorian Studies* 47.2 (2005): 204–214.

Sturrock, June. "Murder, Gender, and Popular Fiction by Women in the 1860s: Braddon, Oliphant, Yonge." *Victorian Crime, Madness and Sensation*. Ed. Andrew Maunder and Grace Moore. Aldershot: Ashgate, 2004. 73–88.

"Unsigned Notice." *Nation* (March 10, 1881). Rpt. in *Anthony Trollope: The Critical Heritage*. Ed. Donald Smalley. London: Routledge, 1999.

Van, Annette. "Ambivalent Speculations: America as England's Future in *The Way We Live Now*." *Novel* 39.1 (2005): 75–96.

Vaughan-Pow, Catherine. "A One-Way Ticket? Emigration and the Colonies in the Works of Charlotte M. Yonge." *Imperial Objects: Essays on Victorian Women's Emigration and the Unauthorised Imperial Experience*. Ed. Rita S. Kranidis. New York: Twayne Publishers, 1998. 248–263.

Wagner, Tamara S. *Financial Speculation in Victorian Fiction: Plotting Money and the Novel Genre, 1815–1901*. Columbus: Ohio State University Press, 2010.

Wynne, Deborah. *The Sensation Novel and the Victorian Family Magazine*. Houndmills, Basingstoke: Palgrave, 2001.

Yonge, Charlotte. *The Daisy Chain; Or Aspirations*. 2 vols. McLean, Va.: IndyPublish, n.d.

———. *The Two Guardians; Or, Home in this World*. New York: Appleton and Co, 1871.

———. *The Trial; Or, More Links of the Daisy Chain*. Doylestown: Wildside, n.d.

———. *Life of John Coleridge Patteson: Missionary Bishop of the Melanesian Islands*. 2 vols. London: Macmillan and Co., 1874.

———. *The Pillars of the House*. 2 vols. London: Macmillan and Co., 1875.

Chapter 13
The Return of the Native as Transatlantic Sensation; Or, Hardy Sensationalized

Julia McCord Chavez

At first glance, it might seem unorthodox to think of Thomas Hardy as a transatlantic writer. Best known in his own time for writing about "the lives of a quiet people in one nook of England," Hardy prompted critics to think of him as a quintessentially English writer ("Hardy's Newest Novel" 110). Raymond Williams unhesitatingly writes in *The Country and the City*, "There can be no doubt at all of Hardy's commitment to his own country" (197). More recently, Amanda Claybaugh has identified "insistent localness" as a prevailing characteristic of Hardy's fiction. According to Claybaugh, Hardy "had no interest in, or even much awareness of, the Anglo-American world" (185). In these accounts, Hardy's Wessex novels stand as the epitome of insularity, turning their back on the Anglo-American world.[1]

Categorizing Hardy as a sensation novelist might seem equally unorthodox. Canonized as one of the "great" novelists of the nineteenth century, Hardy has been lauded as a powerful tragedian, not the purveyor of popular fiction—despite the initial publication of many of his novels in popular magazines such as *Belgravia*, the *Cornhill*, *Harper's New Monthly Magazine*, *Littell's Living Age*, the *Semi-Weekly New York Tribune*, and the *Sunday New York Times*. Admitted deviations from the standards of "high" literature in Hardy's work have been dismissed by critics as a byproduct of a crass literary marketplace, the unfortunate result of "compromises ... forced upon his work" by original readers (Wright 115).

In this essay, I break from a longstanding critical tradition and reexamine Hardy from a radically new vantage point: as a popular novelist participating in a complex transatlantic literary culture. Looking first at *The Return of the Native* in its original serialized publication in the London magazine *Belgravia*, and then at the concurrent serialization of the novel in the American magazine *Harper's New Monthly*, this essay will explore the ways in which the sensational qualities of the

---

[1]   Hardy's many transatlantic publications call these accounts into question, however. *A Pair of Blue Eyes* was serialized in the *Semi-Weekly New York Tribune* in 1873. From 1874 to 1875 *Far From the Madding Crowd* was serialized in three periodicals: *Littell's Living Age*, *The Eclectic*, and *The Semi-Weekly New York Tribune*. *The Hand of Ethelberta* was serialized in the *Sunday New York Times* simultaneously with its appearance in *The Cornhill* in 1876. For full details, see Pinck (300). For a convincing argument that Hardy was in fact acutely aware of his American audience and the economics of publishing within an Anglo-American market, see Abravanel (109–122).

novel and its transatlantic context invite a radical reinterpretation of this Wessex tale. When re-read through the lens of transatlantic sensation, *The Return of the Native* sheds its insularity and emerges as an anti-regionalist text that promotes transatlantic reading communities.

When we strip away the baggage of preexisting criticism and consider the facts of initial publication, it is not hard to read *The Return of the Native*—a novel that follows the star-crossed lovers Eustacia Vye and Damon Wildeve from their respective ill-fated marriages to Clym and Thomasin Yeobright until their untimely deaths in a spectacular storm—as sensational. The difficulty Hardy experienced in finding a publisher for the novel suggests that it was originally read in this literary tradition. When Hardy submitted a portion of the unfinished manuscript for publication in the *Cornhill*, editor Leslie Stephen passed (Nash 54). As Hardy records it in his letters, "though [Stephen] liked the opening, he feared that the relations between Eustacia, Wildeve, and Thomasin might develop into something 'dangerous' for a family magazine, and he refused to have anything to do with it unless he could see the whole" (Maitland 276–277). *Blackwood's* and *Temple Bar* passed as well (Nash 54), and Hardy ultimately found his novel serialized in *Belgravia* magazine, "of all places" (F. Hardy 17).

Belgravia, an illustrated London monthly that was first published in November 1866, was designed for a middle-class audience, in particular a "genteel, middle-class, lady public, of low to fair education standard" (Scheuerle 31). In its initial years, the sensation novelist Mary Elizabeth Braddon served as its conductor. During this time, the magazine typically carried serialized sensation novels as well as biographies, travelogues, light essays, and poetry, and it "developed a rather low-brow reputation, closely associated with the sensationalism of [Braddon's] own fiction and the scandal of her private life" (Nash 56). After March 1876, when the magazine was acquired by Chatto & Windus, illustration became a more important feature, and its list of contributors included Charles Reade, Wilkie Collins, Mark Twain, Algernon Swinburne, Bret Harte, and Thomas Hardy (Scheuerle 32). While the well-known Mudie's lending library had been a subscriber, suggesting a modicum of social approval (Scheuerle 31), modern assessments have deemed *Belgravia* a mediocre publication at best. "It had not been a glorious magazine," Daniel Faber and Michael Bornstein conclude, "but had offered readers sensational adventures, tolerably harmless chit-chat, and occasional instruction. Its success vouches for its reliability as an index to one level of Victorian taste" (92–93).[2]

Serialized within *Belgravia*'s pages, *The Return of the Native* found itself sandwiched between murder mysteries by Richard Dowling,[3] sensational essays

---

[2]   For a competing and more nuanced analysis of *Belgravia* magazine, see Bandish.

[3]   These sensational short stories include: "Genius at the Hammer" (February 1878), "The Marine Binocular" (April 1878), "Her Child's Cry" (May 1878), "The Elba of the Thames" (July 1878), and "The Going Out of Alessandro Pozzone" (August 1878).

on science by Richard Proctor,[4] and essays on topics such as premature burial, Turkish slave stories, and theatrical riots.[5] When this original context is considered, the common critical reading of *The Return of the Native* as falling within the elite genre of Greek tragedy seems strangely cut off from reality.[6] The particulars of its serialization suggest that we might think instead about the novel as falling into an alternative generic model: the novel of sensation. According to Henry Mansel writing in 1863, "a sensation novel, as a matter of course, abounds in incident. Indeed, as a general rule, it consists of nothing else. Deep knowledge of human nature, graphic delineations of individual character, vivid representations of the aspects of Nature or the workings of the soul—all the higher features of the creative art—would be a hindrance rather than a help to a work of this kind … The human actors in the piece are for the most part, but so many lay-figures in which to exhibit a drapery of incident" (486). In this fictional world, accident and aberration govern; plot rules supreme.

Admittedly, *The Return of the Native* is not a perfect fit if Mansel's definition is to delineate what counts as sensation fiction. After all, Egdon Heath is depicted so vividly in the opening chapters of the novel that it becomes a character in its own right. Certainly Hardy is interested in "vivid representations of the aspects of Nature" and "the inner workings of the soul"; his novel is more than the simple conglomeration of incident that Mansel denounces. At the same time, as even those critics most attached to a reading of the novel as tragedy have acknowledged, it is a novel of "chance encounters," "misdirected messages," and "overheard conversations" (Chapman 146).

A close reading of the novel as it initially appeared in serial form demonstrates a heavy reliance on the conventions of sensation fiction, including a foregrounding of "incident." While the novel's first installment opens with the memorable description of Egdon Heath "suggesting tragical possibilities" (*Belgravia*, January 1878, 259), it ends squarely with the touchstone of serialized sensation fiction: the cliffhanger. Shifting from the ageless world of the heath and its rural inhabitants, the narrative takes up the aborted marriage between Thomasin and Wildeve, foreshadows the love triangle that will fuel the action of the novel, and ends with Mrs. Yeobright's salacious question to Thomasin, "Now Thomasin … what's the meaning of this disgraceful performance?" (*Belgravia*, January 1878, 287).

---

[4]   Essays by Proctor include: "Living in Dread and Terror" (January 1878), "The Moon's Myriad Small Craters" (August 1878), and "The Sun in His Glory" (November 1878). Other science essays include: "Bird or Reptile—Which?" by Henry O. Forbes (September 1878) and "What I Saw in an Ant's Nest," by Andrew Wilson (October 1878). For a full discussion of this topic, see Onslow.

[5]   G. Eric Mackay, "Premature Burials" (March 1878); F.E.A., "Some Turkish Slave Stories" (April 1878); H. Barton Baker, "Famous Theatrical Riots" (October 1878).

[6]   Defined by one critic as Hardy's "most ambitious book" and another as "one of the greatest novels of English literature," this novel has been studied meticulously in terms of its relationship to a classical five-act tragedy. See Wright (104) and Wheeler (29), respectively.

Readers of the periodical version were of course required to wait another month to obtain the answer to this question. At the end of the first monthly installment, the narrative focus is placed on incident, in keeping with the generic conventions of the novel of sensation.

Although modern critics are quick to downplay this emphasis on incident, contemporary reviews suggest that Victorian readers did not. The *Contemporary Review* judged Hardy's plot, consisting of "three tragic deaths, two marriages, and then a cheerful ending," to be "all but absurd" ("Contemporary Literary Chronicles" 206). Similarly, a reviewer for the *Athenaeum* suggests the resemblance to familiar sensation plots:

> The general plot of the story turns on the old theme of a man who is in love with two women, and a woman who is in love with two men; the man and the woman being both selfish and sensual … [O]ne cannot help seeing that the two persons in question know no other law than the gratification of their own passion, although this is not carried to a point which would place the book on the "Index" of respectable households. ("Novels of the Week" 654)

Reviewers at the *Atlantic Monthly* concurred with British counterparts, albeit more subtly, praising Hardy's "ingenuity in devising unheard-of incidents and wild and memorable scenes" in an early review ("The Return of the Native, and Other Novels" 502) and concluding in a subsequent review that the novel's "plot … is full of … dramatic situations" ("Contributor's Club" 674).

Not all agreed, of course, and a reviewer for *Scribner's Monthly* commented on the weakness of the plot in comparison to traditional sensation novels: "situations managed so as to whet the reader's interest in the plot are entirely lacking, and that makes the book one which editors of magazines might hesitate to use" ("Hardy's 'Return of the Native'" 910). Notwithstanding this assertion about a lack of focus on plot, the last paragraph of the review ultimately characterizes *The Return of the Native* as sharing some of the same qualities as popular sensation fiction, notably its audience: "the novel has such excellent qualities that one feels that here is an author who has wasted great gifts, perhaps a great name in literature, for the present advantages that come with the writing of a book of regulation length, calculated more for the demands of a three-volume public than for enduring fame" (911).

More certainly than his use of plot, Hardy's characterization of his "dark" heroine, Eustacia Vye, strongly aligns his novel with a tradition of sensation fiction.[7] Most obviously, Eustacia is presented as an exotic, dangerous outsider, the daughter of a transient foreign bandmaster who has only recently come to the heath. According to a reviewer for *Harper's*, she is "an exotic from a more advanced state of society, who has been planted on this unattractive wild and among its simple folk by circumstances which she could not control, and against which she unceasingly rebels, and whose nature is a singular compound of contradictions—of fierceness and gentleness, resolution and vacillation, love and

---

7   See Hughes for an extended discussion of Hardy within the sensation tradition.

inconstancy, coldness and passion, strength and weakness" ("Editor's Literary Record" 627–628). For the insular "simple folk" of Egdon Heath, Eustacia is a sinister presence, literally a witch who threatens their harmonious existence.[8] In Hardy's own words from a letter to his illustrator, Arthur Hopkins, Eustacia is the "wayward & erring heroine" who plays opposite the "*good* heroine" Thomasin (*Collected Letters* 1.52–53).

Contemporary reviews place Hardy's heroine directly within a lineage of earlier sensation heroines. Both the *Nation* and the *Athenaeum* note Eustacia's resemblance to Gustave Flaubert's Madame Bovary ("The Return of the Native," *Nation* 155; "Novels of the Week" 654). This resemblance, in turn, connects Eustacia to other sensation heroines who also draw their inspiration from the dynamic Emma Bovary. As Christopher Heywood has pointed out, Eustacia possesses many affinities with Isabel Sleaford, the heroine of Braddon's 1864 novel *The Doctor's Wife*.[9] Eustacia, like Isabel, is a "dreamy heroine … walking alone in a provincial landscape by twilight and moonlight, and brooding impetuously on marriage" (Heywood 92). Again like Braddon's heroine, Hardy's restless Eustacia longs to be a citizen of the world and to enjoy all that civilization has to offer: "music, poetry, passion, war, and all the beating and pulsing that is going on in the great arteries of the world" (*Belgravia*, September 1878, 263). Eustacia fetishizes Paris as the symbol of the cosmopolitan world, and her marriage to Clym represents a misguided attempt to realize a fantasy of escape from a regional insularity that stifles her, just as Isabel's marriage to the prosaic George Gilbert represents a failed attempt at a more exciting life. In this way, Hardy calls attention to a dearth of options for women in much the same way that sensation authors like Braddon did. As a reviewer for the *Atlantic Monthly* astutely claims, Hardy's representation of Eustacia shows him to be "keenly appreciative of the feminine *situation* as well as temperament" ("Contributors' Club" 673).

In addition, Hardy's "Queen of Night," like Braddon's Isabel, is characterized largely through a series of arguably satiric allusions to her literary preferences. According to the narrator:

> Her high gods were William the Conqueror, Strafford, and Napoleon Bonaparte, as they had appeared in the Lady's History used at the establishment in which she was educated. Her chief-priest was Byron: her antichrist a well-meaning polemical preacher at Budmouth, of the name of Slatters. Had she been a mother, she would have christened her boys such names as Saul or Sisera in preference to Jacob or David, neither of whom she admired … At school she used to side with the Philistines in several battles, and had wondered if Pontius Pilate were as handsome as he was frank and fair. (*Belgravia*, February 1878, 506)

---

[8]   For a reading of Eustacia "as [a] figure of threatening abnormality who the people of Egdon must … control," see Malton (150).

[9]   Braddon's novel was serialized in *Temple Bar* magazine from January to December 1864.

‘ *She lifted her left hand.’*

Fig. 13.1   *She lifted her hand."* Arthur Hopkins. *Belgravia* 34 (February
1878), facing page 493. Courtesy of the University of Wisconsion-
Madison.

This network of allusions suggests a slightly silly woman, whose imagination far
outweighs reason or common sense.

Hopkins's illustrations of Eustacia for the serialized novel reinforce these
sensational tendencies. While Pamela Dalziel has argued that the illustrations were
intended to draw readers' attention away from the more salacious aspects of the
story (91), many of the images bring out the qualities in Eustacia that connect her
with the typical sensation heroine. In the illustration for the February installment of
the novel, for example, Eustacia is depicted as a solitary figure on the heath with a
spyglass in her hand and a cluster of crop ponies in the background (Figure 13.1).

This image of a solitary, brooding woman taps into the recognizable stereotype
of sensation fiction's darkly passionate heroine/villainess (Hughes 178). It has
been argued that the inclusion of the ponies suggests a dangerously unrestrained
sexuality, perhaps reminding us of Braddon's earlier connection between women
and horses in sensation novels such as *Aurora Floyd*. According to Dalziel,
Hopkins in the end "chose to focus not on the faultless goddess but on the less
than ideal woman" in this unflattering illustration (93).

The August and October illustrations connect more explicitly with novels of
sensation by depicting Eustacia as a contemporary "woman of fashion" (Jackson
90) (Figures 13.2 and 13.3).

In these images, Hopkins dresses Eustacia in a black and white striped dress of distinctive cut, thus identifying her within a very specific time and locale. Interestingly, Hardy himself preferred this depiction of Eustacia over the style of representation in the initial illustration. In a letter to Hopkins on February 8, 1878, Hardy wrote, "It is rather ungenerous to criticise, but since you invite me to do so I will say that I think Eustacia should have been represented as more youthful in face, supple in figure, &, in general, with a little more roundness & softness than have been given her" (Dalziel 95). In August 1878, Hardy wrote of the new Eustacia: "I think Eustacia is charming—she is certainly just what I imagined her to be, & the rebelliousness of her nature is precisely caught in your drawing" (Dalziel 100). The version of Eustacia that Hardy favored was the contemporary woman who faces her dilemmas melodramatically, with parasol and teacup in hand and eyes turned upward to the sky.

Contemporary reviews of the novel indicate the degree to which the Braddonesque Eustacia captured the imagination of readers, despite her faults. According to the *Literary World*, "neither the vigorous simplicity of Clym, nor the wild-flower sweetness of Thomasin … interest us as do the passionate and unruly shiftiness of Wildeve, or the incomparable Eustacia, which latter portrait, disagreeable though it be, is drawn with all the fire and dash of Fortuny, combined with the finish of a Meissonier" ("The Return of the Native" 37). *Scribner's* unabashedly calls her "the main figure of the book," and comments that "she is of an excellence that throws other heroines into the shade. Like the Trojan ancients before Helen of Troy, we understand how men are infatuated with her despite her manifest naughtiness, and are forced to lament the fate that such conduct brings in its wake" ("Hardy's 'Return of the Native'" 911). In this sense, Eustacia is perceived as embodying some of the most basic qualities of the femme fatale of sensation fiction (Bouhelma 50). The dark Eustacia seems a kindred spirit to the likes of Lydia Gwilt in Wilkie Collins's *Armadale*,[10] a woman who does not mind wearing a disguise to achieve her ends. In fact, Eustacia relishes the idea of cross-dressing as a Turkish knight in the Mummer's performance, for "[h]ere was something to do: here was someone to see, and a charmingly adventurous way to see him" (*Belgravia*, April 1878, 247). Contemporary readers saw Eustasia, like the prototypical sensation heroine, as "a woman of extreme beauty, of a certain sinister sort, possessed with a devouring yet petty ambition to 'better her condition'" ("The Return of the Native," *Nation* 155).

All of this is well and good, but one might ask at this point whether there is really anything at stake in viewing *The Return of the Native* as a sensation novel. Why should the novel be reconsidered in these terms, instead of the paradigm of tragedy in which it has traditionally been viewed? My answer is that reading *The Return of the Native* as a sensation novel shifts the narrative center so as to give voice to a critique of insularity that forms an important subtext throughout. With Eustacia at the center of the novel, rather than the nominal hero Clym, the

---

[10]   This novel was serialized in *Cornhill Magazine* from November 1864 to June 1866.

'Unconscious of her presence, he still went on singing.'

Fig. 13.2   "Unconscious of her presence, he still went on singing." Arthur
Hopkins. *Belgravia* 36 (March 1878), facing page 238. Courtesy of
the University of Wisconsin-Madison.

'*He brought the tray to the front of the couch.*'

Fig. 13.3   "He brought the tray to the front of the couch." Arthur Hopkins. *Belgravia* 36 (October 1878), facing page 506. Courtesy of the University of Wisconsin-Madison.

central problem in Hardy's fictional world becomes the insularity embodied in the returned "native," not the menacing forces of the outside world. In this reading, what is truly dangerous—even deadly—is the community that cannot tolerate contact with the outside world.

On its surface, Hardy's novel conspicuously marks cosmopolitan yearnings as "wayward & erring," dangerous and destructive. Those in the novel who long to travel and who see merit in other cultures are also the most errant characters— Eustacia and Wildeve. Surely it is no coincidence that Paris, a city of legendary immorality in British minds, captures the imagination of each. Although Eustacia "had never once told Wildeve of the Parisian desires which Clym's description had sown in her," he too designates it "the central beauty-spot of the world" (*Belgravia*, September 1878, 278). Not surprisingly Clym, the purported "light" or moral anchor in the novel, takes an opposite attitude towards this city. Discounting his Parisian life of "selling trinkets to women and fops" as flimsy and effeminate (*Belgravia*, June 1878, 487), he presents a clear statement against cosmopolitanism by urging that "there is nothing particularly great in [life's] greatest walks" (*Belgravia*, August 1878, 240), and thus no reason to leave the heath. The climax of the novel lends this position greater support, for the errant wanderers Eustacia and Wildeve perish in Shadwell Weir while Clym survives his near drowning. Forces converge in Hardy's novel to destroy Eustacia, the symbolic outsider.

The final book of the novel, which "shortly relates the gradual righting of affairs after the foregoing catastrophe" according to its headnote (*Belgravia*, December 1878, 234), appears to reinforce this insular position and endorse regionalism. In this book, Thomasin—the character after Clym most closely associated with Egdon Heath—achieves a happy ending with a loving husband and wealth, yet refuses to move from the heath or give up her "countrified" ways (*Belgravia*, December 1878, 246). She is a proudly regional character, yet one that cannot be dismissed as a foolish rustic, and she triumphs in the end when affairs are "righted." In contrast to the rebellious Eustacia, who fruitlessly longs to become a citizen of the world, the complacent Thomasin is content to remain a citizen of the heath. Moreover, the narrator depicts Thomasin's position as the more reasonable one. Speaking of her response to the threatening storm on the night of Eustacia's death, the narrator explains:

> there were not, as for Eustacia, demons in the air, and malice in every bush and bough. The drops which lashed her face were not scorpions, but prosy rain; Egdon in the mass was no monster whatever, but impersonal open ground. Her fears of the place were rational, her dislikes of its worst moods reasonable. At this time it was in her view a windy wet place, in which a person might experience much discomfort, lose the path without care, and possibly catch cold. (*Belgravia*, November 1878 23)

This passage equates regionalism with reasonableness, and cosmopolitanism with inflated gothic fantasies that render an individual incapable of coping with life. Here, cosmopolitan wandering aligns with the errant and the irrational, and ultimately leads to destruction.

The novel's explicit endorsement of regionalism is somehow dissatisfying, however, and Hardy seems to have recognized this when he "retracted" his happy ending in the 1912 Wessex Edition of the novel through an enigmatic footnote urging readers "with an austere artistic code" to "choose" the better ending (Penguin edition 427). Alleging that Thomasin's happy ending was a byproduct of "certain circumstances of serial publication," Hardy retroactively recasts his Wessex novel as closing with the death of Eustacia in Shadwell Weir (427). Viewed from this perspective, one that valorizes Hardy's wayward heroine, *The Return of the Native* makes a strong case for the merits of wandering cosmopolitanism. If one is sympathetic to Eustacia, as contemporary readers were,[11] her climactic death can be read not as punishment for cosmopolitan longings, but rather as a deplorable side-effect of a stultifying regionalism that cannot tolerate individuality or difference. Although the novel transparently associates regionalism with the pragmatic Thomasin Yeobright, seeming to promote isolationism, it simultaneously portrays another, more sinister regionalism that is linked with the uneducated and superstitious heath folk featured both visually and verbally in the very first installment of the novel. This destructive brand of regionalism becomes graphically embodied later in the novel through Susan Nonsuch and her savage, voodoo folk practices, which involve "cutting and twisting, dismembering and re-joining the incipient image" of Hardy's errant heroine (*Belgravia*, November 1878 16).

Hardy's quiet critique of insularity, which emerges most poignantly when the novel is read as sensation fiction, becomes more pressing when one considers the novel's original serial appearances in magazines that resisted insularity themselves by actively participating in transatlantic literary exchange. While billing itself as a "London magazine," the content of *Belgravia* was self-consciously cosmopolitan, and more specifically transatlantic.

During the period in which *The Return of the Native* was serialized, *Belgravia* included multiple articles by American authors. In particular, *Belgravia* featured stereotypically American trickster tales by Mark Twain, Julian Hawthorne, and Bret Harte. Twain's short story in the March 1878 issue, "The Loves of Alonzo FitzClarence and Rosannah Ethelton," relates the humorous anecdote of a man and woman from Maine and San Francisco who fall in love and marry over the telephone after a villain tries to separate them through telephone trickery. The May 1878 issue of *Belgravia* follows up this tale with another piece by Twain, "Fables and Their Sequels," as well as Hawthorne's story, "An Automatic Enigma." Bret Harte's own trickster tale, "A Tourist from Injianny," appeared in the October 1878 issue, and relates the story of a poor mechanic from Indiana who travels to Europe on his wits and manages to marry his daughter to an English aristocrat by cleverly throwing her into the aristocrat's line of vision.

---

[11]   A reviewer at the *Atlantic Monthly*, for example, wrote: "Eustacia and her lover Wildeve, in the Native, are alike vain, selfish, and lawless, yet our instinctive sympathies are allowed to go with Eustacia under the burst of her blameless husband's terrific wrath …" See "The Return of the Native and Other Novels" (502.)

To emphasize further this transatlantic exchange, America is referenced, either centrally or incidentally, in numerous pieces by *Belgravia*'s British authors. The unsigned essay, "An Epicurean Tour" (April 1878), chronicles a professor's culinary tour of America. This essay uses the term "trans-Atlantic" frequently, and refers to the uncomfortable relations between England and America by pointing out the animosity between the latter and its "unnatural old parent" (156). An article by J. Arbuthnot Wilson, titled "Among the Thousand Islands" (October 1878), provides another kind of American tour essay. This time the subject is camping among the islands located between New York and Canada. Wilson brings America into focus more obliquely in a farcical essay, "The Empress of Andorra" (September 1878), which specifies that its heroine, an opera-singer turned political leader, was born in America.

Transatlantic movement is highlighted in *Belgravia*'s simultaneously running serial novels, as well. Surprisingly, in *The Return of the Native*, Wildeve suggests Wisconsin as the location to which he and Eustacia might escape, were they to leave Edgon Heath together. America is similarly a place of escape, and perhaps opportunity, in Wilkie Collins's novel *The Haunted Hotel*. The first installment of this novel suggests a connection between the British aristocracy and the American economy when the brother of the aristocrat whose murder forms the central mystery is "away, looking after his interests in some mining property which he possessed in America" (June 1878, 407). In the next two installments, the villain of the story travels to the United States to see recent discoveries about chemistry (July 1878, 114; August 1878, 141). In the September installment, the current changes, and Collins gives readers an American guest in Europe, staying at the converted Venetian hotel where the murder took place (362).

Although some of *Belgravia*'s shorter essays appear to solidify British cultural capital by emphasizing the boorishness of Americans like Harte's tourist from Injianny or Wilson's silly Empress of Andorra, America plays a slightly different role in the novels. Here, America is recognized as providing important avenues of exchange with Britain—a safety valve for those who cannot assimilate into British society, a location of potential wealth, and a location of scientific discovery. While transatlantic exchange is mocked within some pages of *Belgravia*, it is surely recognized as beneficial in others. In choosing to carry the literary wares of American authors, essays about America, and novels that include America as a part of their fictional landscape, *Belgravia* rejects insularity and becomes the locus of transatlantic exchange.

Hardy's decision to serialize concurrently in the American magazine, *Harper's New Monthly*, further reinforces the novel's critique of insularity, for the act of transatlantic publication overcomes purely regional affiliations notwithstanding the subject of the novel. Hardy may have been writing about and even nostalgically recreating "one nook in England" ("Hardy's Newest Novel" 110), but his intended audience was by no means so limited. In many ways, *Harper's* embodies the same cosmopolitan ideals that one sees in *Belgravia*. *Harper's* was launched in 1850 as an "accessory" to the Harper brother's prosperous book publishing business

(Perkins 166), and it was patterned after popular British periodicals (Cyganoski 17).[12] Like *Belgravia, Harper's* carried serialized novels, as well as short stories, popular science articles, travel accounts, wood engravings, and a "Monthly Record of Current Events" compiled by the editor (Perkins 166–167).

Harper's self-proclaimed role was to be a popular educator and to "place within the reach of the great mass of the American people the unbounded treasures of the Periodical Literature of the present day" ("A Word at the Start" 1–2), and it held particular appeal for "the aspiring educated elite who were keen to broaden their knowledge on a variety of topics and to entertain themselves with the latest literary creations of the day" (Wyckoff and Nash 10). When the magazine was initiated, it appeared to some to be "the mirror of Victorian literature" (Alden 961). Twenty-eight years later, when Hardy's novel appeared, a strong British influence was still manifestly present. According to Laurel Brake, "although [*Harper's*] *Magazine* abandoned its exclusion of American fiction soon after 1850, under a barrage of native protests, it stalwartly maintained perceptible links with Britain, both in continuing to include British authors and in paying regular attention to social and political—as well as cultural—events in Britain" (106).

In addition to carrying serial installments of *The Return of the Native, Harper's* featured numerous articles by and about Britain. Many of these touched on literary or artistic topics, such as "Joseph Mallord William Turner" (Conant, February 1878), "Milton's L'Allegro" (April 1878), and "An Adventure in a Forest; Or, Dickens's Maypole Inn" (Payn, July 1878). Others, like the serialized novel *Macleod of Dare* by William Black (February 1878 to January 1879), "The Story of Jean Malcomb" (Weiss, May 1878), and "An English Bride in Roumania" (Larimer, September 1878), featured British characters. A third category touched on British cultural issues. These essays included "The English Civil Service" (Morse, May 1878), "A First Week in England" (Walton, July 1878), and "England's Great University" (Conway, December 1878). Thus, like *Belgravia, Harper's* was the site of transatlantic literary exchange. Looking back after 100 years of publication, one writer asserts that *Harper's* had been from its early days "not only a showplace for English fiction but a mirror of American life and ideas as well" (Allen 28). Pushing the argument further, Jennifer Phegley has persuasively demonstrated in *Educating the Proper Woman Reader* that *Harper's* used British fiction to develop American culture.

The transatlantic publication of Hardy's novel brought Wessex to America; it also promoted a distanced reading experience that fostered unexpected connections within a transatlantic reading community. The transatlantic publication of *The Return of the Native* opened up the possibility for cosmopolitan reading, a kind of reading that K. Anthony Appiah identifies as worthwhile because it allows "common conversations about … shared objects" even when culture itself is not

---

[12] For a compelling argument that *Harper's* was originally patterned after Charles Dickens's *Household Words* and that it then influenced the format of later British literary monthlies, see Phegley (32–33).

shared (224). Responses to Hardy's novel in Britain and America suggest just this kind of common conversation.

While reviewers on both sides of the Atlantic were enthusiastic about Eustacia as a character, as I have noted earlier, responses to the novel as a whole were quite different. Initial responses to *The Return of the Native* were generally unfavorable (Pinck 293), and readers on both sides of the Atlantic found the novel alienating and artificial. As one might expect, American reviewers expressed a distinct inability to connect with Hardy's delineation of Wessex and its inhabitants. The reviewer in *Lippincott's* concludes that "a certain romantic interest attaches to these characters, but, while they are consistently portrayed, they scarcely appeal to our everyday sympathies" ("Literature of the Day" 392). This distance is exaggerated when it comes to describing the rustic characters. While *Scribner's* graciously allows that "the Shakesperian talk of these dwellers on Egdon Heath is said to be quite true to life" ("Hardy's 'Return of the Native'" 911), the *Nation* openly questions the accuracy of this treatment ("The Return of the Native" 155) and the *Atlantic Monthly* boldly asserts, "his characters talk like nobody either in life or in books except the clowns in Shakespeare" ("The Return of the Native, and Other Novels" 500). While there is some evidence that Hardy's portrayal of these characters is essentially accurate—a fellow native of Dorset wrote for instance that "Mr. Hardy knows every minutest detail of Dorset life, each convolution of Dorset brain" (Pinck 297)—it was completely beyond the ken for American readers.

What is perhaps more surprising about the reviews is the fact that British readers felt much the same way about the novel. Rather than identifying with Hardy's rustic characters, British reviewers found them to be universally wanting. The *Contemporary Review*, providing the most generous assessment, merely commented that Hardy's "Wessex rustics are framed on the old inconsistent but striking model" ("Contemporary Literary Chronicles" 205). *Blackwood's* condemned these characters as artificial: "those humorous peasants who used sometimes to remind us of Shakespeare's gravediggers and Dogberrys begin to talk like books—that is to say, like Mr. Hardy's books" ("Contemporary Literature" 338). The *Athenaeum*, too, found fault with his characterization and complains of "the clumsy way in which the meaning is expressed. People talk as no people ever talked before, or perhaps we should rather say as no people ever talk now. The language of his peasants may be Elizabethan, but it can hardly be Victorian" ("Novels of the Week" 654). Thus, in Britain as in America, the perceived distance between lived experience and Hardy's depiction of rural life resulted in a lack of personal investment in the story. As a reviewer for the *London Times* characterized it: "we feel rather abroad there, and can scarcely get up a satisfactory interest in people whose history and habits are so entirely different to our own" (qtd. in Pinck 297). British reviewers apparently saw themselves in the camp of sophisticated cosmopolitans, not provincial locals. Like their American counterparts, they read Hardy's characters as Shakespearean caricatures, separated from themselves by an impassible gap. In this way, British reviewers unmoored themselves from a national tradition and aligned themselves instead with others— in this case Americans—who shared their cosmopolitan sensibilities.

If we can take the reviews as representative of a transatlantic reading community, what is most striking is the degree to which readers on both sides of the Atlantic characterize Hardy's novel as essentially alien. For both American and British readers, entering his novel is like traveling "abroad." In this sense, *The Return of the Native* can be seen as the vehicle for creating a shared experience between transatlantic readers, one that reinforces the cosmopolitan agenda of the magazines in which it appeared by uniting a certain group of British and American readers against what they perceived as an outmoded insular community. Rather than being a text with which readers identify, *The Return of the Native* alienates readers from differing geographic regions. In relation to the text, both British and American readers find themselves in a similar vantage point, that of the more sophisticated outsider.

Significantly, this alienation caused readers to find themselves in the same vantage point as the novel's sensation heroine, Eustacia. For contemporary readers, identification with the returned native Clym was difficult, if not impossible. As a result, the novel flopped as a tragedy with this hero at its center. Its limited success arose, instead, from its sensational qualities. For Hardy's transatlantic reading community, setting did not translate into a comprehensible experience; the heath and its inhabitants were too alien, too otherworldly. In contrast, the sensational elements of the novel, embodied most forcefully in its errant cosmopolitan heroine, transcended a moribund setting that touched neither American nor Londoner. Readers from both sides of the Atlantic could connect with this "exotic" heroine. From this perspective, *The Return of the Native* reads as a cautionary tale against, not for, insularity. In this nontraditional reading of the novel, its sensational register provides common ground between Hardy's American and British readers and lays the foundation for a transatlantic reading community.

Works Cited

Abravanel, Genevieve. "Hardy's Transatlantic Wessex: Constructing the Local in *The Mayor of Casterbridge*." *Novel: A Forum on Fiction* 39 (Fall 2005): 97–117.

Alden, Henry Mills. "Editor's Study." *Harper's New Monthly* 119 (November 1909): 960–964.

Allen, Frederick Lewis. "One Hundred Years of Harper's." *Harper's New Monthly* 201 (October 1950): 23–36.

Appiah, K. Anthony. "Cosmopolitan Reading." In *Cosmopolitan Geographies: New Locations in Literature and Culture*. Ed. Vinay Dharwadker. New York: Routledge, 2001. 197–227.

Baker, H. Barton. "Famous Theatrical Riots." *Belgravia* 36 (October 1878): 470–483.

Bandish, Cynthia. "Bakhtin's Dialogism and the Bohemian Meta-narrative of *Belgravia*: A Case Study for Analyzing Periodicals." *Victorian Periodicals Review* 34 (Fall 2001): 239–262.

Black, William. *Macleod of Dare. Harper's New Monthly* 56 (Feb. 1878) to 58 (January 1879).

Bouhelma, Penny. *Thomas Hardy and Women: Sexual Ideology and Narrative Form*. Madison: University of Wisconsin Press, 1985.

Braddon, Mary Elizabeth. *Aurora Floyd*. Oxford: Oxford University Press, 1996.

———. *The Doctor's Wife. Temple Bar* 10 (January 1864) to 13 (December 1864).

Brake, Laurel. *Subjugated Knowledges: Journalism, Gender & Literature in the Nineteenth Century*. New York: New York University Press, 1994.

Chapman, Raymond. "The Worthy Encompassed by the Inevitable: Hardy and a New Perception of Tragedy," In *Reading Thomas Hardy*. Ed. Charles P.C. Pettit. Basingstoke, Hampshire: Macmillan, 1998. 138–155.

Claybaugh, Amanda. *The Novel of Purpose: Literature and Social Reform in the Anglo-American World*. Ithaca, N.Y.: Cornell University Press, 2007.

Collins, Wilkie. *Armadale. Cornhill Magazine* 10 (November 1864) to 13 (June 1866).

———. *The Haunted Hotel: A Story of Modern Venice. Belgravia* 35 (June 1878) to 37 (November 1878).

Conant, Helen S. "Joseph Mallord William Turner." *Harper's New Monthly* 56 (February 1878): 381–401.

"Contemporary Literary Chronicles." *Contemporary Review* 34 (December 1878): 197–208.

"Contemporary Literature." *Blackwood's* 125 (March 1879): 322–344.

"Contributor's Club." *Atlantic Monthly* 44 (November 1879): 672–674.

Conway, Moncure D. "England's Great University." *Harper's New Monthly* 58 (December 1878): 17–37.

Cyganowski, Carol Klimick. *Magazine Editors and Professional Authors in Nineteenth-Century America: The Genteel Tradition and the American Dream*. New York: Garland, 1988.

Dalziel, Pamela. "Anxieties of Representation: The Serial Illustrations to Hardy's *The Return of the Native*." *Nineteenth-Century Literature* 51.1 (June 1996): 84–110.

Dowling, Richard. "The Elba of the Thames." *Belgravia* 36 (July 1878): 83–98.

———. "Genius at the Hammer." *Belgravia* 34 (February 1878): 434–439.

———. "The Going Out of Alessandro Pozzone." *Belgravia* 36 (August 1878): 211–226.

———. "Her Child's Cry." *Belgravia* 35 (May 1878): 351–365.

———. "The Marine Binocular." *Belgravia* 35 (April 1878): 191–203.

"Editor's Literary Record." *Harper's New Monthly* 58 (March 1879): 627–628.

"An Epicurean Tour." *Belgravia* 35 (April 1878): 154–166.

Faber, Daniel and George Bornstein. *British Periodicals of the 18th and 19th Centuries*. Ann Arbor, Mich.: University Microfilms, 1972.

F.E.A. "Some Turkish Slave Stories." *Belgravia* 35 (April 1878): 167–183.

Forbes, Henry O. "Bird or Reptile—Which?" *Belgravia* 36 (September 1878): 317–331.

Hardy, Florence. *Life of Thomas Hardy*. London: Studio Editions, 1994.

Hardy, Thomas. *Collected Letters of Thomas Hardy*. Vol 1. Ed. Richard Little Purdy and Michael Millgate. Oxford; New York: Clarendon, 1978–1988.

———. *The Return of the Native*. *Belgravia* 34 (January 1878) to 37 (December 1878).

———. *The Return of the Native*. *Harper's New Monthly* 56 (February 1878) to 58 (January 1879).

———. *The Return of the Native*. Ed. Tony Slade. London; New York: Penguin, 1999.

"Hardy's Newest Novel." *New York Times* December 28, 1878: 110.

"Hardy's 'Return of the Native' and Black's 'Macleod of Dare.'" *Scribner's Monthly* 17 (Apr. 1879): 910–911.

Harte, Bret. "A Tourist from Injianny." *Belgravia* 36 (October 1878): 424–431.

Hawthorne, Julian. "An Automatic Enigma." *Belgravia* 35 (May 1878): 294–306.

Heywood, Christopher. "*The Return of the Native* and Miss Braddon's *The Doctor's Wife*: A Probable Source." *Nineteenth-Century Fiction* 18 (June 1963): 91–94.

Hughes, Winifred. *The Maniac in the Cellar: Sensation Novels of the 1860s*. Princeton, N.J.: Princeton University Press, 1980.

Jackson, Arlene M. *Illustration and the Novels of Thomas Hardy*. Ottowa: Rowman and Littlefield, 1981.

Larimer, E.W. "An English Bride in Roumania." *Harper's New Monthly* 57 (September 1878): 533–545.

"Literature of the Day." *Lippincott's Magazine* 23 (March 1879): 390–392.

Mackay, G. Eric. "Premature Burials." *Belgravia* 35 (March 1878): 95–103.

Maitland, Frederic William. *Life and Letters of Leslie Stephen*. New York: G.P. Putnam's Sons; London: Duckworth and Co., 1906.

Malton, Sara A. "'The Woman Shall Bear Her Iniquity': Death as Social Discipline in Thomas Hardy's *The Return of the Native*." *Studies in the Novel* 32.2 (Summer 2000): 147–164.

Mansel, Henry. "Sensation Novels." *Quarterly Review* 113 (April 1863): 481–514.

"Milton's L'Allegro." *Harper's New Monthly* 57 (April 1878): 705–717.

Morse, F.H. "The English Civil Service." *Harper's New Monthly* 56 (May 1878): 929–932.

Nash, Andrew. "The Serialization and Publication of *The Return of the Native*: A New Thomas Hardy Letter." *The Library* 2 (2001): 52–59.

"Novels of the Week." *Athenaeum* 23 Nov. 1878, 654–655.

Onslow, Barbara. "Sensationalising Science: Braddon's Marketing of Science in *Belgravia*." *Victorian Periodicals Review* 35.2 (2002): 160–177.

Payn, James. "An Adventure in a Forest; Or, Dickens's Maypole Inn." *Harper's New Monthly* 57 (July 1878): 298–302.

Perkins, Barbara M. "Harper's Monthly Magazine." In *American Literary Magazines*. Ed. Edward E. Chielens. Westport, Conn.: Greenwood, 1986. 166–171.

Phegley, Jennifer. *Educating the Proper Woman Reader: Victorian Family Literary Magazines and the Cultural Health of the Nation*. Columbus: Ohio State University Press, 2004.

Pinck, Joan P. "The Reception of Thomas Hardy's *The Return of the Native*." *Harvard Library Bulletin* 17 (July 1969): 291–308.

Proctor, Richard. "Living in Dread and Terror." *Belgravia* 34 (January 1878): 288–303.

———. "The Moon's Myriad Small Craters." *Belgravia* 36 (August 1878): 153–171.

———. "The Sun in His Glory." *Belgravia* 37 (November 1878): 27–46.

"The Return of the Native." *Literary World* 10 (February 1, 1879): 37.

"The Return of the Native." *Nation* 28 (February 27, 1879): 155.

"The Return of the Native, and Other Novels." *Atlantic Monthly* 43 (April 1879): 500–506.

Scheuerle, William H. "Belgravia." In *British Literary Magazines*. Ed. Alvin Sullivan. Westport, Conn.: Greenwood, 1983. 31–33.

Twain, Mark. "Fables and their Sequels." *Belgravia* 35 (May 1878): 326–331.

———. "Loves of Alonzo FitzClarence and Rosannah Ethelton." *Belgravia* 35 (March 1878): 39–55.

Walton, E.C. "A First Week in England." *Harper's New Monthly* 57 (July 1878): 229–238.

Weiss, Susan Archer. "The Story of Jean Malcomb." *Harper's New Monthly* 56 (May 1878): 829–835.

Wheeler, Otis. "Four Versions of *The Return of the Native*." *Nineteenth-Century Fiction* 14.1 (June 1959): 27–44.

Williams, Raymond. *The Country and the City*. Oxford: Oxford University Press, 1973.

Wilson, Andrew. "What I Saw in an Ant's Nest." *Belgravia* 36 (October 1878): 450–464.

Wilson, J. Arbuthnot. "Among the Thousand Islands." *Belgravia* 36 (October 1878): 412–423.

———. "The Empress of Andorra." *Belgravia* 36 (September 1878): 335–351.

"A Word at the Start." *Harper's New Monthly* 1 (June 1850): 1–2.

Wright, T.R. *Hardy and His Readers*. Houndmills, Basingstoke, Hampshire: Palgrave Macmillan, 2003.

Wychoff, William and Chantelle Nash. "Geographical Images of the American West: The View from Harper's Monthly, 1850–1900." *Journal of the West* 33 (July 1994): 10–21.

Chapter 14
Violent Passions:
Anglo-American Sensationalization
of the Balkans

Ana Savic Moturu

On the morning of September 3, 1901, when Miss Ellen Stone, an American missionary to Turkey, said farewell to the small Protestant congregation of Bansko, a village in the Slavic provinces of the Ottoman Empire, she could hardly imagine that she would soon become a figure of national honor in America and the subject of intense diplomatic negotiations among the great powers. Her capture by a band of Macedonian revolutionaries in one of the narrow passes at the foot of the rugged Pirin Mountain for an exorbitant ransom of 25,000 Turkish liras (110,000 U.S. dollars) shocked both the missionaries and the natives and caused an even greater sensation at home. The whole Western world followed anxiously her six-month ordeal with the brigands in snow-covered Balkan mountains in the company of only one friend, her fellow-captive, Mrs. Katerina Tsilka, a native nursing teacher who was five months pregnant when they were captured. A real-life story that seemed to have sprung straight from the pages of a dime novel or a penny dreadful, Stone's kidnapping seized the headlines all across America and other Western countries, lending itself to wild speculations and sensational interpretations.

A deeper reason why Stone's kidnapping drew such extraordinary international attention is that it raised the ghost of the Eastern Question, a political issue that plagued European diplomacy for most of the nineteenth century. Since the decline of the Ottoman Empire in the late eighteenth century, the emergence of Balkan states on the European political stage after centuries of Ottoman colonial rule and their conflicts over still fluid national boundaries threatened to destabilize the relations of power in Europe.[1] Portrayed by the press as "a seething caldron" of ethnic tensions that threatened to spill over into a full-scale international conflict, the Balkans had already been branded in the West as a region of violence and

---

[1] Russia and Austro-Hungary vied for the sphere of influence over the newly recognized and emerging Balkan states, while Britain and France, although not having territorial pretensions, strove to check other powers' influence in the region. Macedonia, a land inhabited by a medley of nationalities, Bulgarians, Macedonians, Greeks, Albanians, and Serbs, was particularly volatile, with two revolutionary organizations agitating for Macedonian independence from the Ottoman Empire.

ethnic conflicts (notwithstanding the fact that great powers were often directly or indirectly responsible for those conflicts). Stone's kidnapping threatened to entangle the United States, a new global power, into the Balkan crisis and with old-world political rivalries.

By focusing on the newspaper coverage of Stone's kidnapping, I will examine the role of sensational journalism in shaping American popular response to the Balkan crisis and in redefining America's relationship with other major powers, particularly Great Britain. The centrality of sensational journalism to late nineteenth-century culture is best exemplified by the fact that two popular newspaper magnates, William Randolph Hearst and Joseph Pulitzer, were accused of drawing the country into the Cuban War in 1898 as they competed for sensational and thrilling news, though these claims are largely exaggerated. Since its emergence in the 1880s, new journalism has been critiqued for compromising moral and aesthetic standards to increase circulation and for its ability to influence public opinion through exciting stories rather than reasoned and informed argumentation. However, the sensational techniques attributed to new journalism were in fact not new. Rather, this mode of journalism is indebted to cheap penny papers that emerged in the 1830s and that thrived on reportage of shocking crimes and thrilling stories whose goal was to entertain with little to no concern for educating or morally uplifting its readers (Reynolds 169). While penny papers are associated with the emergence of urban mass culture, critics point to the central place of imperial dilemmas and racial anxieties in penny papers and other popular cultural productions.[2] In my analysis of the journalistic coverage of Stone's kidnapping. I will highlight the continuities between reports about Stone's kidnapping and earlier sensational representations of interracial encounters in Indian captivity narratives, frontier adventures, and historical romances—fictional or purportedly real—published in penny papers or in other popular formats.[3] I will argue that the sensational rhetoric dominating journalistic reports on Stone draws on these earlier narratives inscribing the story of her kidnapping within a larger narrative of American empire building.[4] Mobilizing anxieties about America's more overt imperialistic pretentions following the U.S. victory in the Cuban War,

---

[2]   See Shelley Streeby, *American Sensations: Class, Empire, and the Production of Popular Culture* (Los Angeles: University of California Press, 2002).

[3]   For more on Indian captivity narratives in the nineteenth century see Gary L. Ebersole, *Captured by Texts: Puritan to Postmodern Images of Indian Captivity* (Charlottesville: University Press of Virginia, 1995) 190–237; for more on frontier adventures see Streeby, *American Sensations*; and for more on how historical romances played into imperial aspiration in the late nineteenth century see Amy Kaplan, *The Anarchy of Empire in the Making of U.S. Culture* (Cambridge, Mass.: Harvard University Press, 2002) 92–121.

[4]   Karen Roggenhamp's *Narrating the News: New Journalism and Literary Genre in Late Nineteenth-Century American Newspapers and Fiction* (Kent, OH: Kent State University Press, 2005) illuminates the relationship between popular literary forms and new journalism.

journalistic discourse on Stone refashions these anxieties into patriotic visions of America's special status among global powers.[5]

Moreover, by presenting the incident as an ideological rationale for the political rapprochement between the United Sates and Great Britain, the accounts of Stone's captivity served to strengthen Anglo-American cultural and racial solidarity by highlighting the urgency to "defend" Western civilization from the barbaric other(s).[6] However, while sensationalized representations of the "primitive" Balkans seem to justify imperial policy, the sensational mode functions as an ambivalent rhetorical tool that destabilizes the discourse it ostensibly promotes. As a low-brow genre, sensational journalism—like sensational literature—suggests an unacknowledged intimacy between the audience and the subject revealing that the representations of the "barbaric" Balkan other function as a screen for deeper anxieties about racial difference underlying the imperial enterprise.

The imagery in the newspaper coverage of Stone's kidnapping plays upon fears about American vulnerability as a global power and, in line with the tradition of captivity narratives and adventure stories, casts the other as primitive and barbaric. William Randolph Hearst's *Journal-American* draws on these narratives in its first major coverage of Stone's kidnapping rearticulating the established imagery about otherness through the symbols associated with the Balkan region. The Sunday edition of September 22, 1901, devoted a whole page to the Stone incident in a highly sensational article entitled "Miss Stone of Boston Carried off Into Captivity by the Sultan's Brigands" (16). While the title draws the reader in by the unlikely and disconcerting geo-political connection between Boston and the Ottoman Empire, the accompanying collage of drawings and photographs of Stone, native Christian converts, and native brigands focuses the attention on the barbaric "Sultan's brigand," evoking terror and thrill through exaggerated imagery (Figure 14.1).

The action-packed image showcases a fierce-looking brigand with swarthy Middle-Eastern features whisking off a young lady in a white dress on a wild, neighing horse. With his markedly devil-like expression, arched eyebrows, and a pointed beard, the brigand is represented as the embodiment of evil, conjuring traditional representations of Turks as bloodthirsty and barbarous. Both the title and the image evoke the memory of the Armenian atrocities of 1895, when the Turkish irregular troops or Bashi-Bazouks, notorious for their ruthlessness,

---

[5]   The U.S. victory over Spain in the Cuban and the Philippine wars of 1898 and its preoccupations with capitalist expansion in the European-dominated China clearly revealed the U.S. imperialist pretensions, a sign of abandonment of its professed policy of nonintervention, and already, though unwillingly, involved the United States in European diplomatic rivalries.

[6]   In the last years of the nineteenth century, Britain sought the U.S. support in restraining Russia and other powers in China; in return, Britain made concessions to the United States by helping resolve the isthmian canal question in American favor guaranteeing U.S. strategic dominance in the Caribbean (see Samuel Wells, *The Challenges of Power: American Diplomacy, 1900–1921*, Lanham, Md.: University Press of America, 1990).

Fig. 14.1   *Journal American* (22 September 1901). Courtesy of the Harry
              Ransom Humanities Research Center at the University of Texas at
              Austin.

brutally suppressed the rebellion of the Armenians, a Christian minority in the
Asian reaches of the Ottoman Empire. The sensational discourse these historical
references evoke and the exaggerated image accompanying the article fictionalize
reality, inviting the reader to view the incident within a mythologized discourse
on otherness.

It is interesting that both the Turkish brigand and the Bulgarian brigand are
placed at a higher angle in relation to the reader, accentuating the fact that they are
in the position of power as a threatening presence not only to Stone but indirectly

to the public at home. The article further emphasizes this reversal of roles when the reporter claims in the opening lines that Stone's fate is "a matter of dread and uncertainty." The feeling of terror and the sense of a loss of control pervade the report, especially when the commentator, talking about the local brigands' practice of seizing travelers and holding them for ransom, claims that "a far worse fate is perhaps in store for this unfortunate missionary." He goes on to say that "[i]nstead of merely being a prisoner, like a medieval princess, till armed forces or a princely purse comes to her rescue, Miss Stone may fall a victim to the most relentless fiends in the world" (16). While the account unsettles the reader's sense of security by portraying the brigands as an uncontrollable force and as opponents that do not recognize Western principles of war conduct, the allusions to the discourse on chivalry represent an attempt to restore the balance of power by asserting Western moral authority. In addition, by describing the brigands as fiends, the article further sensationalizes the incident by casting it within the religious framework of the struggle between good and evil.

However, despite the moral idealization of the West, the account raises a disturbing question about the nature of American relationships with other nations that resonated with the American public. Stone's kidnapping took place just three days before the assassination of President William McKinley at the famous Pan-American Exposition at Buffalo. While the exposition celebrated America's imperial success and conjured a vision of Pan-American harmony, the assassination committed by Leo Czolgosz, a Polish immigrant and self-proclaimed anarchist, challenged the vision of national unity and global leadership promoted by the exhibition. Similarly, Stone's kidnapping destabilized the myth of national glory by exposing the discrepancies in the vision of America as a respected global leader. Just as captivity narratives and adventure stories explore problematic aspects of America's westward expansion, this article about Stone from the *Journal-American* shows, through imagery foregrounding terror and suffering, to what extent the idea of empire is fractured and unstable.

The layout of the images accompanying the article exposes the contradictions in the vision of America as a benevolent leader by accentuating the contrast between the wild world of the brigands and the decorous world of the kidnapped Miss Stone. The image of the fierce brigand is juxtaposed against a framed image of Miss Ellen Stone and her chaperone Mrs. Tsilka in Victorian poses of elegance and sophistication. The round wavy frame adds softness to their features, and the symmetrical arrangement of figures in the photograph and their dignified postures stand in stark contrast to the distress and turmoil of the other scene. The dignity and calmness that Stone and Tsilka exude reasserts Western authority and moral fortitude. Nevertheless, the image of the invading brigand threatens that authority—visually, the horse's open muzzle seems to chip off a part of the frame of Stone's photograph, suggesting that the myth of imperial glory is a fiction. The illusion that the horse seems to be galloping over the photographs of the mission school and of native converts reinforces the perception of brigands as hostile towards Western cultural legacy. Thus the article builds suspense by exploiting the tension between the perceived threat posed by the brigands and the ability of the "civilized" world to absorb it.

The reports of Stone's kidnapping play out this tension between the "civilized" and the "barbaric" through the motif of the violation of the female body that features prominently in captivity narratives and imperial adventure stories. A few days after the news of the kidnapping reached the American public, the Reverend John W. Baird remarked: "What those two women will suffer can be imagined. May God guard them" (qtd. Carpenter 36). The horror that his remark excites intensifies not only the fear about the fate of the two women, but on a symbolic level it deepens the anxiety about racial boundaries. On October 2, the *Journal-American* published a sensational report by a Paris correspondent who claimed to have interviewed Stone and learned from her that the brigands declared that if the ransom was not received, she would have to choose between death or marriage to one of the brigands ("Ransom" 3). According to Gary L. Ebersole, the threat of sexual violence or coerced marriage, a common motif in captivity narratives, functions within a complex matrix of cultural associations concerning the cult of womanhood and the constructions of the racial other. Since nineteenth-century patriarchal ideology assigns women a special role as guardians of national culture and transmitters of tradition, the representations of the violation of the white female body conjure fears about racial contamination through the female domain. While the theme of captivity in these narratives evokes fears about female vulnerability and moral weakness, potentially calling into question the cultural superiority of Western civilization predicated on patriarchal ideals of female virtue, the representations of women as victims who unflinchingly uphold the Western ideal of womanhood and choose death over life in shame allay the fears about racial purity (217–222). The assurances about Stone's virtue and heroism serve to reassert Western moral superiority, and the presentations of her predicament through the metaphor of rape or forced marriage is a particularly potent symbol for mobilizing patriotic feelings constructing the white male as the chivalrous rescuer of the "damsel-in-distress." The fact that the report about the brigands' ultimatum to Stone proved to be a hoax highlights to what extent the Stone coverage participates in a symbolic exchange with existing narratives about racial encounters that structured not only the presentation but also the interpretation of the incident within the established discourse on otherness.

Both the sensational press and more reputable newspapers such as the *New York Times* engaged in fantastical speculations about the horrors that Stone faced, thus intensifying racial anxieties by employing the familiar motif of the mutilation of the human body. The adoption of the sensational techniques by quality newspapers is due to the fact that by the turn of the century most newspapers had recognized the power of emotional appeals in shaping public opinion and enhancing circulation figures (Fulton 11). On October 7, both the *Journal-American* and the *New York Times* published sensational accounts of a statement made by Z.T. Sweeney, Ex-Consul General to Turkey, in which he claims that the brigands will cut off Miss Stone's finger and then an ear and send it to her family if the ransom is not paid.

Finally, he goes on, "her head will be put upon a pike pole in some little village of Turkey" ("$60,000 Raised" 1; "Brigands Give Miss Stone a Month More" 1). The horrific images of the violation of the human body serve not only to prove the savage and cold-hearted nature of Stone's captors but also help to consolidate the body politic by mobilizing national sympathies for Stone.

However, the sensational genre in which these newspaper reports were written complicates the racial boundaries that they attempt to erect. In his book about sensationalism in the New York press, John D. Stevens argues that lurid details in the sensational press "do not so much inform readers as allow them to share in the feelings of the actors of the real-life Grand Guignol" (5). The shame the readers feel about their "guilty pleasures" is then transformed into moral outrage at the perpetrators of the criminal act. Likewise, Ebersole argues that captivity narratives held a particular fascination for the audience because the author's condemnation of Indian customs allowed readers to retain their assumptions of cultural superiority, while episodes that describe the protagonist's life among the Indians enabled them to indulge vicariously their fascination with the primitive without the fear of being morally implicated or of compromising their racial superiority (196). Just like penny-paper stories, the sensational accounts of Stone's captivity allow the readers to experience the thrill of adventure and transgress their cultural norms while restoring their own sense of virtue through open disavowal and condemnation of the racial other. By presenting the transgressive as simultaneously fascinating and threatening, the sensational press exacerbates the anxieties about American imperialism. Cumulatively, the sensational images of the brigands help to assuage these anxieties by naturalizing their representations as inherently evil and barbaric and by highlighting American civility and moral superiority.

Through sensational speculations about the identity of Stone's kidnappers, the press transposes this sense of moral outrage onto the political plane, molding attitudes towards the Balkans based on America's relationship with great powers. The first theories about Stone's abductors revolved around Turkish impoverished troops who, it was supposed, captured Stone to boost their income. Even though the Turkish government tried to disperse these speculations by pointing to the inconsistencies in the accounts of the eyewitnesses and arguing that the captors were only trying to impersonate Turks in order to conceal their true identity, newspapers continued to blame the Ottoman regime for the kidnapping. The American press relied on Oriental images of unbridled sexuality and bestiality in the portrayal of Stone's captors. The *Journal-American* even published photographs of Turkish brigands ("Governments" 65) implicitly reaffirming Turkish involvement, while the *New York Times* featured a sensational report from a Sofia correspondent claiming that Sultan Abdul Hamid himself had ordered Stone's kidnapping ("One Report" 1).

While the condemnation of the Ottoman regime potentially reveals a readiness to side with the native brigands and see them as fighters for freedom from Ottoman oppression, the representations in the press are complicated—and complicate—American political attitudes towards the Balkans. Along with allusions to Turkish brigands, newspaper articles refer to Boris Sarafov, the leader of the Macedonian Revolutionary Committee with a seat in Bulgaria, as the mastermind behind the kidnapping. No mention was made in the media of the Internal Macedonian Revolutionary Organization, which was actually responsible for the kidnapping, partly because no one believed that the organization was capable of executing the action and partly because in the West not much distinction was made between the two organizations. Although both organizations fought against the Ottoman regime in Macedonia, the Macedonian Committee wanted to annex Macedonia to Bulgaria, while the Internal Macedonian Revolutionary Organization desired to establish Macedonian autonomy within the Ottoman Empire (Perry 38). It was believed that the Macedonian Committee was under Russian patronage, and perhaps for that reason the activities of the organization attracted more attention. Stoking fears of Russian expansion, the *Journal-American* reports a statement by a Russian diplomat saying that "American missionaries have no business here and that the people should not be disturbed in their religious beliefs" ("Brigands May Set Miss Stone Free" 9). Bulgarian and Macedonian cultural and racial affiliations with Russia and the perceived threat of Russian political influence in the region play a significant role in structuring American representation of the Balkan crisis.

Numerous descriptions of the Bulgarian brigands as outlaws liken them firmly to American anarchists and define them as a threat to stability in the Ottoman Empire and the wider region. America, like Britain, was hostile to the creation of new states in the Balkans because it feared that they could become Russia's satellites. At the same time, unlike Britain where at least some politicians voiced open support of the Ottoman Empire, the United States kept its political and diplomatic distance. This political condemnation of the Ottoman Empire accounts for the hesitation in the early reports to attribute blame to the Bulgarian brigands, creating ambivalent attitudes to the Balkans that are symptomatic of the larger crisis of identity in the new empire. America's ambivalence about the Balkan struggles for independence suggests that by seeking the position of global leadership, America finds itself in danger of compromising its foundational ideal of liberty. The merging of the imagery associated with the Turkish brigands and the Bulgarian brigands and the easy shifting of responsibility for the kidnapping from Turkish troops to Bulgarian brigands assuages this crisis of identity. The image of the brigand as a composite monstrosity that embodies both the threat of anarchism and the threat of old, decaying empires transforms the mystery about the brigands' identity into a vehicle for asserting the uniqueness of the American empire. The brigands' ethnic ambivalence makes them a repository for the qualities that the United States defines itself against, revealing to what extent American representations of the Balkans are determined by geo-political constellations and the need of the fledgling empire to articulate its identity against the established powers.

The interpretation of the incident as an outrage against the outpost of Western civilization—the American Board of Commissioners for Foreign Missions— further solidifies the dichotomy of the civilized and the primitive while obfuscating the political context that structures the coverage of Stone's kidnapping. While the missionaries provided financial support for the Eastern-Orthodox Church in Armenia, one of the major reasons for establishing the Board was political in nature: the missionaries were to attract native Christians to the Protestant faith and to exert evangelical influence on the Muslims (Hall 3). In this light, even the Board's humanitarian dedication to strengthening the Eastern-Orthodox Church reveals traditional beliefs about Orthodox Christians as semi-oriental. The brigands' attack on the American missionary reasserted these old associations of Balkan Christians with oriental or heathen traditions. Despite, or perhaps because of, the hostility of the brigands and some portions of the native population towards American missionaries, the press emphasizes the need for American involvement in the Balkans. In this way, the anxiety about American imperial involvements is channeled into a sense of righteous mission.

These sentiments are most effectively conveyed through the narrative surrounding Katerina Tsilka, Stone's companion in captivity. A Macedonian native educated in the United States, Tsilka was feared to be in even greater danger than Stone because of her conversion to Protestantism. With the established barbarity of the Balkan brigands, it seems only natural for the *Journal-American* reporter to claim that "The fate of this pretty young convert may possibly be worse than Miss Stone's, as the outlaws will see no possibility of gaining a large reward for a poor native young woman. They may also hate her for the Protestant religion, which she has adopted" ("Miss Stone" 16). Concerns for her life and the life of her newborn baby, little Elena, born in captivity, paint the brigands in an even more demonic light and provide justification for American interference in the internal affairs of Turkey. Tsilka's suffering legitimizes the American mission in the Balkans, adding a sense of righteousness and urgency to it. Significantly, her devotion to Stone fits within the pattern of racial relations established in captivity narratives and frontier adventures revealing a continuation of imperial aspirations. Just as the white captives and white frontiersmen exert a civilizing influence on the Indians and the Mexicans, Stone is represented as a benevolent teacher to the natives who are willing to embrace Western culture. Tsilka comes to symbolize the fruits of American mission to the Balkans, implicitly calling for American involvement in the Balkan affairs as a means of protecting defenseless natives from barbaric native men.

The emphasis on America's civilizing mission naturalizes America's status as a new global power and the inheritor of the declining Old World empires. However, justifying American involvement in the internal affairs of other countries as a "conscientious duty," critics strive to define the United States against the principles on which European empires were built. Pointing to the self-interest of the European powers in their attitudes towards the Ottoman Empire and the Christian minorities under Ottoman rule, Urbain Gohier, a contributor for the *American Review*, states that American intervention "would give a lesson of human solidarity to effete Europe" (626). Clearly viewing the United States as a power that has superseded old European empires, Gohier asks: "Would it not be a worthy endeavor for the United States to attempt what Europe has declined to do?" (625). Emphasizing America's fundamental difference from the old empires and imagining the American empire as benevolent and protective, Gohier states that American involvement "would not be a work of a conqueror, but the action of a noble heart" (626). The newspaper accounts also display a heightened sense of America's global importance and its status among great powers. Sensationalizing the conflict by evoking the spirit of the crusades, the press helped transform the meaning of the incident from a threat into an opportunity for the United States to claim its supreme role in the world: "All the world is looking at this Nation. This is the first time that all Christian nations have been thus brought together upon the ground of a heathen country. Underlying this is a confidence in God" ("Public Meeting" 7). This passage reinforces the belief that the United States has no equal and that therefore its duty is to act as a leader of the civilized Christian world.

Apart from presenting the United States as a benevolent power, the Christian rhetoric provides a more nuanced view of the relationship among Western powers helping cement the incipient friendship between the United States and Great Britain. It is important to notice that when the U.S. commentators refer to Christianity, they often mean only its Protestant branch. A *New York Times* commentator notes that "Miss Stone's case excited the sympathy of the whole Protestant world" ("Public Meeting" 7). Protestantism stands for Anglo-American civilization, implicitly excluding two other major powers, Catholic France and Eastern-Orthodox Russia, from the supreme position in the Western world. Protestantism further resonates with the myth of Anglo-Saxon racial superiority that was founded on the idea that the descendants of the Anglo-Saxons—the British Empire and then the United States—have been the bearers of the most advanced political and social institutions. Since the late nineteenth century, this theory was used as the ideological basis for Anglo-American political rapprochement and as a tool for legitimizing Anglo-American imperial interests (Frantzen and Niles 210). In 1897, commenting on Russia's influence in the Balkans, Benjamin Ide Wheeler appeals to this myth to endorse American support of the British policy in the Balkans: "[the Balkan] conflict concerns this question: Who is the leader and champion of Occidentalism in the twentieth century—shall it be the Anglo-Saxon or the Slav" (721). By rearticulating the Eastern Question as the mythical conflict between the Orient and the Occident, Wheeler masks the imperial reasons for American support of Britain, representing them as a highest call of moral duty to save the whole Western civilization from the semi-barbarous Russia and its allies.

Similar to American representations of Stone's kidnapping as an attack on Western civilization, the British press engages the same rhetoric in its reports on Stone even though the importation of American sensational techniques into the British press was fiercely contested earlier in the century.[7] While cultural critics and quality newspaper proprietors often described the phenomenon of sensational

---

[7]   See Joel H. Wiener, ed., *Papers for the Millions: The New Journalism in Britain, 1850s to 1914* (New York: Greenwood Press, 1988).

journalism as a result of excessive freedoms and a disregard for traditional authority in America, and thus a marker of a fundamental difference between the British Empire and America, British representations of Stone's kidnapping exhibit a move towards an ideological and political reconciliation. The sensational imagery that constructs the Bulgarian brigands as the savage other and as a threat to civilization helps to align British political interests and national sympathies with America. In a full-page illustration on its front cover remarkably similar to the previously discussed image from the *Journal-American*, The *Penny Illustrated Paper and Illustrated Times*, a cheap British weekly newspaper, depicts Stone tied to a galloping horse and surrounded by the brigands. Both the image and the accompanying article on the next page underscore Stone's physical suffering at the hands of the brigands. Intensifying fears about Stone's plight through moral denigration of the brigands, the author asserts that "The ransom would certainly not be handed over until she was safely delivered, as her captors might murder her after the receipt of the money, in order to seal her lips forever" ("Bulgarian Brigands" 3). By emphasizing Stone's suffering through sensational imagery and rhetoric, the article reinforces the representations of the brigands as savage and primitive.

Interestingly, in contrast to the American representations of Stone that highlight on the threat of the brigand and often use illustrations that portray Stone as a young woman, the front-page illustration in the British newspaper shows an elderly Stone and focuses the reader's attention on Stone's face, emphasizing her emotional pain and suffering. While both visual and verbal imagery is more subdued, Stone's unsettling gaze directly at the reader creates psychological drama. The shock and fear inscribed in Stone's face reflect a different set of anxieties that structure British attitudes towards the Balkan crisis. While American representations dramatize the contradiction between American political ideals and its imperial pretensions, British coverage reveals anxieties about waning imperial power. Significantly absent in this article is the emphasis on Stone's moral superiority. While assertions about the superiority of Western civilization in both American and British representations of the incident help to restore Western sense of power, this article highlights Stone's utter helplessness. Thus, it foregrounds deeper fears about the consequences of imperial expansion and implicitly questioning America's imperial pretensions on moral grounds. Despite their professed friendship, other British newspaper accounts express more overtly an anxiety about America's new position as a global power. A *London Times* commentator deliberates whether America will, like France, take the interests of the European powers into consideration when it decides on the course of action towards the Ottoman Empire ("The United States" 3). Concerns about America's imperial success play into a larger set of anxieties exacerbated by the *fin-de-siècle* fears about the inevitable decline of great civilizations.

Paradoxically, despite British apprehensions about American emergence as a global power, the press alleviates anxieties about British imperial decline by emphasizing cultural and racial similarity between Britain and the United States.

In a tone decidedly critical of Western political practices but also expressive of disconcerting similarities between the Balkans and the West, a *London Times* commentator remarks that the politically motivated kidnapping is not different in spirit from political intrigues in Britain and America ("Court Circular" 7). However, what is striking is that this recognition does not lead to a deeper insight about commonalities in human nature but functions as another vehicle for reasserting Anglo-American superiority. The writer is not reassured that the brigands are up to the moral standards required of their task as liberators of their land, and he doubts that they will treat Stone with the courtesy and consideration due to their "lofty motives." On the contrary, asserting Anglo-American cultural superiority and implicitly dismissing the brigands' ability to treat Stone in a civilized way, the author focuses on describing the "chronic disorder that reigns in the Balkan Peninsula" ("Court Circular" 7). The images of ethnic conflict, political disorder, and violence represent the brigands as savage and primitive: "Throughout these distracted regions one looks in vain for any power or influence that makes for order and progress. Besides Macedonian discontent, Bulgarian intrigue, Albanian violence, and Turkish incapacity, we have the restless ambitions of Greeks and Serbs and Montenegrins" ("Court Circular" 7). By evoking fears of anarchism which George Holyoake, a contributor to the journal *Nineteenth Century and After*, defines as "a reversion to the savage state" (686), these images reassert Balkan barbarity and implicitly underscore Britain's status as a higher civilization. The sensational images of the Balkans serve to affirm Britain's solidarity with the United States and allay the fears about Britain's perceived imperial decline by highlighting Britain's affinities with the rising American empire.

To what extent these sensational representations in the British and American press are constructions that conceal deeper anxieties about racial difference is revealed best in Stone's memoir, published shortly after her release, and the travel narrative of Edith Durham, a British relief worker who visited Macedonia after the Ilinden uprising funded in part by the money from Stone's ransom. After her release on February 23, 1902, Stone surprised the West with her open endorsement of the Macedonian revolutionary movement and her tireless agitation for raising the awareness about the condition of Macedonians under Ottoman rule. Her memoir *Six Months Among Brigands*, published in the *McClure's Magazine* in five installments from May to October 1902, destabilizes racial hierarchies established in the press. While the press accounts conflate the Ottoman troops with Macedonian brigands, Stone explains the conditions that have led to Macedonian brigandage, drawing attention to the plight of the Balkan Christians under Ottoman rule and the Ottoman government's failure to implement the reform measures stipulated by the great powers at the Berlin Congress in 1878.[8] In contrast to the newspaper accounts that dismiss the brigands as outlaws, Stone describes them as romanticized fighters for freedom who take to arms because "numberless women and children in Turkey suffer nameless outrages and are put to death daily!" (104).

---

[8]   For more on Balkan struggles for independence see Barbara Jelavich, *History of the Balkans: Eighteenth and Nineteenth Centuries* (Cambridge, Mass.: Harvard University Press, 1988).

Stone's memoir presents a departure from nineteenth-century sensational narratives in that she does not engage to the same extent established motifs and images that confirm racial stereotypes. Instead, Stone gives a human dimension to the brigands when she describes their simple kindness: one day they presented her and Tsilka with a bouquet of wild cyclamen; on Thanksgiving holiday they surprised her with turkey for dinner; and on another occasion they helped her and Tsilka dry baby clothes by the fire (11, 106, 230). Moreover, Stone does not express fears about going native, a motif that pervades much of the writing about Indian captivity. In her memoir, Stone explains how the native dances that the brigands played for entertainment seemed to her strange at first but that she came to appreciate their beauty admitting that they "provoke[ed] merriment in us all" (103). Unlike the nineteenth-century captives who, even when they adopted Indian culture maintained upon return that they did so only to save themselves, Stone acknowledges her affinities with at least some aspects of the brigands' culture.

Despite her revision of the image of the Balkan brigands and her open championship of their cause, Stone's treatment of the brigands is nevertheless indicative of her pride in the American imperial mission and demonstrates some important continuities with previous narratives about racial encounters. Engaging the theme of civilizing mission, Stone's narrative participates in rearticulations of American imperial policy as a matter of cultural leadership. While she connects with the brigands on a human level, she nevertheless asserts her superiority by assuming the role of a guide or a teacher and by insisting on giving them religious instruction. Even though markedly romanticized and sensational in itself, Stone's alternative view of the Balkans challenges the images of the Balkans as savage by exposing their constructed nature and by demystifying their role in establishing normalcy in the face of racial anxieties.

More than Stone's memoir, Edith Durham's travel narrative *The Burden of the Balkans* questions the very basis of Western notions of racial superiority. While Durham frequently remarks that she feared Stone's fate, reinforcing the idea of Anglo-American solidarity by invoking the sensational discourse of Stone's kidnapping, her narrative self-consciously plays upon sensational representations of the Balkans, subverting the notions of Western superiority promoted by the press. At the opening of the narrative, Durham admits that living in the Balkans and reading daily news was as engrossing as reading a penny-dreadful. While she reinforces a negative view of the Balkans by associating the region with cheap sensational stories of no literary value, she is equally sarcastic about the West. Adopting the low-brow genre for parodic purposes, Durham observes that primitive and "un-Western" passions govern Western fascination with the Balkans:

> All the land around was a hell of misery! We lived on a thin crust of quiet, beneath which surged a lava-bed of raw primæval passions and red-hot race hatreds into which no Power dare thrust its fingers for fear of having them burnt off. It was a position of such absorbing interest that, with apologies to my friends, I must confess I never wanted either European comrades or books. (167)

To a greater extent than Stone's memoir, Durham's narrative cheerfully enacts the *fin-de-siècle* nightmare of turning native. While she perpetuates the racial stereotypes of the Balkans as savage by describing the region as a "hell of misery," her frank admission that she desires to be a part of the "primitive" culture upsets Western ideas of racial hierarchies. By using the volcano metaphor in an ambiguous way she complicates the representations of the Balkans as a volatile region implying that the image stands not only for Balkan savagery but also for mounting anxieties about British identity. Durham's recognition of her own "raw primæval passions" shows that Western identity is just a thin veneer or "thin crust" of artificially constructed racial identity. In this way, Durham's narrative is indicative of a larger change in the intellectual mood in the early twentieth century marked particularly by disillusionment with the Enlightenment belief in progress and by more pervading doubts about the superiority of Western civilization. By employing the sensational structure of feeling for parodic purposes, Durham's narrative makes explicit the idea that the moral outrage at the Balkan other conceals fears about the primitive in Western identity.

While American and British journalistic reports of Stone's kidnapping paint the Balkans as savage and primitive, the underlying narratives about imperial anxieties suggest that Western images of the Balkans are created in response to artificially constructed self-perceptions of racial superiority. Just as the sensational stories restore the social order by displacing the guilt about moral faults onto scapegoat characters who are punished in the end,[9] the press denigrates the Balkan other who destabilizes racial boundaries by challenging Anglo-American notions of racial superiority and self-perceptions of America as a benevolent empire. However, this dynamic is marked by an ambiguity insofar as the sensational genre suggests an implicit bond between the reader and the crime described: after all, the story of the crime is created for the reader's pleasure. In this sense, the moral outrage at the primitive Balkan other conceals a fascination with the barbaric that is feared to reside in the civilized self. This ambiguous pattern of relations continuously calls into question the reestablished racial hierarchies perpetuating the need for new stories that will reaffirm racial difference.

Works Cited

"$60,000 Raised of the Fund to Rescue Woman from Bulgarian Bandits." *Journal-American* October 7, 1902: 1.

Brantlinger, Patrick. "What is 'Sensational' about the 'Sensation Novel'?" *Nineteenth Century Fiction* 37 (1982) 1–28.

"Brigands Give Miss Stone a Month More." *New York Times* October 8, 1901: 1.

"Brigands May Set Miss Stone Free." *Journal-American* October 23, 1901: 9.

"Bulgarian Brigands." *Penny Paper Illustrated and Illustrated Times* October 26, 1901:1.

---

[9]   See Patrick Blantlinger, "What is 'Sensational' about the 'Sensation Novel'?" *Nineteenth-Century Fiction* 37 (1982): 1–28.

"The Capture of Miss Stone." *Times* November 13, 1901: 5.

Carpenter, Terasa. *The Miss Stone Affair: America's First Modern Hostage Crisis.* New York: Simon & Schuster, 2003.

"Court Circular and News." *Times* October 18, 1901: 7.

Durham, Edith. *The Burden of the Balkans.* London: Thomas Nelson & Sons, 1905.

Ebersole, Gary L. *Captured by Texts: Puritan to Postmodern Images of Indian Captivity.* Charlottesville: University Press of Virginia, 1995.

Fulton, Richard D. "Sensational War Reporting and the Quality Press in Late Victorian Britain and America." In Joel H. Wiener and Mark Hampton, eds. *Anglo-American Media Interactions, 1850–2000.* Houndmills: Palgrave, 2007.

Frantzen, Allen J., and John D. Niles, eds. *Anglo-Saxonism and the Construction of Social Identity.* Gainesville: University Press of Florida, 1997.

Gohier, Urbain. "American Intervention in Turkey." *North American Review* November 1901: 618–626.

"Governments Strive for Miss Stone Release." *Journal-American* September 29, 1902: 65.

Hall, William Webster. *Puritans in the Balkans: The American Board Mission in Bulgaria, 1878–1918, A Study in Purpose and Procedure.* Sofia: Cultura, 1938.

Holyoake, George. "Anarchism." *Nineteenth Century and After* 296 (1901): 683–686.

Jelavich, Barbara. *History of the Balkans: Eighteenth and Nineteenth Centuries.* Cambridge: Cambridge University Press, 1988.

Kaplan, Amy. *The Anarchy of Empire in the Making of U.S. Culture.* Cambridge, Mass.: Harvard University Press, 2002.

"Miss Stone of Boston Carried off Into Captivity by the Sultan's Brigands." *Journal-American* September 22, 1902, 16.

"One Report from Sofia." *New York Times* October 23, 1901: 1.

Perry, Duncan M. *The Politics of Terror: The Macedonian Liberation Movements, 1893–1903.* Durham, N.C.: Duke University Press, 1988.

"Public Meeting Held in Aid of Miss Stone." *New York Times* October 14, 1901: 7

"Ransom for Miss Stone Must Be Paid in Six Days." *Journal-American* October 2, 1901: 4.

Reynolds, David S. *Beneath the American Renaissance: The Subversive Imagination in the Age of Emerson and Melville.* New York: Alfred A. Knopf, 1988.

Roggenhamp, Karen. *Narrating the News: New Journalism and Literary Genre in Late Nineteenth-Century American Newspapers and Fiction.* Kent, OH: Kent State University Press, 2005.

Stevens, John D. *Sensationalism and the New York Press.* New York: Columbia University Press, 1991.

Stone, Ellen. "Six Months Among Brigands." *McClure Magazine* May 1902: 1–16; June 1902: 99–109; July 1902: 222–231; September 1902: 404–471; October 1902: 562–570.

Streeby, Shelley. *American Sensations: Class, Empire, and the Production of Popular Culture*. Los Angeles: University of California Press, 2002.

"The United States and Turkey." *Times* October 29, 1901: 3.

Wells, Samuel. *The Challenges of Power: American Diplomacy, 1900–1921*. Lanham, Md.: University Press of America, 1990.

Wheeler, Benjamin Ide. "Greece and the Eastern Question." *Atlantic Monthly* 476 (1897): 721–733.

Wiener, Joel H., ed. *Papers for the Millions: The New Journalism in Britain, 1850s to 1914*. New York: Greenwood Press, 1988.

Index